Democracy's Chief Executive

Democracy's Chief Executive

INTERPRETING THE CONSTITUTION
AND DEFINING THE FUTURE
OF THE PRESIDENCY

Peter M. Shane

UNIVERSITY OF CALIFORNIA PRESS

University of California Press
Oakland, California

© 2022 by Peter M. Shane

Library of Congress Cataloging-in-Publication Data

Names: Shane, Peter M., author.
Title: Democracy's chief executive : interpreting the constitution and defining
   the future of the presidency / Peter M. Shane.
Description: Oakland, California : University of California Press, [2022] |
   Includes bibliographical references and index.
Identifiers: LCCN 2021047026 (print) | LCCN 2021047027 (ebook) |
   ISBN 9780520380905 (cloth) | ISBN 9780520380912 (epub)
Subjects: LCSH: Presidents—Legal status, laws, etc.—United States. |
   Executive power—United States. | Democracy—United States. |
   Constitutional history—United States. | Constitutional law—United
   States. | United States—Politics and government.
Classification: LCC KF5051 .S53 2022 (print) | LCC KF5051 (ebook) |
   DDC 342.73/062—dc23/eng/20211028
LC record available at https://lccn.loc.gov/2021047026
LC ebook record available at https://lccn.loc.gov/2021047027

Manufactured in the United States of America

31   30   29   28   27   26   25   24   23   22
10   9   8   7   6   5   4   3   2   1

To Martha, Beth, and Eric

CONTENTS

TOWARD A PRO-DEMOCRACY
CONSTITUTIONAL PRESIDENCY

Democracy's Chief Executive explains how wrongheaded ideas about expansive executive authority under the Constitution have helped to create within our national government an organizational psychology of presidential entitlement that threatens American democracy and the rule of law. Right-wing judges and lawyers since the Reagan administration have been the theory's primary, though not exclusive champions. The dangerously antidemocratic administration of Donald J. Trump stands as the most extreme version so far of an "entitled presidency." But even with Trump out of the White House, his successors will have to decide how far to embrace his administration's constitutional vision. Unless the theories underlying extreme presidentialism are exposed, analyzed, and rejected, the dangers of unchecked presidential power will persist. *Democracy's Chief Executive* is intended to provide general readers with an accessible guide to the ideas that have enabled the present moment and to argue for a vision of executive power that returns the presidency to the constitutional discipline of checks and balances.

Following current constitutional debates about the state of the American presidency can be a daunting challenge. Among lawyers, judges, and academics, three debates about the office of our chief executive are occurring simultaneously. One is a debate about how the Constitution should be interpreted as a general matter. The second is a debate about the founding generation's understanding of the presidency. The third is a debate about what institutional design for the presidency would best serve the national interest in our time. At the risk of oversimplification, each of these debates can be described in terms of opposing camps.

On the interpretive debate, the contending positions are generally *originalist* versus *adaptive*. For originalists, the meaning of the Constitution was fixed at its enactment, and legal decision-makers today may legitimately enforce only that fixed meaning.[1] As questions arise, for example, about the scope of presidential authority to deploy U.S. military forces abroad or as to the kinds of abuses of office that count as impeachable "high crimes and misdemeanors," originalists argue that the twenty-first-century answer should be whatever the 1787 answer happened to be. By way of contrast, "adaptivists"—sometimes called "living constitutionalists"—regard the meaning of the Constitution as subject to change. In an adaptive approach, historical arguments may be instructive, but are not controlling. Instead, the great strength of the Constitution is that its frequent ambiguity permits interpretation to achieve results that are normatively compelling given changing circumstances and contemporary needs. In asking whether the president should be able to control all federal criminal prosecutions personally or whether a presidential self-pardon would ever be permissible, we would want to know about Founding-era debates. But ultimately, twenty-first-century interpreters should resolve any textual ambiguity in favor of whichever answer is most consistent with twenty-first-century knowledge, values, and experience.

The second debate—the dispute over the Framers' original expectations— is a debate about constitutional history. One camp, the *presidentialists*, typically adheres to a view known as unitary executive theory, which ascribes to the president complete authority to command how every officer of the federal executive branch implements whatever discretion he or she has with regard to carrying out federal law. Unitary executive theorists most often, though not always, also embrace broad readings of the president's explicit Article II powers, such as the pardon power or the president's authority as commander in chief of the armed forces. A handy name for adherents to the opposing camp is harder to come by, but they might usefully be called *constitutional pluralists*. Pluralists recognize, of course, that we have only one president, but tend not to ascribe to the Founders any hard and fast expectations for the president's unilateral powers. Instead, pluralists emphasize the priority of Congress in setting the terms by which executive power is to be exercised, as well as the authority of the judiciary to review whether presidential action is lawful.

The opposing camps in the contemporary design debate tend to pose visions of a presidency either tightly or loosely centralized. On one side are those who think the country is best served by a president relatively unfettered in his or her decision-making with regard to the conduct of government. In this view, the president is "the decider."[2] What the president says, within the bounds of the law, goes. Against this position stands an argument for a more diffuse and accountable vision of presidential power. The presidency, viewed through this lens, operates best when the executive branch is transparent, congressional oversight is vigorous, and the president's reins over adminis- trative agencies are more lightly held. This vision of the presidency is thus not just hierarchical, but also collaborative. Executive power is checked and balanced by co-equal branches, and also by checking mechanisms internal to the executive branch.[3] In a balanced presidency cognizant of shared power, the president's success depends not only on centralized authority, but also on energizing and coordinating the initiative of others.

As table 1 on the next page shows, anyone thinking about these three concurrent debates might, in principle, find themselves holding any of eight different combinations of positions. In an important sense, life is easiest for those whose views track the combination in line 1. If line 1 describes your convictions, then you are in the happy position of thinking the Constitu- tion originally intended and thus commands an institutional presidency you regard as still best for the nation. Not only is this a set of views likely to appeal to activist presidents, but it would take little congressional initiative to secure, and the views of an originalist judiciary will reinforce the highly centralized, unilateral vision. My own view is that the soundest positions are to be found in line 8, but, as we shall see, securing that vision depends on a degree of commitment and initiative from the legislative branch that can hardly be taken for granted.[4]

On September 7, 2018, I had the privilege of appearing as a witness before the Judiciary Committee of the United States Senate to testify in opposition to the nomination of Brett M. Kavanaugh to serve as an Associate Justice on the US Supreme Court. Now-Justice Kavanaugh inhabits line 1, and the committee's Democratic minority had invited me to address what they and I took to be then-Judge Kavanaugh's dangerously indulgent ideas about the scope of presidential power under the Constitution. I entertained no illu- sion when I testified that my analysis would derail the Kavanaugh nomina- tion. The political solidarity among Senate Republicans left little doubt in anyone's mind as to the hearing's eventual outcome.

One may therefore reasonably ask why anyone should bother with pro- moting now a critical analysis of executive power that proved dead on arrival at the Kavanaugh hearings. The answer is that what becomes con- ventional wisdom about the Constitution is not simply a matter of sound research and academic acceptance. The originalist position on constitutional

TABLE I Competing positions in concurrent contemporary
debates on the constitutional presidency

	How should the Constitution be interpreted?	What was the founding generation's vision of the presidency?	What model of presidential power best serves twenty-first-century needs?
1	Originalist	Unilateral	Highly centralized
2	Originalist	Unilateral	Shared
3	Originalist	Pluralist	Highly centralized
4	Originalist	Pluralist	Shared
5	Adaptive	Unilateral	Highly centralized
6	Adaptive	Unilateral	Shared
7	Adaptive	Pluralist	Highly centralized
8	Adaptive	Pluralist	Shared

interpretation was fairly marginal fifty years ago. Prior to the 1970s, its animating ideas took root not in the academy, but in the "politics of postwar constitutional conservatism."[5] As documented by political scientist Calvin TerBeek:

> Political originalism was the collective work of, among many others, Barry Goldwater, *National Review*, James Kilpatrick, and conservative media impresarios Dan Smoot and Clarence Manion. It was *these* actors and institutions who first devised the content of what conservative legal elites in the Department of Justice and legal academy would call "originalism."[6]

And the attraction of originalism to political conservatives of the 1950s did not arrive randomly or because of the inherent persuasiveness of the theory. Instead, "non-legal actors set upon" originalism as "an ostensibly non-racialized first constitutional principle to delegitimize *Brown* [*v. Board of Education*]," the Supreme Court's unanimous 1954 decision declaring the intentional racial segregation of public schools to be in violation of the Fourteenth Amendment.[7] What legal academics have since contributed to the enterprise has been both the crystallization of originalism as a constitutional theory and its refinement with philosophical, historical, and linguistic argument. Originalism originally gained force, however, significantly because of its political valence.

Academics have played a similar role with regard to the currently ascendant "unitary executive theory," a cornerstone of modern-day presidentialism. Although earlier presidents and justices had made statements consistent with the claims of unitary executive theory, the theory was not "explicitly named or consciously promoted until the 1980s."[8] And just as with originalism, "unitary executive theory" has come to be widely accepted as conventional wisdom in large measure because of a "conscious, long-term intellectual investment of legal elites."[9] TerBeek's account of the particular dynamic through which originalism became dominant turns out to be an equally accurate description of the symbiotic relationship between politics and academic development in the ascendancy of unitary executive theory: "Parallel to legal elites' legitimization of [the construct] as a jurisprudential and academic theory, it was institutionalized by the GOP in the Supreme Court, Departments of Justice, Solicitors General, lower federal and state court judges, presidents and agency heads."[10] It is also true that, whatever the theoretical merits (or demerits) of presidentialism turn out to be, it gained traction in no small part because it seemed congenial for a political agenda—a program to yank the federal government rightward, away from the liberalism of the 1960s and 1970s.[11]

I thus offer the analysis in this volume as part of what I hope will prove an ultimately successful investment in an adaptavist view of the Constitution— a view that simultaneously corrects the unpersuasive originalist arguments for presidential unilateralism and moves past them to argue for institutional reforms in the name of greater executive-branch transparency and more robust checks and balances. As with the competing visions of constitutional originalism and presidential unilateralism, the vision offered here also has political roots. The political scientist Steven Skowronek has written that "a new construction of the presidency gains currency when it legitimizes the release of governmental power for new political purposes."[12] With regard to the theory offered in this volume, the "new political purposes" I have in mind involve the strengthening of American democracy in the wake of an astonishingly anti-democratic presidency between 2017 and 2021. One could thus say that the ideas that follow, like those that came together in support of originalism, have roots in racial politics—but in this instance, a politics of inclusion and equality.

I have organized the argument into three parts. Part 1, which I call, "Aggressive Presidentialism: Originalism Done Badly," comprises three chapters. Chapter 1 explores how the legal ascendancy of presidentialist ideas has helped enable the increasing slide toward an authoritarian executive we have witnessed since 1981. Chapter 2 explains how one especially dangerous tenet of the presidentialist creed—exclusive presidential control over criminal prosecution—cannot be squared with the originalist interpretive method on which it purports to rest. Chapter 3 then explicates a host of separation-of-powers issues that have been affected by the rise of presidentialism and spells out how their resolution following presidentialist premises threatens to make the presidency yet more autocratic.

Part 2, "Constitutional Interpretation for Democracy," turns to the theory and practice of constitutional interpretation. Chapter 4 is a critique chapter. It argues that originalism, generally speaking, does not support presidentialist theory. It goes further, however, to argue that the cure for originalism done badly is not just originalism done competently. Unvarnished originalism, I argue, runs the risk of (a) improperly locating authority to determine constitutional meaning in the past instead of the present, (b) pretending that the meaning of language is unchanging, and (c) obscuring the element of discretionary judgment entailed in all constitutional interpretation. Chapter 5 offers my alternative: an adaptavist approach to interpretation that values historical inquiry, but which also candidly prioritizes democratic values in resolving interpretive ambiguities.

Part 3, which, like the book, is called, "Democracy's Chief Executive," contains two chapters. Chapter 6 applies the method urged in chapter 5 to the problem areas identified in chapter 3, as well as some others. Chapter 7 tries to set out the conditions under which it is imaginable that democratic constitutionalism generally and my vision of Article II, in particular, might actually become a dominant understanding. These conditions are as much social, economic, and political as legal, but the core idea is easily stated: The shift from an authoritarian to a democratic presidency requires democratic reform in the larger society, not just legal reform within government itself.

More than one friend of mine reminded me: "No one votes for a president to do nothing. Voters expect presidents to accomplish things." Their implication is that there is no constituency for presidential modesty in the exercise of power; voters want restraint only in the pursuit of those policies with which they disagree. I persist in the hope that my friends' assessment is too one-sided. Like many Americans, I personally would wish for any number of profound changes in the direction of public policy in the United States. But I also believe in constitutional checks and balances and the rule of law. We should want the presidency to evolve in ways that protect those timeless values and, as this book tries to explain, the battle for that kind of presidency will in large part be a battle against bad constitutional ideas.

PART ONE

Aggressive Presidentialism

ORIGINALISM DONE BADLY

ONE

From the "Unitary" to
the "Entitled" Executive

ON JULY 25, 2019, when Donald J. Trump conducted his fateful phone call with Ukraine president Volodymyr Zelensky, he no doubt thought he was doing nothing wrong. He later dubbed it a "perfect call."[1] He surely had no expectation he would ever be held accountable for the contents of his conversation. The president's insouciance would have been nurtured both by his limitless self-regard and by his numerous prior successes in dodging comeuppance for so many breaches of political norms (and perhaps violations of law) that would have doomed other politicians. But feeding his confidence also would have been the explicit assurances his lawyers had provided in numerous contexts about a president's place in the American constitutional system. Trump would likely have believed that he need never disclose the contents of any conversation with a foreign leader, that the conduct of foreign diplomacy was his singular prerogative, and that he had unlimited discretion in the direction of the federal government's investigative powers regardless of his motives.

Trump would have enjoyed such legal assurances because, for the last forty years, the executive branch of our federal government—especially, but not exclusively when in the hands of conservative Republicans—has been in thrall to a constitutional theory that misreads the Constitution's grant of executive power and threatens American democracy. As I wrote over a decade ago, this theory, which I call aggressive presidentialism, turns out in practice to be a form of institutional ambition that feeds on itself.[2] It reflects and encourages a psychology of entitlement within and beyond the White House. From the Reagan administration forward, various of its proponents have sought to assure skeptical Americans that strong institutional norms and our constitutional system of checks and balances would prevent presidentialism from slipping into authoritarianism. But the administration of Donald J. Trump dramatized dangers previously treated as hypothetical. Aided and abetted by lawyers willing to make extreme arguments in support of presidentialism, we have seen how a chief executive scornful of competing institutions and conventional governance norms can subvert constitutional democracy.

Even with the Trump administration now behind us, the dangers posed by aggressive presidentialism are real. Voters want presidents to accomplish things, and Trump no doubt acclimated the American people to expect grand claims for what presidents can achieve through unilateral action. To be fair, Trump was to some extent echoing the rhetoric of his immediate predecessors, who sometimes claimed as personal accomplishments what were really the initiatives of a complex federal bureaucracy. Bill Clinton, for example, claimed it was his initiative to authorize FDA regulation of tobacco.[3] George W. Bush took it to be his personal prerogative to decide what stem cell lines should be allowable subjects of federally funded fetal tissue research.[4] But for the number and dishonesty of his misleading claims, Trump stood in a class by himself. Every successor going forward will be aware of the precedents Trump set and of the extent to which he got away with his braggadocio.

Trump's performance also showed why his behavior would not count as a boon to political accountability even under the least nuanced model of electoral democracy. Although the endorsement of a popular vote majority cannot itself guarantee that a president will represent a national majority on every issue, Trump lacked even that mandate. His brand of partisanship catered chiefly to an extreme minority. His record shows how the combination of big money influence in our elections, the malapportionment built into the electoral college system, the operation of party primaries, and various forms of vote suppression can yield presidents more loyal to a factional party base than to the national electorate as a whole. I will explore this theme in detail in chapter 5.

Notorious for his outsized self-regard, Donald Trump presumably did not need the subservience of misguided lawyers to nurture his personal sense of entitlement. His narcissism and self-dealing were on display long before he launched his political career.[5] But time and again, Americans witnessed how Trump, as president, echoed the rhetoric of his legal counsel to claim some "absolute right" to engage in conduct that was destabilizing and even corrupt.[6] Whether it is the law or an exaggerated sense of personal privilege that leads any president to undermine democratic norms, Trump's success in doing so and the legal theories that enabled him have set institutional precedents that may work in support of antidemocratic initiatives in the future undertaken even by "normal" presidents.

In the face of real-world threats to the operation of America's democratic institutions, it may seem an academic indulgence to point out that the constitutional interpretation on which presidentialism is founded is largely wrong. But it is important to point it out nonetheless. The insistence of presidentialism's proponents that the constitutional text penned in 1787 compels their conclusions is easily challenged. But a broader claim is just as critical: not only are "originalist" arguments for extreme presidentialism unfounded, but the methods by which contemporary originalists seek to frame the presidency in 1787 terms are wrongheaded in principle. What we are facing, in short, is an accelerating threat of dangerous claims for presidential power based on poor legal arguments that, in turn, reflect an approach to constitutional interpretation that itself is not justified. These bad legal ideas are threatening American democracy.

THE RENAISSANCE OF UNITARY EXECUTIVE THEORY

Looking back to the Reagan administration, it should be not surprising that, for conservative Republicans in 1981, a presidentialist view of the Constitution—a vision in which a president could work his will on public policy without interference from Congress or much accountability to the courts—would have been an easy sell. Although the Watergate scandal and President Gerald Ford's subsequent pardon of Richard Nixon had laid the groundwork for a Democratic presidential victory in 1976, the White House remained the likeliest point of leverage to move the country in a more right-wing direction. Watergate and the Ford pardon would fade from political salience. Richard Nixon's electoral strategy of 1968 had not lost its promise. The election of 1980 produced a Republican victory for Ronald Reagan, the dominant right-wing politician of his age.

In returning the presidency to GOP control, Reagan's win over Jimmy Carter seemed to vindicate the title of a much-discussed 1969 volume, *The Emerging Republican Majority*.[7] In that influential work, political strategist Kevin Phillips had provided a rigorous basis for optimism (among Republicans, at least) regarding near-term Republican dominance of presidential politics. By way of contrast, even though the 1980 election had returned the Senate to GOP control for the first time since 1955, the House remained in Democratic hands with no obvious prospect for any imminent Republican takeover. Senate filibuster rules combined with Democratic control of the House would mean that any conservative shifts in policy direction initiated by Congress could come only with Democratic support, which would hardly be reliable. As a result, anything truly revolutionary that Republican presidents might be able to accomplish in terms of reversing the country's moderate-to-liberal national politics would have to be accomplished within the domain of unilateral presidential authority.

This is not to say that either the government lawyers or legal scholars arguing for the "imperial presidency" in the 1980s were the first to promote some version of such ideas or that they were self-consciously arguing in a partisan way. But part of the human condition is the inevitability of what cognitive psychologists call "motivated reasoning."[8] We are most likely to take at face value evidence and reasoning consistent with what we want to believe is true. If you think it likely that presidential unilateralism is your surest path to political success, you will find the legal arguments on behalf of presidential unilateralism appealing. You will meet them with too little skepticism. Between 1981 and 1993, the Reagan and then Bush Justice Department became the crucible for honing what has come to be known as "unitary executive theory," a key pillar of aggressive presidentialism.[9] The basic tenet of "unitary executive theory" is that the president is entitled to tell any and every member of the executive branch of government how to do their jobs and to fire them if they do not comply.[10]

Among the early modern champions of unitary executive theory are two current Supreme Court Justices, Chief Justice John G. Roberts Jr. and Associate Justice Samuel Alito. From 1981 through early 1982, Roberts worked as a special assistant to Reagan's first attorney general, William French Smith. From 1982 to 1986, the future Chief Justice served as associate White House counsel.[11] Alito, for his part, spent the first Reagan Administration as an assistant to Solicitor General Rex Lee, the lawyer in Reagan's Justice Department with primary responsibility for shaping the administration's constitutional arguments to the US Supreme Court. From 1985 to 1987, Alito served as a deputy assistant attorney general in the Office of Legal Counsel under Assistant Attorney General Charles J. Cooper, also a devotee of unitary executive theory.[12] The Office of Legal Counsel, known widely as OLC, provides "outside counsel" to the White House and executive branch administrative agencies on issues of constitutional interpretation, as well as complex statutory problems.[13]

Meanwhile, with the blessings of such conservative legal figures as Edwin Meese, who served first in the Reagan administration as a counselor to the president and from 1984 on as attorney general, conservative law students at Yale and the University of Chicago in 1982 founded the Federalist Society for Law and Public Policy Studies.[14] Both well-organized and well-funded, "FedSoc" went on to become an influential incubator of constitutional theory—including unitary executive theory—as well as a powerful network for amplifying the visibility and promoting the careers of conservative and libertarian lawyers.

Among FedSoc's roster of favorite government officials is William Barr, President Donald Trump's second confirmed attorney general. Barr had done a stint on President Reagan's Domestic Policy Council in 1982 and 1983, but first became a major Justice Department figure in the George H. W. Bush administration. Starting as assistant attorney general in charge of OLC, Barr rose quickly to be the deputy attorney general and then, from 1991 through the end of the administration, attorney general.[15] It was in his OLC years, however, that he made what is arguably his most important early contribution to unitary executive theory, a 1989 memo entitled, "Common Legislative Encroachments on Executive Branch Authority."[16] His analysis, prepared for an interagency group of the administration's agency general counsels, discusses what Barr argued were "a variety of common provisions of legislation that are offensive to principles of separation of powers, and to executive power in particular, from the standpoint of policy or constitutional law."[17] To anyone familiar with the customary ways in which the federal government has operated over the centuries, some of these claims are startling. Barr argued, for example, that Congress violates the president's appointments authority by requiring "a fixed number of members of certain commissions be from a particular political party."[18] Yet such requirements of political balance are a feature of virtually every so-called independent federal agency. Likewise, Congress supposedly violates the Constitution by requiring the president to submit recommendations for its legislative consideration. In Barr's view, "Because the President has plenary exclusive authority to determine whether and when he should propose legislation, any bill purporting to require the submission of recommendations is unconstitutional."[19] Again, such legislative requirements have been utterly routine since the founding. Barr's 1989 memo thus foreshadowed the forcefulness with which he would be prepared to make even far-fetched constitutional arguments thirty years later on behalf of a President Trump. Barr actually told the Federalist Society in November 2019 that "by the time of the American Revolution, the patriots well understood that their prime antagonist was an overweening Parliament," not the king.[20] This trivialization of the revolutionaries' anti-monarchical fervor would have come as no small shock to the patriots signing the Declaration of Independence, who laid out twenty-seven specific grievances against George III.[21] Likewise with Thomas Paine, the author of Common Sense, who described the king as a "hardened, sullen-tempered Pharaoh" and the "Royal Brute of Great Britain."[22]

THE DOCTRINAL PILLARS OF LEGAL PRESIDENTIALISM

"Unitary executive theory"—the President's supposed authority to control the entire federal bureaucracy—is one of three key interlocking doctrines or interpretations of the Constitution that undergird twenty-first-century presidentialism. Although the other core claims are not customarily labeled as such, they are easily recognizable. One asserts the unlimited scope of any discretionary power vested in presidents by the Constitution, such as the pardon power.[23] I will call this the "plenary discretion principle." The other posits the president's assertedly unilateral prerogative to conduct the nation's foreign affairs and national security policy making; I will call this principle, "national security unilateralism."[24] According to their champions, all three are rooted in the original 1787 understanding of Article II of the Constitution, even though all three are deeply opposed to the notion of checks and balances and the principle of presidential accountability to the other branches of government.

Unitary executive theory actually comes in a variety of forms, although its proponents commonly assert at least two propositions. One is that Article II of the Constitution guarantees presidents the power to fire at will any subordinate officer within the executive branch.[25] The second is that, to the extent Congress has vested any administrative official with policy-making discretion of any kind, the president is constitutionally entitled to command that official as to how his or her discretion must be exercised.[26] A good example of the theory in practice involves the Reagan administration's response to a statute requiring the director of the Centers for Disease Control to prepare and disseminate an informational pamphlet on AIDS without clearance by any other official or office, including the White House.[27] In an opinion signed by OLC's Charles Cooper, the Justice Department insisted it would be unconstitutional to keep the president out of the loop, so to speak, even for drafting an expert pamphlet on AIDS: "The Director of the CDC, as a subordinate executive branch officer within the Department of Health and Human Services, is subject to the complete supervision of the President with respect to the carrying out of executive functions."[28] In asserting the president's entitlement to edit CDC pamphlets, OLC said: "It matters not at all that the information in the AIDS fliers may be highly scientific in nature."[29] In other words, any delegation of authority to any agency to do anything is effectively, in the presidentialist view, a delegation of power to the president.

At first blush, these propositions of presidential authority may not seem threatening. Their implications for actual government practice, however, are radical. For one thing, so-called independent administrative agencies, the leaders of which are protected from presidential firing except for good cause, would be unconstitutional under unitary executive theory.[30] Dozens of long-standing agencies, such as the Federal Reserve System, the Federal Communications Commission, and the Federal Trade Commission would be unconstitutional as currently structured. Moreover, the supervisory power to which the unilateralists subscribe would guarantee presidents the authority to control criminal investigations of potential wrongdoing even by themselves and their closest associates.[31]

To make things yet more ominous, enthusiasts for unitary executive theory tend also to be advocates for extensive and unreviewable presidential authority in other respects, including the conduct of national security surveillance and the deployment of US military forces abroad. It is this latter cluster of views that I call "national security unilateralism." Belief in these views played a major part in Justice Department memos that advised the George W. Bush administration on the "enhanced interrogation" of enemy combatants (including practices that we would surely call "torture" if perpetrated against Americans),[32] Bush's supposed authority to ignore the Geneva Conventions in America's treatment of al Qaeda,[33] and the permissibility of engaging in forms of electronic eavesdropping that were then in violation of the Foreign Intelligence Surveillance Act.[34]

In tandem, unitary executive theory and national security unilateralism envision a presidency largely unconstrained by either Congress or the judiciary. But they are bolstered yet further by what I have called the "plenary discretion principle." The idea is that, if the Constitution vests any discretionary power in the president, Congress may not regulate its exercise, even indirectly. To put the point differently, the manner in which the president's constitutionally vested discretion is exercised, no matter how corrupt or in violation of constitutional values, cannot ever be deemed unlawful. This is what Richard Nixon meant when, with regard to the defense of national security, he told interviewer David Frost: "When the president does it, that means that it is not illegal."[35]

In an extraordinary 2006 address, former vice president Al Gore laid out in compelling detail how the claims of presidential authority by the George W. Bush administration along the lines I just laid out threaten to upend the government of laws ideal.[36] Taking note of how a dangerous theory of constitutional interpretation was enabling the Bush administration's worst abuses, he spoke in terms even more salient now: "[The Bush] Administration has come to power in the thrall of a legal theory that aims to convince us that this excessive concentration of presidential power is exactly what our Constitution intended."[37] Gore explained that, once unilateralism spawns disrespect for legal constraint, authoritarianism looms:

> Unless stopped, lawlessness grows. The greater the power of the executive grows, the more difficult it becomes for the other branches to perform their constitutional roles. As the executive acts outside its constitutionally prescribed role and is able to control access to information that would expose its mistakes and reveal errors, it becomes increasingly difficult for the other branches to police its activities. Once that ability is lost, democracy itself is threatened and we become a government of men and not laws.[38]

Fortunately, advocacy for an excessively presidentialist view of the Constitution has had to contend over the centuries with a competing tradition rooted in the commitment to checks and balances. Scholars I call "constitutional pluralists" interpret our checks and balances system to emphasize the roles that the Framers assigned to the multiple institutions of our national government in holding each other to account.[39] In the pluralist view, the scope of permissible presidential initiative depends very much on the actions of Congress and the courts. It is through the commitment to checks and balances and the constraining force of the competing branches that the rule of law is preserved.

I am saving for later chapters a more detailed account of how presidential unilateralists misread the Constitution and why the pluralist view is superior. Yet it is important to state at the outset that our modern presidents' pretensions to power hardly conform to any original consensus as to the design of the presidential office. When scholars or pundits try to persuade you that the presidency of Donald J. Trump somehow vindicated the constitutional design of 1787, beware.

One of the most important scholarly works to date in support of unitary executive theory has the provocative title, *Imperial from the Beginning: The Constitution of the Original Executive*.[40] Its author, Professor Saikrishna Prakash, argues that the Framers created an "elective monarch," with powers of "law execution; control of foreign affairs; command of the military; and the creation, appointment, and direction of officers involved in implementing" those powers.[41] But in its particulars, the argument is considerably overstated. The eleven-year span between the Declaration of Independence and the Constitutional Convention did witness a renewed appreciation of the value of an efficient executive power not wholly beholden to the legislature. But the idea that Americans, having just overthrown George III, would have embraced a presidency modeled on his powers is more than a little counterintuitive. James Wilson, an early Supreme Court Justice who had signed the Declaration of Independence and who had served as an influential participant in the Philadelphia Convention of 1787, specifically took the view during the convention that "the Prerogatives of the British Monarch" were not "a proper guide in defining the Executive powers."[42] Despite his role in urging "unity in the executive," Wilson

> said that Unity in the Executive instead of being the fetus of Monarchy would be the best safeguard against tyranny. He repeated that he was not governed by the British Model which was inapplicable to the situation of this Country; the extent of which was so great, and the manners so republican, that nothing but a great confederated Republic would do for it.[43]

Especially striking among modern-day presidentialists is the opposition to almost any sort of presidential accountability to Congress. For its legal defenders, the logic of presidential resistance often observes the following two-step doctrinal dance. Step Number One: Construe any aspect of how the Constitution describes the presidency as precluding any legislative measure that would impinge on that description. For example, because the Constitution authorizes the president to nominate "Officers of the United States," it is supposedly unconstitutional to limit the pool of nominees to individuals with particular qualifications.[44] Because the Constitution authorizes the president to recommend to Congress "such measures as he shall judge necessary and expedient," it is supposedly unconstitutional for Congress to mandate informational reports from anyone in the executive branch.[45] Because the Constitution imposes specific qualifications for the presidency based on citizenship, age, and residency, Trump's lawyers argued that Congress may not impose as "additional qualifications" any limitations on presidents' financial conflicts of interest.[46] (In actuality, historical practice runs entirely counter to each of these positions.)

Step Two: Because there is rarely any judicial authority substantiating these arguments, resort to a legal strategy for reading statutes called "constitutional avoidance." This ordinary rule for interpreting statutes holds that, if possible, statutes should not be read in a way that would raise a serious question as to whether they are constitutional. For example, if the wording of a law is ambiguous enough that it could either be read broadly, but in a way that might violate the First Amendment, or narrowly, in which case it would not limit free expression, judges will adopt the second reading. Following that logic, aggressive presidentialists use "constitutional avoidance" to read any statute narrowly if its broader reading would raise questions about the legislative restriction of executive power they have argued is unconstitutional under Step One.[47] To trigger such narrow readings, the unilateralist arguments I have cataloged need not be authoritative to be consequential; they need only be "serious." If a statute can somehow be read so narrowly as to leave the president unregulated—see Step One—then the president's lawyers will insist that is how the law should be read in order to avoid a highly contrived, but "serious" constitutional question.

The Trump administration was especially successful in its early years in deploying an analogous approach to avoiding Congress's oversight questions. Instead of actually claiming executive privilege to withhold specific information from Congress, various witnesses, facing interrogation from congressional committees, refused to answer on the ground that the information sought *might* be subject to privilege and the president *might* want to claim privilege.[48] In this manner, they not only avoided disclosures the administration could find politically embarrassing, but they avoided immediately raising an issue that Congress could take to a court for resolution. Between the extreme narrowing of statutes and playing dodgeball with congressional oversight, the unilateralists' constitutional avoidance techniques generate a protective zone for presidential power that goes way beyond what sound constitutional interpretation would itself require. Thus are the seeds planted for an authoritarian presidency.

The legal theories against which I am arguing did not spring from nowhere in 2017. Accelerating presidential claims to unaccountable power and the risks they pose to democracy have older roots and will stand as troubling precedents well after Trump's departure. The relevance of the Trump administration is that it took the risks of extreme presidentialism that observers had hypothesized under his predecessors and turned them into real-life examples of constitutional abuse.

Although, like its predecessors, the Trump administration was aggressively presidentialist in foreign and military affairs—a topic we will revisit in chapter 6—it is really in domestic affairs that Trump and his lawyers elevated aggressive presidentialist arguments to extreme new heights. The best publicized example springs from Trump's resistance to the investigation of Russian interference in the 2016 presidential election. The final report of Special Counsel Robert S. Mueller, III highlighted ten areas in which evidence was available that might support criminal obstruction of justice charges against Trump.[49] Prosecutors "found multiple acts by the President that were capable of exerting undue influence over law enforcement investigations, including the Russian-interference and obstruction investigations."[50] The report noted, however, that factual assessments regarding a sitting president face a unique complication. As head of the executive branch, a president has many opportunities afforded by his ordinary constitutional powers to influence official proceedings, subordinate officers, and potential witnesses. Showing that a president has obstructed justice thus requires prosecutors to show more than a presidential exertion of attempted influence. They would have to show corrupt motive.[51]

In line with presidentialist doctrine, however, the president's lawyers insisted that, if the Constitution authorizes the president to do something— anything—within his discretionary powers, his motivation is irrelevant to legality. This is the "plenary discretion principle" at work. White House counsel argued, for example, that the president possesses a constitutionally vested power to fire any subordinate official within the executive branch and to terminate any criminal investigation, within his complete discretion. On that basis, Trump's lawyers made "a categorical argument" to the Special Counsel "that 'the President's exercise of his constitutional authority . . . to terminate an FBI Director and to close investigations . . . cannot constitutionally constitute obstruction of justice,'" even if corruptly motivated.[52] In other words, we are supposed to believe that, no matter what our criminal statutes may say, a president cannot be acting illegally in preventing the investigation of his own criminality or that of his family and associates.

The Mueller report refutes Trump's legal arguments in detail, and the arguments will be discussed in greater detail in chapter 2. It is astonishing, however, that anyone would expect arguments like these to be taken seriously in what purports to be a rule of law-based system like ours. The obstruction of justice statutes cover "[w]hoever corruptly . . . obstructs, or impedes or endeavors to influence, obstruct, or impede the due and proper administration of the law."[53] To act "corruptly," is to act with an impermissible purpose. Proof of obstruction does not require that the act manifesting corrupt purpose be unlawful on its own. It is enough that the proscribed act was done for a dishonest or improper end.

Nothing in the Constitution authorizes a president to act corruptly. Whatever the president's ordinary powers may be regarding criminal prosecution, it remains true, as the Mueller Report insists, that:

> the proper supervision of criminal law does not demand freedom for the President to act with a corrupt intention of shielding himself from criminal punishment, avoiding financial liability, or preventing personal embarrassment. To the contrary, a statute that prohibits official action undertaken for such corrupt purposes furthers, rather than hinders, the impartial and evenhanded administration of the law.[54]

Moreover, the president's oath requires him to execute his office "faithfully," and his constitutional mandate with the furthest domestic reach is the charge to "take care that the laws be faithfully executed." To argue that the president's corrupt exercise of constitutional powers is outside the reach of the law would make the oath meaningless.

Equally ambitious have been legal claims on Trump's behalf that, beyond his salary, a president may pocket direct and immediate financial benefits while in office, at least if he is not explicitly taking money for specific services rendered.[55] Implying just the opposite, the Constitution has two provisions intended to prevent sitting presidents from receiving "emoluments" beyond their government salary. The Domestic Emoluments Clause provides that the president is to receive "Compensation" "for his Services," but not "any other Emolument" from the United States or from any State.[56] The obvious purposes are to prevent either presidential self-dealing in managing federal finances or resort by individual states to financial inducements for presidential favoritism. Under the Foreign Emoluments Clause, "no Person holding any Office of Profit or Trust under [the United States], shall, without the Consent of the Congress, accept of any present, Emolument, Office, or Title, of any kind whatever, from any King, Prince, or foreign State."[57] Here, too, the Constitution's purpose is clear, namely, to prevent foreign powers from compromising any federal official's sole allegiance to the United States.

Litigation has targeted Trump for ignoring both clauses. The alleged violations include:

- Holding a 76 percent interest in Trump International Hotel, which markets itself to the international diplomatic community;
- Profiting from foreign states and foreign officials patronizing Trump Tower and Trump World Tower in New York City;
- Getting income from real estate projects in which the Trump Organization is engaged in the United Arab Emirates and Indonesia; and
- Receiving a benefit for the Trump International Hotel from the General Services Administration, which allowed Trump to remain on the hotel's lease, notwithstanding a lease agreement between the hotel and the government which provides that "no ... elected official of the Government of the United States ... shall be admitted to any share or part of this Lease, or to any benefit that may arise therefrom."[58]

It has also been alleged that the State Department and U.S. Embassies promoted the Mar-a-Lago Club, a Trump-owned business in Palm Beach, Florida, which regularly rents its facilities to federal, state, and local governments.[59] Trump infamously announced what became a short-lived decision to hold a U.S.-hosted meeting of the G-7 heads of state at his Doral Golf Club in Miami, rather than at a government-owned venue.[60] Millions would have had to have been spent on security precautions to protect leaders from Canada, France, Germany, Italy, Japan, and the United Kingdom—security precautions already in effect in the government-owned presidential retreat at Camp David.[61]

Seeking to preserve Trump's ability to enrich himself while in the White House, Justice Department lawyers argued in court that "emolument" in the Constitution should be narrowly construed to mean only "profit arising from an office or employ."[62] In other words, the only "emolument" prohibited by the Constitution would be an outright bribe. The argument is nonsense. In an extensive scholarly opinion, a federal trial court judge in

D.C. found that the Justice Department position "disregards the ordinary meaning of ["emolument"] as set forth in the vast majority of Founding-era dictionaries; is inconsistent with the text, structure, historical interpretation, adoption, and purpose of the Clause; and is contrary to Executive Branch practice over the course of many years."[63] According to the judge, the government's arguments ignored the "overwhelming evidence pointing to over two hundred years of understanding the scope of the Clause to be broad to achieve its purpose of guarding against even the possibility of 'corruption and foreign influence.'"[64]

The Justice Department's campaign against presidential accountability in the emoluments suits, however, appears modest compared to the arguments both OLC and Trump's private lawyers made in resisting congressional efforts to review Trump's business practices while in office. Given his obvious potential conflicts of interest, Trump's foreign financial entanglements, and his possible evasion of the Constitution, House committees subpoenaed Trump's banks and accountants to obtain his financial records. The House Ways and Means Committee, pursuant to federal law, requested and then subpoenaed the Internal Revenue Service to turn over Trump's federal tax records.[65] The wording of federal law unconditionally entitled the House Ways and Means Committee to the records it sought. Treasury Secretary Steven Mnuchin, however, directed IRS not to comply.[66]

In defense of his stonewalling, Mnuchin proffered an OLC opinion truly shocking in its brazenness.[67] OLC conceded that the relevant statute, 26 U.S.C. § 6103(f), did not require the House Ways and Means Committee to specify any reason for requesting the president's tax returns.[68] It likewise acknowledged that the committee chair and various members had nonetheless "offered many different justifications" for the demand, including a desire to "inform tax reform legislation" and "expose any alleged emoluments received from foreign governments."[69] Nonetheless, OLC argued, Treasury was within its rights in withholding Trump's records because of a unilateral executive branch determination that the reasons offered by the committee— reasons they were under no statutory obligation to provide—were merely pretextual, and that the committee's real purpose was to facilitate public disclosure of the president's returns, a purpose that OLC argued would be constitutionally illegitimate.[70]

In Trump's private lawsuits seeking to stop his banks and accountants, and the State of New York, from releasing his records, Trump's lawyers went even further. Congress, they insisted, could not legitimately pursue Trump's tax returns to ascertain whether he violated the law, since the purpose of such disclosure would be "law enforcement," and only the executive branch and the courts are allowed to participate, they argue, in law enforcement.[71] Moreover, Congress could not legitimately seek Trump's records as part of legislative deliberations over whether to strengthen conflict-of-interest laws because, they contended, Congress may not constitutionally impose conflict-of-interest laws on the president.[72] The supposed reason for this, unbelievable as it may sound, is that imposing ethical requirements on the president while in office would impermissibly add to the exclusive constitutional requirements for the presidency, namely, that the president be a natural-born citizen and at least thirty-five years of age.[73] Under this view, the president would be above the law for the astonishing reason that Congress would not be entitled to make any law regarding the president.

These examples of Trump's aggressive presidentialism—his claim to be above the obstruction statute, his disregard of the Emoluments Clauses, and his attempt to stonewall congressional demands for his financial records—are but the best publicized examples of how arguments in support of extreme presidential power have metastasized. How these arguments, if accepted, would undermine checks and balances and the rule of law is more or less apparent as soon as the arguments are stated. They are, however, only part of the story. As chapter 3 will explore, Trump's record also demonstrates how legal arguments about the president's relationship to the federal bureaucracy can be deployed in more obscure contexts to undermine genuinely democratic governance. Unfortunately, the very complexity of these arguments works in favor of any overreaching president. As long as the constitutional debates and their implications remain obscure to all but legal experts, the prospects for pushing back politically on aggressive presidentialism are correspondingly diminished.

DEMOCRATIC NORMS AND THEIR VULNERABILITY TO ATTACK

Scholars supporting extreme views of presidential power sometimes urge us to be assuaged by three supposedly mitigating factors. One is the possibility that Congress is authorized to impeach and remove the president for high crimes and misdemeanors. Unfortunately, however, this leaves open a vast realm of potential abuse of power that might be dangerously antidemocratic, but not at the "high crime and misdemeanor" level. It also overlooks the serious political hurdles to taking such a step against even a deserving target.

The second is the supposed power of other institutions to check abuse, including government structures such as courts, Congress, and the administrative bureaucracy, and independent bodies, including, preeminently, the press.

The third is the constraining force of governance norms, both within the executive branch and as between the other branches and the president. Norms are the unspoken, but commonly held values and rules of engagement that enable people and institutions to get along. No law bars my neighbors from painting their house purple adorned with massive green polka dots, but they do not. Likewise, I always park my car in front of my house, never theirs. These are courtesies of mutual accommodation, not enforceable obligations. Similarly unenforceable, but widely expected value norms and customary practices of governance are supposed to check unduly aggressive claims to unilateral presidential power.[74]

Unfortunately, Trump's assault on the values and institutions that might check his powers was relentless. His administration's attitude toward informal constraints on the exercise of power seemed to be, "Norms are for losers." That his behavior and utterances frequently lacked the weight, courtesy, and truthfulness that we associate with "acting presidential" tells but a fraction of the story. The most dangerous precedents lay with behaviors and utterances plainly subversive of those values that are central to governance in a constitutional democracy.

Among the most defining norms in any working democracy are respect for the rule of law and its implicit promise of evenhandedness in the administration of justice. Thus, for example, although it is widely assumed that presidents may appropriately influence their respective administrations' general law enforcement priorities—focusing resources more or less on, say, white collar crime or drug enforcement—it has likewise been axiomatic that presidents should not interfere in individual cases. To reinforce the idea of prosecutorial independence and as a specific reaction to the Watergate scandal, every president since Jimmy Carter has adopted policies to limit interaction between the Justice Department and the White House.[75]

Yet Trump's disdain for the law and his scorn for prosecutorial independence could hardly have been clearer. He was in office less than two weeks when he fired Acting Attorney General Sally Yates because she refused to defend the first, sloppily drafted incarnation of his travel ban executive order.[76] He was less than four months in when he fired FBI Director James Comey because of unhappiness with the FBI's investigation of Russian involvement in the 2016 presidential campaign.[77] (Comey's discharge was all the more notable because Congress, after Watergate, gave FBI Directors a statutory ten-year term, precisely to reinforce the norm of investigative independence.[78]) Trump famously and without foundation called for criminal investigations of Hillary Clinton, former UN Ambassador Susan Rice, Joe and Hunter Biden, and Justice Department lawyers he held responsible for pursuing the Russia investigation.[79] He engaged in relentless public attacks against his first attorney general, Jeff Sessions, because Sessions recused himself from that inquiry.[80] Indeed, the toughest issue posed by Trump's attempts to sideline the Russia investigation was not whether he acted inappropriately, but whether his actions were so provably corrupt as to constitute a criminal obstruction of justice.[81]

Trump's contempt for law was evident also in his use of the pardon power. Bypassing the normal process for the evaluation of pardon applications, Trump repeatedly used the pardon power to curry favor with his right-wing Republican base. In April 2018, he pardoned Scooter Libby, the former chief of staff to Vice President Dick Cheney who had been convicted of perjury and obstruction of justice in 2007 in connection with the investigation into who leaked the identity of CIA officer Valerie Plame.[82] Six weeks later, Trump pardoned Dinesh D'Souza, a right-wing author who had pleaded guilty in 2014 to knowingly making illegal campaign contributions.[83] D'Souza had been fined $30,000 and sentenced to five years' probation, including eight months in a supervised "community confinement center."[84] In May 2019, Trump pardoned former Army 1st Lt. Michael Behenna, who was convicted and sentenced to twenty-five years in prison by a military court in 2009 for killing an Iraqi prisoner.[85] Trump indicated he was considering pardons for several American military members accused of war crimes.[86]

Among Trump's most troubling pardons, however, was arguably his very first—for the former Maricopa County sheriff Joe Arpaio, who had been found guilty of criminal contempt, but not yet sentenced, for disregarding a court order in a racial-profiling case.[87] Arpaio, a vocal Trump supporter during the 2016 campaign, who echoed Trump's "birtherism" claims regarding Barack Obama, was notorious for treating inmates brutally and for harassing Hispanic Arizonans based on their perceived immigration status. As summarized in an ACLU study, "People who encountered Arpaio's detention system faced gruesome conditions and humiliating practices, and they were denied basic necessities and health care. For instance, female inmates reported that officers made them sleep in their own menstrual blood and assaulted pregnant women."[88] He had become infamous for his treatment of those he held in an outdoor jail he called his "Tent City," where inmates were compelled to wear pink underwear and work in chain gangs.[89]

What was most pernicious about the Arpaio pardon—a pardon issued without any Justice Department review—is that it was so obviously intended to subvert the authority of the judiciary to enforce its lawful orders. At a rally prior to the pardon, Trump implicitly condoned the civil rights violations that prompted the court order as Arpaio "doing his job."[90] It began a pattern of using pardons—or the possibility of pardons—as political favors or worse. At one point, he publicly acknowledged the possibility of a pardon for his former campaign manager, Paul Manafort, who had been convicted of eight felonies and who pled guilty to two more in the course of the Mueller investigation.[91] At the time, Manafort was presumably being pressured to provide information to the Special Counsel that could have been damaging to Trump. Following his defeat in the 2020 election and with but a month left in his term, Trump finally issued Manafort's pardon, along with pardons for Charles Kushner—the father of Trump's son-in-law, Jared Kushner—and Roger J. Stone Jr., a longtime adviser. He had earlier commuted Stone's sentence for lying to Congress to cover up his efforts to find out about hacked emails relating to Trump's 2016 election opponent.[92] So much for the rule of law.

Also foundational are the norms that embody respect for the value of those institutions that can serve as a check on presidential abuse—namely, the press, the other branches of government, and the civil service. The press affords a check through its independent reporting and analysis. Congress protects against abuse through oversight and the imposition of regulatory restraints on executive power. Courts can afford relief from arbitrary executive action in properly brought litigation that surfaces violations of the law. The civil service, though part of the executive branch, can serve a checking function by promoting values of expertise, deliberation, consensus building, and political neutrality.[93]

Trump has assiduously resisted all of these institutions. He has belittled the press relentlessly, describing mainstream media as "the enemy of the people."[94] He has ridiculed and sought to humiliate individual journalists.[95] And he has spewed lies and half-truths at a mind-boggling rate.[96] Ominously, Trump has even sought to persuade his supporters that any journalism casting him or his administration in a light less than glowing is "fake news."[97]

This pattern even includes his repeatedly denying saying and doing things that videos unmistakably show him to be saying and doing.[98] Describing a totalitarian regime, George Orwell famously wrote in the novel *1984*, "The party told you to reject the evidence of your eyes and ears. It was their final, most essential command."[99] Trump has said no less. He also reversed his predecessors' policies of routinely making public his daily schedule, his agenda of phone calls with foreign leaders, and his roster of White House visitors.[100]

Having tried to undermine public trust in the press, Trump similarly called into question the legitimacy of any judge who ruled against his signature initiatives, just as during his campaign he attacked U.S. District Court Judge Gonzalo O. Curiel, who had issued some unfavorable rulings in a case involving the largely fraudulent Trump University.[101] Candidate Trump insisted he American-born Judge Curiel was biased against Trump because of his "Mexican heritage." As president, when the lower federal courts blocked the initial versions of Trump's ban on entry for travelers from a number of Muslim-majority nations, he tweeted that US courts are "slow and political!"[102] When a federal trial judge blocked his executive order seeking to punish sanctuary cities, he declared: "The rule of law suffered another blow, as an unelected judge unilaterally rewrote immigration policy for our Nation."[103] On November 20, 2018, when Judge Jon Tigar of the Northern District of California ordered the administration to accept asylum claims regardless of where migrants entered the country: "Trump called the decision 'a disgrace,' attacked Tigar as 'an Obama judge,' and critiqued the Ninth Circuit as 'really something we have to take a look at because it's not fair,' adding, 'That's not law. Every case that gets filed in the Ninth Circuit we get beaten.'"[104]

With regard to Congress, the Trump White House tried to stonewall any committee oversight related to the president's finances, Russia's involvement in the 2016 election, or Trump's pressuring the government of Ukraine to investigate the business activities of Hunter Biden. It often refused to respond to subpoenas for documents, claimed absolute immunity against compelled testimony by current White House personnel, and pressured White House employees—current and former—either not to testify or to testify only within the narrowest possible subject-matter constraints.[105]

Arguably most surprising, however, was Trump's assault on the executive branch itself. He failed to follow standard agency review processes in developing some of his most controversial policies. He tried to place his then political advisor Steve Bannon on the so-called Principals Committee of the National Security Council—while actually removing the director of National Intelligence and chairman of the Joint Chiefs of Staff from that committee.[106] He repeatedly nominated key cabinet and subcabinet officials without relevant policy experience, but who had a high public profile of supporting Trump politically. As of October 2019, one out of every fourteen of his political appointees had been a lobbyist—281 in all.[107] He relentlessly attacked the professionalism and reliability of the federal law enforcement and intelligence communities and routinely heaped ridicule on his first secretary of state, Rex Tillerson, and first attorney general, Jeff Sessions[108]—both of whom he had selected for their respective offices. He left many important positions unfilled and exploited legal loopholes in order to fill key posts with "acting" administrators, thus circumventing the Senate confirmation process.[109] The last strategy was clearly deliberate, even with regard to cabinet-level officers; as Trump told an interviewer: "I like 'acting' because I can move so quickly. It gives me more flexibility."[110]

Trump made it evident early that he values sycophancy over qualifications. His impulse to appoint his political defenders, in combination with weak White House vetting, led to a significant number of nominees who had to be withdrawn in embarrassing circumstances. A perfect example involved Rep. John Ratcliffe, a Texas Republican, who Trump indicated would be his nominee to become director of national intelligence after his original appointee, former Senator Dan Coats, resigned over policy disagreements with the White House.[111] Ratcliffe had been a vigorous defender of Trump in questioning Robert Mueller during a House committee hearing, but had little experience relevant to the DNI position, having served in federal law enforcement for only four years as an assistant, and then acting United States attorney for the Eastern District of Texas.[112] Ratcliffe withdrew when it became clear that his official biography greatly exaggerated the significance of his limited antiterrorism work in that office.[113] But just as telling was a comparison of Ratcliffe's background with those of the five prior directors. Two had served in important ambassadorial roles, among other important government posts, and three had multi-decade military careers, with significant high-level intelligence responsibilities.[114] Ratcliffe's prior public service consisted of eight years as mayor of Heath, Texas, a town of about 7,000 in population.[115] Trump clearly preferred to be surrounded by family members and flatterers, rather than advisers who could bring to bear on their job performance their own extensive knowledge and experience. Quite remarkably, nearly seven months after Ratcliffe withdrew from consideration, Trump resubmitted his nomination, and he was confirmed.[116]

But beyond Trump's hostility to the rule of law and his scorn for institutions positioned to check presidential abuse, Trump also demonstrated, in a variety of ways, his contempt for the most elementary norm of a democratic presidency: a commitment to being a president of and for all Americans. He abandoned the norm of "other-focused leadership"—not being president of just those who support you, and certainly not using the presidential office to line your own pockets. Instead, he unabashedly used his office to promote his private interests and those of his family, while attempting to humiliate and intimidate anyone critical or just insufficiently loyal—whether in the press, the bureaucracy, the private sector, or even his own party. He appointed family members to White House posts and played fast and loose with security clearances.[117] He also set up trusts in a way that permitted him to withdraw funds from private Trump Organization enterprises without disclosure.[118] Under his watch, the government spent millions on events held on Trump-owned properties.[119]

Among the most galling displays of Trump's favoritism was his apparently differential sympathy to those of his fellow citizens suffering the aftermath of natural disasters depending on whether they lived in primarily Republican or Democratic jurisdictions. In the midst of 2018 California wildfires, he tweeted: "There is no reason for these massive, deadly and costly forest fires in California except that forest management is so poor. Billions of dollars are given each year, with so many lives lost, all because of gross mismanagement of the forests. Remedy now, or no more Fed payments!"[120] In the face of two devastating hurricanes hitting Puerto Rico, Trump, without foundation, denied the reports of three thousand deaths on the island and lied about the extent of federal aid.[121] Yet when Hurricane Harvey wreaked havoc on Louisiana and Texas, Trump's response was what one might expect from a normal president: "We are one American family. We hurt together, we struggle together and believe me, we endure together."[122]

Undoubtedly Trump's grossest departure from a norm of inclusive presidential concern lay in his repeated stoking of racial resentment and refusal to stand up to white nationalist extremism. Whether insisting there were "good people" on "both sides" when the white supremacist "Unite the Right" rally turned violent in Charlottesville,[123] using racist remarks to attack four congresswomen of color,[124] or maligning a majority-black Baltimore district as a "rat and rodent infested mess,"[125] Trump's rhetoric repeatedly and unapologetically gave aid and comfort to the most extreme forms of white identity politics.

Trump's persistent attacks on these norms led to a kind of trickle-down hostility to democracy and the rule of law that permeated his administration. Both his first EPA chief, Scott Pruitt, and interior secretary, Ryan Zinke—chosen because of their hostility to the statutory missions of their respective agencies—were forced to resign because of multiple ethics probes.[126] The Government Accountability Office found that Housing and Urban Development Secretary Ben Carson violated the law by lavishly refurnishing his office.[127] The Office of Government Ethics refused to certify a legally required financial disclosure by Commerce Secretary Wilbur Ross—a highly unusual step—because he continued to own a stock he claimed to have sold.[128] A State Department inspector general report found that Trump appointees were engaged in a pattern of politically motivated harassment of career professionals.[129] When accused of violating the Hatch Act because of her partisan tweeting, Department of Housing and Urban Development Regional Administrator Lynne Patton—a former Trump events planner—said: "It may be a Hatch Act violation. It may not be. Either way, I honestly don't care anymore."[130] When repeated Hatch Act violations led the Trump-appointed head of the independent U.S. Office of Special Counsel to call for the dismissal of White House counselor Kellyanne Conway, Trump made clear his intention to ignore her transgressions.[131]

Trump's repeated pattern of approving appointments for ideologues and loyalists without apparent qualifications, his public cultivation of overt shows of sycophancy by his staff and cabinet, and his own norm-breaking behavior sent an impactful message throughout the executive branch—and to GOP legislators in Congress—about his priorities. Nowhere was the message more pernicious than with regard to the administration's lawyers. The quality of government counsel is essential for the rule of law to be meaningful because, for the overwhelming majority of administrative decisions, government lawyering is the exclusive avenue through which law is brought to bear on decision-making. Most government decisions are too low in visibility or too diffuse in impact to elicit judicial review or congressional oversight as ways of monitoring legal compliance. Government lawyers thus provide a key bulwark against lawlessness. They shoulder a unique obligation to balance their roles as advisers and advocates. If they abandon their duty to protect the institutions they serve, not just the temporary incumbents who hold public office, there will frequently be no one else effectively situated to do the job of assuring diligent attention to the law.[132]

Yet Trump made clear his view of lawyers as enablers, as fixers who ignore or lie their way around legal limits in order to give the president room to do whatever he wants.[133] He expected his attorney general would shut down the threat of the Russia investigation just as his former private attorney, Michael Cohen, had tried to shut down the threat of embarrassing stories of Trump's extramarital affairs. It should have come as no surprise that lawyers down the ladder got the point—that Justice Department attorneys, for example, started to make implausible arguments in court to eviscerate the Affordable Care Act[134] and to deny the tools of basic hygiene to immigrant children in American detention.[135] Lower-level bureaucratic functionaries showed they get the message, too, for example, by ignoring court orders at odds with the Trump Administration agenda.[136]

My point in cataloging so extensive a set of troubling behaviors is not just that the Trump administration was dangerous for democracy, although it was. My point is that these behaviors were directly enabled and encouraged by government lawyers' embrace of aggressive presidentialism as a constitutional philosophy. That philosophy starts with the view that any exercise of discretionary power by the president that is not explicitly barred by constitutional text falls, for that reason, into the basket of exclusive executive power that Article II vests in the president and which the other branches of government may not discipline. From this premise, Trump's politically motivated pardons, his attacks on the press, the courts, and the civil service, his nepotism, his subversion of agency missions, his acts of intimidation, humiliation, and favoritism—all of that—were supported as not merely lawful, but constitutionally protected against genuine accountability. Whether Trump's behavior would have been more constrained had his lawyers offered him a different view of his authorities is unknowable. But no such view existed in the Trump administration. When Trump said he had the "absolute right" to pardon himself for any crime or the "absolute right" to declare a national emergency at our southern border, he was parroting his lawyers' advice.[137] Their counsel no doubt informed his insistence that he could have fired Special Counsel Mueller because "Article II allows me to do whatever I want."[138] Asked by a gaggle of reporters about the Mueller investigation, Trump even said, "Take a look at one other thing. It's a thing called Article II. Nobody ever mentions Article II. It gives me all of these rights at a level that nobody has ever seen before."[139] Unitary executive theory may be, in a sense, just words, but from the mouths of presidents, words matter.

As dangerous as the Trump administration proved to be, his was not the first administration whose behavior should provoke anxieties about the corrupting potential of unitary executive theory and national security unilateralism. When Richard Nixon told David Frost that a president has authority to break the law if he deems it in the national interest, he was no doubt revealing his own frame of mind when he ordered not only warrantless wiretapping, but also burglary—so-called black bag jobs—to get compromising material on anti-war protestors.[140]

The philosophy of national security unilateralism likewise infected the Reagan administration, leading to the Iran-Contra scandal. Between 1984 and 1986, Congress prohibited the use of military or intelligence appropriations to aid military forces seeking to overthrow the government of Nicaragua. The Reagan administration responded with a covert scheme to raise money for the Contras independently of Congress (in evasion of Congress's fiscal powers), to facilitate that fundraising through arms sales that flouted applicable federal law (in evasion of Congress's legislative powers), and to lie about it, even under oath (in evasion of Congress's investigative powers).[141]

In November 1986, while denying that the deals represented a trade of "arms for hostages"—American hostages held by radical Islamic groups in Lebanon with ties to Iran—President Reagan confirmed reports that the United States over the previous two years had facilitated six sales of anti-tank missiles, antiaircraft missiles, and spare parts for missile systems to Iran that were unlawful under various statutes regulating the international sale of arms. When the web of operations became public, NSC staffer Lt. Col. Oliver North and a host of other officials, including National Security Adviser John Poindexter and former National Security Adviser Robert McFarlane, lied to Congress, destroyed evidence, and unlawfully withheld information from investigators. Seven officials were convicted of these crimes, although the convictions of North and Poindexter were set aside judicially on the ground that the cases against them were tainted by evidence that they had supplied voluntarily to Congress under a grant of immunity. A prolonged independent counsel probe came to an end in 1993, after President George H. W. Bush, following his loss in the 1992 elections, pardoned six high officials who had either been convicted of Iran-Contra offenses or were under continuing investigation.[142]

Bush glibly minimized Iran-Contra's threat to constitutional governance, dismissing the independent investigation as nothing other than the "criminalization of political differences." By his own admission, William Barr, then Bush's attorney general, strongly supported all the pardons. In a 2001 interview, he told the University of Virginia's Miller Center for the Study of the Presidency: "The big [pardons] obviously were the Iran Contra ones. I certainly did not oppose any of them. I favored the broadest—There were some people arguing just for Weinberger, and I said, No, in for a penny, in for a pound."[143]

The George W. Bush administration was yet more aggressive in its embrace of aggressive presidentialism. Based on theories of national security unilateralism, Justice Department opinions—some later withdrawn—were used to justify the harsh interrogation of enemy detainees after September 11 and the conduct of warrantless electronic surveillance, both in violation of statute. In addition, Bush vastly expanded the use of presidential "signing statements"—formal utterances on the occasion of signing Congress's bills into law—to assert the existence of constitutional problems with the very same statutes Bush was signing.[144] Over the course of his two terms of office, Bush levied nearly 1,500 constitutional objections against 1,070 provisions of law scattered across 127 statutes.[145] Fewer than a hundred of these objections related to problems other than asserted incursions into the authority of the executive. Just over four hundred of the separation of powers objections related to the president's asserted powers over military command, foreign policy, or national security. The remaining thousand or so made frequently unprecedented claims based on no legal authority whatsoever and often in objection to wholly familiar forms of statutory command, such as requirements for executive branch reports to Congress on a variety of topics. The Bush administration thesis that congressional requirements for executive branch reports somehow violated the president's power to recommend measures for congressional consideration would rather have shocked Alexander Hamilton, who happily functioned effectively as the House of Representatives' chief adviser on ways and means during his time as our first Treasury Secretary.[146] Three hundred eighty of Bush's objections mentioned unitary executive theory explicitly. The administration's audacious claims of presidential power directly reflected the well-documented determination of Vice President Dick Cheney and his counsel, David Addington, to use national anxiety after September 11 as a lever for strengthening at every turn the president's legal authorities, both foreign and domestic.[147]

I have so far omitted mention of the two post-Reagan Democratic presidents, Bill Clinton and Barack Obama. They, too, played a role in the upward trajectory of executive power, but mostly in a somewhat different manner from the Republican presidents. The Democratic Party, which is generally more pluralist and pro-government than the contemporary Republican Party, is less instinctively hostile to constitutional arrangements that force presidential compromise and accountability. Thus, especially in the wake of Watergate, Democrats have been slower to claim unrestricted constitutional power in the presidency. Democratic presidents, however, are at least as willing as their Republican counterparts to assert arguably attenuated readings of existing statutory law as delegating to the executive branch broad administrative power.

Thus, for example, with regard to presidential authority to deploy U.S. military force abroad, both the Clinton and Obama administrations made dubious claims of statutory license to deploy such force without explicit authorization. The furthest-reaching such argument by the Clinton administration purported to find congressional appropriations authority to engage in the bombing of Kosovo notwithstanding a section of the War Powers Resolution seeming to contradict such a claim.[148] For its part, the Obama administration claimed dubiously that its involvement beyond sixty days in a military campaign against the Kaddafi regime in Libya was consistent with the War Powers Resolution because its activities no longer qualified as "hostilities" under that Act.[149]

In domestic affairs, both Clinton and Obama extended the reach of the White House in guiding executive branch regulatory policymaking, further blurring the line between presidents as chief supervisors of the executive branch and presidents as the final decision maker on policy judgments Congress had delegated to others. Opponents frequently argued that the Obama administration also, in order to achieve its policy objectives, would sometimes ignore statutory provisions that appeared to limit its administrative strategies. This was especially true with regard to its efforts to implement the Affordable Care Act, a.k.a., Obamacare, despite the opposition of congressional Republicans.[150]

In a sense, the Clinton and Obama presidential power moves may seem less threatening to constitutional checks and balances because, with few exceptions in domestic affairs, the Democratic administrations did not dispute the power of Congress, in principle, to regulate the executive branch or the authority of courts to hold the executive branch to account. But

Clinton and Obama were no less eager to position themselves, in turn, as the pivotal actors in driving all significant executive branch policy. Neither pushed back in any significant way on the constitutional theories of their predecessors. At most, they briefly and unevenly decelerated the accretion of presidential power. Yet the trajectory continued upward. That is why, unless the public, its elected representatives, and the judiciary stand up against the legal claims of unitary executive theory, the plenary discretion principle, and national security unilateralism, aggressive presidentialism will outlive the Trump administration, no matter who succeeds it.

THE THREAT TO DEMOCRACY

Asked to defend aggressive presidentialism as a good idea, not just as a technical reading of the Constitution, its proponents typically rely on the president's status as the sole government official who brings to bear on his or her office a national mandate and perspective. In other words, presidentialism supposedly advances the cause of democracy.

This is an argument we shall revisit later, but the Trump administration beautifully illustrates just how empty it is. We have, as is well known, no national election, but fifty-one elections that choose the electors in each state and in the District of Columbia who are, in turn, the only Americans who directly vote for president. The two most conspicuously norm-breaking administrations in recent decades—the Trump administration and the first George W. Bush administration—came to power despite the president-elect losing the national popular vote. In the case of Bush, notwithstanding the machinations that produced his Electoral College victory, it is all but certain that a plurality of voters in the pivotal state of Florida believed when they cast their votes that they had effectively voted for the Democratic candidate, Vice President Al Gore.[151] Moreover, in both elections, the overall victor had actually failed to carry a majority of voters even in the states that awarded them electors on a winner-take-all basis.[152] In short, the winner-take-all state contests combined with the absence of any runoffs to assure a majority winner in the individual states meant that the Electoral College almost certainly produced an overall winner in 2000 and in 2016 without a genuine national mandate.

To make things worse, the Trump administration also demonstrated the feasibility—and from its point of view, the desirability—of a policy strategy catering entirely to the most ideologically committed base of a single political party. Rather than having his policy stances moderated by a national perspective, Trump resolutely prioritized his base voters' priorities. Congressional Republicans largely acquiesced in his aggressiveness lest they face opposition in Republican Party primaries when they seek reelection. In short, the combination of gerrymandered congressional districts, voter suppression, dark money–driven campaign financing, and the electoral college has produced an electoral system in which the president need not have a genuinely national perspective either to win election or to govern. Aggressive presidentialism only magnifies the value of winning the prize of White House occupancy for an undemocratic president.

How can America get out of this mess? The answer—as explored in the chapters that follow—has two big parts, one internal to government and one in the hands of the American people. Within government, we need courts, elected leaders, and the lawyers who serve or argue before them to push back against aggressive presidentialism. We need those who implement the Constitution in their official roles to embrace a view of the constitutional presidency that adapts an eighteenth-century text to the needs of twenty-first-century democratic governance.

To get to that place, however, we also need an electorate that understands what has happened and why. We need Americans to be disabused of the idea that our pathological chief executive is what the Constitution, properly interpreted, demands. We need voters who believe in a living, adaptive constitutionalism, not just because it produces a set of preferable or more progressive outcomes, but because it represents the sounder approach in principle to implementing the government design we inherited. We need the people of the United States to take up the future of democracy as their own cause and to empower and hold accountable representatives who will protect constitutional checks and balances. Reform demands a virtuous circle. As citizens become frustrated with unchecked presidential abuse, they can put into office politicians amenable to democratic reform. As those elected leaders create new avenues for public democratic engagement, yet more Americans will be motivated to get in on the action.

A colleague once asked me during a conversation on these topics what could make things better, and he added, "Don't say, 'a motivated and informed public.'" That is like asking how to lose weight without eating less food or how to learn to swim without getting in the water. We have dug ourselves into a hole or acquiesced while others dug for us. Climbing out of that hole will require vigilance and initiative, both individual and collective. It also requires understanding how we got to this moment. We can advance the prospects for democratic renewal by rescuing public understanding of the constitutional chief executive from the misguided theorizing of aggressive presidentialists.

TWO

The "Chief Prosecutor" Myth

SIX MONTHS BEFORE Donald Trump announced his intention to nominate William Barr to succeed Jeff Sessions as attorney general, Barr wrote a remarkable letter to two Justice Department officials—Rod Rosenstein, then the deputy attorney general supervising Robert Mueller's investigation of Russian interference in the 2016 presidential election, and assistant attorney general, Steven Engel, the head of the Justice Department's Office of Legal Counsel (OLC).[1] Barr admitted he was "in the dark" about relevant facts.[2] But he went on to urge the view—in nineteen single-spaced pages—that Trump's firing of FBI Director James Comey could not, as a matter of constitutional law, amount to obstruction of justice. Barr argued from unitary executive theory that the president enjoyed "illimitable . . . law enforcement discretion."[3] The president was entitled—indeed, required—to supervise any and all criminal prosecutions. Barr wrote that "because the President alone constitutes the Executive branch, the President cannot 'recuse' himself" from supervising any criminal investigation, even an investigation focusing on the President and the President's closest associates.[4] Based on the principle of plenary discretion, Barr further insisted that because the Constitution vests the president with "illimitable" discretion over the firing of a criminal prosecutor, such a firing decision cannot be regulated by Congress regardless of its motive:

> The authority to . . . remove principal Executive officers . . .[is] quintessentially Executive in character and among the discretionary powers vested exclusively in the President by the Constitution. When the President exercises these discretionary powers, it is presumed he does so lawfully, and his decisions are generally non-reviewable.[5]

In other words, even if the reasons for firing a prosecutor were entirely corrupt—for example, to forestall an investigation of the president or the president's family—the discharge could not be deemed unlawful: "The President's exercise of its [*sic*] Constitutional discretion is not subject to review for 'improper motivations' by lesser officials or by the courts."[6] Thus did Barr preview for the Trump administration just how forcefully he would be willing to push legal arguments to subvert institutional accountability for the misconduct of Donald Trump.

Beginning a dissection of presidentialism with the debate over criminal prosecution makes sense for three reasons. First, criminal prosecution is the gravest of the federal government's civilian powers. The stakes in allocating control of prosecution could hardly be higher. Second, the issue of presidential control over prosecution provides an interesting test of the presidentialists' actual commitment to the method. Unlike many questions we pose to the Constitution—for example, does the Fourth Amendment protect cell phone data,[7] or is the president entitled to full policy control over the Nuclear Regulatory Commission[8]—questions over the constitutional status of criminal prosecutions are not anachronistic. The founding generation actually was familiar with criminal prosecutions. Criminal prosecutions are not the consequence of some unforeseen technological invention or convulsive social change that the founding generation could not have anticipated. The question, "Does the new Constitution guarantee the President complete control over all federal criminal prosecution?" would thus have been entirely comprehensible to late eighteenth-century voters. Asking about their expectations or understanding regarding Article II in this specific respect is a logically coherent undertaking. Third, precisely because criminal prosecution is a discrete governmental function with which the Framers were familiar, the arguments for and against the presidentialist position are simply easier to follow and to assess than the more arcane, albeit highly consequential arguments chapter 3 will review on presidential control over the entire administrative bureaucracy.

Barr's memo offered aggressively presidentialist answers to the three constitutional questions raised by Trump's decision to fire FBI Director Comey and by that decision's potential conflict with federal obstruction of justice law:

- Does the Constitution permit presidents to recuse themselves from criminal investigations targeting themselves or close associates?
- Does the Constitution require such recusal?

- If a president is not recused from supervising a criminal investigation that poses a conflict of interest, may Congress nonetheless regulate or limit how the president exercises his supervisory discretion—constraining, for example, his discretion to fire a prosecutor?

Barr's negative answer to these questions—the presidentialist answer—purports to be rooted in the original meaning of the 1787 constitutional text.[9] And the memo just takes for granted that Americans in 2019 are bound by the supposed 1787 interpretation.

Barr's memo provides a fine launching pad for understanding what has been wrong with extreme presidentialism both in theory and in how it has been practiced for the last forty years. First, insofar as presidentialism purports to bind us tightly to understandings of government power forged in the eighteenth century, it diverts attention from any inquiry into what would be the most appealing answers to the relevant constitutional questions if we considered ourselves free to interpret the Constitution in light of contemporary values. With regard to the president's relationship to criminal law enforcement, the most appealing answer is not Barr's.

Second, it turns out that, on questions of the president's relationship to criminal law enforcement, the historical view advanced by the extreme presidentialists is wrong. As with many of the questions we will examine in later chapters, to accept the presidentialist account of history of criminal prosecution requires us to ignore a host of relevant evidence that points in a contrary direction. When advocates for a constitutional view purport to be bound by history, but explore history so inadequately, it is hard to escape the feeling that their pre-commitment to a particular conclusion is driving their search for evidence, not the other way around.

TAKING HISTORY SERIOUSLY

The presidentialist argument against limiting presidential control over prosecution purports to rely on a historically based reading of the Constitution rooted in what its advocates call "original public meaning."[10] The method rests on a deceptively straightforward-sounding logic: What turned the Constitution into binding law were the votes of those who ratified the Constitution. When they ratified the Constitution, they presumably understood its words to mean what an educated American reader of 1787 would have thought them to mean. Therefore, we should regard ourselves, in the early decades of the twenty-first century, as still bound by that meaning. The late Supreme Court Justice Antonin Scalia played an outsized role in popularizing this approach to constitutional interpretation.[11]

The method is rife with problems, which will be reviewed in depth in chapter 4. But its superficial logic is clear. For presidentialists, the historical foundation for presidential control over criminal prosecutors is rooted in a syllogism: "Executive power," in the late eighteenth century, meant "not legislative" and "having the power to put in act the laws."[12] When Article II thus vested "the executive power" in "a" president, it thus vested in a single individual all executive power, comprehensively and indivisibly. Vesting that authority in "a" president meant that it would be shared by no other individual, and any person assisting the president in the exercise of executive power must be removable by the president at will. Criminal prosecutors help to enforce the law; therefore, the president has constitutionally based control over them and can fire them for any reason.

The presidentialists' syllogism rests unfortunately on an artificially constricted focus on that one snippet of constitutional text. But its fallacy runs even deeper. The theory sensibly focuses on what the 1787 draft signaled to its ratifiers; after all, their votes and not the subjective intentions of the Framers are what turned the Constitution into law. But what the Constitution meant to them cannot be discerned deductively from dictionaries. People ascribe meaning to words in context pragmatically. That is, they reason from the behavior they observe or in which they themselves engage when the words are used in relevant contexts. For example, if I see a sign on a restaurant door that reads, "No shirt. No shoes. No service," I do not infer that this is an establishment offering neither shirts, nor shoes, nor service; I understand that customers may receive service at this restaurant only if their torsos and feet are covered. I likewise understand, dressing as I do as a conventional cis-gendered male, that I am not relieved of the obligation to wear pants or shorts. I even understand that a customer wearing a dress will not be denied service because she is not wearing a shirt. Yet none of this is discernible from the text of the sign alone. I have enriched the meaning of the sign based on my knowledge of its context and purposive intent. It is not the dictionary that primarily guides my understanding; it is my experience of restaurants and my understanding of contemporary mores.

In contemplating the newly proposed constitutional text between 1787 and 1789, those Americans enfranchised to vote on its ratification would have likewise brought to their understanding of "executive power" more than dictionary definitions. They would also have had their experience of living under executive power as exercised under state constitutions, which would have greatly colored what they thought they were voting on. They would have been familiar with the operation of criminal prosecutors. Yet these experiences, under constitutions worded similarly to the U.S. Constitution, would not have left the impression that grants of "executive power" guaranteed complete authority over criminal prosecution.[13] Instead, the classification of criminal prosecution within a typology of government functions would have been at least ambiguous. Voters would likely have regarded prosecution as partaking of judicial power as much as executive power, and they would have expected legislative bodies to have considerable control over its operation. For these reasons, the "original public meaning" of Article II "executive power" would not have guaranteed presidents the power to control prosecutorial discretion regardless of the dictionary definition of "executive."

In short, if we consider the experience of eighteenth-century Americans to be a guide to their likely interpretation of the Constitution's vague phrases, what is critical is that Americans in 1787 would not have experienced on our side of the Atlantic either a widespread commitment to concentrated executive power in general or a specific expectation that the direction of government lawyering was centrally an executive function. If the founding generation thought state prosecutors were inherently exercising executive power, one would have expected state attorneys general or other state prosecutors to be appointed by governors and made legally accountable to them. Yet the early state constitutions, some drafted before and some drafted after 1789, commonly authorized the legislature to appoint certain civil officers directly or to determine by statute how officers should be appointed.[14] Insofar as those constitutions provided specifically for the legislative appointment of officers we would conventionally identify as "executive," the likeliest targets included attorneys general and state attorneys. Six of the first thirteen state constitutions specifically mention an attorney general, and each of them speaks of the attorney general in the same breath, as it were, as it refers to state judges.[15]

Pre-1787 state constitutions providing explicitly for the legislative appointment of attorneys general were in effect in New Jersey, North Carolina, and Virginia.[16] This was so even though the North Carolina Constitution and the Virginia Bill of Rights mandated the separation of powers explicitly, which the federal Constitution does not.[17] Again, if representing the government in court were an inherently executive function, then one would not expect constitutions declaring a state's allegiance to the separation of powers to put their appointment in the hands of the legislative branch.[18]

The 1796 Constitution of the new state of Tennessee explicitly provided for the legislative appointment of the state's attorneys.[19] Yet other constitutions left it to the discretion of the state legislature as to how state officers would be appointed or provided for appointments of administrative officers by councils made up predominantly of state legislators. In Vermont, for example, the state's attorneys, one in each county, were legislatively appointed and accountable to the courts, not the governor, for certification of their reimbursable expenses.[20] Connecticut provides an especially intriguing example. Continuing to operate under its 1662 charter until well after ratification of the federal Constitution, Connecticut provided by statute in 1784 for the judicial appointment of state's attorneys.[21] This practice continued until 1854, notwithstanding an 1818 constitution that said nothing on the subject and also contained an explicit separation of powers provision.[22]

Among legal scholars, there are two common ripostes to this evidence that government lawyers involved in executing the law were frequently not subordinated to a governor's executive power. One is that the federal Constitution of 1787 was understood to be a rejection of the weak executive model established by the pre-1787 state constitutions.[23] This proposition, however, does not resolve the questions concerning to what degree and in which respects the president would be a stronger executive than the governors who operated under the earlier state constitutions. The Framers clearly rejected the idea of sharing the leadership of the executive branch between a chief executive and a council, as had been the case in a number of states. But clarity on that point does not resolve the ambiguities surrounding those powers that the chief executive would exercise. It also makes puzzling the persistence of divided control over state's attorneys in *post*-1787 state constitutions, notwithstanding executive-power-vesting clauses paralleling the now-ratified federal text.[24] If the wording of the federal Constitution implied complete presidential power over criminal prosecution, it seems weird that states after 1787 would adopt essentially identical wording but take control over state legal officers away from their respective governors.

The second riposte is that explicit state constitutional clauses fragmenting gubernatorial control over executive functions supposedly testify to a common understanding that, without such explicit exemptions, executive power would be unitary. In other words, because some state constitutions spelled out limitations on gubernatorial power that were not replicated in the federal Constitution, the federal Constitution must not have intended any such limitations.

In response, however, it must first be pointed out that such an argument cannot explain the Connecticut practice of judicial appointments for state's attorneys; no provision for such appointments appears in the 1818 Connecticut Constitution. State authorities simply accepted the appropriateness of such appointments. In other words, even though their state constitution was just as silent on the question as the federal Constitution, Connecticut continued to assume that the judicial appointment of government lawyers was consistent with the separation of powers framework embodied in both documents.

But just as important, the presidentialist argument does not follow the way in which the Supreme Court derives lessons from the early state constitutions. For example, in *District of Columbia v. Heller*, the Court drew on state constitutions that explicitly linked the right to bear arms to individual self-defense as confirming that the Second Amendment does so as well, even though the Second Amendment contains no such wording.[25] In other words, the explicit references in early state constitutions to individual self-defense did not demonstrate to the Court that self-defense was beyond the concerns of the Second Amendment.[26] The Court rather inferred that late eighteenth-century constitutional drafters, deliberating on the right to bear arms, concluded that self-defense was embraced by that right, sometimes explicitly, sometimes implicitly. Similarly, the fact that state constitutions were often explicit in setting up the independence of certain executive officers from gubernatorial control suggests that, when deliberating on the nature of executive power, late eighteenth-century constitutional drafters regarded a degree of administrative independence from the chief executive as consistent with the separation of powers. At the very least, the idea of criminal prosecution as central to constitutional grants of executive power is undermined by the common practice of vesting the appointment of attorneys general and state's attorneys elsewhere than in the state governors.

The conclusion that criminal prosecution was not central to constitutional grants of executive power is buttressed by the way in which the First Congress dealt with federal law enforcement. As numerous scholars have recounted, Congress's approach to the creation of federal legal officers was dramatically different from the care with which Congress defined and established the departments of Foreign Affairs, War and Treasury.[27] The centrality of both foreign and military affairs to the constitutional grant of executive power was clear to the First Congress, which gave the president explicit and broad powers to direct the cabinet departments holding those portfolios and did little to specify their internal structure. By way of contrast, Congress spelled out the structure of the Treasury Department in considerable detail and created a number of significant offices within the department. Although the Treasury Act allowed presidential removal of the Treasury secretary, there was no indication, unlike the secretaries of Foreign Affairs and of War, that the Treasury secretary's responsibilities would be defined by presidential orders. The secretary was charged by statute with a series of specific duties, about which that officer would be required to report not only to the president, but also to Congress directly.[28] Such arrangements quite likely were rooted in the idea, embodied in many of the early state constitutions, that the government's treasurer ought to have special accountability to the legislature.[29]

Yet in stark contrast to all of this, Congress devoted just a single, albeit long sentence in Section 35 of the Judiciary Act of 1789 to the newly created office of attorney general. The Act provided:

> [T]here shall ... be appointed a meet person, learned in the law, to act as attorney-general for the United States, who shall be sworn or affirmed to a faithful execution of his office; whose duty it shall be to prosecute and conduct all suits in the Supreme Court in which the United States shall be concerned, and to give his advice and opinion upon questions of law when required by the President of the United States, or when requested by the heads of any of the departments, touching any matters that may concern their departments, and shall receive such compensation for his services as shall by law be provided.[30]

District attorneys, the forerunners of United States attorneys, got two sentences:

> [T]here shall be appointed in each district a meet person learned in the law to act as attorney for the United States in such district, who shall be sworn or affirmed to the faithful execution of his office, whose duty it shall be to prosecute in such district all delinquents for crimes and offences, cognizable under the authority of the United States, and all civil actions in which the United States shall be concerned, except before the supreme court in the district in which that court shall be holden. And he shall receive as compensation for his services such fees as shall be taxed therefor in the respective courts before which the suits or prosecutions shall be.

That's it. The Judiciary Act conveys no clear idea on behalf of its drafters as to the centrality of these officials to the new government or, indeed, to executive power. There is not yet a Department of Justice for the attorney general to lead, nor any mandatory supervision by the attorney general over the district attorneys. Indeed, the original draft of the Judiciary Act would have had each court appoint the attorneys who appeared before them on behalf of the United States.[31] It is not clear on what basis the Congress was persuaded to abandon that proposal. The first district attorneys were attached to the Department of State, which apparently exercised little supervision over their functions.[32] And for what it is worth, there is no point looking to Publius for further guidance on these questions. The roles of a federal attorney general or district attorney or criminal prosecutor go entirely unmentioned in *The Federalist*.

Ambiguity in the constitutional status of the federal government's new law enforcers appears a lot less mysterious once we understand that the public prosecutor was generally a far less significant government figure throughout the late eighteenth and most of the nineteenth centuries than today, and most definitely was not seen as an inherent bearer of executive power. The British common law tradition was one of private prosecution.[33] Although a variety of public prosecutors appeared during the colonial period, private prosecution in the United States persisted throughout much of the nineteenth century.[34] The early version of the public prosecutor in the United States was considered a judicial officer: "At the beginning of the nineteenth century in America, the district attorney was viewed as a minor figure in the court, an adjunct to the judge. His position was primarily judicial, and perhaps only quasi-executive."[35] Moreover, in contrast to the unilateralist theory of hierarchical control over prosecution, the norm with regard to public prosecution in both the colonies and early states was one of local control. As explained in the leading history of criminal prosecution in early America:

> Even where the Attorney General was nominal head of state prosecution, in reality the local prosecuting attorney was swiftly drifting toward his own island of localized power. Local courts and local appointments or recommendations hastened this trend, which was also marked by a concomitant decline in the centralized power of the Attorney General.
>
> The federal system of prosecution established in 1789 provides a freeze-frame of the trends and philosophies that were predominant in criminal prosecution at the beginning of the American nation. The Attorney General was a weakened office relegated to vague supervisory power, advisory capacity,

and limited appellate jurisdiction. Primary responsibility for prosecution was in the hands of local officials.

In the first 30 years of the new republic there were few changes in the duties and responsibilities of the prosecuting attorney.[36]

Given this history of decentralized prosecution[37] and its common classification as a judicial function, it is a dubious proposition at best that the Vesting Clause of Article II communicated to those ratifying the federal Constitution that they were signing on to a system of criminal prosecution to be administered within the complete and illimitable discretion of the new chief executive. Indeed, against this backdrop, the early history of the attorney general's office and its relationship to our first district attorneys— later called U.S. attorneys—looks less like a failure to live up to a founding text on executive power and more like a direct continuation of state patterns that would have guided how those ratifying the Constitution understood its implications.[38]

Susan Bloch's study of the attorney general's early role tells much of this story.[39] The district attorneys were part-time functionaries, whose chief source of income was their private practice.[40] The Judiciary Act did not provide the attorney general any supervisory power over them, and the lack of a "fixed relation" between the attorney general and the district attorneys was a powerful source of frustration to George Washington's first attorney general, Edmond Randolph.[41] Randolph sought and received Washington's support for proposed legislation that would have required district attorneys to notify the attorney general of all cases they handled that involved foreign nations or "in which the harmony of the [state and federal judiciaries] may be hazarded."[42] Randolph also sought authority to direct the district attorneys in their handling of such cases.[43] After the Senate, however, would go no further than requiring district attorneys to keep the attorney general informed on lower court litigation, no legislation expanding the attorney general's authorities was enacted.[44] Renewed efforts under later Presidents Jackson and Pierce to consolidate supervisory control by the attorney general failed similarly.[45]

The first congressional provisions for supervisory direction over the district attorneys gave that role, in a limited form, not to the attorney general, but to the Treasury Department. The motivating concern was not one of criminal law enforcement, but the handling of litigation with implications for the federal fisc. Thus as Jed Shugerman recounts:

In 1797, Congress gave the Comptroller of the Treasury significant prosecutorial authority over district attorneys in directing suits over revenue and
debts. In practice, district attorneys were not really supervised at all. Active
supervision was impossible over such long distances, with such limited transportation and communication. They also had too little work to require much
attention.[46]

Concerned that this system had proved inadequate to maintain control
over federal accounts, especially in the wake of the War of 1812, Congress
charged the president in 1820 with designating an officer of the Treasury to
direct and superintend suits for the recovery of money or property.[47] President Monroe selected for this purpose a non-lawyer, Stephen Pleasanton,
the Fifth Auditor of the Treasury, who was apparently overwhelmed when
district attorneys sought instructions at too great a level of detail.[48] Attorney General Wirt, who claimed no supervisory power of his own, advised
Mr. Pleasanton that he was obligated to provide instructions only on when
to proceed, not how.[49]

Notwithstanding this account of early ambiguity as to the nature of prosecutorial power and the persistence of independence among the early district
attorneys, two points might be made for the presidentialists. First, notwithstanding the looseness of the early federal law enforcement network, presidents did issue directions to district attorneys in some especially important
cases, consistent with the vesting of executive power in the president.[50] Second, neither the relative lack of executive supervision in practice, nor historical ambiguity about the characterization of prosecutorial power belie the facts
that Congress did place prosecution in the executive branch and ultimately
did consolidate supervision of the district attorneys in the attorney general.

Such arguments, however, deal only with Article II in what should be
considered its "authorizing character," not its "protective character." That is,
each of the first three articles of the Constitution—the articles that establish
the respective powers of government—has a kind of dual nature. Each has
an *authorizing* character, in the sense that it affirmatively authorizes one or
more of the respective branches to implement certain powers. But each also
has a *self-protective* character, in that it signals some domain of legislative,
executive, or judicial power, respectively, beyond the authority of any other
branch to regulate or impede. For example, Article III leaves to Congress
the jobs of configuring a Supreme Court and structuring the inferior courts
entirely.[51] But the Supreme Court has interpreted the grant of "judicial
power" as foreclosing legislation that would undo final judgments in cases

already decided.[52] Article II similarly authorizes the president to exercise certain managerial powers with regard to the executive branch. He nominates, appoints, and commissions civil officers, may seek the opinions of heads of departments, and "takes care that the laws be faithfully executed."[53] At the same time, the president is given a textually unlimited pardon power and a veto power extremely difficult in practice to override.[54] The dual character of each article is crucial because, without each branch's self-protective powers, a system of checks and balances could not work; one branch could vitiate the checking powers of the other branches.

The facts that presidents, in the absence of any statutory bar, issued directions to district attorneys or that Congress allowed the district attorneys to be presidentially appointed speak only to the authorizing character of Article II with regard to executive power. The precedents that presidentialists cite may support presidential assertions of supervisory authority in the absence of congressional restraint, but they say nothing about any presidential entitlement to direct prosecution in defiance of legislative limits. As late as 1831, the Jackson administration thought it necessary to secure an opinion from Attorney General Roger Taney as to whether he could properly direct the district attorney in New York to discontinue a prosecution—and Jackson sought the opinion despite the obvious foreign policy implications of the matter at hand.[55]

Moreover, the constitutionally ambiguous nature of prosecutorial power still found expression in federal law even as supervisory power over district attorneys was eventually conferred on the attorney general. An Act of August 2, 1861, finally provided:

> That the Attorney-General of the United States be, and he is hereby, charged with the general superintendence and direction of the attorneys and marshals of all the districts in superintendence the United States and the Territories as to the manner of discharging their respective duties; and the said district-attorneys and marshals are hereby required to report to the Attorney-General an account of their official proceedings, and the state and condition of their respective offices, in such time and manner as the Attorney-General may direct.[56]

Yet two years later, in "An Act to give greater Efficiency to the Judicial System of the United States," Congress codified a statutory role for courts in the appointment of these very same officials:

> In case of a vacancy in the office of marshal or district attorney in any circuit, the judge of such circuit may fill such vacancy, and the person so appointed

shall serve until an appointment shall be made by the President, and the appointee has duly qualified, and no longer.[57]

The authority of courts to appoint US attorneys in cases of vacancy remains a part of federal law today, testifying to the ongoing ambiguous character of the power they exercise.[58]

And far from rejecting the ambiguous line between executive and judicial power, the Supreme Court in 1879 both acknowledged and embraced it. In the so-called Second Enforcement Act of February 28, 1871, Congress required federal circuit court judges, on petition, to appoint federal election supervisors for any congressional election in a city or town with a population of at least twenty thousand persons.[59] When five Baltimore election judges were indicted for election irregularities, they sought habeas corpus on a number of grounds, including the supposed constitutional impropriety of having election supervisors chosen by judges, rather than within the executive branch.[60] The Supreme Court rejected the argument, specifically noting the executive-judicial ambiguity:

> It is no doubt usual and proper to vest the appointment of inferior officers in that department of the government, executive or judicial, or in that particular executive department to which the duties of such officers appertain. But there is no absolute requirement to this effect in the Constitution; and, if there were, *it would be difficult in many cases to determine to which department an office properly belonged*. Take that of marshal, for instance. He is an executive officer, whose appointment, in ordinary cases, is left to the President and Senate. But if Congress should, as it might, vest the appointment elsewhere, it would be questionable whether it should be in the President alone, in the Department of Justice, or in the courts. The marshal is pre-eminently the officer of the courts; and, in case of a vacancy, Congress has in fact passed a law bestowing the temporary appointment of the marshal upon the justice of the circuit in which the district where the vacancy occurs is situated.[61]

The precise same argument could be made with complete validity regarding judicially appointed prosecutors.

Twenty-first-century federal law continues to respect in other important ways the special judicial tie to prosecution. For example, the Supreme Court has held that federal prosecutors are absolutely immune from tort liability in connection with their official duties as prosecutors. For example, no prosecutor may be sued for intentionally slandering or even negligently targeting an innocent defendant. Yet what gives rise to the absolute immunity from civil liability in tort is precisely the prosecution's tie to the judicial function: "A United States attorney, if not a judicial officer, is at least a quasi-judicial officer, of the government. He exercises important judicial functions, and is engaged in the enforcement of the law."[62] It is on this basis that the Supreme Court has upheld not only the prosecutor's absolute immunity from tort liability, but also the extension of that liability to civil rights suits under 42 U.S.C. § 1983.[63]

Additionally, federal courts retain the authority to appoint prosecutors to handle cases of criminal contempt. Explicit authority for such appointments appears in Rule 42 of the Federal Rules of Criminal Procedure.[64] Rule 42 is rooted in what has long been recognized as the "inherent power of the judiciary to appoint disinterested private attorneys as special prosecutors to pursue criminal contempt proceedings . . . when government prosecutors are unwilling or unable to perform that function."[65] Of course, enforcing the law against criminal contempt is no less "execution of the laws" than any other criminal prosecution, which is precisely why Justice Scalia denied that the judiciary has any such power.[66] But no other Justice has joined his position.

To sum up: The vesting of executive power in the president would not have communicated to readers in 1787 that the president would be guaranteed complete supervisory control over criminal prosecution. The founding generation would have thought criminal prosecution as much as a judicial power as an executive power. That is why so many state constitutions, for example, explicitly made government attorneys directly accountable to the judicial or legislative branches, rather than to the governor. That is why, even now, federal law permits the judicial appointment of U.S. attorneys, a practice going back to 1863. That is why criminal prosecutors enjoy the same immunities from tort liability as do judges. The "original public meaning" of executive power simply does not support a reading of Article II that guarantees presidents complete control over federal criminal prosecution.

A MODERNIST VIEW

Imagine now that we can put aside what the founding generation thought the Constitution meant and simply look through a modern-day lens at the constitutional text and its implications for the questions Barr addressed. A logical starting point would be noting that the Constitution explicitly provides twice for an obligation of presidential honesty in the administration of the laws. The president's oath includes a promise "faithfully" to execute the office of president, and the president's most broadly stated Article II obligation is to "take care that the laws be faithfully executed."[67] A presidential decision to abstain from supervising a criminal investigation implicating either the president or the president's close personal or political associates would seem squarely in line with these obligations of faithfulness to law. Implementing the maxim that no one should be the judge in their own cause would fulfill, not defeat the duty of faithfulness.[68] It seems plain that the Constitution would *permit* a presidential recusal.

An arguably harder question—again, putting history aside—is whether the Constitution actually *demands* recusal from any criminal prosecution posing a direct conflict of interest for the president. What makes the question tricky is not whether recusal is appropriate; again, the avoidance of judging one's own culpability answers the question of propriety. The issues are issues of limits and of enforceability. As to limits, conscientious presidents might find themselves in a quandary if they could not fire or instigate the firing of prosecutors who are themselves violating the law. A president ignoring a lawless prosecutor, even one conducting an investigation of the president, might not be taking care that the laws be faithfully executed. Such a predicament is highly unlikely, however. A president's dissatisfaction with the course of a criminal investigation is all but certainly likely to focus on disagreements over policy, not legal transgression. Conceding a president's entitlement to discharge a lawless prosecutor is not, in practical terms, conceding much.

The issue regarding enforceability is whether it makes sense, as a matter of principle, to view a constitutional norm as an actual obligation if no one can effectively force compliance. That is, even if a president persisted in personally supervising a prosecutorial investigation that implicates a direct conflict of interest, it would probably be impossible to find any individual person so injured by the president's supervision as to entitle that person to seek a court's review of the president's decision to remain involved. If "constitutional duties" encompass only obligations enforceable by litigation, it must be conceded that no court will ever enjoin a recalcitrant president to forbear from supervising a particular criminal prosecution.

I think it the better view, however, that the Constitution implies a broader view of governmental duty. Article V of the Constitution requires all government officers, both state and federal to "be bound by Oath or Affirmation, to support [the] Constitution."[69] The president's oath includes the rhetorically more forceful commitment to "preserve, protect and defend" the Constitution.[70] Promises to "preserve, protect and defend"—even to "support"—the Constitution plainly commit officeholders to do something more than merely "observe" or "formally comply with" the Constitution. To "support" is to "enable to function," or, as James Madison wrote, to help "in giving effect to the federal Constitution."[71] Should presidents fail to observe constitutional norms implicit in the rule-of-law ideal, it is hard to see how they are enabling the Constitution to function. A promise to defend or support the Constitution is not much of a promise unless one is obliged, at least as a matter of honor, to keep that promise. It is thus at least arguable that the Constitution, properly interpreted, mandates a president's recusal from prosecutorial supervision when a conflict of interest is presented, even if such a mandate could be enforced only through impeachment or electoral defeat.

That leaves the question of whether Congress may regulate how presidents supervise prosecutors when faced with a conflict of interests. In other words, if a president interprets the Constitution not to mandate recusal, and if the president declines to recuse him- or herself voluntarily, may Congress nonetheless limit the extent of the president's discretion in how supervision of the prosecution is carried out? With regard to the investigation of Russian interference in the 2016 election, the one seemingly pertinent statutory limitation was the ban on obstruction of justice. Federal law threatens with criminal sanction anyone who

> corruptly, or by threats or force, or by any threatening letter or communication influences, obstructs, or impedes or endeavors to influence, obstruct, or impede the due and proper administration of the law under which any pending proceeding is being had before any department or agency of the United States.[72]

It would thus follow that a president may not fire a criminal prosecutor "corruptly," with the intent to "impede the due and proper administration of the law."

Unless we are historically bound to some contrary view, it is difficult to see how applying to the president this statutory limitation on the corrupt exercise of discretion could possibly be unconstitutional. The Constitution explicitly authorizes Congress not only to "make all Laws which shall be necessary and proper for carrying into Execution" Congress's constitutional powers, but also "all other Powers vested by this Constitution in the Government of the United States, or any Department or Officer thereof."[73] The president is an officer of the United States. Barring the president from exercising his constitutional powers corruptly would seem, almost by definition, to be a "necessary and proper" regulation of his authority. Prohibiting the corrupt exercise of power is merely the flip side of the explicit constitutional requirement that presidents exercise their powers "faithfully."

This conclusion is amply reinforced by the Supreme Court decision that is most at odds with the thesis of the Barr letter—*Morrison v. Olson*.[74] That 1988 decision upheld, by a 7–1 vote, the constitutionality of the Ethics in Government Act, which established the post-Watergate independent counsel system.[75] Mindful of the Saturday Night Massacre, Congress enacted a system in 1978 to limit direct presidential influence over criminal prosecutors investigating wrongdoing by the president or members of the president's close political circle. Although amended several times in its technical details, the essential framework for the system remained in place until Congress allowed the statute to lapse in 1999.[76]

The Act would be triggered if the attorney general received specific information that the president or another covered individual had committed a serious federal offense.[77] Upon receiving that information, the attorney general would then have ninety days to investigate.[78] At the end of ninety days, the attorney general would have to reach a determination either that further investigation was not warranted, that further investigation was warranted, or that the attorney general's preliminary investigation had not reached a definitive conclusion one way or another.[79] An attorney general making either of the latter two determinations would be required to apply to a special panel of the U.S. Court of Appeals for the District of Columbia Circuit to appoint an independent counsel.[80] Such counsel would be required, in conducting his or her further investigation, to follow the Justice Department's general policies on criminal prosecution.[81] But the attorney general's power—and thus the power of the president—over the independent counsel would be quite limited. Specifically, an independent counsel could be removed from office:

> other than by impeachment and conviction, only by the personal action of the Attorney General and only for good cause, physical or mental disability (if not prohibited by law protecting persons from discrimination on the basis of such a disability), or any other condition that substantially impairs the performance of such independent counsel's duties.[82]

Because of this limitation, a president who was unhappy with how an independent counsel was performing could not either fire or require the firing of the independent counsel solely because of that sense of dissatisfaction.

It is notable how carefully Congress crafted the Ethics in Government Act to provide a response to presidential conflicts of interest without carving too deeply into the ordinary prosecutorial discretion that Congress delegates to the executive branch. First, the Act applies only if information arises about federal crimes allegedly committed by a relatively small universe of elected officials and high-level political appointees and campaign managers. Second, the sole judge of whether the allegations received are genuinely worth pursuing is the attorney general, a presidential appointee. The attorney general's determination is final. Should the attorney general find that the proffered information is too vague or general or that, following preliminary investigation, no further prosecutorial initiative is warranted, no court is empowered to overturn the attorney general's conclusion. Under carefully prescribed circumstances specified in the law, the attorney general would be compelled to seek a special prosecutor, but it would also be the attorney general who determines the scope of that prosecutor's jurisdiction. The president is not allowed personally to fire an independent counsel, even for good cause. But if good cause exists, as defined in the statute, and the attorney general fails to remove the independent counsel, the president has authority to remove the attorney general. In sum, Congress carefully protected the president's capacity to take care that the laws be faithfully executed, and significant decision-making with regard to prosecutions implicating presidential conflicts of interests was lodged with an official, the attorney general, likely to be a close presidential associate.

It is true, of course, that the statutory limitation on direct presidential control over independent counsels opened up the possibility that such prosecutors would enjoy some significant discretion to make decisions with which, as a matter of policy, the president might disagree. That was the very point of the statute. For its part, however, the Supreme Court concluded: "[W]e simply do not see how the President's need to control the exercise of that discretion is so central to the functioning of the Executive Branch as to require as a matter of constitutional law that the counsel be terminable at will by the President."[83] If it is constitutional for Congress to limit all but entirely the president's policy control over a federal criminal prosecutor in cases posing a serious conflict of interest, a less aggressive limitation—such as a bar on firing prosecutors corruptly in order to interfere with federal law enforcement—seems even more obviously permissible.

All of the analysis thus far points to the conclusion that, examined through a modern lens, limiting presidential control over prosecutors pursuing investigations that pose a presidential conflict of interest advances the faithful execution of the laws and is consistent with both the spirit and letter of the Constitution. William Barr's conclusions to the contrary rest chiefly on two propositions, namely, that prosecution is part of the executive power vested by Article II in the president and that, because the president solely is invested with the executive power, "the President alone constitutes the Executive branch."[84] The second of these arguments is absurd on its face. Article II authorizes the president to "require the opinion, in writing, of the principal officer in each of the executive departments, upon any subject relating to the duties of their respective offices."[85] The Constitution does not enumerate the "executive departments"; creating and authorizing those establishments is left to Congress. But the reference to "executive departments" explicitly signals that the president is not the entirety of the executive branch, constitutionally speaking.

As for whether the "executive power" itself encompasses complete control over criminal prosecution, Barr's argument runs into an obvious ambiguity. Putting aside the historical argument we have already traversed, the phrase is incontestably vague as to its content. If we assume the "executive power" means the power to execute the laws, "the laws" presumably includes the Constitution itself and, insofar as they respect constitutional limits, the statutes that Congress enacts. Thus if the Constitution itself requires presidential recusal from prosecutions posing conflicts of interests, then a president who opts out of supervising a prosecution targeting the president is, by definition, executing the law. Should Congress enact a statute limiting the president's supervision of prosecutions, the president's observance of such statutory limits would likewise be executing the laws. There is simply nothing in the text of the Constitution, read through a modern-day lens, which precludes an attractive interpretation of Article II to protect the rule of law against presidential conflicts of interest. Indeed, given the stakes in terms of presidential legal accountability, permitting presidential recusals as well as statutory limits on presidential supervisory discretion would seem the clearly preferable reading.

Because originalist interpretation happens to coincide in this instance with modernist interpretation, I will put off to chapter 4 the question which mode of interpretation is preferable in conceptualizing the constitutional presidency. The quasi-judicial element of criminal prosecution has other separation-of-powers implications, which I will take up in chapter 6. For now, I simply ask what is to be made of the presidentialists' insistence that it is the original understanding of our 1787 Constitution that not only entitles presidents to supervise criminal prosecutions, but also bars Congress from regulating the exercise of that supervision? At the very least, the historical case is dubious. And if history does not bind us to a constitutional interpretation that limits our present-day capacity to combat presidential corruption, we are free to interpret the text as it makes sense in light of contemporary needs and values. Permitting presidents to recuse themselves from supervising prosecutions that pose conflicts of interest, and legitimating statutory limits on supervisory discretion that are well tailored to prevent the undue politicization of law enforcement, are both moves which accord with the best contemporary constitutional understanding. In insisting that history demands otherwise, the presidentialists are wrong about history; they are allowing their preference for presidentialism to blind them to the contrary evidence. The current benefits to the rule of law in recognizing the permissibility of limiting a president's control over criminal prosecution are so obvious that it seems absurd to deny contemporary constitutionalists the authority to be guided by those benefits in interpreting the constitutional presidency.

THREE

Politicizing the "Deep State"

PRESIDENTS AND THE BUREAUCRACY

IN TURNING FROM whether the president is constitutionally in charge of criminal prosecution to whether the president is constitutionally in control over all federal administrative policy making, it is helpful to begin at a particular historical moment. In the early months of 1981, I was a government lawyer just four years out of law school and working as an assistant general counsel at the federal Office of Management and Budget. It was heady stuff, not least because of the venue—a structure now called the Eisenhower Executive Office Building, but which was then known only as the Old EOB. An elaborate late nineteenth-century edifice situated just west of the White House, the Eisenhower EOB, its web page boasts, possesses a "flamboyant style," which "epitomizes the optimism and exuberance of the post–Civil War period."[1]

Among my tasks was helping to review proposed executive orders—orders that are typically presidential directives to the rest of the executive branch—to make sure they were consistent with existing law. On February 18, I was invited to attend a meeting called for the general counsels of executive branch administrative agencies to familiarize them with one such order. The meeting was held in the EOB's august Indian Treaty Room. Surrounded by the room's French and Italian marble-paneled walls and beneath the stars painted on its ceiling, a roomful of lawyers was presented with copies of an early Reagan order with the modest title, "Federal Regulation."[2] Many took out pens and started making notes in the margins—presumably marking suggested items for comment or change—until the fastest reader in the group got to the end of his copy. As I recall the scene, the silence in the room broke with a confused muttering: "My copy has the president's signature on it!" Jim Miller, an economist who had advised the Reagan campaign and who had served in OMB as a key strategist behind the order, ran the meeting. He replied: "I think you may have misunderstood the purpose of our meeting. What you have is not a draft for comment. It's an executive order that the president has already signed."

In the normal course of business, OMB, at least in those days, would have shared draft executive orders with the agencies likely to be affected.[3] The goal would be a policy consensus as to their content. The higher-ups in Reagan's OMB feared, however, that this order—Executive Order 12,291—would attract such deep-seated resistance from career bureaucrats throughout the administrative agencies that its issuance might be postponed indefinitely. It was not a silly fear. Executive Order 12,291, although building on earlier steps in the Nixon, Ford, and Carter administrations, profoundly altered the relationship of administrative agencies to the White House.[4] It institutionalized a system of centralized oversight of the agencies that became the most significant innovation in federal policy-making process in the last third of the twentieth century.

With regard to the president's role as chief of the executive branch, as with Trump's claims for presidential prerogative regarding crime and prosecution, the Trump administration took potentially dangerous ideas about executive power to unprecedented extremes. But with regard to presidential control of the larger civil bureaucracy—that is, the bureaucracy beyond just the criminal prosecutors—Trump's initiatives had roots going back as far as the Nixon administration and to conceptions of presidential authority that started to take serious hold in the Reagan administration, manifested in part by Executive Order 12,291. The story is a complicated one with two key subplots: the intensification of White House review of general regulatory policy and increasing political control over the administrators who decide individual cases. But the bottom line can be easily stated: In the years between the Nixon presidency and the Trump presidency, we moved from (a) a balanced, pluralistic approach to federal public administration—in which diverse voices, some political and some expert, worked toward fact-based, even if politically inflected solutions to public problems to (b) a potentially more authoritarian approach in which the whole of the federal government's administrative apparatus is supposed to follow the policy preferences—perhaps the whims—of a single person, the president. According to the presidentialists, even administrative judges—administrative officials who decide thousands of individual cases that may never get to court—are supposed to be personally accountable to the chief executive, not wholly independent. The risks that these developments reveal for government in the public interest are real but obscured by the story's legal intricacy. This chapter is designed to tell that story, including how presidentialist ideas about the constitutional presidency nurtured the move from pluralism toward authoritarianism. The next chapter will look at those ideas on their merits and explain why our recent presidents' case for constitutional presidentialism stands on weak ground.

THE CIVICS LESSONS HIGH SCHOOL RARELY TEACHES

Among the sadder, but most robust findings of social science researchers over the decades is how little adult Americans recall of basic civics facts. In 2021, the annual Annenberg Constitution Day Civics Survey recorded the highest percentage of adult Americans ever since the survey launched in 2006 who could name all three branches of the federal government—56 percent. A fifth of those surveyed could name none.[5] Unfortunately, even those who accurately name the branches may not understand how government works and be able to spot the significant power shifts in its processes.

Those who do recall their high school civics will remember being taught that the Constitution creates a legislative branch—namely, Congress; an executive branch headed by the president; and a judicial branch comprising the Supreme Court and whatever lower courts Congress may create. As a starting proposition, they will also have heard that Congress makes law, the executive branch implements the laws that Congress enacts, and the courts decide cases, which often involve applying Congress's statutes to specific sets of facts.

But here's what basic civics often leaves out: If by "law," we mean the complete body of official rules and standards that bind individuals and firms on penalty for disobedience, it is not Congress that directly creates most federal "law." The Constitution does provide Congress with extensive lawmaking authority, including powers to spend for the general welfare, to regulate interstate commerce, and to protect civil rights.[6] But the Constitution says very little about how these powers are to be implemented. Instead, the text provides that Congress has the power "to make all Laws which shall be necessary and proper for carrying into Execution [its constitutionally vested] Powers, and all other Powers vested by this Constitution in the Government of the United States, or any Department or Officer thereof."[7] Congress has used this Necessary and Proper Clause authority to create administrative agencies in the executive branch and to provide those agencies a range of procedural tools through which they, in turn, generate the largest volume of rules and standards that govern Americans. In a technical legal sense, what they do is "administration," not "lawmaking." But as Chief Justice John Roberts has written: "[T]he citizen confronting thousands of pages of regulations—promulgated by an agency directed by Congress to regulate, say, 'in the public interest'—can perhaps be excused for thinking that it is the agency really doing the legislating."[8]

One long-standing tool that Congress permits many agencies to use is administrative adjudication—decision-making in individual cases. Such cases may eventually wind up in court, but they are not decided in the first instance by judges in robes. They are decided initially by a wide array of administrative officials, often called administrative judges or administrative law judges.[9] These officials typically report their decisions to the commissioners or directors of the federal agencies that employ them. The various agencies' lead officials then decide whether or not to follow whatever their first-level adjudicators have recommended. If the party involved is disappointed with the agency's final decision, it is after that final decision that they may finally bring their case to court.

The other and arguably more potent tool is administrative rulemaking—the power, following specific statutory processes, to issue sometimes far-reaching rules that bind the public. Among the best publicized of these administrative rules are the rules to combat air and water pollution. But Congress has created over a hundred agencies with some degree of rule-making authority, and their rules address virtually every segment of our economic and political life.[10] To lawyers and non-lawyers alike, these regulations often read in the same language of command one expects to find in congressional statutes—and they have the same force of law. Yet the production of such administrative rules typically far outnumbers Congress's yearly output of statutes.[11] Moreover, they are the product of the executive branch and not of the legislature.

In conducting either administrative adjudication or administrative rule-making, agencies must operate within the scope of authority Congress has provided. They are Congress's "agents," and Congress is their "principal." The Supreme Court thus requires Congress to give agencies at least some limiting standard in their authorizing statutes to guide how they use their adjudication or rulemaking powers.[12] The federal courts are typically available to halt agency action that overflows the legally authorized channels Congress has provided.[13]

But the statutes that Congress enacts vary widely in how much discretion they give agencies to design rules or adjudicate cases. Some are specific, like recipes. They are fairly detailed not only as to Congress's regulatory goals, but also as to the steps Congress wants an agency to follow in achieving those goals. Classic examples include what are called the Delaney Clauses in the Federal Food, Drug and Cosmetic Act.[14] With regard to food additives, for example, Congress has given the Food and Drug Administration—an agency Congress has created—a quite specific instruction: If a food or color additive is found, through appropriate testing, to cause cancer in humans or animals, the FDA must ban it. As statutes go, the Delaney Clause offers the agency a clear instruction.

A great many statutes, however, are more like guidelines than recipes. If you give a chef a recipe, he or she will know what ingredient to use and in what amounts, how the ingredients are to be combined, and for how long and at what temperature they are to be cooked. But you could also tell a chef that you would like a "balanced and nutritious meal." You might give "balanced" and "nutritious" some general definitions and rule out foods you don't like. At that point, however, you trust the judgment of the chef to come up with a meal that satisfies your goals of balance and nutrition. That is a much broader swath of authority, and many statutes have just this sort of feel.

Agencies can use adjudication to turn guideline-type statutes into much more specific law. For example, the Federal Trade Commission Act exemplifies the guideline-style statute. It authorizes the FTC to root out "unfair or deceptive trade practices," but it does not specify what is "unfair" or "deceptive."[15] Over the decades, the FTC has used its authority to conduct administrative adjudication to prosecute businesses it has deemed to be acting in a manner that is "unfair" or "deceptive." At different times, the Commission has changed its mind whether "deceptive" means "having the capacity to deceive" or "likely to deceive."[16] Lawyers can consult the administrative orders that emanate from these adjudicative proceedings, just as they would read court decisions, to find out specifically the kinds of deals the FTC now rejects as unfair or deceptive. Thus, these FTC decisions represent a kind of lawmaking, even though they emerge from an agency acting under a rather general license from Congress. (Of course, many administrative adjudications focus less on policy formation than on the sound application of preexisting rules to specific facts; social security disability claims are typical. Social security adjudications are not intended to make policy, but to apply already specific law.)

Other agencies use rulemaking to give specific content to Congress's demands. The National Traffic and Motor Vehicle Safety Act, for example, authorizes the secretary of transportation to "prescribe motor vehicle safety standards," which "shall be practicable, meet the need for motor vehicle safety, and be stated in objective terms."[17] The Act defines "motor vehicle safety" to mean:

> the performance of a motor vehicle or motor vehicle equipment in a way that protects the public against unreasonable risk of accidents occurring because of the design, construction, or performance of a motor vehicle, and against unreasonable risk of death or injury in an accident, and includes nonoperational safety of a motor vehicle.[18]

Congress has generally not spelled out, however, which parts of a motor vehicle present safety concerns, much less how great a risk of accidents is to be deemed reasonable or unreasonable. The Department of Transportation has used this authority to promulgate detailed rules involving dozens of motor vehicle components, such as brakes, windshields, tire pressure monitoring, and much else.[19] This again is "law" made in the executive branch.

All of the statutes by which Congress "hires" the executive branch to create public policy—whether the statutes read like recipes or like guidelines—leave room for the executive branch to exercise its best judgment in fulfilling the missions Congress has assigned. Under statutes as broad as the FTC Act or the Motor Vehicle Safety Act, the room for judgment that Congress leaves open—what lawyers would call "discretion"—is conspicuous on the face of the statute. But even a direction as specific as the Delaney Clause—ban all food additives that appropriate testing shows are carcinogenic—leaves important questions unresolved. For example, what counts as appropriate testing? Indeed, what is a food additive? Do food additives include chemicals that may be transferred to food from its packaging? When you contemplate the vast realm of human activity that Congress has rendered subject to executive branch regulation and add up all the "room for best judgment" within which agencies are allowed to maneuver under the law, you realize that the volume of discretion that the executive branch exercises is vast. How that discretion is directed within the executive branch can and will have profound impacts on the scope and nature of regulation affecting every aspect of our health, safety, and welfare. Add to that the discretion agencies often have to decide which problems to address and investigate in the first place, what projects to fund, and which priorities to emphasize, and you realize administrative agencies have a lot of power that is not tightly controlled by congressional recipe-like statutes.

Congress over the centuries has created a highly complex network of administrative bodies to exercise the discretionary power of the executive branch. Rather than authorizing all the important decisions to be made by a single person or a small group, Congress has erected a vast executive establishment including dozens of agencies.[20] These agencies are headed by political appointees whom the Constitution explicitly envisions will be nominated for office by the president and then appointed by the president with the Senate's consent.[21] Civil servants, however, will do most of the work. These include many federal officers who are formally appointed by agency heads, but who are actually chosen apolitically based on their skills and expertise. Between the corps of "career civil servants" and the agency heads, there is likely to be in most agencies an intermediate leadership layer, including some careerists and some officers appointed by each new presidential administration.

What this institutional design is intended to accomplish is ambitious and, in some respects, subtle. For one thing, assigning different areas of social concern to different agencies enables the government to attack problems with the benefit of specialized expertise in different areas. That is, the FTC can employ economists, the Federal Communications Commission can employ technologists (and economists), the Environmental Protection Agency can employ scientists (and economists), and so on, who are chosen because of their particular skill sets. By virtue of their professional training and, over time, by virtue of their experience with their respective agencies, these experts can help political leadership in framing issues and analyzing potential courses of action impartially and based on the best research.

Congress has also mandated procedures for agencies to follow that are intended to foster impartiality and to generate a record of administrative decision-making that will help ensure accountability. An agency engaged in rulemaking, for example, typically has to publish its proposed rules for public comment, provide the public a meaningful opportunity to respond, and publish each final rule along with an explanation of its substance and how the agency responded to the significant issues raised during the "notice and comment period."[22] Agencies engaged in adjudication often have to follow even more elaborate procedures that resemble judicial trials.[23] Moreover, if agency rules or adjudicative decisions are challenged in court, an agency has to show not only that it followed all legally required procedures, but also that its strategies for statutory implementation were reasonably related to Congress's goals, as shown by the facts presented to the agency when it made its decision. Courts may set aside agency "law making" if it is "arbitrary" or "capricious," either in its fact-finding or policy logic.[24]

But there is also room in this system for political values to play a part. After all, it is the president who is constitutionally charged with appointing all agency heads, subject to Senate advice and consent. For most agencies, Congress authorizes the president to select additional members of a leadership team that interacts both with the agency head and with career staff. All of these officials are constrained by law, but they may, and are expected to, bring to their decisional processes the general values and priorities for which the president stands. Keeping in mind all the discretionary room agencies have to exercise best judgment, the potential impact of the leadership team is tremendous.

Imagine, for example, an objective assessment by career employees of the Department of Transportation that leads engineers and statisticians to predict, with an 80 percent confidence level, that a particular safety improvement in a specific automobile component will reduce the likelihood of fatal accidents caused by that part's failure by 30 percent. But imagine further that fatal accidents attributable to this part are already rare, affecting perhaps one in every five million motorists, although the improvement, if required by an agency rule, would raise the cost of manufacture by only $50 per vehicle. Should that improvement be required by regulation? One might expect a secretary of transportation who has been appointed by a free-market enthusiast president to think the additional cost would not be worth it, given the small number of people who are possibly, but not definitely going to be affected. Another secretary of transportation, appointed by a more safety-oriented president, might decide that even a small risk of accidents from the unimproved component is, indeed, "unreasonable," because the cost of preventing such accidents is so low. These cabinet members are likely to come to different decisions—each of them potentially lawful—because of the different value frameworks within which they each assess the factual record presented to them. When pundits say, "Elections matter," this is what they mean—to the extent policy formation entails value judgment, the values with which presidents and their appointees approach administrative decision-making will affect the details of agency rules and orders, not to mention their priorities for action.

To be an agency head in this system—for example, the secretary of labor, the administrator of the Environmental Protection Agency, or the chair of the Federal Communications Commission—is to perform a complex balancing act. On one hand, you got your job through the president, and your careers are now intertwined. You would not have been selected were it not for some basic compatibility between your policy outlook and the president's. To some extent, what the president wants to accomplish is what you want to accomplish or you would not have taken the job. Your values and the president's values largely mesh.

On the other hand, now that you are in office, you find yourself being pulled in multiple directions, perhaps some at odds with the president's preferences. An agency head appointed by a free-market president still must confront the unions and the consumer and other public interest groups who routinely focus on his or her agency's policy agenda. The cabinet secretary appointed by a president more enthusiastic about federal public interest requirements will still have to deal with industry, trade associations, and free market think tanks weighing in against a more intensively regulatory agenda. Moreover, every agency head will be dependent, to some extent, on the knowledge and input of career civil servants who have collectively served both Democratic and Republican presidents and whose focus on the agency mission may not align precisely with anyone's political platform. And on top of this, the agency head must deal with Congress's oversight and appropriations committees—including committees in either house of Congress that may not be controlled by the president's party, but which wield considerable power over the agency's budget and authorities. Agency officials who have been confirmed by the Senate are likely, at their confirmation hearings, to have pledged their responsiveness to Congress when it seeks information from them.

Given these realities—the availability of highly significant lawmaking discretion in the hands of appointed administrators and political tugs in multiple directions both toward and away from the president's policy preferences—it is no surprise that every president wants to augment the gravitational pull of the White House. For its part, Congress, in a variety of ways, seeks to give the agencies they have created more room to maneuver. In some cases, Congress does so by making the agencies "independent," which is really a misnomer because almost all the agencies implementing Congress's statutes through rulemaking and adjudication are part of the executive branch. There is no "independent" administrative branch of government.

But independent agencies can operate, if they choose, with more distance than other agencies from the president's policy advisors.

Congress may increase the potential autonomy of agencies from presidential command in a variety of ways. Congress may put an agency in the hands of multiple commissioners, no more than a half-plus-one of whom may belong to the president's political party.[25] Congress may give administrators terms of office longer than a single presidential term. Most important, Congress may protect administrators from being fired by the president at will by saying or implying via statute that the administrator may be removed only for "inefficiency, neglect of duty, and malfeasance," which translates roughly to incapacity, wrongdoing, or failure to do the appointed job.[26] It has long been understood that such tenure protection would prevent presidents, say, from firing an administrator simply over a policy disagreement. Members of the Federal Trade Commission,[27] the National Labor Relations Board,[28] the Consumer Product Safety Commission,[29] and many other important agencies enjoy that level of protection.[30]

Since the Reagan administration, however, presidentialists have been attacking not only Congress's decisions to counterbalance presidential policy control of the agencies, but the constitutionality of even trying to do so. Despite the breadth of the Necessary and Proper Clause of the Constitution that I quoted earlier, presidentialists have insisted that the president's complete policy control over the discretionary decision-making of administrative agencies is constitutionally mandated, and Congress may do little, if anything, to augment the president's accountability to anyone else.[31] The Trump administration represents the zenith so far of that effort, but you could see the seeds of the future planted in the Eisenhower EOB Treaty Room in 1981, as well as in other legal stands that presidents have endorsed as far back as the 1980s.

CHOOSING PERSONNEL I: WHO GETS TO APPOINT?

With regard to the president's relationship to the federal administrative bureaucracy, the easiest way to state the question separating the presidentialist camp from the checks-and-balances or pluralist camp is this: To what extent does the president get to tell federal administrators how to exercise their statutory authority, including all the discretion just described? Almost all presidentialists would argue that the president has constitutional authority to fire anyone who does not follow the president's policy lead, even if Congress, by statute, provides otherwise.[32] The most aggressive view of presidentialism even holds that Congress's delegations of authority to particular agencies are really delegations to the president, constitutionally speaking.[33] In this view, any president so inclined could personally take over whatever decision-making Congress has assigned to a subordinate administrator. The president would not have to fire anyone to prevail in a policy disagreement; he or she could simply perform the administrative function himself.

The checks-and-balances camp would say it is up to Congress whether the president may fire most officials at will or whether some administrators get tenure protection under something like an "inefficiency, neglect of office, or malfeasance" standard. Further, even when Congress has not given an official protection from at-will removal, the president cannot simply take over an administrator's assigned role. If the president wants something done that an administrator refuses to do—and if Congress has not limited the president's power to fire the administrator at will—then the president, to get his or her way, must go ahead and fire the person and to take whatever are the political repercussions for such a move.

For better or worse, however, courts have so far not gotten to resolve this dispute clearly. Because modern presidents have not yet tried to perform personally the administrative tasks of others, no case has yet presented a judicial challenge to a president's power to do so. Likewise, presidents have rarely exercised whatever firing power they have, and those rare officials who have left their posts under pressure have almost never sued to challenge the legality of their discharge.[34] Yet the Supreme Court has confronted a series of challenges to statutes that limit either the president's role in the appointment of administrative officers or the president's discretion to fire them. Constitutional lawyers have looked to these cases for clues to the question, "To what extent is the president constitutionally entitled to control other administrators' discretion?"

In a Constitution largely silent about the organization of the executive branch of government, the major exception is the Appointments Clause of Article II. In early state constitutions written both before and after 1787, it was common for governors to share the appointments power with some sort of executive council and for state legislatures to retain some appointment authorities themselves, especially regarding state treasurers.[35] Article II, however, contemplates neither of these arrangements. In the major power-granting section of Article II, the Framers provided that the president would "nominate, and by and with the advice and consent of the Senate, shall appoint ambassadors, other public ministers and consuls, judges of the Supreme Court, and all other officers of the United States, whose appointments are not herein otherwise provided for, and which shall be established by law: but the Congress may by law vest the appointment of such inferior officers, as they think proper, in the president alone, in the courts of law, or in the heads of departments."[36]

Parsing the Article II text, one can discern two rules from the Appointments Clause. One is a rule for "officers" who are not "inferior"; these are now typically described as "principal officers."[37] Principal officers must be nominated by and, if the Senate consents, appointed by the president. For officers of "inferior" status, by which the text presumably means something like "subordinate," Congress has four choices. In establishing "inferior" officers, Congress may fall back on the default process of presidential nomination with Senate advice and consent. Alternatively, it can leave the president with appointment power that does not require consent, place the appointment power in the head of a department, or authorize appointment by a court.

Applying these rules in sound fashion, however, requires attending to two problems of categorical definition. The first, which is immediately evident from the text, is the need to differentiate between officers who are "principal" and officers who are "inferior." For example, should someone like the "deputy attorney general" be deemed "inferior" just because of the "deputy" status, or does that officer's critical and wide-ranging role in Justice Department operations and policy making justify treating the office as a principal one? In other words, can someone be a principal officer by virtue simply of the importance of their statutory mission rather than their technical position on a departmental organization chart?

The second question relates to the scope of the term "officer." If every person who performs any function at all on the federal payroll were to be deemed an officer, then one of the four constitutional appointment methods would come into play for every executive branch secretary, messenger, or cleaning staff member. Given the intuitive improbability of such a conclusion, the Supreme Court long ago observed that some executive branch functionaries are merely "employees," who presumably may be hired through any reasonable process that Congress designs.[38]

How these categories are differentiated has direct implications for presidential impact on the executive bureaucracy. Put simply, to the extent Congress can place administrative tasks in the hands of inferior officers or employees, it may also limit the president's direct role in selecting such personnel. Prior to the Watergate era, however, there was little constitutional litigation on these points. A turning point was the Ethics in Government Act enacted as a response to Nixon's Saturday Night Massacre.[39] That statute provided for independent counsel to be appointed by the U.S. Court of Appeals for the District of Columbia Circuit, rather than by the president. Given the text of Article II, excluding the president from the appointments process in such cases would be permissible only if the independent counsel were an inferior officer. In the 1988 case of *Morrison v. Olson*, one of Mr. Olson's challenges to his prosecution was that the court-appointed independent counsel, Alexia Morrison, could not be deemed an "inferior" officer because the Ethics in Government Act made her very difficult to fire, and the president could not directly fire her at all.[40] Her autonomy, in essence, supposedly made her a principal officer.

The Supreme Court rejected Olson's argument. The seven majority justices ruled that she was an "inferior" officer, based on four factors. First, she was, in fact, legally removable by the attorney general, a higher official. Second, she had only limited duties, specified in advance by the attorney general's application for her appointment. She bore "no ongoing responsibilities that extend beyond the accomplishment of the mission that she was appointed for and authorized by the Special Division to undertake."[41] Third, her office was temporary, "in the sense that an independent counsel is appointed essentially to accomplish a single task, and when that task is over, the office is terminated, either by the counsel herself or by action of the Special Division."[42] Finally, in the performance of her duties, she was bound by the Ethics in Government Act to follow as much as possible the existing policies of the Justice Department; she was not herself an executive branch policy maker.

For his part, Justice Scalia—*Morrison*'s sole dissenter—vigorously challenged the majority's conclusion. He argued, based on what he took to be the plain meaning of "inferior," that Article II called for a categorical test of whether the challenged individual was truly subordinate to higher officials. Because the point of allowing an independent counsel's removal from her job only for incapacity or other "good cause" was precisely to protect her decision-making autonomy, Scalia insisted she was effectively not "subordinate."[43]

The issue could have continued to be politically salient in dividing the presidentialists, like Scalia, from the checks-and-balances camp, except that the Ethics in Government Act fell out of political favor. The Act had a sunset date of 1999.[44] By that time, both Republicans and Democrats felt aggrieved by what they believed to be the mistreatment under the Act of Presidents George H. W. Bush and Bill Clinton, respectively. Bush, though not a target of investigation, effectively shut down the work of the Iran-Contra independent counsel, Lawrence Walsh, by pardoning six key individuals indicted and, in some cases, already convicted in connection with the scandal: Caspar Weinberger, Elliott Abrams, Duane Clarridge, Alan Fiers, Clair George, and Robert McFarlane.[45] When Walsh in 1992 secured the indictment of former defense secretary Caspar Weinberger, Republican accusations intensified that Walsh sought only a political vendetta against President Reagan. Walsh's opponents derided his efforts, in the oft-repeated phrase of Oliver North, as no more than "the criminalization of political differences." The timing of certain revelations regarding Weinberger's private notes concerning Iran-Contra policy meetings seemed to support the attack on Walsh. It was late in the 1992 presidential election campaign that the independent counsel alleged that the notes belied President Bush's prior explanations of his own role in and knowledge of the Iran-Contra affair. For their part, half a dozen years later, Democrats accused Independent Counsel Kenneth Starr with equal vehemence of effectively campaigning for Clinton's impeachment after the initial focus of his investigation, the financial transactions referred to as "Whitewater," turned up no prosecutable offense.[46]

In a 1997 low-profile case involving the Coast Guard Court of Criminal Appeals, Justice Scalia had the chance to write a majority opinion that set forth his preferred test for "inferior"-ness, without necessarily reversing *Morrison* on the point.[47] Yet unless Congress rediscovers its enthusiasm for court-appointed independent prosecutors, there will not be politically significant battling over the line between principal and inferior officers.

The more important legal issue for presidential control of the bureaucracy turns out to be the boundary between "inferior officers" and "employees." And it is most important because of a class of federal functionaries who receive little public attention outside the profession: administrative judges. Administrative judges, who may have many different titles, are the executive branch officials charged with dispute resolution, sometimes between private parties, but more often between a private party and the government.[48] Nearly all such adjudications are reviewable by regular courts if a losing private party seeks review, but few are. As a result, in terms of volume, administrative adjudications overwhelm court decisions as vehicles for the implementation of law. There are nearly five thousand administrative adju-dicators of various types in the executive branch, as compared to about eight hundred sixty permanently authorized federal court judges.[49] They decide over seven hundred fifty thousand cases annually, probably about double the number of civil and criminal felony case filings in federal district court.[50]

Congress has set up so wide a variety of these programs—and has most often done so piecemeal without any vision of procedural uniformity—that simply cataloging the different schemes and the features they have in common (or on which they differ) has been a major scholarly project.[51] But all those who are employed by agencies to resolve disputes between those agencies and private parties have an obvious common problem, namely, the appearance of partiality. For example, if an adjudicator appointed and paid by an admin-istrative agency is the official who gets to decide if the agency's complaint against some person or firm is well-founded, that individual or firm could well wonder if the adjudicator is already biased in favor of the agency. Within the large group of administrative adjudicators throughout the executive branch, however, is a special sub-group called "administrative law judges," or ALJ's. Congress has given ALJ's significant legal guarantees to protect relatively independent decision-making. Congress has created special rules to govern their hiring and removal, as well as the degree to which they interact with other agency personnel. Their pay is set by statute and by regulations issued by the federal Office of Personnel Management, and agencies cannot affect an ALJ's pay by giving bonuses or, conversely, poor performance reviews.[52]

The ALJ system is rooted in congressional deliberations that started in the 1930s and 1940s, which led to the eventual enactment of our most significant statute on federal administrative process, which is called the Administrative Procedure Act.[53] The system Congress eventually adopted sought to balance two conflicting goals. One was to provide the ALJ's suf-ficient guarantees of independence to assuage public concerns over their partiality to the agencies that employed them. On the other hand, as noted earlier, administrative adjudications are a tool—until recent decades the primary tool—through which administrative agencies advance their policy values. Hence, Congress gave agency heads who employed ALJ's significant powers to review and even overrule their decisions.[54] However, because the ALJ decisions are written and based on a record also available for review in court, an agency decision to overrule an ALJ is also subject to judicial challenge should a private party that wins at the ALJ level find its victory overturned when appealed to the agency's principal officers.

Entirely reliable data are not available as to the number of ALJ's employed in the executive branch as opposed to the number of other administrative judges who do not have their statutory protections. In 2010, however, there were sixteen hundred federal ALJ's, of whom thirteen hundred worked for the Social Security Administration. By comparison, as of 2002—the last year for which a comprehensive survey is available—there were thirty-three hundred administrative judges in a less protected status.[55] The agencies running important administrative adjudication programs with these less protected functionaries include the Departments of Agriculture, Energy, Health and Human Services, and Veterans Affairs, as well as the Equal Employment Opportunities Commission, the Environmental Protection Agency, the Executive Office of Immigration Review, and the U.S. Patent and Trademark Office.[56]

For presidentialists, the hiring scheme designed to help ensure the political independence of ALJ's is problematic. Until 2018, the system worked as described by Professor Kent Barnett:

> Agencies may appoint them but only after the OPM has winnowed a list of candidates. ALJ candidates must be licensed attorneys, have seven years' litigation experience in courts or administrative agencies (but not necessarily in matters related to the hiring agency), and pass an examination that the OPM administers. The OPM then ranks candidates based on examination scores, experience, and veteran status. The OPM then prepares, under what is known as the "Rule of Three," a list of the three highest-scoring candidates from which the appointing agency can select its ALJ. The goal of this OPM-led process is to render the appointments nonpolitical.[57]

Agencies had some limited avenues to increase their ALJ options. They could borrow or hire ALJs who already work in another agency or wait until several vacancies exist to obtain a larger register of candidates. But most ALJ's were hired through the OPM process.

In 2018, however, the Supreme Court was confronted with a case—*Lucia v. SEC*—involving an agency's efforts to insulate ALJs from the appearance of partiality to even a greater degree.[58] Rather than determine directly who shall be its ALJ's, the Securities and Exchange Commission hired a Chief ALJ, who would select the Commission's other ALJ's, subject to approval by the Commission's Office of Human Resources. This would be a constitutionally permissible scheme if the ALJ's were "employees," but not if they are "officers." As inferior officers, they would have to be appointed through one of the Article II methods, which would include appointment by the Securities and Exchange Commission itself. But the SEC could not delegate its authority to other officials inside the agency.

Lucia is the sort of case about which the average American surely knows nothing, but in which potentially big issues of presidential power are lurking. The Trump Justice Department, whose job would ordinarily be to defend the Securities and Exchange Commission, took the other side. The Supreme Court had to appoint a lawyer to make the argument that the Commission's scheme was constitutional. But by a vote of 7–2, the SEC lost.

This case is potentially important for at least three reasons. First, it means the president's political appointees—the principal officers in each agency—cannot delegate to others within the agency the primary role in appointing agency adjudicators. The selection of agency adjudicators must, to that extent, be politicized. Second, as discussed below, the categorization of ALJ's as "officers" will subject them to a greater likelihood of being dismissed for political reasons. Third, as a "mood setter," a case like this signals to presidents that agency adjudication is not altogether off limits for White House interference.

There is no doubt the Trump administration was interested in subjecting agency adjudication to tighter policy control from the top. In less than a month after the *Lucia* decision, Trump used his general statutory authority over civil service rules to sharply curtail OPM's role as an honest broker in the hiring of ALJ's. Executive Order 13,843 eliminates OPM's examination and rating requirements for ALJ's.[59] It removes ALJ's from a merit-based competitive vetting process and substitutes a political selection process in its stead.

Furthermore, although the Executive Order recognizes that agencies are still bound by the removal processes Congress has enacted to protect ALJ's, the Justice Department that same month rolled out an interpretation of the removal standard that would allow political appointees to fire ALJ's for failing "to follow agency policies . . . or instructions," apparently without regard to the nature of those policies or instructions.[60] In briefing the *Lucia* case before the Supreme Court, the Department tried without success to get the Court to address the president's removal authority and interpret the tenure protections for ALJ's as narrowly as presidentialists insist that the Constitution requires.[61] The Court declined to discuss the issue at all.

Reflecting the new mood regarding the legitimacy of White House concern with administrative adjudication, Trump issued in October 2019 yet another executive order that actually purported to limit what agencies could decide through adjudication.[62] The Supreme Court long ago held that adjudication could be used to determine that a private party's past conduct violated a new standard of conduct so long as the agency did not impose any penalty for the past infraction. The FTC, for example, could determine through adjudication that a new form of artificial intelligence–driven, but misleading online commercial practice was "unfair and deceptive," even though the novelty of the practice meant there was no rule yet explicitly forbidding it. Such a use of adjudication to announce a new view of the law would be permissible so long as it resulted only in future-oriented orders and not retrospective penalties.[63] The agency could tell a firm, "Don't do this again!" but could not fine the firm for failing to have anticipated what the FTC eventually decided.

The Trump order purports to tell agencies, including independent agencies, they may no longer do so.[64] This order, taken at face value, would limit not just ALJ's and other varieties of administrative judges, but the agency heads who make the ultimate decisions on agency adjudication. It is by no means clear that the president has any such restrictive power.

One need not look far back in our political history to see the risks of opening up administrative adjudication to further political control from the top. Among the most important groups of administrative adjudicators in the federal system who are not protected by ALJ tenure rules are our Immigration Judges. Administrative hearings and appeals in immigration cases are handled by the Executive Office of Immigration Review (EOIR), a division of the Department of Justice.[65] Adjudicatory hearings are held in Immigration Courts, presided over by immigration judges, who work under the supervision of a chief immigration judge. Decisions of immigration judges may be appealed to the Board of Immigration Appeals (BIA), also within the Justice Department. The BIA is authorized to consist of twenty-one members headed by a chairperson. The EOIR director may also appoint temporary Board members for a term not exceeding six months. Temporary members are present or retired immigration judges, retired BIA members, or senior EOIR attorneys. In addition to hearing administrative appeals, the BIA may certify cases for decision by the attorney general.

Our system of immigration adjudication has been excoriated by both federal judges and scholars for severe backlogs, long waiting times, and poor decision-making.[66] A 2005 decision of the U.S. Court of Appeals for the Seventh Circuit, *Benslimane v. Gonzales*, written by Judge Richard Posner, offered a sample of judicial criticisms expressed in other cases:[67]

- "The [immigration judge's] opinion is riddled with inappropriate and extraneous comments."
- "This very significant mistake suggests that the Board was not aware of the most basic facts of [the petitioner's] case."
- "The procedure that the [immigration judge] employed in this case is an affront to [petitioner's] right to be heard."
- The immigration judge's factual conclusion is "totally unsupported by the record."
- The immigration judge's unexplained conclusion is "hard to take seriously."
- "There is a gaping hole in the reasoning of the board and the Immigration Judge."
- "The elementary principles of administrative law, the rules of logic, and common sense seem to have eluded the Board in this as in other cases."[68]

Posner noted that, in the year ending on the date his case was argued, different panels of the Seventh Circuit had reversed decisions of the Board of Immigration Appeals in whole or part "in a staggering 40 percent of the 136 petitions to review the Board that were resolved on the merits."[69] In the *Benslimane* case, the court set aside a deportation order the Board issued against an alien because "he failed to produce a document that was both peripheral to his claim to be allowed to remain in this country by virtue of his marriage and already in the possession of the immigration authorities."[70]

A few months after *Benslimane* and not quite a year into his tenure as attorney general, Alberto Gonzales promised to implement twenty-two "key reforms needed to improve the performance and quality of work of the nation's immigration court system."[71] His goals increased additional funding, the imposition of a qualifying test for new hires, the administration of annual performance reviews for incumbent judges, and improved training. Unfortunately, a practice that started in 2004 and continued even under these reforms involved the improper use of political and ideological criteria for selecting immigration judges, who are supposed to be apolitical civil service employees. A 2008 report by the Justice Department's inspector general concluded:

> In the spring of 2004, [the attorney general's chief of staff, Kyle] Sampson created and implemented a new process for the selection of IJs. The new process ensured that all candidates for these positions were selected by the Attorney General's staff. Under this process, staff in the [Office of the Attorney

General (OAG)] would identify and select candidates for these positions using the Attorney General's direct appointment authority. Sampson implemented the new process and it [was followed by the Department's White House Liaisons, [Jan] Williams and then [Monica] Goodling. . . .

We determined that, under the process implemented by Sampson and followed by Williams and Goodling, the OAG solicited candidates for IJ positions and informed EOIR who was to be hired for each position. The principal source for such candidates was the White House, although other Republican sources provided politically acceptable candidates to Sampson, Williams, and Goodling. All three of these officials inappropriately considered political or ideological affiliations in evaluating and selecting candidates for IJ positions. For example, we found that Goodling screened the candidates using a variety of techniques for determining their political affiliations, including researching the candidates' political contributions and voter registration records, using an Internet search string with political terms, and asking the candidates questions regarding their political affiliations during interviews.[72]

A follow-up investigation by the *New York Times* found that a total of thirty-one immigration judges were hired through the politicized process, and that the sixteen of them who had decided enough asylum cases to allow meaningful statistical comparison had "ruled against asylum-seekers significantly more often than colleagues who were appointed, as the law requires, under politically neutral rules."[73] Both Goodling and Sampson resigned in 2007 while the scandal was unfolding.

The more the hiring of administrative adjudicators is placed in political hands, the greater the risks of this kind of abuse. And although the immigration judge example stems from the George W. Bush administration, the Trump administration augmented the possibilities for White House politicization of agency hiring. For example, in creating the constitutional prospect for inferior officers to be appointed by "heads of departments," the Framers no doubt envisioned that these heads of departments would be principal officers whom the president had nominated, but whom the Senate has vetted. The Trump administration, however, showed how the use of "acting administrators" can be used to evade the Senate's role.

Continuity in government creates the obvious problem that vacancies will occur that cannot be filled immediately by individuals nominated and confirmed for those precise positions. The Constitution explicitly provides for one temporary fix, namely, recess appointments. Under Article II, § 2: "The President shall have Power to fill up all Vacancies that may happen during the Recess of the Senate, by granting Commissions which shall expire at the End of their next Session."[74] That option, however, does not fit all circumstances; for example, vacancies often occur when the Senate is not in recess. As a consequence, as early as 1795, Congress has also specified through statute who may serve in an "acting" capacity during a hiatus between regularly confirmed incumbents.[75]

The most recent such statute, the Federal Vacancies Reform Act (FVRA),[76] authorizes the president in most cases to fill vacancies in advice-and-consent positions with temporary "acting" administrators. Trump repeatedly used the FVRA in unprecedented ways to expand his potential influence over agencies. The first matter involved the Consumer Finance Protection Bureau. It is unusual among independent agencies because only a single head administers it. When the position became vacant in November 2017, Trump used FVRA authority not to appoint a different individual from within the agency to become acting head, but rather to appoint as acting director the Senate-confirmed head of a different agency—specifically, OMB Director Mick Mulvaney, who had proved an unfailing political ally.[77] Mulvaney served nearly thirteen months in that "acting" position until the Senate confirmed as his CFPB replacement another Trump nominee, who had actually worked under Mulvaney at OMB. The new director took the position that she regarded herself as serving at the president's pleasure.[78]

President Trump made a second unusual FVRA appointment after his first attorney general, Jeff Sessions, resigned under presidential pressure in November 2018. In this instance, Trump used the FVRA to appoint as acting attorney general a member of Sessions's staff who had not been confirmed to any position at all in the Trump administration.[79] Trump relied on a statutory provision that entitled him to name as the acting attorney general any employee of the Justice Department who had served in the department for at least ninety days and whose pay grade was at least equivalent to that of a GS-15 official.[80] Trump bypassed then deputy attorney general Rod Rosenstein, whose supervision of the Special Counsel investigation into the 2016 election had drawn Trump's criticism, in favor of Matthew Whitaker, Attorney General Sessions's chief of staff. What was unusual was not the designation of a non-confirmed acting agency head—such temporary appointments are common during the early days of a new administration—but rather the designation of a non-confirmed acting agency head not rendered necessary by the inauguration of a new president.

The third unusual high-profile vacancy appointment occurred following what was universally seen as the forced resignation in April 2019, of Homeland Security Secretary Kirstjen Nielsen. Trump indicated that she would be succeeded by Kevin McAleenan, the commissioner of Customs and Border Protection, serving as acting secretary.[81] In order to facilitate this transition, Acting Deputy Under Secretary Claire Grady, who would have been Nielsen's statutory successor in line, also resigned.[82] This appeared to be part of a larger pattern of avoiding Senate involvement in the high-level staffing at DHS. At one point, eight of the top twelve DHS positions supposed to be filled by Senate-confirmed appointees were being filled either by "acting administrators" or by senior officials holding other posts, but exercising so-called "delegated authority"; none had been confirmed to the jobs to which they had been promoted.[83] Trump made clear what he took to be the advantages of non-Senate-confirmed officials. He said in a television interview, "I like 'acting' because I can move so quickly. It gives me more flexibility."[84]

The picture that emerges from these complex developments is potentially revolutionary for administrative adjudication. A president following Trump's example could staff the cabinet for significant periods of time with acting heads of departments who had not been confirmed by the Senate and who owe their career advancement entirely to the president alone. Thanks to the *Lucia* case, these functionaries could be the ones to sign off on the hiring of the government's administrative adjudicators. Under Trump's rules, they would not have to deal with the Office of Personnel Management in deciding who is qualified. Because the adjudicators are civil servants, they are not supposed to be hired based on political criteria. Yet the immigration judge example shows the difficulty of monitoring that practice. A combination of statutes Congress has enacted plus a presidentialist reading of Article II could wind up tethering our corps of administrative adjudicators far more closely to the White House than has ever previously been imagined.

CHOOSING PERSONNEL II: WHEN MAY THE PRESIDENT FIRE?

Years before the Supreme Court decided its most important cases interpreting the Article II powers of appointment, it weighed in on presidential firing authority and on the power of Congress to limit that authority. This is trickier business because the Constitution says nothing explicit about administrative removals, except by impeachment, and the topic was little discussed at the time of the founding. The question of removal authority is plainly important because presidential power to remove an administrator at will directly enhances the prospects for exercising leverage over how that administrator exercises his or her policy discretion.

In 1926, in a case called *Myers v. United States*, a 6–3 Supreme Court opinion threw out a statute that required the president to seek Senate advice and consent to remove any officer whose appointment had also required advice and consent.[85] Ironically, in writing his contributions to *The Federalist* to persuade New York voters to ratify the Constitution, Alexander Hamilton had represented that this is precisely how the new Constitution would work. He asserted "one of the advantages to be expected from the co-operation of the Senate, in the business of [administrative] appointments" was that "the consent of that body would be necessary to displace as well as to appoint."[86] Such a requirement, Hamilton then argued, would lead to stability in administration notwithstanding a change in presidents. Nonetheless, practice after 1789 had been to the contrary, and the Court's 1926 opinion, written by Chief Justice William Howard Taft, a former president, concluded that inserting a requirement of Senate consent to presidential removals invaded the president's executive power.

Chief Justice Taft's opinion, one of the longest in Court history, represents the Court's most thorough embrace of unitary executive theory. Although the only issue presented was whether Congress could reserve for itself an active role in deciding on officer removals, the Taft opinion argued that the president's obligation to "take care that the laws be faithfully executed" was an obligation he could not fulfill without the power of at-will removal over *all* officers of the executive branch.

Taft argued that the First Congress had authoritatively reached that conclusion in creating the first three departments of government: Foreign Affairs, War, and Treasury.[87] During their deliberations, an extended debate occurred over whether the bill creating the Department of Foreign Affairs should specify that the secretary of state was removable by the president. Some argued the president had only such removal power as Congress allowed. Others insisted that the Constitution guaranteed the president complete at-will removal power and that spelling out his removal power for one department might imply wrongly that the president needed Congress's permission to exercise at-will removal in others. The text that came out of the House, reflecting what historians have called the Decision of 1789, referred indirectly to what should happen once the president removed the secretary.[88] In that way, the statute supposedly made clear Congress's assumption that the president had removal power without a strong implication that the president derived that authority from Congress. Ultimately, all three bills referred included oblique references to presidential removals, which is why Taft insisted that the First Congress endorsed the view of an illimitable presidential removal power. Justice McReynolds in a dissent of roughly equal length disputed Taft's history.[89] As I will discuss further in chapter 4, the Decision of 1789 provides a weak foundation on which to support an aggressive theory of presidential removal power.

In any event, the Court's endorsement of so broad a theory of presidential removal power did not last a decade. In 1935, a unanimous Supreme Court—including four justices who had joined in Taft's 1926 opinion—upheld Congress's entitlement to restrict the president's removal power to cases of "inefficiency, neglect of office, or malfeasance."[90] Congress had written that tenure protection into the statute creating the Federal Trade Commission. Franklin Roosevelt, in his first year as president, sought to remove from the FTC a Hoover-appointed commissioner, William E. Humphrey, without suggesting any impropriety in the execution of his office. Roosevelt had written to Humphrey only that "the aims and purposes of the Administration with respect to the work of the Commission can be carried out most effectively with personnel of my own selection," and, "You will, I know, realize that I do not feel that your mind and my mind go along together on either the policies or the administering of the Federal Trade Commission, and, frankly, I think it is best for the people of this country that I should have a full confidence."[91] When Humphrey declined to resign, Roosevelt fired him. Following Humphrey's death, his estate sued for the pay he would have earned had he been allowed to complete his seven-year term.

It fell to the Court how to distinguish Humphrey's case from that of Frank Myers, the decedent postmaster of Portland, Oregon, whose estate had successfully sued for his back pay after he was fired without the Senate's consent on the direction of President Wilson. The facts of the two cases were easy to distinguish. In Myers's case, Congress had essentially given itself the power to veto a presidential removal decision. Today, this would be called unconstitutional "aggrandizement." In the FTC Act that protected Humphrey, Congress had not reserved for itself any such role. It had simply narrowed the grounds on which the president could implement his removal power. As a consequence, the Court felt free to ignore parts of Taft's 243-page opinion that went further than necessary to decide Myers's challenge: "In the course of [the *Myers* decision], expressions occur which tend to sustain the government's contention [in *Humphrey's Executor*], but these are beyond the point involved and, therefore, do not come within the rule of *stare decisis*. In so far as they are out of harmony with the views here set forth, these expressions are disapproved."[92]

The *Humphrey's Executor* Court, however, further distinguished the cases in a superficially more puzzling way. As a postmaster, the Court said, Myers was a "purely executive officer."[93] Congress had more leeway with regard to FTC commissioners because they did a different kind of job:

> The Federal Trade Commission is an administrative body created by Congress to carry into effect legislative policies embodied in the statute in accordance with the legislative standard therein prescribed, and to perform other specified duties as a legislative or as a judicial aid. Such a body cannot in any proper sense be characterized as an arm or an eye of the executive. Its duties are performed without executive leave and, in the contemplation of the statute, must be free from executive control.[94]

In other words, unlike the "purely executive" Myers, Humphrey was performing a task mostly "quasi-legislative" or "quasi-judicial." The puzzle posed by this language is twofold. First, every agency, including the Post Office, is "an administrative body created by Congress to carry into effect legislative policies embodied in the statute in accordance with the legislative standard therein prescribed." That is quite literally the definition of an administrative agency, and the FTC is identical to the Post Office in this respect. Further, even if the FTC's administrative activities resemble those of Congress (rulemaking) or a court (adjudication), the FTC is plainly neither Congress, nor part of the judiciary. There is really no branch of the federal government to which the FTC could belong other than the executive branch.

For over half a century, *Humphrey's Executor* settled the constitutionality of independent agencies without serious challenge. The Court further determined that Congress could create an independent agency by implication—by virtue of its assigned quasi-judicial mission—even if the relevant statute did not explicitly protect the members of the agency from at-will removal. But Theodore Olson, the respondent in *Morrison v. Olson* discussed in the last chapter, thought he could still use *Humphrey's Executor* to hold independent prosecutors unconstitutional on the ground that a prosecutor, like a postmaster, is "purely executive."

Based on the historical evidence reviewed in chapter 2, the Court might have rebuffed Olson precisely on this point. Despite many offhand judicial statements to the contrary, there is a good case, as chapter 2 explains, that the founding generation thought of prosecutors as being as much judicial as executive officers. The *Morrison* Court, however, took a different tack. Justice Rehnquist's opinion for a seven-justice majority said the labeling of the officer's function could not determine the constitutionality of protecting their tenure. Instead, "the real question is whether the removal restrictions are of such a nature that they impede the President's ability to perform his constitutional duty."[95] Applying this test, the Court upheld a for-cause removal protection for the independent counsel, concluding that the control and oversight measures provided—in particular, the attorney general's ability to remove the officer for cause—were adequate "to ensure that the President is able to perform his constitutionally assigned duties."[96] The Court reached this result even though the counsel performed an executive law enforcement function involving "no small amount of discretion and judgment."[97]

Morrison is the Supreme Court decision that modern-day presidentialists most dislike. It not only reaffirmed, but arguably broadened *Humphrey's Executor*. Moreover, the sole dissenter, Antonin Scalia, is an iconic figure in right-wing jurisprudence. The stentorian tone of his dissent makes for powerful reading, if not for persuasive logic. Since *Morrison v. Olson*, however, every justice in the majority has left the Court, and right-wing Republican presidents have appointed five—or perhaps six—strongly presidentialist justices since that 1988 decision: Thomas (succeeding Thurgood Marshall, who had been in the majority), Roberts (succeeding Rehnquist, who had written the majority opinion), Alito (succeeding O'Connor, who had voted with the majority), Gorsuch (succeeding Scalia, who had dissented), Kavanaugh (succeeding Kennedy, who had recused himself). The possible sixth Republican-appointed presidentialist may turn out to be Barrett (succeeding Ginsburg, who had herself replaced Byron White, a member of the *Morrison* majority). It is quite likely all the new presidentialist justices would have decided *Morrison v. Olson* differently.

Indeed, in 2010 and with Scalia and Kennedy still on the Court, the presidentialist justices got to express their discomfort with the outlook of *Humphrey's Executor* without overruling it.[98] Congress had created an agency called the Public Company Accounting Oversight Board (PCAOB), which was to be appointed and closely supervised by the Securities and Exchange Commission (SEC). Even though our federal Securities Acts are silent on the point of SEC commissioner tenure, SEC members are generally regarded as having implicit statutory protection from at-will presidential discharge. It is, in that sense, an independent commission. As it happens, however, Congress gave the PCAOB the same tenure protection against the SEC. As a result, the president could not fire SEC members except for good cause, and the SEC could not remove PCAOB members except on the same terms.

The Court held that the double layer of protection from at-will removal was an unconstitutional abridgement of the president's constitutionally granted supervisory powers: "By granting the Board executive power without the Executive's oversight, this Act subverts the President's ability to ensure that the laws are faithfully executed—as well as the public's ability to pass judgment on his efforts. The Act's restrictions are incompatible with the Constitution's separation of powers."[99] One obvious problem with this analysis, however, is that subjecting the PCAOB members to at-will removal by the SEC augments the president's supervisory power only in one limited circumstance—namely, when the president wants to remove a PCAOB member for whom good cause does not exist, and the SEC, though independent, is inclined to fulfill the president's wish. If the PCAOB member is not actually removable on grounds of inefficiency, neglect, or malfeasance, then SEC members—themselves protected against at-will removal—could not be fired by the president for keeping the PCAOB member in place.

Brett Kavanaugh, then a conservative member of the U.S. Court of Appeals for the District of Columbia Circuit, proved eager to deploy the general language of *Free Enterprise Fund* to advance his aggressive view of presidentialism—ironic, given that Kavanaugh made his name in conservative circles as a deputy to Whitewater independent counsel Ken Starr, whose position Kavanaugh presumably would now say was unconstitutional.[100] Judge Kavanaugh was not just an enthusiast for presidential power; he was a campaigner. He elaborated presidentialist theories in cases that did not require constitutional analysis at all. He wrote law review articles urging Congress to expand and protect presidential power. He was a key White House official when the George W. Bush administration made some of its most outlandish claims for presidential authority under Article II of the Constitution.

Judge Kavanaugh's most noteworthy judicial opinions on the unitary executive were rendered in disputes where no constitutional issue should have been addressed. One was his concurrence at a preliminary stage in *In re Aiken County*, a suit that required no constitutional analysis.[101] Judge

Kavanaugh's concurrence offered a detailed explanation why, in his view, the creation of independent administrative agencies like the Nuclear Regulatory Commission departed from a proper reading of Article II—a reading in which the president would be deemed singly and personally responsible for all "execution of the laws." Although insisting that his point was "not to suggest that [*Humphrey's Executor*] should be overturned," he suggested that the earlier case might best be regarded dismissively as a decision "by a Supreme Court seemingly bent on resisting President Roosevelt and his New Deal policies."[102] At a later stage in the litigation, he detailed at length his expansive view of the president's prerogatives regarding criminal prosecution—before concluding that the NRC could not use that prerogative to defend the challenged NRC decision at issue.[103] This presumably came as no surprise to the NRC, which had never raised the issue in its briefs.

In another decision, Judge Kavanaugh demonstrated that unitary executive theory could well be promoted—and Congress's design for agency independence undermined—not by overturning *Humphrey's Executor*, but by inventing wholly new theories that would enable courts to work around it. *PHH Corp. v. Consumer Finance Protection Bureau* involved a challenge by a mortgage lender against the CFPB's imposition of a massive penalty for an alleged impropriety.[104] The three-judge D.C. Court of Appeals panel to which Judge Kavanaugh belonged concluded unanimously on statutory grounds that the CFPB's order was improper. But Judge Kavanaugh used the case as occasion to cut a new theory from whole cloth as to why the CFPB's structure as a single-headed independent agency was unconstitutional under the separation of powers.

Recognizing that *Humphrey's Executor* precluded his holding the CFPB unconstitutional simply on the ground that the president could not fire its director at will, Judge Kavanaugh manufactured an entirely new rationale for *Humphrey's Executor*, namely, that "in the absence of Presidential control, the multi-member structure of independent agencies acts as a critical substitute check on the excesses of any individual independent agency head—a check that helps to prevent arbitrary decision making and abuse of power, and thereby to protect individual liberty."[105] He then determined that a single-headed independent agency lacks the supposed liberty-protecting features of multimember agencies and proceeded to hold the CFPB structure unconstitutional on that ground—a conclusion the D.C. Circuit reversed en banc.[106] Arrogating to a court the power to determine whether a congressionally designed administrative structure is sufficiently protective of liberty under a wholly subjective metric was extraordinary enough. Equally remarkable, however, was that the author of a judicial opinion five years earlier that decried the constitutionality of multimember agencies like the Nuclear Regulatory Commission then offered in his *PHH* decision the most robust policy defense in the history of U.S. jurisprudence of the wisdom of multimember independent administrative agencies.

In 2018, Judge Kavanaugh was elevated to the Supreme Court, where he is no longer bound to follow precedent. Yet another case—*Seila Law LLC v. Consumer Finance Protection Bureau*, brought to the Supreme Court in 2020 the question whether the CFPB is constitutionally structured.[107] Not surprisingly, Kavanaugh helped form a presidentialist majority which, in a 5–4 decision, determined that the single-headed structure of the CFPB was impermissible. Should Congress reinstitute an independent counsel system, it remains to be seen whether the presidentialists would rely on *Seila Law* as having so undercut the rationale for *Morrison v. Olson* as to warrant overruling it. This is a dangerous possibility.

CHOOSING POLICY: INTENSIFYING WHITE HOUSE CONTROL OVER RULEMAKING

Because of the leverage presidents derive from their powers of both appointment and removal, the legal battles regarding the interpretation of those constitutional powers are important for the exercise of power within our checks and balances system. But even a president with judicially sanctioned at-will removal power will not find the threat of firing to be a consistently useful tool of day-to-day management. The enormous volume of agency regulatory activity poses a challenge for White House monitoring, and the difficulties of replacing recalcitrant administrators means they cannot credibly be threatened with discharge over every possible policy disagreement with the White House.

The sixties and seventies spawned a number of social movements that spurred Congress to create new agencies with broad rulemaking powers— agencies such as the Department of Transportation, the Environmental Protection Agency, the Consumer Products Safety Commission, and the Equal Employment Opportunity Commission. Congress also vastly expanded the rulemaking powers of existing agencies, such as the Department of Health, Education, and Welfare, which was eventually split into the Department of

Education and the Department of Health and Human Services. The civil rights movement, the consumer movement, and the environmental movement were all instrumental in instigating Congress's grants of rulemaking power to the executive branch. The procedural norms surrounding rulemaking, which more closely resembles the work of legislatures than courts, are not as hostile to political oversight as are the expectations associated with adjudication.

With the expansion of executive branch rulemaking activity, presidents inevitably recognized that the regulatory initiatives of the federal agencies would affect their own political fortunes. Even if Congress assigned the job of combating pollution, for example, to the administrator of the EPA, how the EPA performed that task would reflect on the president. Richard Nixon, under whom the EPA was created, did not want the White House taken unaware by EPA regulatory initiatives. He presumably wanted an agency vigorous enough to earn the votes of environmentalists, but not so aggressive as to provoke political backlash by those who thought environmental regulation could cost jobs, boost inflation, or simply limit their business opportunities. Nixon therefore took a first step toward centralizing regulatory oversight in the White House by creating a so-called "Quality of Life Review" process in OMB.[108] In essence, this review process amounted to a White House requirement that the EPA engage in informal discussions of any proposed new rules with representatives of other federal agencies that might counsel less ambitious EPA approaches in order to accommodate their own competing missions. As a move toward White House oversight, this was more of a nudge than a new command structure.

By the time of Nixon's resignation from office, however, inflation had become a pressing political concern, intensified by the Arab oil embargo of 1973. President Gerald Ford adopted the view that regulation could worsen inflation and also that a focus limited to the impacts of environmental regulation was not enough. He thus issued an executive order requiring that all "major proposals for legislation, and for the promulgation of regulations or rules by any executive branch agency must be accompanied by a statement which certifies that the inflationary impact of the proposal has been evaluated."[109] Ford authorized the director of OMB to develop criteria for the evaluation of new regulations or legislative proposals, as well as to prescribe processes for the evaluations to be conducted. He did not, however, require agencies to use these evaluations in any particular fashion, and quality control over the analyses was generally left to the agencies.

President Carter went further. A fervent believer in the prospects for bureaucratic reform, he came to office amid a developing bipartisan consensus that commercial transportation, for example, had been over-regulated and that in critical sectors, such as energy and antitrust, a multiplicity of agencies and regulatory schemes had created undue compliance costs and might be stifling innovation.[110] In 1978, he took several institutional measures to achieve regulatory reform. One was establishing a cabinet-level Regulatory Analysis Review Group (RARG) to review important regulations.[111] That cabinet-level body was granted review authority over the most important regulations agencies proposed, although it had no formal powers over the regulatory agencies. The Council on Wage-Price Stability conducted most of the RARG's analytic work, overseen by the RARG's major players—senior officials in OMB, the Council of Economic Advisers, and other parts of the Executive Office of the President.

In addition, Carter revoked Ford's Executive Order No. 11,821 and replaced it with a far more detailed order requiring, among other things, that executive agencies prepare analyses of all major proposed regulations to help assure simplicity, clarity, and cost-effectiveness.[112] These regulatory analyses, available to the public in both proposed and final form, were to indicate alternative regulatory approaches that the agency considered, the anticipated economic impacts of each, and "a detailed explanation of the reasons for choosing one alternative over the others."[113] Carter's new Executive Order No. 12,044 also imposed obligations on agencies to review existing regulations for possible improvement but left to each agency the task of developing a review process. Like Ford, Carter did not attempt to apply his requirements to the independent regulatory commissions.

Finally, Carter created a Regulatory Council, consisting of representatives from twenty executive departments and eighteen independent agencies.[114] Their main task was preparing a semiannual schedule of proposed regulations, as Carter's executive order had required.

The cumulative effects of the measures taken by Presidents Nixon, Ford, and Carter were to accelerate notification of the White House when administrative agencies were considering major regulatory initiatives, to intensify the internal agency processes of regulatory analysis, to require the sharing of those analyses outside each agency, and to amplify the voice of White House officials in advising agencies of the president's policy preferences. None of these measures, however, called into question the final authority of the agencies to make the regulatory decisions entailed in implementing

Congress's statutes. They relied heavily on the president's explicit constitutional authority to seek information from executive departments regarding the performance of their official duties.

President Reagan's Executive Order No. 12,291—the order signed with virtually no agency input from any agency beyond the Reagan White House—made a dramatic leap forward in terms of centralizing control. That leap is exactly why the draft order had been withheld from the agencies that would usually have been consulted. Members of the Reagan transition had identified what they took to be two shortcomings of the Carter system.[115] First, even though copies of the agencies' regulatory analyses were to be shared with OMB, there was no centralized quality control. The rigor of any agency's analysis was pretty much left up to the agency. Moreover, although agencies were required to analyze the costs and benefits of their proposals for rule making, they were not bound in their choice of regulatory strategy by the results of their analysis. Specifically, agencies were not required to use their analyses to maximize the ratio of regulatory benefits to regulatory costs.

The lawyers and economists on the Reagan team, working with James J. Tozzi, a veteran federal policy analyst who had helped implement the Carter administration reforms, came up with the draft order to remedy these two supposed defects. Henceforth, agencies would be told that, to the extent permitted by law, they would have to hold off on the publication of any significant new regulatory proposal until OMB was satisfied with the quality of its cost-benefit analysis. This gave the White House a centralized quality control that the review process had previously lacked. Moreover, to the extent an agency's statutes permitted, each agency would be bound by presidential order to pursue its regulatory objectives in the most cost-effective way.

The lawyers involved in vetting the order, not only in OMB, but also in the Justice Department's Office of Legal Counsel (OLC), were aware that this level of White House intervention in the regulatory process was breaking new ground. Congress had not passed any statute authorizing the White House initiative. As a result, the constitutionality of requiring agencies to perform OMB-approved "regulatory impact analyses" would depend on plausible arguments that the president was acting within the "executive power" that Article II of the Constitution vests in the president and his constitutional duty to "take care that the laws be faithfully executed." President Reagan, like Presidents Nixon, Ford, and Carter, could point to the president's explicit entitlement to obtain information from the executive departments. Quite obviously, however, neither the information-gathering power, nor any other clause in Article II unambiguously signified a presidential entitlement to manage the policy-making discretion of the agencies to which Congress had delegated its wide variety of regulatory assignments.

In signing off on the legality of the Reagan executive order, the Justice Department turned to an influential analytical framework derived from Justice Robert Jackson's opinion in the famous 1954 Supreme Court case of *Youngstown Sheet & Tube Co. v. Sawyer*.[116] The *Youngstown* Court held unconstitutional an executive order issued by President Harry S. Truman that authorized the secretary of commerce to take control of U.S. steel plants and assure their continued operation in the face of a steelworkers' strike. Truman insisted the measure was needed to maintain steel production in order to sustain the U.S. military effort in Korea. He had earlier sought without success to have Congress explicitly give the president the power to respond to strikes in just this way.

Six of the nine justices on the *Youngstown* Court voted to overturn the Truman order, but they produced six separate opinions stating somewhat different rationales for doing so. Over time, the most influential has been the opinion by Justice Robert Jackson because his mode of analysis is potentially applicable to every unilateral presidential initiative. Jackson argued that presidential initiatives could roughly be seen as falling into three categories—those authorized by statute, those in violation of statute, and those about which our statutory law is silent.[117] The president, he pointed out, is on strongest constitutional ground when acting within the first category and weakest when acting in the second, which is where Jackson placed the Truman order. In the third category, he said, where Congress has not spoken, the president's authority to act was uncertain. Jackson implied, however, that a case for presidential initiative might be upheld in this "zone of twilight" if there were at least a plausible constitutional argument in the president's favor, and the initiative met a legitimate national need without either invading individual rights or destabilizing the constitutional system of checks and balances.

The drafters of the Reagan order had gone to notable lengths to avoid conflict with any existing federal statute. They placed management responsibility in OMB, in which Congress had already vested other oversight powers with regard to how the various agencies imposed information-reporting obligations on the public.[118] The order eschewed any interference in agency adjudications, which are typically subject to their own statutory procedural requirements—including limits on communication with outside parties.[119] Agencies were directed to comply with the order's requirements only "to the extent permitted by law."[120] And notably, Reagan, like Carter, exempted from his order the so-called independent agencies—that is, the agencies whose members the president was not entitled to fire at will.[121]

Most important, at least in theory, the order formally respected Congress's assignment of regulatory decision-making to agencies, not to OMB. The order contemplates that agencies will perform regulatory impact analyses in connection with both their original public proposals and in support of each regulation as finally drafted. With regard to the former, the order authorizes the director of OMB to request that an agency refrain from publishing its preliminary Regulatory Impact Analysis (RIA) or notice of proposed rulemaking until OMB's review of the analysis was complete.[122] Should the agency's final regulatory impact analysis not be in complete accord with OMB's views, the order directs the agency to "refrain from publishing its final Regulatory Impact Analysis or final rule until the agency has responded to the director's views, and incorporated those views and the agency's response in the rulemaking file,"[123] which is available to the public. The order states, however, that neither of these requirements "shall be construed as displacing the agencies' responsibilities delegated by law."[124]

Despite the order's reassuring phrases, the potential challenges it posed to each agency's customary room to maneuver were obvious. "Requests" not to publish a proposed rule until the agency's RIA was approved and directions to hold off on a final rule until the director had submitted comments and the agency had prepared a formal response could obviously be turned in practice into an indefinite hold on specific regulations—at least if no statute mandated a particular timetable for agency action. Moreover, the direction to agencies to follow the dictates of cost-benefit analysis would itself limit an agency's regulatory options—otherwise the requirement would be of no import. The order would seem to tailor the agency's range of discretion more narrowly than Congress might have contemplated.

The Justice Department, however, adopted the view that the order did not transgress constitutional grounds—a view I agreed with in my first published article as a law professor.[125] It is widely conceded that the vesting of executive power in the president, along with the president's charge to take care that the laws be faithfully executed, entails some supervisory relationship with administrative agencies.[126] Although the requirement of cost-sensitivity might seem to narrow an agency's options, the plasticity of cost-benefit analysis would typically leave agencies considerable leeway, in principle, to justify their preferred regulatory approaches. Moreover, the president's supervisory role placed him in a constitutionally unique position to try to coordinate and bring coherence to the multiple and often overlapping missions of the many regulatory agencies. Requiring agencies to adhere to cost-benefit analysis could be seen, or so I argued, as an aid to this coordinating function because it would help minimize the prospect that any one agency's initiatives could make it more difficult for other agencies to accomplish the objectives they were pursuing under their respective administrative portfolios.

In other words, we lawyers recognized that the impact of the order would increase the White House's gravitational pull in the struggle for influence over agency policy making. But the respect formally paid to the statutory assignment of responsibility to each agency, the order's specific provisions to avoid conflict with any relevant statute, and the plausibility of the order's compatibility with a president's supervisory role added up, in our view, to a constitutionally sufficient justification for the order. It moved the needle toward centralization but intruded on no one's constitutional rights and did not destabilize checks and balances or upset the constitutional separation of powers. Or so we believed.

Importantly, the 1981 Justice Department did not purport to defend the Reagan order based on "unitary executive theory" or any particularly novel or aggressive ideas about the presidency.[127] At that moment, however, the department was under the leadership of William French Smith, who had been the president's lawyer in California. Smith was a committed Reagan Republican, to be sure, but not himself an ideological warrior. With service on the boards of both corporations and cultural nonprofits, as well as such bodies as the U.S. Advisory Commission on International Educational and Cultural Affairs, the board of directors of the Los Angeles World Affairs Council, and the Legal Aid Foundation of Los Angeles from 1963 to 1972, Smith was a classic, civic-minded establishment Republican.[128] Theodore B. Olson, Smith's law partner, served as head of OLC during most of the first Reagan administration. Although he took a strong view in that role of the president's constitutional powers and privileges, Olson operated very much as a "lawyer's lawyer," not advancing novel and aggressive executive power claims as a first line of attack.

Lawyering in the second Reagan administration took a different tone. Smith's successor as attorney general was Edwin Meese III, who had served during the first Reagan administration as a senior White House advisor and who relished the prospect of using control of the Justice Department to give greater weight and influence to right-wing legal ideas that had been largely marginal to mainstream constitutional law prior to the 1980s. It was Meese's Justice Department and the OLC leadership of another hard-line conservative, Charles J. Cooper, which truly embraced the idea of unitary executive theory as the right way to understand the original Constitution. The OLC opinion discussed in chapter 1, which asserted the supposed unconstitutionality of insulating from White House control the pamphlet-writing responsibilities of the Centers for Disease Control, is a telling artifact. Its premise was explicit: "As head of a unitary executive, the President controls all subordinate officers within the executive branch. The Constitution vests in the President of the United States 'The executive Power,' which means the *whole* executive power."[129] Such was supposedly "the framers' original intent."[130]

But Meese's Justice Department went beyond pushing its constitutional theories as necessary to address individual controversies. Through a series of official documents, it expressly promulgated a systematic creed of constitutional interpretation it directed lawyers to follow. These included the 1987 "Original Meaning Jurisprudence: A Sourcebook,"[131] the 1988 "Guidelines on Constitutional Litigation,"[132] and a report that same year titled, "The Constitution in the Year 2000: Choices Ahead in Constitutional Interpretation."[133] Meese's doctrine clearly embraced a hard-edged interpretation of separation-of-powers principles, which would insure the president's complete control over the executive branch. But his department also saw litigation as a way to educate judges on the "right" way to think about constitutional issues. In every constitutional brief, lawyers were told to include a section defending their position based on the original meaning of the constitutional text:

> The inclusion of an original meaning section will help to refocus constitutional analysis on the text of the Constitution. Not only will it serve to ensure that government attorneys give careful consideration to the original meaning of the constitutional provisions at issue, it will help to focus judges on the text of the Constitution and away from their personal preferences or from incorrectly reasoned court precedent as the appropriate basis for decisionmaking. Instead of looking exclusively to years of questionable precedents and their equally questionable accretions, the courts will at least be more likely to review the original constitutional text.[134]

One will search Meese-era documents in vain for any notice of the profound problems, as discussed in the next chapter, with originalism as a method of interpretation.

Meese's turn toward a more aggressive defense of presidential prerogative did not mark any change in the defenses offered for White House regulatory review because no more aggressive defense was needed. No litigation ever challenged the president's authority to issue the order. And even though the Democratic Party controlled both Houses of Congress throughout the Reagan administration, formal pushback against the order was limited to the rare insertion into a regulatory statute of an exemption of a particular regulation from this form of OMB oversight.[135] In a way, Congress's use of such a device had the impact of legitimating the 12,291 process. After all, if Congress could expressly exempt a regulation issued under one particular statute from 12,291 review, the absence of such an exemption in every other regulatory statute enacted since 1981 might be read to imply Congress's acceptance of the new process.

For his part, Reagan's successor, George H. W. Bush, felt no need to reinvent the Reagan executive order. As Reagan's vice president, he had chaired a Task Force on Regulatory Relief created by Executive Order No. 12,291 to oversee its implementation, and Bush obviously supported the system. Yet complaints by congressional Democrats about what they saw in the second Reagan administration as a dangerous lack of transparency posed a critical political obstacle to the ongoing process.

Seemingly as a result, Bush created a separate Council on Competitiveness, which Vice President Dan Quayle would chair, and which would largely take over the role of pressuring regulatory agencies to roll back legal requirements and set less ambitious standards going forward. Although the council was composed of the administration's major economic advisers, it functioned chiefly through the vice president's staff as a source of pressure on OMB and other agencies, especially EPA, to take account of economic impacts in the course of regulatory policy making.[136]

The council was not content merely to react to agency proposals for regulation. It took the initiative in identifying controversial areas of regulatory activity on which to focus its sustained attention, while at the same time maintaining a high degree of secrecy. No executive order or other formal document "chartered" the Council on Competitiveness. A "Fact Sheet" released in April 1989 by the Office of the Vice-President was the sole public document marking its establishment and structure.[137] There is no indication that, while in operation, the council followed regular procedures, published or otherwise. It had no formal or informal agreement with Congress over legislative access to the documentation of its deliberative contributions. It established no controls on the degree or nature of its substantive contacts with outside interests. Yet by interagency memo, it asserted its jurisdiction over "not only regulations that are published for notice and comment, but also strategy statements, guidelines, policy manuals, grant and loan procedures, Advance Notices of Proposed Rulemaking, press releases and other documents announcing or implementing regulatory policy that affects the public."[138] Given the council's limited resources, the percentage of actual activities the council could review was presumably quite small compared to the entire regulatory output of the federal executive. Nonetheless, according to the vice president's self-expressed mandate, there was virtually no policy-making activity that the council regarded as categorically beyond its reach.

A number of political circumstances coalesced between 1990 and 1992 to give the council special policy-making prominence. First, contrary to President Bush's deregulatory rhetoric, the Bush administration entered 1990 and 1991 with a record of significant increases in the number of new regulations being issued. Given the sensitivity of that activity to the business community, plus the vice president's widely acknowledged need for enhanced credibility, the council provided the vice president a significant forum through which to demonstrate his substantive heft and his political clout. Second, the OMB regulatory review process got caught in crossfire over the 1989 reauthorization of the Paperwork Reduction Act.[139] That statute authorized creation of the Office of Information and Regulatory Affairs (OIRA), the OMB office that had been delegated the function of carrying out regulatory review under Executive Order 12,291. With the statutory authorization for funding OIRA set to expire, critics sought to insert into the reauthorization bill a set of procedural constraints for OIRA regulatory review. These included comprehensive "logging" requirements for all OMB activities and communications relating to review, the imposition of deadlines for the conduct of reviews, and a requirement for OMB to explain in writing its reasons for suggesting changes in any proposed regulation. When OMB threatened to recommend a veto of any such requirements, Richard Darman, the director of OMB, and Rep. John Conyers, Chair of the House Government Operations Committee, reached a "sidebar" agreement to delete the statutory requirements in return for an OMB promise to implement the proposed changes administratively. Although the Darman-Conyers pact appeared to clear the path for House support of reauthorization, the administration informed Rep. Conyers that it could not support the Darman deal because its provisions "would seriously interfere with the president's constitutional duty to supervise the Executive Branch."[140]

In retaliation, the Democratic Congress refused either to reauthorize OIRA or to confirm a presidential appointee to succeed Wendy Gramm, who had departed as OIRA administrator in 1989. As a consequence, OIRA throughout the Bush administration lacked an advice-and-consent appointee to wield its authority over executive agencies. Although OIRA continued to operate its regulatory review operation without an express statutory charter, the Council on Competitiveness stepped in to fill the political void and to set the tone of regulatory review in a way that OIRA could not.

Outside commentators credited Allan B. Hubbard, the council's executive director, with significantly institutionalizing the council's regulatory review operation. Hubbard's appointment provoked criticism, however, from Congress and from environmentalists because, as part-owner of an Indiana chemicals company and a significant holder of utilities stocks, he was thought to have both financial interests and ideological predispositions hostile to the environmental regulations that occupied most of the Council's agenda.

There is no doubt the Council had significant impact on the content of regulatory policy making. As summarized by one commentator, the council "convinced agency heads to weaken, and in some cases eliminate, regulations relating to commercial aircraft noise, the protection of wetlands, mandatory recycling, and air pollution."[141] Its impact was well illustrated by the Environmental Protection Agency's (EPA) experience in issuing regulations under the Clean Air Act Amendments of 1990 to limit the effect of new municipal incinerators as sources of air pollution. Among other things, the EPA originally proposed to require:

> operators of [such] new sources of air pollution to achieve a twenty-five per cent reduction by weight of unprocessed waste by separating out some or all of the following recoverable/recyclable materials: paper and paperboard combined; ferrous materials; nonferrous metals; glass; plastics; household batteries; and yard waste.[142]

EPA would further have required the recycling of all lead-acid batteries—the source of 60 percent of the lead in U.S. garbage—and prohibited their incineration by municipal incinerators. These proposals were based on three cost-benefit studies with which the Council on Competitiveness disagreed.

The Council persuaded EPA to change the agency's view regarding the merits of the waste separation proposal. EPA abandoned its waste separation requirement because of its revised conclusion that "emissions reductions resulting from materials separation were not only difficult to quantify but were in fact relatively small."[143] The D.C. Circuit subsequently determined that EPA had sufficient support in the record to justify this change in view as nonarbitrary.[144]

As paraphrased by the D.C. Circuit, the council also had argued to EPA that EPA's waste separation plan "would violate principles of federalism because waste management is traditionally a state and local concern," and would not impose a "standard of performance" as authorized by the Clean Air Act, because the rule would set "a strict standard rather than allowing flexibility in meeting a particular goal."[145] The D.C. Circuit did not rule on these arguments because EPA did not rest its final rule upon them.

The D.C. Circuit did, however, invalidate EPA's decision not to ban the incineration of lead acid batteries.[146] Public records are not available to substantiate how much of EPA's rationale for retreat emanated from the Council, but it is reasonable, given the political context, to infer a close relationship between the thinking of the Council and the rethinking by EPA.

Among the council's other most controversial deregulatory initiatives was vetoing EPA's proposed implementation of a Clean Air Act requirement for industry to secure state permits to increase emissions of any pollutant. Although the EPA proposal seemed to track closely the logic of the statute, the Competitiveness Council successfully urged a change under which any company could significantly increase its emission of a pollutant beyond its current permit levels simply by notifying state regulators of an intent to do so in seven days.[147] This approach effectively circumvented both EPA's express statutory authority to object to particular applications for permit applications, as well as a legislatively implied notice and comment period. Such was also the conclusion of EPA's General Counsel, expressed in a written opinion, which was essentially overruled post hoc by a Justice Department legal opinion issued after EPA was forced to change its regulatory approach.[148]

The pattern of anti-environmental changes achieved through Competitiveness Council intervention in other regulatory proposals is entirely consistent with these examples. The council helped to derail an EPA effort to reduce sulfur dioxide emissions from the Navajo Generating Station, which, among other things, had obscured the view of the Grand Canyon. The council tried to press upon EPA a revised definition of protected "wetlands," which, by one estimate, would have lowered protections on one-third of American wetlands as earlier defined, including a majority of forested wetlands. The council intervened to persuade the Federal Aviation Administration to relax its requirements for phasing out noisy aircraft under the Airport Noise and Capacity Act of 1990.[149]

Such was the regulatory oversight system dedicated most faithfully to a categorical view of presidential power that, in turn, was touted as advancing the cause of accountability. But even without careful parsing, the record suggests obvious accountability issues. First, it was the conclusion of the most extensive journalistic study of the Competitiveness Council that it intervened in "dozens of unpublicized controversies over important federal regulations, leaving what vice presidential aides call 'no fingerprints' on the results of its interventions."[150] The White House's efforts to avoid public disclosure of its oversight activity took multiple forms: resisting FOIA disclosure of documents belonging to President Reagan's Task Force on Regulatory Relief on the ground that the Task Force (and, by implication, the council) was not an "agency" covered by FOIA; resisting congressional access to information about the council beyond published fact sheets and the testimony of individuals who did not participate in council deliberations; and keeping decisions at staff level to shield them from the greater publicity that would likely follow cabinet-level involvement. Intriguingly, only one council decision—pressuring EPA on pollution permit modifications—ever escalated to actual presidential involvement; the usual, albeit tacit, rule was to avoid appeals to the president wherever possible. It would not seem unrealistic that behind this approach lay a desire to buffer the president from criticism for council policies, especially given a campaign promise to be the "environmental president." Obscurity would, of course, impede accountability.

The covertness of the Competitiveness Council's approach is troubling not only because of its seeming inconsistency with customary norms of regulatory process, but also because evidence suggests extraordinary access to the council for special business interests. The council's recommended modifications to EPA's permit amendment regulations were essentially identical to suggestions earlier made to the EPA by Indiana-based pharmaceutical company Eli Lilly, the Pharmaceutical Manufacturers Association, and the Motor Vehicles Manufacturers Association. One of the vice president's closest personal advisers, though not on the council, was Mitch Daniels, former political director in the Reagan White House and an Eli Lilly vice president.[151]

When Bill Clinton succeeded Bush, he inherited the hostility of congressional Democrats to what they perceived as a too-secret, too-antienvironmental system of regulatory review. Yet the Clinton administration was no less interested than its predecessors in intensifying White House supervision of the regulatory agencies. It abolished the Council on Competitiveness. But it proceeded to redraft the Reagan order into a new version, Executive Order 12,866, which followed much the same strategy of regulatory review.[152]

The Clinton order did make some significant changes to address the criticisms of Democratic skeptics. For example, while reaffirming the Reagan language on possible regulatory burdens, the order took a rhetorically more balanced view of regulation. According to the Clinton order, regulation can "protect and improve . . . health, safety, the environment, and well-being [as well as] improve the performance of the economy."[153] The Clinton preamble went on to underline the administration's commitment not to compromise the decision-making primacy of line agencies, not to cloak the regulatory oversight process in secrecy, and not to allow the integrity of the regulatory review process to be jeopardized.[154]

Leaving aside the hortatory language of the preambles, the Reagan executive order directed agencies to regulate only where regulatory benefits outweigh the costs and to choose regulatory means that minimize the net costs of any administrative initiative.[155] The Clinton order kept that mandate but added both nuance and additional values. For example, the Clinton order cautions against overreliance on "hard variables," and articulates a number of regulatory benefits that are not easily monetizable.[156] In addition, agencies are meant to consider a host of factors that are not directly related to the costliness of regulation, including innovation, consistency, predictability, flexibility, distributive impacts, and equity.[157] This broader value structure was less antagonistic toward the values that underlay much of the regulatory state whose actions OIRA is to oversee.

In setting out regulatory review procedures, the Clinton order also made some important changes from the Reagan model. The Reagan order, for example, like the Clinton order, targeted OIRA resources on "significant" regulations. But under the Reagan order, significance was measured entirely in monetary terms. By contrast, the Clinton order treated as significant not only those regulations of high monetary value, but any regulation that could "significantly hurt the environment, public health, or safety, or diminish the rights of individuals receiving government entitlements, grants, or loans."

Moreover, the Clinton order was sensitive to the critique of Reagan and Bush regulatory review—that is, that it was interminable and resulted in "paralysis by analysis." The Clinton order included a tight timetable within which the review process had to proceed.[158] If OIRA at OMB failed to meet the deadlines, the executive order gave agencies the green light to proceed.[159] Moreover, any analysis or objections raised by OIRA were required to be provided in writing and to set forth the pertinent provision of the executive order on which OMB was relying.[160]

Finally, the Clinton order made the regulatory review process at least superficially more transparent. It contained disclosure provisions and protections against ex parte contacts by interested parties.[161] The Clinton order thus sought to protect agencies' rulemaking processes from undisclosed pressures brought to bear through OMB rather than through the notice and comment proceeding at the agency. It also required disclosure of significant information while the review process is ongoing.

In two respects, however, the Clinton order intensified the push toward policy centralization. Reagan had been advised that, with regard to the independent agencies—the administrators of which enjoyed statutory protections against removal—he could demand informational reports from them, but he could not require that they follow his substantive policy instructions.[162] Congress is especially protective of its relationship to those agencies. Presumably because Reagan thus thought it politically risky to assert any control over independent agencies, he did not impose any requirements on them at all. Clinton essentially took the legal advice that Reagan's Justice Department gave him in 1981. He did not impose any substantive requirements on the independent agencies, but he did require that they submit information regarding the status of their proposed and ongoing rulemaking activities as part of the government's Unified Regulatory Agenda.[163]

The order also arguably strengthened the bar on agency publication of final or proposed rules without OMB signoff. As noted earlier, the Reagan order authorized the Director of OMB to request delay in the publication of a proposed rule until OMB concluded its review of the agency's regulatory impact analysis. Reagan then directed agencies, before publishing their final rules, to give the OMB director time to submit his or her views for the administrative record and to prepare a response to the director's views.[164] In contrast, the Clinton order directed agencies to the extent permitted by law to refrain from publishing any regulatory action until the OMB review was completed or the order's prescribed time periods had elapsed without an OMB request that the agency rethink its approach.[165] An agency head determined to publish a rule without complying with this direction was directed to "request Presidential consideration" of the agency's preferences, which would be handled by the vice president.[166] Were such a dispute to arise, a purported presidential demand over an agency's objection not to promulgate a rule would be difficult to reconcile with the order's further provision that "[n]othing in this order shall be construed as displacing the agencies' authority or responsibilities, as authorized by law."[167] It would be difficult to construe such a presidential command in any other way unless one accepted the theory that all powers delegated by Congress to an agency could be commandeered and performed by the president himself.

President George W. Bush left the Clinton order all but entirely intact, leaving it to other instruments of administrative management to steer his administration's regulatory policy in a different philosophical direction. He did make two seemingly significant amendments to the executive order in 2007. One was a requirement that each agency "designate one of the Agency's Presidential appointees" to serve as the agency's "regulatory policy officer," namely, the point person within the agency who would promote agency compliance with the executive order regulatory review process.[168] The second change reflected agencies' increasing enthusiasm for steering public behavior through so-called "guidance" documents. These documents, while not formally binding, could well influence the actions of regulatory parties by revealing an agency's understanding of the law (including its own regulations) and enforcement priorities. The White House, perhaps suspecting that the popularity of these documents had something to do with the prospects they afford for avoiding OMB regulatory review, amended Executive Order 12,866 to require OMB review of "significant guidance documents."[169]

The election of Barack Obama appeared to many in 2008 as a repudiation of the Bush administration's aggressive claims to unilateral presidential power, especially in military affairs. There was thus a widespread expectation, regarding domestic affairs, that Obama would significantly revise the OIRA regulatory review process. Obama fed that expectation with a memorandum issued on April 23, 2009, which "direct[ed] the Director of OMB, in consultation with representatives of regulatory agencies, as appropriate, to produce within 100 days a set of recommendations for a new Executive Order on Federal regulatory review."[170] Moreover, he nominated to be his first head of OIRA law professor Cass Sunstein, the most prolific and one of the most influential contemporary administrative law scholars in the United States. Intriguingly, before entering the academy and as an OLC lawyer just after his Supreme Court clerkship, Sunstein had been one of the Justice Department lawyers advising on the constitutionality of the Reagan order on federal regulation. His appointment, however, was unlikely to betoken a withdrawal from White House assertiveness in regulatory review. As a scholar, Sunstein has been identified with a school of thought suggesting that the unitary executive model of the presidency, while not the Framers' vision, is actually the best model for accomplishing accountable administrative government.[171]

In the end, however, no such rewrite of the Clinton order ever happened. Obama issued several executive orders regarding regulatory review, but they functioned chiefly to reiterate what the administration took to be the most salient aspects of Executive Order 12,866. A January 2011 directive, Executive Order 13,563, entitled, "Improving Regulation and Regulatory Review," added an additional statement as to the administration's philosophy of regulation.[172] The order told agencies that, where possible, they should allow at least sixty days for public comments on proposed regulations. It further required agencies to come up with plans for reviewing existing regulations to determine if any needed to be modified or repealed in order to improve effectiveness or to achieve regulatory goals in a less burdensome way. A follow-up Executive Order 13,579, issued in July 2011, asserted that the independent agencies "should" follow the principles of the earlier order and likewise required such agencies to develop a plan for reviewing existing regulations.[173] But neither order broke truly new ground in calibrating the relationship between administrative agencies and the White House.

Focusing on the progress of the regulatory review process from Reagan through Obama reveals several key points. One is the enthusiasm of all five presidents to institutionalize practices of White House oversight yet more intrusive than those inherited from Presidents Nixon, Ford, and Carter. In theory, however, the system continued to operate within the legal framework provided by OLC to justify the original Reagan order. That is, the president's role was permissible because it was formally a matter of information gathering and coordination; key policy decisions were still being made, at least in principle, by the agencies.

One can observe, for example, the Obama administration's legal fastidiousness with regard to White House relationships with agency administrators in a much-publicized 2011 episode involving the Environmental Protection Agency. EPA was on the verge of issuing ambitious new ambient air quality rules with regard to ozone. These would impose significant costs on industry, and it is likely the Obama White House was worried that an aggressive environmental regulatory initiative a year before Obama's reelection campaign would make him vulnerable to the challenge that he tilted too far against business in making environmental policy. He did not, however, directly order EPA Administrator Lisa Jackson to stand down. Instead, OIRA Director Sunstein sent Jackson a letter stating: "The President has instructed me to return [the ozone] rule to you for reconsideration. He has made it clear that he does not support finalizing the rule at this time."[174] Sunstein proffered "good government" reasons. He questioned whether a new final rule in 2011 would make sense, given that EPA would be facing a statutory mandate to reconsider the issue in 2013 in any event. Further, he suggested that there might soon be available to EPA yet more current scientific data on which to base its standards.

In terms of bureaucratic protocol, however, three things were notable: First, the president was confining his "direction" to telling Sunstein—an official within the Executive Office of the President—what to do. Second, what Sunstein was asking was Administrator Jackson's "reconsideration." Third, because the request came from Sunstein, appeal to the president remained possible, but as Sunstein conveyed, Obama did not support finalizing her rule "at this time." Jackson thus could have approached Obama with a threat to resign—a threat of some significance given Jackson's strong credibility within the environmental community—but she would have been warned not to expect the president to back down. This is pressure, to be sure, but it falls short of the president formally dictating agency policy, much less purporting to take over the rule-writing authority himself.

Focusing on the executive order process alone, however, does not tell the full story. Additional means of intensifying White House control over agency policy making helped further set the stage for more extreme steps still to come under Trump. For example, in addition to updating the Reagan order, Clinton innovated in other ways to increase the gravitational pull of the White House on agency policy making. The classic description of his initiatives is a law review article written by Justice Elena Kagan while still a law professor. Kagan, who had served as deputy director of Clinton's Domestic Policy Council, wrote:

> More important [than changes Clinton made to the Reagan executive order], the Clinton White House sandwiched regulatory review between two other methods for guiding and asserting ownership over administrative activity, used episodically by prior Presidents but elevated by Clinton to something near a governing philosophy. At the front end of the regulatory process, Clinton regularly issued formal directives to the heads of executive

agencies to set the terms of administrative action and prevent deviation from his proposed course. And at the back end of the process (which could not but affect prior stages as well), Clinton personally appropriated significant regulatory action through communicative strategies that presented regulations and other agency work product, to both the public and other governmental actors, as his own, in a way new to the annals of administrative process.[175]

Kagan was a fan of what she called "presidential administration," although she did not believe the Constitution guaranteed presidents the kind of aggressive policy control Clinton advanced. Her argument instead was that, where Congress's statutes permitted, it should be presumed that Congress intended to permit the president's directive supervision. She argued such a presidential rule would improve public administration, a claim to be discussed later.

For his part, even though he left Clinton's order intact, George W. Bush embraced the rhetorical style of claiming agency work as his own and advanced "presidential administration" in other ways. First, like his father, he allowed his vice president the opportunity for policy influence to be exerted through a largely secretive, albeit shorter-lived coordinating committee. In 2001, Dick Cheney's National Energy Policy Development Group prepared a report setting forth the new administration's energy policy.[176] In addition to Cheney, the Task Force comprised the secretaries of Agriculture, Commerce, Energy, Interior, State, Transportation, and the Treasury, along with other senior administration-level officials. According to a report by the Government Accountability Office, these members held ten meetings with petroleum, coal, nuclear, natural gas, and electricity industry representatives and lobbyists.[177] Yet the vice president refused to disclose the identities of any of these consultants either in response to congressional oversight or in litigation brought by both liberal and conservative public interest groups. (Cheney was partly following in the footsteps of the Clinton administration's 1993 Health Reform Task Force chaired by Ira Magaziner and Hillary Rodham Clinton. Like the Cheney group, the Clinton group conducted much of its work confidentially, although it also held public hearings and hundreds of consultations with stakeholder groups.[178])

Moreover, Bush tried to reset the organizational psychology of the executive branch by issuing an unprecedented number of signing statements in connection with the congressional enactments he was signing into law. Specifically, Bush exploded the use of such statements to register constitutional objections to provisions of the bills he was nonetheless legally approving—

most often, objections to the potential impact of the bills on what the president insisted were his inherent constitutional powers. With regard to laws enacted between 2001 and 2009, Bush objected to 1,070 provisions embodied in 127 statutes.[179] Hundreds of these objections reflected dubious theories of presidential administrative entitlements—challenges to congressional reporting requirements as supposed violations of the president's power to recommend measures to Congress (219), to congressional specifications of the qualifications required of certain administrative officeholders as supposed violations of the president's power of nomination (37), and to a variety of measures Bush deemed in violation of his power to require the opinions of heads of departments (30) or simply violations of the supposed "unitary executive" principle (380). It is unclear how many, if any of these objections led to executive branch defiance of statutes. Their main purpose seems to have been habituating the executive branch and most especially, its lawyers, to asserting unilateral presidential power at every plausible instance.

Where President Obama broke new ground was in the use of so-called "policy czars." The notion of a policy czar itself was not novel—their use goes back at least to World War I. And there may be a dispute as to the number of "czars" in any White House, because "czar" is not likely to be in the advisor's official title, the term lacks precise definition, and at least a few advisors whom the press has labeled "czars," are actually Senate-confirmed officials with statutory titles.[180]

Yet if we take czars to be "policy advisors appointed by the president to coordinate and oversee White House policy in a particular area, irrespective of Senate confirmation," the Obama use of czars was distinctive in two respects. First, he appointed more czars very early in his presidency than had any prior president, including nearly thirty such appointments in the first year of his administration. Congressional Republicans were thus alarmed that he was effecting an end-run around the Senate confirmation process. Second, Obama created within the White House "several new czar-led offices 'designed to advance central elements of his campaign's agenda.'"[181] Three such offices were created by executive order: a climate czar, an urban affairs czar, and a health czar. To the extent czars such as these are not Senate-confirmed, they would likely feel the policy tug of Congress less acutely than the Senate-confirmed administrators on whom they may be keeping tabs and whose work they would be coordinating in the president's name. It is true that Obama early on abandoned the Bush enthusiasm for using signing statements to assert the unconstitutionality of provisions of statutes he was signing into law; over eight years, he issued only about three dozen.[182] But the hands-on approach of his White House to key areas of policy making showed an intensification, not a relaxation of the president's intent to use his informal powers to govern how administrative agencies did their statutory jobs.[183]

Trump, as in other areas, blew past all prior administrations in seeking to control agency policy making through OMB. Specifically, Trump overlaid the Reagan-Clinton system with two additional sets of requirements that are unwise and arguably unlawful, and which operate in even greater obscurity. They appear in an early Trump executive order, Executive Order 13,771.[184] One of the two new mandates is called regulatory budgeting.[185] An agency's regulatory "budget" is the arbitrary ceiling that Trump's OIRA places on the total economic cost that the agency is allowed to impose in a single year through all of its new regulations. This is gross cost, not net cost—no accounting for benefits is permitted. The premise of the program is that compliance costs are a burden on the economy and, therefore, aggregate cost ceilings will improve the economy. For Fiscal Year 2019, OIRA used the cost-ceiling mandate to require agencies to actually produce negative regulatory cost.[186] If followed, the costs of new regulations would have to be more than offset by savings from regulations canceled.

The second Trump requirement is known in D.C. as "cut-go." It is a requirement that, before issuing any new regulation, an executive agency must identify for OIRA two regulations appropriate for revocation.[187] Both cut-go and regulatory budgeting had been proposed in GOP-sponsored "regulatory reform" bills that Congress never enacted.[188]

Regulatory budgeting and cut-go may sound appealing, except for three profound problems. First, cost ceilings take no account of regulatory benefits, which, of course, are supposed to be half the focus of the agency's regulatory analysis under the Reagan-Clinton system. Second, it makes no sense for an agency intent on ramping up protection for the country's health and safety to have to sacrifice existing protection for health and safety as part of its strategy. And finally, Trump's order has no legal foundation in the Constitution or any federal statute.

Like its Reagan and Clinton predecessors, Trump's executive order recites that "nothing in this order shall be construed to impair or otherwise affect . . . the authority granted by law to an executive department or agency, or the head thereof."[189] But unless it is understood as limiting the authority of administrative agencies, the order is meaningless. No congressional statute instructs agency heads to concern themselves with the aggregate cost of their total regulatory program in deciding how or whether to fulfill its statutory duties. Nor does any statute condition the issuance of new regulations on the revocation of old ones.

The Trump order, taken at its word, seemingly requires agencies to violate the ordinary rules of administrative law. The Administrative Procedure Act effectively bars agency regulation that is "arbitrary, capricious, [or] an abuse of discretion."[190] As interpreted by the Supreme Court, this standard requires that agencies engaging in administrative policy making must base their policies on factors that are legally and factually relevant.[191] But there is no statute under which an agency can claim it is relevant to the merits of a new regulation whether the agency is meeting an arbitrary cost ceiling for its regulatory program as a whole or whether the cost of a new regulation is offset by the revocation of two older rules. OIRA thus appears to be forcing agencies to make decisions based on legally irrelevant considerations.

The regulatory budget system also rests on faulty economic logic. Presumably, by keeping regulatory costs low, the plan is to free up private resources to pursue other investment opportunities. Yet as Richard J. Pierce, one of the nation's foremost administrative-law experts, has noted, OIRA has historically reported "total benefits [from regulation] that are approximately seven times as great as total costs."[192] Assuming agency rules have been rigorously vetted before being issued, there is no likelihood that the resources devoted to compliance would yield a better return on investment when devoted to other ends. Blanket deregulation will not help the economy.

The Trump Justice Department issued no public opinion setting forth a theory as to the order's legality. In litigation challenging the order, the department argued that various plaintiffs lack the technical standing to bring their lawsuits. Still, no theory in support of the order's legality has come forth. Unlike the requirements imposed by the Reagan and Clinton orders, the requirements imposed by 13,771 cannot be justified as straightforward exercises of the president's power to obtain agency information or his authority simply to coordinate agency action for maximum effectiveness. Trump is asserting the authority to make substantive agency decisions himself through the device of OIRA review.

But like Bush and Obama, Trump has not relied on the OIRA review process alone to control the regulatory tasks that Congress has assigned to the various federal agencies. He started by appointing campaign supporters as czars in three key policy areas: regulation, trade, and immigration.[193] In addition, the congressionally created Office of National Drug Control

Policy, the director of which is usually called the "Drug Czar," went without a Senate-confirmed leader for nearly three full years under Trump.[194] During that time, control over the administration's opioids agenda went not to the office's career staff, but to Kellyanne Conway, a counselor to the president, acting director Rich Baum, and a newly appointed deputy chief of staff, Taylor Weyeneth, a recent college graduate in his early twenties with no obvious qualifications. Key career staff resigned.[195]

Trump also initiated a practice, ultimately abandoned, of installing what has been called "a sort-of shadow cabinet to monitor the loyalty and progress of his various appointees." As recounted by Jerry Mashaw and David Berke: "These 'shadow' advisors—who are not subject to Senate confirmation, and are allegedly selected more for political allegiance than policy expertise—were installed at each agency but report directly to senior White House policy advisors in the [Executive Office of the President]."[196] Within months the White House backed off on this practice because of friction with the cabinet officers Trump also chose. Yet their deployment revealed that, despite the personal loyalties of Trump's cabinet appointees and their deep identification with his policy agenda, the White House had worried that the president's lack of a personal relationship with many department heads might compromise their reliability.

Finally, Trump sought to cement his control of his cabinet's agenda with executive orders dictating their substantive policy priorities. These included directives on immigration,[197] implementation of the Affordable Care Act,[198] the review of past national monument designations,[199] and the fast-tracking of infrastructure projects requiring environmental analysis.[200] For example, Executive Order 13,813, issued in October 2017, variously directed the secretaries of the Treasury, Labor, and Health and Human Services to "consider" within specified time frames new proposed rules to expand access to so-called "association health plans," expand the availability of short-term, limited-duration insurance, and expand the availability and permitted use of employer-provided health reimbursement arrangements—all as supposed reforms to the operation of Obamacare.[201]

THE STATE OF THE POST-REAGAN UNITARY EXECUTIVE

We can sum up this chapter's complex tour through the administrative state by turning again to a moment in not-too-distant history. For a little over two years prior to taking the OMB position I described at the beginning of this chapter, I was an attorney-adviser in the Carter Justice Department's Office of Legal Counsel. During that time, the office received a formal inquiry from the secretary of the interior regarding whether he and members of his department's Office of Surface Mining Reclamation and Enforcement had acted lawfully in meeting with members of the president's Council of Economic Advisers to discuss a proposed rule.[202] That rule, a truly major administrative project, "intended to establish 'a nationwide permanent program for the regulation of surface and underground mining operations by the States and the Federal Government as required by'" the Surface Mining Control and Reclamation Act of 1977.[203]

Let this sink in a bit: The secretary of a cabinet department—not an independent agency—that was engaged in a policy-laden rulemaking, not an adjudication, wanted formal guidance as to whether it had been permissible for him to meet off the record *at all* with White House advisers in connection with that rulemaking. Although I did not work on this particular opinion, I am certain from the number and intensity of office conversations of which I was aware that this was not considered a question with an obvious answer. After careful analysis, OLC concluded "that no prohibition against communications within the executive branch after the close of the [rulemaking's public] comment period exists; [and] that nothing in the relevant statutes or in the decisions of the D.C. Circuit Court suggests that full and detailed consultations between parties charged with promulgating the rules and the President's advisers are barred."[204] However, because "it may be inappropriate for interested persons outside the executive branch to conduct ex parte communications with the Secretary and his staff," it might be important that "advisers to the President [not serve] as a conduit for such ex parte communications."[205]

Forty years later, there exists a fully institutionalized White House rulemaking oversight process that entails substantial communication, much of it confidential, between the non-independent rulemaking agencies and OMB personnel on every significant rule. Presidents Reagan, Clinton, Obama, and both Bushes had asserted their right to remain informed as to all rulemaking activity percolating within the agencies and to require agency observance of general cost-benefit principles. Trump went further, demanding that these agencies identify, for every proposed new regulation, at least two that they would eliminate. Trump additionally asserted the right of the White House to impose aggregate annual limits to the costs any executive agency could impose on the economy by virtue of its regulatory activity. If the Trump administration generated legal opinions supporting these initiatives, they were not made public. There was no public acknowledgment that White House control of administrative discretion at this level of intensity even raised important legal issues.

How did we get from "here" to "there"—from a world in which presidents presumed some need for deference to their administrators and in which the constitutionality of independent agencies was beyond doubt, to a world in which presidents show greater and greater comfort claiming all of administration as their own and, bit by bit, the safeguards for independent administrative policy making are called into constitutional question?

Three key factors have coalesced since the Reagan administration. First, the Republican right wing, empowered by corporate donors who now understood aggressive presidentialism to be a powerful tool, ironically, for shrinking government, got behind an ideological campaign for presidentialism as constitutional theory. Reagan's second attorney general, Edwin Meese, used the Justice Department as a staging ground for the deployment of so-called constitutional originalism, claiming it favored the presidentialist view. The Federalist Society emerged not only as an incubator for presidentialist ideas, but also as a recruiting base for ambitious conservative lawyers to find their way into influential government positions.

Second, aggressive presidentialists such as John Roberts, Samuel Alito, Neil Gorsuch, and Brett Kavanaugh became members of the federal judiciary. They found themselves positioned to advance presidentialist ideas through judicial opinions casting doubt on the long-term vitality of cases like *Humphrey's Executor* and *Morrison v. Olson* as precedents.

Third, the political context was favorable. Following the ambitious legislative work of the 1960s and 1970s, presidents from Reagan forward frequently found themselves struggling to produce achievements consistent with their campaign promises, while facing a Congress controlled in whole or in part by the opposition party. Such a political configuration undoubtedly increased every president's temptation to use nonstatutory, but increasingly aggressive means to manage the exercise of whatever policy-making discretion earlier Congresses had delegated to the executive branch. This was true not only for the Republican presidents who set up the OIRA regulatory review process or who exploded the use of presidential signing statements to promulgate radical new claims of executive authority, but also for Democratic presidents who strengthened White House oversight processes and joined Republicans in the use of czars and nontransparent commissions as devices for centralizing White House policy control. Notably, both Democratic and Republican presidents from Clinton forward began the expanded use of presidential rhetoric to claim agency activity as their own.

In the wake of what might now be considered the incremental consolidating steps of the Reagan through Obama administrations, the Trump administration was both a natural evolution and a radical step forward. The administration's philosophy regarding presidential initiative seems to be that whatever the other branches of government cannot stop is perforce lawful. If other presidents could nudge, Trump could command. The mood of presidential entitlement nurtured most unabashedly by the Bush signing statements or more subtly by Supreme Court victories such as the *Free Enterprise Fund* and *Lucia* decisions has congealed into a legal doctrine that Trump announced baldly, "I have an Article II, where I have the right to do whatever I want as president."[206] Trump's choice of William Barr, an early warrior for presidentialism in the George H. W. Bush administration, to be his attorney general perfectly bookends the period.

The trajectory toward more and more presidential control is unlikely to reverse itself spontaneously. While Republicans have been enthusiasts for presidentialism as a tool to shrink the administrative state, Democratic presidents will feel pressure to use the same tools to advance more proregulatory aims. The distinguished presidential scholar Harold Bruff has said that the precedents presidents care about most are examples of what their predecessors were or were not able to get away with.[207] No president is elected to do nothing.

Yet part of the presidentialist conceit, especially as propounded in Republican administrations, has been, "This is what the original Constitution required." In reaching that conclusion, Republicans have insisted they are being "originalist," faithful to how the Framers themselves would have understood the text they made into law. As conservatives, this is a claim they might seem philosophically compelled to make lest a more avowedly creative method for constitutional interpretation appear to legitimate expansions of individual liberties in ways that conservatives disfavor, such as reproductive freedom and gay rights. Chapter 4 shows, however, that conservative originalism is largely bogus and does not provide a sound foundation for separation-of-powers jurisprudence. Chapter 5 argues for what I am calling democratic constitutionalism, an adaptive, "living Constitution" view, which likewise does not support the Trumpian view of the presidency. Chapter 6, which surveys a variety of constitutional controversies concerning the presidency, returns to the issues of bureaucratic control reviewed in this chapter, among others, to offer a portrait of the constitutional presidency in tune with the needs of twenty-first-century American democracy.

PART TWO

Constitutional Interpretation for Democracy

FOUR

The Originalist Mirage
of Presidential Power

ONCE THE REAGAN ADMINISTRATION launched the modern campaign for presidentialism, it became politically necessary for right-wing
presidentialists to argue that their interpretation of Article II is dictated not
by modern needs, but by the Framers' original vision. Republican presidents
from Reagan forward have championed a form of constitutional jurisprudence called "originalism," which conservatives embraced in opposition
to what they took to be the excessive interpretive creativity of the Warren
Court.[1] The embrace of originalism compels right-wing champions of presidentialism to argue that their view of "executive power" is rooted either in
the unadorned text of the Constitution or in some version of its historical
meaning; otherwise, they could be accused of the same creativity in constitutional interpretation that led the Warren Court to strike down racially segregated schools and to expand free speech rights or that supported the Burger
Court's embrace of women's reproductive freedom. This would not do.

Chapter 1 identified three tenets central to contemporary presidentialism.
Two are substantive claims about particular bundles of authority. "Unitary
executive theory" is the proposition that the Article II Vesting Clause, in
combination with the "Take Care" or Faithful Execution Clause, entitles the
president to complete supervisory control over the entire executive branch.
Implicit in that supposed guarantee is a presidential entitlement to dictate
how all legal discretion vested in the executive branch is to be exercised
and to remove any civil officer of the United States who fails to follow the
president's direction. "National security unilateralism" is the sum total of
frequently asserted presidential authorities in foreign and military affairs.
These include a supposed presidential authority to deploy military force

anywhere in the world if, in the president's judgment, such a deployment would serve a substantial national security interest of the United States.[2]

The third proposition, which I have called the "plenary discretion principle," is really a way of reading any of the president's explicit Article II authorities. The idea is that, if the Constitution names a specific presidential power, Congress is not entitled to channel or restrict its exercise.[3] For example, if one is to believe the Bush-era signing statements, the president's express constitutional authority to nominate all principal officers within the executive branch supposedly makes unconstitutional any Congressional attempt to specify qualifications for those whom the president may nominate. Or, as explained in chapter 2, presidentialists argue that the supposed vesting in the president of executive power to supervise criminal prosecutions makes it impermissible to criminalize any such supervision, even if performed in a manner that corruptly obstructs justice.

Chapter 2 used the argument about presidential control of criminal prosecution as a kind of case study of the wrongheadedness of presidentialism. Criminal prosecution was an inviting place to begin our exploration because it is a form of public administration with which the founding generation was familiar. There is a straightforward pragmatic argument, consistent with constitutional values, in favor of allowing Congress some authority to protect the independence of criminal prosecution. But there is also historical evidence available to shed light on how early Americans thought about criminal prosecution. One can see, even without wading too deeply into the weeds of constitutional theory, how that history belies the originalist claim to illimitable presidential power over criminal prosecution.

Chapter 3 documented, however, that the ambitions of unitary executive theory go way beyond control of criminal prosecution. That chapter detailed how presidents from Reagan forward have sought to consolidate control in the White House over all discretionary executive-branch policymaking, whether in the form of administrative rules or regulations or even how agencies conduct administrative adjudication. The steps taken in that direction depend on a series of claims about presidential authority, some of which—like the president's authority to demand information from the heads of administrative agencies—are well-established, while others—like the president's allegedly comprehensive removal power—have so far not prevailed in court.

Thinking about how to apply the historical Constitution to presidential control of the entirety of the twenty-first century administrative state is, however, to ask an utterly anachronistic question. The smallest federal cabinet department of the early twenty-first century probably employs nearly as many people as the entire federal government at the cusp of the nineteenth century.[4] To ask how the founding generation understood their text would apply to a context they surely could not have imagined is to ask what, on its face, is a question bordering on incoherence.

To see what is wrong about the range of presidentialist claims applied to the modern administrative state, it is therefore helpful to think more conceptually about the whole enterprise of applying an old Constitution to new problems. Giving originalism its due requires some detailed attention to the variety of approaches that go by that label. This chapter will seek to demonstrate, using those approaches, that originalism, by its own terms, cannot justify unitary executive theory. But it will also explain why the proper interpretive cure for presidentialism is not "better originalism," but a sound version of adaptive or "living" constitutionalism.

ORIGINALISM AND THE COMPLEXITY
OF COMMUNICATION

Contemporary originalism comes in a variety of forms. After all, everyone interpreting the Constitution is, in some sense, an originalist, beginning their analysis with the same historic document. Constitutional arguments are invariably tethered to some part of that document and are defended as consistent with the values underlying the original text taken at an appropriate level of generality.[5] Presidentialists, however, most frequently link their interpretation to a highly formalist version of originalism they advertise as genuinely constraining. Such originalism starts with the premise that the meaning of any part of the constitutional text is fixed at the time of its ratification. Originalism counsels that, to avoid deciding cases according to their subjective personal values, judges (and, by implication, others who interpret the Constitution) should give the text's fixed meaning the primary role in deciding how the Constitution ought to be applied today. Judicial constraint is widely taken to be the central value of the typically conservative brand of originalism.[6]

Those who write about constitutional originalism generally distinguish between two approaches, each of which is highly formalist. (What I mean by "formalism" is exclusive reliance on a limited range of history-based evidence that purports not to take account of changing conditions or practical consequences. Formalists regard such materials as giving discernible, fixed content to the Constitution's categories of authority: legislative, executive, and judicial.) Old originalism, which might also be called intent-based originalism, seeks to find behind the constitutional text the founding generation's expectations for the application of that text, using whatever historical evidence is available.[7] Perhaps the most glaring example of intent-based originalism in the Supreme Court is its reading of the Eleventh Amendment. In quite specific language, the amendment forbids federal courts to exercise jurisdiction over cases brought in federal court against states by citizens of other states.[8] The Supreme Court has held, however, that the intent behind the Eleventh Amendment was to restore a tacit baseline understanding among the Framers concerning the states and sovereign immunity generally.[9] In view of this imputed intent, the Court reads the Constitution—with limited exceptions[10]—as not authorizing federal suits brought against a state, whether by its own citizens or citizens of other states, and whether in state or federal court.[11] There is no plausible reading of the text of the Eleventh Amendment that yields that meaning. Yet the Court believes its doctrine reflects what those who framed the amendment had in mind.

Prior to the 1980s, critics of old originalism dissected at length its inherent conceptual difficulties. The most basic is the difficulty of finding a coherent collective intent behind a document, the legal status of which reflects not only the handiwork of its drafters, but also the understandings of the various state ratifying conventions.[12] Majorities coalesced around the adoption of a particular text, but voters may have done so with very different expectations as to the application of that text in practice. Old originalism has also been critiqued as ironically inconsistent with the founding generation's preferred methods of interpretation.[13] That is, there is good reason to think that the Framers did not expect their subjective intentions to govern future constitutional interpretation.

Largely in response to these critiques, a new originalism emerged in the 1980s and 1990s, which purports to be linked not to the drafters' or ratifiers' subjective intentions, but instead to the so-called "original public meaning" of the relevant text. Original public meaning is said to be the meaning of the text as it would have been understood by then-contemporary competent readers in the population at large, as evidenced by dictionaries or other indicators of popular usage.[14] New originalism resonates with the old originalism in that its advocates would insist that original public meaning is also the best evidence of intent. But, in any event, to the extent there is an ascertainable original public meaning, that meaning would presumably be what people voting on ratification thought they were voting for or against.[15]

There is a deep problem, however, with drawing from a text's semantic meaning the most reasonable inferences as to what the words implied to those who read them. Consider that, as chapter 2 explained, the foundation of unitary executive theory is a syllogism rooted in what its advocates offer as the "original public meaning" of "executive power": "Executive power," in the late eighteenth century, meant "not legislative" and "having the power to put in act the laws."[16] In his famous *Morrison v. Olson* dissent, Justice Scalia added that the vesting of such power "does not mean *some of* the executive power, but *all of* the executive power."

But Victoria Nourse has gone a long way toward demonstrating how this reading of the Article II Vesting Clause is far less straightforward than it appears.[17] When any text is sparse, as Article II certainly is, she explains, "interpreters are likely to interpolate or add to the meaning of raw text when seeking to apply the text to a particular context."[18] Drawing on philosophy of language, she calls this process "pragmatic enrichment,"[19] and notes that such enrichments are "hypothesized meanings—they are not the 'actual' meaning of the text but attempts to apply the raw text to a particular context, by the addition of meanings."[20] Recall my "no shirts, no shoes, no service" example. The realization that such a sign does not preclude wearing dresses is an act of pragmatic enrichment. "Shirts" is taken to signify a covering up of the upper body with an appropriate garment, whether or not literally a "shirt." Persuasive interpretation of any document requires readers to be alert to the degree to which they are engaging in pragmatic inference and to be open to evidence within the document that contradicts that inference.[21]

As Professor Nourse explains, the unilateralist "enrichment" of the Article II Vesting Clause, exemplified by Justice Scalia's *Morrison* dissent,[22] is reading into it a vesting of *all* the power of executing law, even though the word "all" or something similar is not actually part of the text.[23] But other aspects of both Article I and Article II bedevil this reading. Perhaps the most obvious is that the Senate has roles to play in both the appointment of officers of the United States and in the approval of international treaties, powers otherwise explicitly conferred on the executive branch.[24] So at most, the Vesting Clause can be read to mean, "The executive Power shall be vested in a President of the United States of America, *except as this Constitution explicitly assigns executive power elsewhere.*" But once we surface that the unilateralists have enriched the meaning of the Vesting Clause with an implied exceptions clause in the manner I have crafted, the question is immediately posed as to why the *explicit* vesting of executive power elsewhere is the only constitutionally permissible limitation on executive power. Might there also be *implicit* powers vested elsewhere to check the executive?

The semantic possibility that the Vesting Clause does not preclude legislative checks on executive power would also seem to follow directly from the wording of the Necessary and Proper Clause, which gives Congress authority "To make all Laws which shall be necessary and proper for carrying into Execution the foregoing Powers [of Congress], and all other Powers vested by this Constitution in the Government of the United States, or in *any Department or Officer thereof*."[25] If the vesting of executive power gave the president *all* the executive power and the entire executive branch were to be viewed as merely an extension of his authority, one might have thought the organization of the executive branch would itself have to be left to the president.[26] Yet the Necessary and Proper Clause says otherwise, and it says so with the word "all," a signaling of comprehensiveness that does not appear in Article II.

What makes this yet more complicated is that Justice Scalia, in line with the unilateralist school, wants to infer not just that the president is vested with all the power of legal execution, but that the lodging in the president of the executive power implies a hierarchical relationship that entitles him to unregulated removal power over administrators, including criminal prosecutors. Article II, however, says nothing about removal, and the Appointments Clause complicates the inference in two respects. First, Congress is authorized to vest the appointment of "inferior officers" in the courts of law.[27] This plainly points to an uncertainty as to the president's constitutionally intended relationship to an entire class of inferior officers. Second, and more profoundly, given the ordinary rule that the power to appoint implies the power to remove,[28] the Senate's role in the appointments process for any officer requiring the Senate's advice and consent would seem to imply a Senate role in removals as well. Indeed, Alexander Hamilton so represented the Constitution to readers of *The Federalist*:

> It has been mentioned as one of the advantages to be expected from the co-operation of the Senate, in the business of appointments, that it would contribute to the stability of the administration. The consent of that body would be necessary to displace as well as to appoint. A change of the Chief Magistrate, therefore, would not occasion so violent or so general a

revolution in the officers of the government as might be expected, if he were the sole disposer of offices.[29]

Joseph Story later acknowledged the logic of this reading, suggesting that, even if practice by the 1830s had settled on the president a power of removing principal officers—the propriety of which he declined to endorse—"in regard to 'inferior officers' . . . the [option] is still within the power of Congress . . . of requiring the consent of the senate to removals in such cases."[30] The persistence of the idea, forty years into the life of the Republic, that Congress could condition presidential removals on Senate consent strongly belies the notion of any "ordinary meaning" interpretation of the Vesting Clause that would give the president unfettered, unilateral removal power.

Beyond these complications lies the puzzle of the Article II Opinions Clause. Article II authorizes the president to "require the opinion, in writing, of the principal officer in each of the executive departments, upon any subject relating to the duties of their respective offices."[31] From a unilateralist perspective, this strikes an obviously odd note because such a power would seem necessarily implicated in the scope of the unilateralists' version of the Executive Power Vesting Clause. Professor Akhil Amar has suggested that the redundancy is there for purposes of emphasis or clarification—a suggestion that itself is a form of pragmatic enrichment.[32] But taking the actual wording of the text seriously generates greater uncertainties. The Opinions Clause would make no sense if it empowered the president to require opinions in writing concerning only those "duties" that the president assigns to principal officers; it would be bizarre for the Vesting Clause to have authorized presidents to personally assign duties to subordinate officers, but not to authorize them to inquire as how those directions were being implemented. Therefore, the "duties" referenced by the Opinions Clause must logically be duties assigned to principal officers by some authority other than the president—presumably by Congress. But if that is so, then the ordinary meaning of the explicit grant of power to seek formal opinions regarding those duties would have two further logical implications that complicate the unilateralist narrative. The first is that duties assigned to "the Heads of Departments" are not to be performed by the president, but rather by those officers explicitly tasked to perform them. The text links duties explicitly to "offices," and Congress, not the president, creates offices.[33] Further, the formality of the opinions that presidents may request supports the idea that the president's relationship to the agencies is, if not at arm's length, then at least not fully integrated. This suggests, as Peter Strauss has argued, that the president's power, upon receiving those opinions, is supervisory, but not directive.[34] His task is to "take Care that the Laws be *faithfully* executed," which on its face is something different from "executed in a manner consistent with the president's policy preferences." Authorizing presidential demands for "opinions in writing" from officials to whom the president may issue direct, substantive orders truly would seem odd and superfluous.

Taking the foregoing textual complications into account, here is a semantically plausible rendering of the Vesting Clause that reads very differently from Justice Scalia's version. The Article II Vesting Clause could be interpreted to convey the following thought:

> To the extent this Constitution does not confer executive power elsewhere, whether explicitly or by implication, the executive power that the Constitution does confer shall be vested in a President of the United States. Should Congress assign duties to executive branch Departments, the President shall supervise their execution.

A point this reading highlights is that the mission of Article II's first sentence is chiefly to signal the choice of a single, rather than a plural chief executive, but not to say what the single chief executive does. Nothing in the "original public meaning" of "executive power" contradicts this reading if we limit our reading to the words' bare semantic content. The reading is perhaps not compulsory, but it reveals both the role of pragmatic enrichment in attaching meaning to the Vesting Clause and the potential for a pragmatic enrichment that gives the legislative branch more leeway to structure the president's relationship to the bureaucracy. It highlights the reality that the Scalia reading of Article II, which purports to follow from the meaning of "executive power," really follows instead from his presupposition that our government has three branches of government with distinct boundaries and that the basket of power in the hands of the executive branch must include plenary supervisory authority over every officer of the United States who participates in the execution of the law. In other words, having predetermined what the Vesting Clause must mean, Justice Scalia just ignores the ways in which other Clauses potentially falsify his reading. It is a precommitment to a presidency empowered in a particularly robust way that produces Justice Scalia's hard-edged reading of the Article II Vesting Clause; it is not compelled by the words.

Because pragmatic enrichment is inevitably involved in our reading of sparse or general texts, an originalist method relying entirely on the settled semantic content of words at a particular point in history cannot fully reveal the likely inferences readers drew from those words. Those inferences will not be completely revealed by dictionaries or even by the advanced techniques of corpus linguistics—"the use of large, searchable databases, or corpora, of computer-annotated texts to ascertain evolving patterns of word use over time."[35] Of at least equal importance will be evidence of how people acted in the wake of a particular utterance—that is, how they implemented their understanding of the words in question. That evidence does not support Justice Scalia's reading of the executive power Vesting Clause.

THE AMBIGUITIES OF "EXECUTIVE POWER" AT THE FOUNDING

Justice Scalia did more than offer an aggressive interpretation of Article II in *Morrison v. Olson*. He treated the unconstitutionality of regulating the exercise of executive power as obvious: "If to describe this case is not to decide it, the concept of a government of separate and coordinate powers no longer has meaning."[36] Unfortunately, his statement is nonsense. Evidence from the Founding makes it abundantly clear that there was no consensus that Article II gave the president "exclusive control over the exercise of" executive power. That evidence includes, of course, the evidence detailed in chapter 2, which revealed how little capacity Congress created for the president or attorney general to supervise the early federal prosecutors; the regularity with which contemporary state constitutions, with relevant clauses nearly identical to Article II, placed the power to appoint prosecutors in legislative or judicial hands; and the general eighteenth century ambiguity as to whether prosecution was actually an executive or a judicial power. Several of the state constitutions that took governors out of appointing state attorneys, unlike the federal Constitution, even had explicit separation of powers provisions and still did not treat prosecution as an exclusively executive function.[37]

In expanding our focus, however, from criminal prosecution to all of federal administration, it should also be noted that there are some disagreements among originalists about the scope of the president's guaranteed supervisory control. Professor Saikrishna Prakash has gone so far as to argue that the Vesting Clause gives presidents the authority, if they so choose, to perform personally any and all administrative tasks Congress delegates to the executive branch.[38] This would accord with William Barr's assertion that, constitutionally speaking, the president alone is the executive branch. But Prakash's analysis is contradicted by opinions of both Federalist and Jeffersonian early attorneys general.[39] A far more common position is that the scope of the president's supervisory authority is implicit in his supposed power to remove any civil officer of the United States, not that the Constitution would permit the president to exercise all of the executive branch's statutorily authorized discretionary tasks personally.

Because, as we have noted, the Constitution makes no explicit reference to the removal of civil officers, except through impeachment, presidentialist arguments for a comprehensive presidential removal power must themselves rest on the supposed implications of other powers. Presidentialist interpreters thus rest their position on readings of the Vesting and Take Care Clauses that they "enrich" through some further exploration of historical context. The typical arguments are that the president has removal authority because the English king had removal authority.[40] Also, a policy decision by the First Congress—the so-called Decision of 1789—supposedly reveals a predominant contemporary understanding that the Constitution vested removal authority in the president.[41]

The argument from English history is rooted in the Framers' acquaintance with William Blackstone's *Commentaries on the Laws of England* and their reliance on his characterization of the king's "executive power."[42] Although not citing explicitly to Blackstone (or, indeed, to any other authority), Chief Justice (and former president) Taft presumably had Blackstone in mind when he wrote in a famous dictum in 1926: "In the British system, the crown, which was the executive, had the power of appointment and removal of executive officers, and it was natural, therefore, for those who framed our Constitution to regard the words 'executive power' as including both."[43] Taft, however, appears to have confused the Crown's possession of a power with the source of that power. In other words, just because kings were empowered to perform a function does not itself reveal whether the power inhered in the monarch or was granted by Parliament.

English law actually recognized Parliament as having legislative control over the king's power of removal.[44] Although many officers in eighteenth-century English government were removable at the king's pleasure, for some of them—those who had originally held their office as a matter of property right—the king's authority was based in reform legislation that granted him a removal power he otherwise lacked.[45] In addition, shortly before the adoption of the U.S. Constitution, Parliament created a number of commissions with extensive powers to audit, investigate, and bind executive departments, yet denied the king removal power.[46] A number of other officers who exercised significant regulatory and law enforcement authority "held their offices in fee simple, for life, or during good behavior."[47] In short, it was simply not the case that the Crown was deemed to have inherent or illimitable removal power over all executive officers despite being the unitary holder of executive power. To put the point another way, English law does not provide a basis for inferring removal power from the vesting of executive power in a single president.

The so-called Decision of 1789 refers to a debate in the First Congress concerning the first three departments it created, the Departments of Foreign Affairs, War, and Treasury. Deliberations regarding the Department of Foreign Affairs (soon changed to "State") revealed a disagreement as to the removability of the secretary of foreign affairs. Different opinions were expressed as to whether the Constitution guaranteed the president the right to remove the secretary at will, whether the president would need Senate consent for the removal, whether Congress could vest removal power in the president, or whether the secretary could be removed only by impeachment.[48] Advocates of the removal-at-will theory objected to a provision in the draft bill directly authorizing presidential removal on the ground that it implied the president needed congressional approval in order to possess removal power. As finally enacted, the new department's organic act referred to presidential removal only obliquely, indicating that a chief clerk of the department would perform the duties of the "principal officer" of the department when "the said principal officer shall be removed from office by the President of the United States, or in any other case of vacancy."[49] Modern presidentialists (including Chief Justice Taft) have deemed this compromise, which satisfied the sensibilities of those arguing for presidential at-will removal power, as somehow authoritatively ratifying the link between Article II executive power and the power to remove.

As noted, however, by Harvard law dean John Manning, "a close reading of the legislative history by prominent legal historians" shows "the House was divided ... with roughly equal numbers believing that (a) the President had illimitable removal power; (b) Congress should get to determine the contours of the power to remove federal officers; and (c) the Senate must give advice and consent to the removal of officers appointed with advice and consent."[50] According to Dean Manning, rather than showing a contemporary consensus as to the meaning of executive power, the debate revealed that, "even to the most informed of the founding generation, the removal question was unsettled."[51]

The absence of consensus among well-informed readers is equally evident in the Senate vote to accept the House language. Senate debates were not recorded at the time, so we do not have direct evidence of the positions that different senators took on the issue. What we do know is that Vice President John Adams twice had to cast tie-breaking votes on motions that would have eliminated from the bill any mention of a presidential removal power.[52] Further clouding the picture, the diary of Senator William Maclay suggests that Senate supporters of the House bill played on its ambiguity to argue that it would not exclude the Senate from participating in removal decisions.[53] It is hard to imagine clearer evidence of lack of consensus about the Constitution's dictates. Indeed, as explained earlier, if one were to rely entirely on Article II's text and given the ordinary rule that the power to appoint implies the power to remove, the Senate's role in the appointments process for any officer requiring the Senate's advice and consent would likely have implied to many ratifiers of the 1787 Constitution a Senate role in removals.

The historical case for a founding consensus around a presidential removal power is weakened further by evidence that the First Congress did not appear to entertain the kind of rigorous view of the president's unitary control of administration that might reasonably imply a power of at-will removal. For example, Congress accepted a proposal by Alexander Hamilton, signed into law by George Washington, to create a so-called Sinking Fund Commission.[54] This body was authorized to purchase U.S. debt on the open market "under the direction of the President of the Senate, the Chief Justice, the Secretary of State, the Secretary of the Treasury, and the Attorney General."[55] Of the five commission members, two—the president of the Senate (that is, the vice president) and the chief justice—were not removable by the president at all. Indeed, prior to ratification of the Twelfth Amendment in 1804, there was no guarantee that the vice president would even be of the same party as the president or of the three cabinet members serving ex officio. The Act required presidential agreement to such purchases of U.S. debt as the commission might approve but gave the president no power to initiate the purchase of debt except at the commission's initiative. Again, the First Congress, which included numerous signatories to the Constitution, enacted without any separation of powers objection this obvious incursion into the president's unitary control of fiscal administration.[56]

Yet other evidence concerning the First Congress's handiwork regarding the structure of the initial administrative departments seems to belie the idea that the Framers intended to mandate a hard version of a unitary executive.[57] For example, although the president was given significant flexibility and control when it came to the new Departments of War and of Foreign Affairs, this was not so regarding the Treasury.[58] The same statute that referred to the treasury secretary as removable created an Office of the Comptroller within the Treasury Department. The Act is silent on the comptroller's removability, and House debates revealed different opinions as to the comptroller's relationship to the president. Although Madison assumed presidential removability despite his own belief that the comptroller's functions were "not purely of an executive nature," Representative William Loughton Smith of South Carolina "approved the idea of having the Comptroller appointed for a limited time, but thought during that time he ought to be independent of the Executive, in order that he might not be influenced by that branch of the Government in his decisions."[59] Even supporters of broad presidential removal authority acknowledge that the treatment of the comptroller "suggests that the Decision of 1789 did not encompass the conclusion that the President had the power to remove all officers of the United States lacking constitutionally granted tenure."[60] Apart from the issue of removal, Congress gave the comptroller significant authority and independence. Initially authorizing the comptroller to superintend accounts and countersign warrants drawn by the secretary of the treasury, Congress later gave that officer power also "to institute suit for the recovery of" a "sum or balance reported to be due to the United States, upon the adjustment of [a tax officer's] account."[61] Over time, Congress continued to expand the comptroller's responsibilities and tenure, experimenting with different types of removal protection.[62]

Another insufficiently appreciated blow to the old originalist case for a hard unitary presidency is the First Bank of the United States. Separation of powers theorists have largely ignored the Bank presumably because, as a kind of public-private partnership, it so obviously does not fit comfortably within any traditional view of the administrative state. Yet there is no doubt the bank wielded government power. Professors Walter Dellinger and H. Jefferson Powell—at the time of their writing the assistant attorney general in charge of the Office of Legal Counsel (OLC) and his former deputy, respectively—have observed that a modern-day OLC opinion on the constitutionality of a national bank would have focused immediately on possible separation-of-powers objections to the bill.[63] The Bank may be inconvenient for originalist defenders of a unitary presidency, but it can hardly be ignored as irrelevant.

As Professor Jerry Mashaw recounts, the Bank of the United States—strongly urged by Framer Alexander Hamilton and modeled after the Bank of England—effectively regulated the money supply.[64] As Mashaw explains:

> The statute authorizing the Bank provided a charter and specified the total capitalization of the enterprise. It also provided voting rules for stockholders, limits on total debt and the amount of interest to be charged, and a limit on the subscription to be made to the Bank by the federal government. But all the Bank's operating policies—including when and where to establish branches—were left to the regulations to be adopted by the Bank's directors, only a minority of whom would be selected by the United States.[65]

"Minority" is here an understatement. The federal government was entitled to name only five of the Bank's twenty-five directors, not even enough by themselves to constitute a quorum for doing business.[66] The Treasury Department enjoyed some limited supervisory authority over the Bank in the sense that the secretary could demand reports and inspect Bank records. There was, however, no provision for presidential or Treasury authority to direct the bank in its operations.[67]

What makes this example of attenuated presidential influence so telling was that enactment of the Bank's charter in 1791 was very much the subject of constitutional debate. James Madison famously opposed the Bank as going beyond the enumerated powers of Congress, recalling that the Philadelphia Convention specifically declined to give Congress an express power of incorporation precisely to avoid the establishment of a national bank.[68] The measure was debated vigorously in the House on constitutional grounds, even though unanimously approved by the Senate.[69] Nor did Congress's adoption of the bank bill end the intra-governmental deliberations. President Washington, who, of course, had presided over the Constitutional Convention, thought the issue of sufficient moment that, prior to signing the Bank's charter, he sought the formal opinions of his attorney general and secretaries of State and of the Treasury on the constitutional issue.[70] We thus have four major statements by leading contemporary figures—Hamilton, Jefferson, Madison, and Randolph—all formally assessing the constitutionality of the bank bill.

Here's the rub: Not one of these opinions mentions the separation of powers as a source of objection or concern. Jefferson, Madison, and Randolph all thought the Bank unconstitutional as going beyond Congress's Article I powers, but none said a word about the lack of presidential supervisory authority or indeed anything about the Bank's attenuated accountability to even the Treasury Department. Hamilton did not acknowledge the executive's attenuated influence over the Bank as something that needed to be constitutionally explained away. He did not mention it at all.

Intent-oriented originalists might challenge the salience of this argument because the Founders might have deemed the Bank a private and not a governmental entity, thus obviously beyond the president's reach. Perhaps it never occurred to the First Congress that the Bank's directors and officers might be thought officers of the United States, subject by constitutional command to presidential appointment, removal, and direction. To the extent this speculation is accurate, however, it would only make the originalist position weaker. It would imply that those most familiar with the Constitution's drafting and the ratification debates were unaware of any authorial intent to confine the delegation of significant government authorities even to purely government institutions. If that's so—and I think it is—then it must follow that there was no authorial intent to confine the delegation of discretionary government authority exclusively to officials whom the president could command and remove. In sum, the First Congress's eclecticism in fashioning different administrative structures with different lines of accountability to different sources of supervision could hardly have been more conspicuous.

In evaluating the case for presidential control over criminal prosecution, chapter 2 already took note that the early state constitutions, some drafted before and some drafted after 1789, commonly authorized state legislatures to appoint certain civil officers directly or to determine by statute how officers should be appointed. Such constitutions thus created an attenuated or at least potentially attenuated relationship between such officers and the governor. This was true despite the prevalence of executive power vesting clauses and clauses identical to or significantly resembling the federal "Take Care" clause. Besides state attorneys and attorneys general, the most common beneficiary of such independence was the state treasurer. Almost all states that drafted constitutions around the time of the federal Constitution excluded the state's treasurer from close gubernatorial supervision and made the treasurer subject to legislative control.[71]

Michael McConnell, a leading conservative legal scholar, has argued in his own work that the Article II Vesting Clause gives the president removal power, in the absence of statutes to the contrary.[72] He concedes, in other words, that implied authorities conveyed by the Vesting Clause are subject to legislative regulation—"defeasible," in legal parlance. He concludes, however, that a presidential power of at-will removal is implicit in the Faithful Execution Clause:

> Unless [the president] can staff the executive with persons of his own choosing, he cannot discharge his executive function. That requires both the ability to appoint and the ability to remove—but the unfettered ability to remove is the more important, because the inability to fire can have the effect of saddling him with an officer hostile or indifferent to his program, while his inability to appoint any one person leaves him with a universe of alternative nominees.[73]

Although the argument McConnell offers was raised in the First Congress, history again fails to substantiate that removal power was implicit in the "original public meaning" of the Faithful Execution Clause. First, it is not obvious that the Faithful Execution Clause was deemed a source of authority for the new president, as opposed to a source of obligation. Legal historians have shown how the faithful execution obligation emerged from a long history of officer oaths that were required of officers both of high and low rank in England, the colonies, and the newly independent states, where "faithful execution" was associated above all with a fiduciary obligation to obey the law and pursue "true, honest, diligent, due, skillful, careful, good faith and impartial" execution.[74] In the context of the federal Constitution, it likely was read as well as a prohibition against the executive suspension of statutes—a ban imposed on the English king in 1689 with the enactment of the Bill of Rights.[75]

Moreover, requirements of faithful execution and bans on the suspension of statutes coexisted in virtually all roughly contemporary state Constitutions that also eschewed a fully unitary executive. Governors in nine early states, the constitutions of which conferred on the legislature powers of appointment with regard to important civil officers, were explicitly required by those same constitutions to take care that the laws be faithfully executed.[76] In those states, it is obvious that the presence of an express faithful execution obligation was not thought incompatible with limiting the governor's direct control of administrators. Four others of the state constitutions that vest administrative appointments in authorities other than the governor but omit faithful execution clauses nonetheless expressly prohibited the executive suspension of statutes.[77] Under this view of faithful execution, thirteen of the sixteen early state constitutions not only vest executive power in a governor, but also impose a faithful execution obligation or its equivalent. There is little here to buttress the notion that drafters of state constitutions equated the vesting of executive power and the obligation of faithful execution of the laws with hierarchical control of public administration directed solely by the governor.

In sum, although inferring a broad presidential removal power from the elliptical text of Article II does no violence to its language, the case that the original public meaning of Article II mandated such power is vaporously thin. Article I of the Constitution explicitly authorizes Congress "to make all Laws which shall be necessary and proper for carrying into Execution . . . all . . . Powers vested by this Constitution in the Government of the United States, or any Department or Officer thereof." Thus did the Framers deliberately leave to Congress extremely broad discretion in designing the institutions and offices the executive branch would comprise. In one of his contributions to *The Federalist*, James Madison wrote that under the proposed new Constitution, "[t]he tenure of the ministerial offices generally, will be a subject of legal regulation, conformably to the reason of the case and the example of the State constitutions."[78] Even if he and others later changed their mind as to the implications of Article II, the Constitution had been authoritatively represented to voters as giving Congress power to limit officer removability. The educated reader of 1787 would likely have inferred that Congress would enjoy great deference in deciding how most reasonably to implement its constitutional powers in creating administrative officers to implement the legislative will.

THE UNBEARABLE LIGHTNESS OF ORIGINALISM

Given the historical evidence just reviewed, you could well be uncertain as to the central flaw in the aggressive presidentialist reading of the Constitution. Is the problem originalism or just "originalism done badly?" Assuming my historical review is accurate, have I not shown on originalist grounds that the Constitution permits Congress to create independent agencies and to limit the president's capacity to direct other officers' exercise of their legal discretion? Why not continue to pursue originalism as the correct interpretive method, but just do it more thoughtfully?

If courts were to define an extremely limited role for the use of historically based interpretation, one could imagine some such approach at least being practicable. The approach would start from the recognition that the Constitution makes certain provisions so specific that there is no real ambiguity as to their application. There is no doubt, for example, as to the age requirement for presidents, as to who presides over a presidential impeachment trial, or as to when each new Congress convenes. For the vaguer provisions, courts could use history to determine whether so strong a contemporary consensus existed regarding the import of the relevant text that the provision in question ought to be treated now as being as specific as the others I have mentioned. In other words, at least hypothetically, historical inquiry could show us that the Fifth Amendment phrase "infamous crime" specifically meant any felony or that the Eighth Amendment ban on "cruel and unusual punishment" specifically forbade flogging. But showing this level of consensus would pose a very heavy burden of proof to carry for challengers to government action.[79] Because the absence of consensus will generally be easier to prove historically than the presence of consensus, this approach would greatly narrow the occasions for courts to overturn government action as unconstitutional. For example, to defend the constitutionality of independent agencies, one would need only to amass enough evidence to cast doubt on whether the presidentialist history established a consensus link between "executive power" and inherent removal authority. It does not, so independent agencies would be constitutional.

As law professor Erich Segall has documented, however, the Supreme Court has never embraced so limited a role for history and has consistently taken a more aggressive stance regarding the scope of judicial review since at least the mid-nineteenth century.[80] To champion originalism coupled with an utterly marginal role for the courts is to wish for a system that never will be.

Yet my own objections to the use of originalism run deeper than a critique of the mediocrity of much historical analysis done by judges. These more fundamental critiques have been well developed in the literature on constitutional interpretation over the last fifty years, although they seem to have had little impact on the thinking of our most aggressively presidentialist jurists.

The first is a matter of authority. The problem was famously, if incompletely articulated by Thomas Jefferson. What Professor David Strauss has called "Jefferson's Problem" is the question why every generation ought not have its own authority to make its own binding laws.[81] In 1789, Jefferson wrote to James Madison:

> We seem not to have perceived that, by the law of nature, one generation is to another as one independent nation is to another. . . . The earth belongs always to the living generation. . . . On similar ground it may be proved that no society can make a perpetual constitution, or even a perpetual law. Every constitution, then, and every law, naturally expires at the end of 19 years. If it be enforced longer, it is an act of force and not of right.[82]

Jefferson's timeline for renewal may have been impractical, but his challenge directly raises the puzzle: By what authority should we now be deemed bound by the text of 1787, 1868, or any other distant year, even if we could objectively ascertain its "original public meaning?"

That question looms especially large for our 1787 text because of the exclusivity of the ratification process and the drafters' decision to make formal amendment extraordinarily difficult. Legislatures in each of the original states authorized elections for delegates to each state's ratifying convention. These legislatures, of course, were entirely white and male in membership, as were the ratifying conventions. Most states imposed property qualifications for voting, which excluded a large number of even white male voters. Women had the franchise in New Jersey.[83] Free Black males who met the property requirements could vote in some places, but not others.[84] In short, the deliberative bodies that transformed the Constitution from a proposed text into binding laws were profoundly undemocratic in ways Americans would never sanction today.

The limited representativeness of the state conventions and the electorates that chose them might seem less of a problem if our contemporary multi-gendered, multi-racial majorities could readily amend their handiwork. The Framers, however, entrenched their prose in a manner that resists formal amendment. First, an amendment must be proposed either with the approval of two-thirds of each House of Congress or by a new constitutional convention called on the "application" to Congress of two-thirds of the states.[85] Any proposal that successfully jumps one of these high hurdles would become part of the Constitution only if thereafter ratified by three-quarters of the states.[86] Bemoaning the authority of "dead white men" may seem like a cliché, but it does seem difficult to agree that a group of propertied dead white men from 1787 should be able to entrench their specific expectations for the law without regard to how diverse majorities of voters in the twenty-first century regard their handiwork.

Consequently, it seems more reasonable to say that the contemporary legitimacy of the Constitution's binding norms must rest on both current circumstances and the lessons of history. If the Framers hit upon something that has proved useful for centuries and still makes sense in current circumstances, the law is well served by heeding that wisdom. If not, however, and if the text is sufficiently capacious to permit an interpretation superior to "original public meaning," there is no obvious reason to forego the more attractive interpretation.

Second, as a matter of principle, there simply cannot have been a consensus understanding as to the meaning of a constitutional provision as applied to a context the drafters did not—often could not—anticipate. We can actually be pretty certain what the founding generation believed an "army" to be. It is inconceivable that Congress's power to "raise and support Armies" could possibly be extended to an Air Force, much less to a Space Force. The only non-land-based force that the Framers would have known about would be a navy, and the Framers provided for distinct explicit authority "to provide and maintain a navy." "Armies" was not a mere metonym for all fighting forces, and fighting from the air or from outer space would surely have seemed outlandish. For all we know, late eighteenth-century Americans would have viewed a military force in outer space as satanic and nothing a good nation should take part in. From a purely textual point of view, it does not really help that the Constitution also authorizes Congress "to provide for the common defence"[87] because that clause presumably was not intended to authorize the creation of entire armed services. If the scope of the clause had been that far-reaching, no separate authorities would have been needed to "raise and support Armies" or to "provide and maintain a Navy."

Thinking through the implications of the phrase "executive power" entails the identical problem of anachronism. Imagine, contrary to the historical evidence discussed earlier, that there really was a founding consensus in favor of comprehensive presidential control over the discretionary decision-making of every officer in the executive branch. Imagine—and this is wholly imaginary—we could identify something like unanimity among the ratifiers in anticipating that Article II would mandate a strictly hierarchical view of executive authority under which Congress's delegations of power to the executive branch were effectively all delegations of power to the president personally. If so, we should also consider that, in 1787, the founding generation faced both the prospect of a federal civil establishment likely to employ at most a few thousand persons and the certainty that the chief executive would be the venerated former commander in chief of the Continental Army. Under those conditions, it is at least imaginable that Americans could have found it both plausible and desirable to institutionalize a hierarchical civil command structure with meaningful accountability effectively vested in a single human manager. In the first quarter of the twenty-first century, however, with a total federal civilian workforce of non-seasonal fulltime permanent employees of nearly two million, not including the postal service, the model is utterly fanciful. The corps of administrative law judges serving the Social Security Administration alone is over half the probable size of the entire federal government in 1800.[88] No president can be expected to keep a genuinely watchful eye and thoughtful, informed perspective on the work done in every corner of the modern executive establishment. To ask if eighteenth-century Americans would have understood the Article II Vesting Clause as giving the president comprehensive supervisory authority over a federal government employing a workforce roughly equal to the entire population of the 1776 United States is to ask a preposterous question.[89]

Third, the most common normative defense for originalism—the idea that originalism prevents judges from resolving constitutional disputes according to their personal and political values—is chimerical. Professor Segall has documented the wide variety of cases in which our contemporary Supreme Court originalists enter into decisions without an ounce of serious originalist support, all but invariably to suit the preferred judicial outcomes for political conservatives.[90] This is dramatically evident, for example, in the free speech and campaign finance areas, as well as in Supreme Court review of Congress's exercise of its commerce powers.[91]

To see why originalism leaves so much wiggle room for judicial creativity, it is helpful to review the analogous development in statutory interpretation. At the same time jurists and scholars are debating the relative merits of originalist versus pragmatic forms of constitutional interpretation, they are also pursuing a similar debate between "textualists" and "purposivists" about the interpretation of statutes. Textualists supposedly hew entirely to the meaning of a statute's words; purposivists expand their focus beyond the bare statutory text with recourse to other evidence of what the enacting legislature hoped its text would accomplish.[92] A major part of that debate concerns the permissibility of deriving interpretive guidance from "legislative history," that is, the body of hearings, committee reports, congressional debates, and earlier drafts, in addition to the language finally adopted. Those opposed to consulting legislative history often point to its frequent ambiguity and the possibility of cherry-picking the evidence to support one's preferred view of what a statute means.[93] The late Judge Harold Leventhal famously quipped that citing evidence from legislative history is like "looking over a crowd and picking out your friends."[94]

The potential for opportunistic evidence choice, however, jumps exponentially when one consults contemporary sources for "original public meaning." The most famous Supreme Court decision in the "original public meaning" mode was *District of Columbia v. Heller*, the 2008 case overturning D.C.'s near-ban on handguns and establishing for the first time that the Second Amendment enshrines a judicially enforceable right to possess guns for self-defense in one's home.[95] The Second Amendment reads: "A well regulated Militia, being necessary to the security of a free State, the right of the people to keep and bear Arms, shall not be infringed."[96] Four other conservative Justices joined a majority opinion by Justice Scalia that purported to resolve the case based entirely on the "original public meaning" of these twenty-seven words. Historians have, for the most part, been hugely critical of Scalia's result.[97] But Scalia insisted he was just following the text. He proceeded first to disconnect what he called the prefatory clause, "A well regulated Militia, being necessary to the security of a free State," from what he called the "operative clause," "the right of the people to keep and bear Arms, shall not be infringed."[98] He insisted, contrary to common sense, that the meaning of the operative clause should not be thought of as confined by the prefatory clause, thus discarding the notion that the subject of the Second Amendment was the right of states to support and arm their own militias.[99] He then resorted to dictionaries to give "keep," "bear," and "arms" their broad, conventional, and nonmilitary meaning.[100]

To test Scalia's inferences, two scholars—Josh Blackman and James C. Phillips—using the "corpus linguistics" approach mentioned earlier, took advantage in 2018 of a database known as the Corpus of Founding Era American English (COFEA), which compiles nearly one hundred thousand texts with over one hundred forty million words from the start of the reign of King George III (1760) to the death of George Washington (1799).[101] What they found is that the "overwhelming majority" of sources using the phrase "bear arms" were referring to their military use. As for "keep . . . arms," about half of the eighteen relevant documents they were able to identify "referred to keeping arms in the military context, roughly a quarter referred to a private sense of keeping arms, and another quarter or so were ambiguous references."[102] Thus it turns out that "bear arms" was overwhelmingly used in a military context, "keep arms" was rarely used at all, but when "keep arms" was used, it was just as likely to be used in a military context as not.

Yet even these findings fail to persuade the two conservative legal scholars that their findings falsify Scalia's reading. They write:

> Linguistic inquiries often fail to account for other evidence that informs constitutional meaning, including the structure of the Constitution and historical practice. And even within the linguistic evidence, we still need to determine whether all sources are treated equal or whether some sources should be seen as more probative of the interpretive question at hand.[103]

In other words, even if the "overwhelming majority" of uses support one interpretation, a judge supposedly bound by original public meaning might consciously or unconsciously ignore the majority of uses in favor of the idea that the most probative sources are in the minority.

And the multiplicity of sources itself does not end the room for cherry picking. As it happens, the history of Supreme Court decisions includes a significant list of decisions no one seriously thinks of overruling, but which cannot be explained on originalist grounds. What this means, however, is that, when originalism points in a direction that a judge does not want to pursue, the judge can invoke *stare decisis* to decide a contemporary case in a manner that remains faithful to non-originalist precedent.[104]

There is, to be sure, pro-originalist commentary purporting to address these problems. For example, the problem of incoherence in treating 1787 (or 1868 or . . .) definitions as settling unanticipated questions in unfamiliar contexts has led various scholars to suggest various kinds of what David Strauss calls "moderate originalism."[105] The various forms of "moderate originalism" supposedly confine interpreters to the drafters' original *principles* or *values*, but not to the specific *applications* of the text they would have anticipated. What this does is elevate the level of generality with which we approach original meaning. For example, proponents of the Fourteenth Amendment did not anticipate that it would command an end to racially segregated schools; we know this because the Congress that proposed the Fourteenth Amendment also maintained racially segregated schools in the District of Columbia. Presumably, they perceived no conflict. Yet it has been offered as an originalist defense of decisions striking down segregated schooling that the Fourteenth Amendment also adopted a principle of "equality" and, if we take equality as the governing value, racially segregated schooling violates this "original" principle.[106]

The problem with "moderate originalism," however, is that it gives away everything distinctive about originalism. No theorist of whom I am aware argues for ignoring constitutional text altogether. No one argues for treating the Tenth Amendment as a recipe for fried chicken. But if we can raise our focus on original textual meaning to the level of original values or principles, there is virtually no limit on what can be defended consistent with originalism. Exhibit A in demonstrating this is a brief filed in the gay marriage case, *Obergefell v. Hodges*.[107] Here legal scholars advanced the argument that the original meaning of the Fourteenth Amendment precluded the limitation of marriage to heterosexual couples.[108] The problem is not just that the 1868 generation would have resolved that issue differently; it is that few would have understood the question as a question. I am delighted that the United States now recognizes the right of same-sex couples to marry. In my view, that is the constitutionally and morally correct result. If, however, it is originalism that justifies *Obergefell*, then originalism can truly justify anything.

One of the most thoughtful originalist theorists, Keith Whittington, has advanced a helpful conceptual distinction between constitutional *interpretation* and constitutional *construction*.[109] As he explains, interpretation involves the search for the original public meaning—the communicative content—of the words themselves. The process of applying the words to answer specific questions, however, does not follow straight from meaning to resolution. That is the process of construction. There may be cases in which the communicative content of the words is so compelling relative to the problem presented that the realm of construction—theorists now call it the "construction zone"—is vanishingly small. Yet in many cases—certainly most litigated cases—the construction zone is large enough so that some additional guideposts are necessary to get from meaning to resolution.[110]

This conceptualization is helpful, however, in articulating why originalism cannot live up to its discretion-limiting claims. In an effort to explain how the construction zone does not permit the kind of creativity in constitutional implementation of which the Warren and Burger Courts are so often accused, originalist scholars have offered a variety of guideposts to keep sound judging in line. A leading libertarian originalist, Randy Barnett, has borrowed from the work of a legal philosopher and contracts scholar, Steven Burton, to argue that the construction zone can be meaningfully constrained by the obligations of good-faith judging.[111] Barnett and coauthor Evan Bernick cast judges as having a fiduciary relationship to the Constitution, which supposedly directs them to adhere to "the spirit of the Constitution," and not to "improve, evade, or get out of" the "deal" the ratifiers made. Judges, they urge, must be especially attentive to the "functions" of the constitutional provisions they interpret.[112] It is imperative that judges, like parties disappointed with their contracts, not seek to "recapture" a "foregone opportunity"—foregone, one supposes, by the Framers or their heirs—"to change or amend the written Constitution."[113]

The Barnett-Bernick view of "good faith," however, accomplishes very little, a point they appear to concede: "As compared to alternative approaches that leave *all* linguistically permissible rules on the table, our approach makes it *marginally* more likely that judges will arrive at rules that are consistent with the Constitution's spirit. The latter is our primary goal."[114] One doubts that Justice Scalia deployed his muscular rhetoric in defense of what he sincerely thought would be merely "marginal" improvement.

There are numerous possible ripostes to the Barnett-Bernick theory, but two loom largest. The first is that the vague phrases of the Constitution are often vague because the Framers had in mind multiple functions for their work that were in tension with one another. Was the "function" of the Recess Appointments Clause to preserve continuity in government or to prevent presidential evasions of the Senate's advice and consent power? Was the separation of powers designed to foster action-slowing deliberation or to free the executive from the kind of parliamentary micro-management that bedeviled government under the Articles of Confederation?[115] The answer to all these questions is affirmative, which makes reliance on the spirit of the Constitution inevitably indeterminate.

Theoretically, however, the Barnett-Bernick view of the fiduciary judge also surfaces the problem I highlighted earlier of lawmaking legitimacy. The drafters of 1787 or 1868 may have "forgone opportunities to change or amend the Constitution," but no one now alive did any such "foregoing." If the drafters used language sufficiently capacious to embrace a more attractive application of the text than the applications they specifically imagined, a good case exists that a living constitutionalist is being perfectly faithful to the Constitution in taking advantage of their deliberate choice to speak in vague, interpretively capacious terms.

It seems no accident that, in Barnett's hands, good-faith construction turns out to coincide with his preferred libertarian outcomes. He finds Justice Scalia's *Heller* opinion to be in good faith in finding an enforceable individual right under the Second Amendment, but not in good faith—or at least in adequate good faith—in asserting the presumptive lawfulness of forms of gun regulation that have existed in the United States for centuries.[116] Another example he would offer of "bad faith" is *Wickard v. Filburn*.[117] That case allows Congress's power to regulate interstate commerce to reach even local, arguably noncommercial activity if, in the aggregate, that activity has a significant impact on interstate commerce. He sees the latter as a bad faith construction of the Constitution because of the breadth of regulatory power it would seem to legitimate. The Commerce Clause, however, was adopted to enable Congress to address national problems beyond the competence of individual states to address. John Marshall early described the bounds of Congress's regulatory competence:

> The genius and character of the whole government seem to be that its action is to be applied to all the external concerns of the nation, and to those internal concerns which affect the States generally, but not to those which are completely within a particular State, *which do not affect other States, and with which it is not necessary to interfere for the purpose of executing some of the general powers of the government.*[118]

If Marshall has correctly stated the appropriate test, there is certainly nothing "in bad faith" about the result in *Wickard v. Filburn*.

When I first encountered the Barnett-Bernick elaboration of good faith, two decisions that clearly fail their criteria jumped to mind: *Bolling v. Sharpe* and *Harper v. Virginia State Board of Elections*.[119] *Bolling*, decided the same day as *Brown v. Board of Education*, held that racially segregated schooling in the District of Columbia violated the Due Process Clause of the Fifth Amendment. *Harper*, decided in 1966, held it unconstitutional to levy a poll tax as prerequisite to voting in a state or local election.

Bolling is impossible to defend on originalist grounds. Even if "moderate originalism" sufficed as a method for holding racially segregated schooling in the states to be violative of the Fourteenth Amendment's Equal Protection Clause, that clause applies only to state governments. The Fifth Amendment does limit the action of the federal government (including the District of Columbia) but includes no Equal Protection Clause. The amendment was adopted in 1791, the same year that the city of Washington was founded. Congress did not create a school system for the District of Columbia until 1804. The issue posed in *Bolling v. Sharpe* would have been almost as unlikely to have arisen in 1791 as the issue of gay marriage in 1868. Yet, the Court in

Bolling recognized what the Court has since called, "the equal protection component of the Due Process Clause of the Fifth Amendment,"[120] clearly a modern invention.

Because the poll tax overturned in *Harper* was a state tax, the Fourteenth Amendment was certainly relevant. The Court treated relevant precedents as establishing that "the Equal Protection Clause of the Fourteenth Amendment restrains the States from fixing voter qualifications which invidiously discriminate."[121] The Court determined that making "the affluence of the voter or payment of any fee an electoral standard" represented just such an invidious discrimination. There were but three conspicuous problems with this wholly just outcome, two of which the majority did not bother even to mention. One unmentioned problem is that the drafters of the Fourteenth Amendment did not regard it as applicable to discrimination in voting,[122] which is why the Fifteenth, Nineteenth, and Twenty-Sixth Amendments were later added. The second unmentioned problem is that the nation had, just two years earlier, adopted the Twenty-Fourth Amendment, which outlawed poll taxes in federal—but only in federal—elections. If the Equal Protection Clause outlawed state poll taxes, then the Twenty-Fourth Amendment was superfluous because "the equal protection component of the Due Process Clause of the Fifth Amendment" would already have outlawed the poll tax in elections for federal office. Excluding state poll taxes from the reach of the Twenty-Fourth Amendment represents as clearly and intentionally "forgone" an opportunity to amend the Constitution as is imaginable. The third problem, which the majority did acknowledge, was that the Court had upheld the constitutionality of state poll taxes just twenty-nine years earlier in a case called *Breedlove v. Suttles*.[123] The Court overruled *Breedlove*, noting only, albeit correctly, that "[n]otions of what constitutes equal treatment for purposes of the Equal Protection Clause do change."

What drove the unanimous outcome in *Bolling* and the six-Justice majority in *Harper* had nothing to do with "original public meaning," and everything to do with the moral intolerability of reaching the opposite conclusion. The Justices no doubt thought it inconceivable in the wake of *Brown* that racially segregated schooling should be preserved in the nation's capital. Nor in the wake of the 1965 voting rights march from Selma to Montgomery could the Court countenance a limitation on the franchise not plausibly related to any individual's qualifications to participate as a member of a political community.

The majority opinion in *Harper* provides a perfect illustration of what David Strauss has called constitutional law as common law. In the common law method, cases are decided chiefly by consulting and analogizing to precedent.[124] The majority cited an earlier decision, *Carrington v. Rash*, for the proposition that a State may not deny the opportunity to vote to a bona fide resident merely because he or she is a member of the armed services.[125] It cited *Reynolds v. Sims*, the one-person, one-vote reapportionment case, for the proposition that a state could not use its citizens' places of residence as a way to give one citizen a weightier vote than another.[126] From these cases, it discerned a principle that distinguishing between voters on grounds "not germane to one's ability to participate intelligently in the electoral process" was impermissible.[127]

Of course, recourse to the analysis of precedent, like "moderate originalism," is only incompletely constraining. In drawing analogies from precedents to a current dispute, judgments must be made regarding the features of prior cases that make them salient to the new controversy. For centuries, common-law judges operating in the fields of torts, contracts and property law would speak as if they were merely "discovering" the law through their handiwork, not "making" law. No one now disputes the creativity in common-law judging.

Like Strauss, I would argue, however, that common-law judging is at least as constraining as moderate originalism and, in contemporary form, more candid. The common-law constitutionalist acknowledges that judgments of "fairness and policy" influence the interpretive enterprise and thus can and should spell out how those factors shape decision making. Originalism constrains its practitioners to exaggerate the degree to which historic meaning commands their outcomes. By contrast, Justice Scalia's rhetorical stance in deciding the *Heller* case implying the irrelevance of his personal sentiments on gun ownership seems like pure artifice.

If I am right about this, the question still arises as to the values that should guide our "moderate originalism" or "common-law constitutionalism" as we seek answers to separation-of-powers questions in precedent, history, and institutional custom. Benjamin Cardozo, whom Strauss recognizes as one of America's finest common-law judges, said, "The final cause of the law is the welfare of society."[128] If separation-of-powers law is to advance the welfare of society, what values should we prioritize in deriving guidance from the past? Democracy, I will argue, provides the path forward.

FIVE

Interpreting Democracy's Constitution

THE LATE JUSTICE ANTONIN SCALIA, probably originalism's most pugnacious advocate, famously insisted that the Constitution is "not a living document," but "dead, dead, dead."[1] He was speaking normatively, about how he thought people *should* read the Constitution. More specifically, he was trying to sell his listeners two ideas: The meaning of the Constitution's words should be viewed as fixed when written, and constitutional interpretation ought to entail no more than applying those words according to their original meaning.[2] Chapters 2 and 4 have both argued against this normative view.

But the "dead Constitution" is also clearly wrong as a matter of description of how courts actually have read the Constitution. As numerous scholars have shown, our prevailing body of constitutional doctrine—the corpus of rules our courts have created for putting the constitutional text into operation—frequently bears no reliable relationship to the original meaning of the text, assuming such meaning can even be discerned.[3] On subject after subject, with regard to both individual rights and the Constitution's structural provisions, our constitutional law has evolved in ways that its Framers and ratifiers could not have anticipated. In at least some of the relevant cases, the Supreme Court has even had the decency not to pretend otherwise.

Fortunately, the "living Constitution" is also normatively superior. In modern parlance, the adaptive Constitution's living quality is a feature, not a bug. As Chief Justice John Marshall wrote in 1819, ours "is a Constitution intended to endure for ages to come, and consequently, to be adapted to the various crises of human affairs."[4] The fact that its drafters saw fit to leave key terms vague—on important questions, as Marshall noted, "only its great outlines" are "marked"—has meant that every generation can renew the Constitution's authority by reinterpreting its phrases according to precedent, custom, and contemporary need, not just text alone.[5] In chapter 4, I argued that the formalist portrayal of originalism—the idea that one could proceed automatically from original meaning to the application of the words—often describes a project verging on incoherence. That is because what the text communicated to readers of 1787 or 1868 depended on contextual factors that have since changed profoundly. Applying a text's semantic meaning without reference to original context means that the application thus fashioned for the contemporary world will frequently have no resemblance to what the original readers of the text imagined the words to be communicating.

Consider the Second Amendment. Some advocates may claim—although I would disagree—that the text communicated to readers in 1791 that people had the right to own any guns that would be useful in military service. If so, then the Second Amendment could today protect the right to own machine guns, which would certainly be useful for military service in the twenty-first century. Justice Scalia's opinion in *District of Columbia v. Heller* dismisses that argument, holding that "the sorts of weapons protected" by the Second Amendment were only those "in common use" when the Second Amendment was adopted, not those that would be useful for military service today.[6] He would thus exclude machine guns from protection, even as the Court concedes "no amount of small arms could be useful against modern-day bombers and tanks."[7] The apparent gap now between the asserted purpose of the language and its application, however, does not change Scalia's reading of the Second Amendment. Scalia writes: "The fact that modern developments have limited the degree of fit between the prefatory clause [i.e., the reference to militia] and the protected right cannot change our interpretation of the right."[8] But that is not an entirely satisfactory response. What the language would have communicated in 1791 would have been contingent on two things: first, reader familiarity with the kinds of 1791 weapons most likely embraced by "the right to bear arms"—muskets, for example, and revolvers—and the fit in 1791 between the signification of those weapons and the purpose of protecting access to them—assuring suitability for effective military service. When the Court indulges an "interpretation" that attends to some specific expectations of the drafters, but not to the purposes behind the choice of words, or vice versa, the language no longer means what it meant to readers originally. "Constructing" such contemporary applications of the Constitution by asking how dead generations understood their text runs the risk of being doubly wrongheaded: It mistakenly locates in past generations the legitimate authority to restrict our contemporary political choices, and it runs the risk of pretending that the communicative content of words is properly ascertainable apart from what would have been their real-world implications when the words were written.

And originalism assumes, of course, that we can also divine an original consensus as to the communicative content of words, even among readers all living in their original real-world context. David Strauss has posited this excellent challenge: Consider the heated controversy that exists today as to what would be the operational consequences of adopting a so-called Equal Rights Amendment prohibiting government discrimination by sex.[9] There is profound disagreement whether language permitting discrimination "on the basis of" or "on account of" sex should be understood to reach discrimination against trans persons.[10] If we cannot discern a contemporary consensus as to the meaning of a vague constitutional proposal drafted in our own time, it suggests we ought to be cautious before imagining there was a contemporary consensus as to the meaning of vague or ambiguous terms uttered centuries ago—or that we could reliably identify one.

THE VALUE OF CANDID VALUES

The truth is that, in the process of applying the Constitution, values activated by the interpreter and that go beyond the technical meaning of the text itself must come into play. There is no other way to operate in what contemporary theorists call the "construction zone."[11] Judges and other interpreters acting in good faith are required to identify for themselves the level of generality at which the Constitution's purposes are to be understood. Adjusting the level of generality is inevitably involved in seeking the "spirit of the Constitution."[12] And the level of generality that seems appropriate to the interpreter will inevitably depend on the values framework being deployed. Similarly, under a "common law" conception of constitutional interpretation, the values that the interpreter brings to bear on interpretation will be factors in identifying which historical precedents ought to inform contemporary interpretation and in deciding which are the salient features of those precedents.[13] There is just no escape from the introduction of values beyond the text in the process of construing the meaning of that text. Judges who genuinely regard restraint as a virtue in judging should not pretend that "the text made me do it." They should be mindful of how extra-textual factors enter their analysis, identify those values, and explain interpretive outcomes with reasons that rely on the values they have identified.

Of course, not all values are created equal when it comes to legitimate constitutional interpretation. Some align better with the Constitution than others. We can get a start on locating permissibly relevant values by considering the nature of the document we are interpreting. In the words of Chief Justice John Marshall, "We must never forget that it is a constitution we are expounding."[14] At a minimum, the Constitution is law, and fidelity to law precludes interpretation that is merely self-regarding. "The Constitution means X in order that I can get rich or do whatever I feel like" is plainly a form of constitutional reading at odds with any rule of law ideal. Nor would it improve matters to change, "I" to "we," if "we" means my family, my sect, my party, my race, and so on. Interpreting the Constitution to give advantage to oneself or to those related to me, look like me, or think like me cannot be reconciled with the "spirit of the Constitution" because no one drafting or ratifying a constitution would ever credit the facilitation of self-dealing as the objective of any legitimate legal system.

To promote legitimacy, the values that inform constitutional construction must be public-regarding values.[15] And, not surprisingly, different eras in Supreme Court history seem much more comprehensible if we understand the Court as having different theories of public welfare and views of public need that have changed over time. This is not to say that, in any given era or even for a single case, only one value can explain the Court's interpretive choices. But it is hard, for example, to survey the work of the Marshall Court and not think that nation building was critical to its jurisprudential outlook.[16] Likewise, the late nineteenth-century Court seemed to be driven, in part, by what it perceived to be the legitimate requirements of industrialization.[17] The New Deal Court recognized the need for a strong federal response to dire economic circumstances and, soon enough, to global war.[18] To different degrees and in different respects, the Warren and Burger Courts can be seen as advancing the value of democratic civic inclusion.[19] The Rehnquist Court revived concerns with federalism and respect for traditional values.[20] The Roberts Court is arguably intent on pursuing a vision of public policy that is libertarian in economics, but protective of tradition—especially conservative religious tradition—in matters of morality.[21] To identify these orientations is not to justify them, but merely to describe them. They illustrate the inevitability that the justices' selection of public values deserving of protection will shape the outcome of constitutional cases.

My forward-looking argument—my roadmap to breaking away from the aggressively presidentialist reconceptualization of executive power that took root in the Reagan administration and metastasized in the Trump administration—starts with rejecting the presidentialists' originalism when it comes to conceptualizing the constitutional presidency and articulating a values framework that should take priority over originalist argument. This may seem strategically unwise for a legal advocate in the 2020s. Originalists, for the moment at least, seem to be running the show from the Supreme Court.[22] And the historical material arrayed in chapters 2 and 4 may have already persuaded you that we could have a presidency less threatening to democracy and the rule of law if we simply practiced "public meaning originalism" with more careful attention to actual history. Why not just try and beat the presidentialists at their own game?

The answer is twofold. First, the historical evidence mustered to refute presidentialist claims has been strong and available for a long time. The failure of those justices who are most indulgent of executive power to engage that history seriously may or may not betoken bad faith.[23] But it certainly does not suggest open-mindedness. The majority's refusal, for example, in *Seila Law v. CFPB*, to engage seriously with the new historical arguments in the dissent is telling.[24] It may simply be a fool's errand to hope better historians can change judicial minds through the force of better argument on the presidentialists' terms.

A deeper answer is that rooting constitutional interpretation in theories that do not hold up either normatively or descriptively is unproductive and even dangerous. It is unproductive to prioritize eighteenth century thinking in assessing proper constitutional arrangements for the twenty-first century. Historical experience may teach lessons, of course, and the historical record is thus always worth considering. The past should not, however, be the omnipresent driving force in interpretation. And originalism is dangerous because it is dishonest for government to assert authority based on empty promises of objectivity. Assurances that originalism will yield determinate answers and exclude interpreter values from constitutional outcomes simply do not hold up.[25] Values that go beyond the text will inevitably affect how the Constitution is applied in controversial contexts. Judges who own up to this reality may or may not make better decisions, but they will certainly advance public understanding of how constitutional interpretation actually works.

INTERPRETING THE SEPARATION OF POWERS THROUGH THE LENS OF DEMOCRACY

My candidate for the motivating value most appropriate to guiding current interpretation of the constitutional presidency is democracy. Courts and lawyers must often resolve constitutional ambiguities about the powers of the presidency or concerning the chief executive's relationship to Congress and the courts. I argue that the choice among interpretive options should be significantly guided by this inquiry: "What would most strengthen both the electoral and deliberative sides of America's hybrid democracy?"

Before defining that inquiry more precisely, let me say why I am emphasizing democracy at all. It is my premise that the object of our Constitution—indeed, of any constitution—is to establish legitimate government. Legitimacy is often used in two different senses.[26] A government has *social* legitimacy if those governed regard the system as worthy of their allegiance and obedience. A government has *moral* legitimacy to the extent it embodies a principled response to the question, "Why are a relatively small group of citizens empowered to coerce legal obedience by all?"[27] One hopes, of course, that the two ideas overlap—that a government's social legitimacy will be rooted in its moral legitimacy, so that improvements in the moral legitimacy of a government will earn it yet greater popular allegiance. It is my premise and certainly my hope that a genuinely free people will not accord social legitimacy to a government utterly lacking in moral legitimacy.

For the overwhelming majority of countries in the world, some version of democracy is deemed to be the basis of morally legitimate government. "Democracy" famously comes in many forms, however. At least in Western nations, the legitimating force of democracy is deemed to rest on two pillars. One is the promise of equal respect for the interests of all citizens in the course of collective decision-making. This does not mean that all decisions must please all citizens equally; public policies will still have winners and losers. But the interests of all who are affected by collective decisions must still be taken seriously. No one's interests may be dismissed out of hand by virtue of characteristics irrelevant to the merits of the decision, such as their race, gender, religion, or partisan affiliation.

The second pillar is the promised opportunity for individual political engagement. That is, another feature of authentic democracy is that each citizen gets to experience himself or herself as an authentically efficacious actor in the formation of the collective will. In the words of Robert Post: "We could not plausibly characterize as democratic a society in which 'the people' were given the power to determine the nature of their government, but in which individuals who made up 'the people' did not experience themselves as free to choose their own political fate."[28] There is, of course, a real-world relationship between the opportunity for effective engagement and the promise of equal respect. A society in which the citizenry has authentic opportunities for engagement ought to be a society in which those governing feel the most pressure to take everyone's interests into serious consideration in making policy.

When democracy is seen in this light, two things become clear immediately. One is the crucial importance of elections. The democratic character of a representative government like our own depends in large measure on the reliability of free and fair elections of relative frequency.[29] Elections are legitimating because they reinforce the accountability of those governing to the people they govern, and participation in elections—not just voting, but also organizing, campaigning, and even running for office—provides critical opportunities for personal political engagement.

But it should be just as obvious that, in the real world, elections are not enough. The volume of policy decisions of concern to any individual is too great for the selection of a single representative to afford any citizen genuine opportunities for influence on all of them. The connection between the voter and policy making becomes even more attenuated when the elected legislators delegate significant policy choice to the unelected bureaucracy, even if, to some extent, elected officials oversee the bureaucrats.

Moreover, electoral rules such as gerrymandering work to effectively insulate certain officeholders from accountability to readily identifiable subsets of the voting public. A Republican or Democratic voter stuck in an electoral district that is populated overwhelmingly by the other party, or a minority voter in a majority-white district in which racial bloc voting predominates, will find that their elected representatives worry little about earning their support by advocating forcefully for their policy preferences.[30] In such packed districts, the representatives' "base" guarantees their reelection. These antidemocratic features of our electoral system, especially when coupled with the influence of special interest money, help ensure that elections offer an insufficient guarantee that elected officials will remain conscientiously attentive to all their constituents' interests over the full range of their decision-making.

Starting in the 1980s, scholars from a wide array of disciplines began taking more seriously the idea that "electoral democracy" is incomplete both as a description of the democracy we have and as a prescription for the democracy we want. In a seminal work, *The Mild Voice of Reason: Deliberative Democracy and American National Government*, political scientist Joseph M. Bessette persuasively discerned in the work of the Framers an intention to create what he called a "deliberative democracy," in which "lawmaking would promote the rule of *deliberative* majorities."[31] In this vision, elected representatives would enact policies that the people themselves would have chosen if they possessed the same degree of knowledge and experience as did their representatives, as well as the time and opportunity for reasoned deliberation over the relevant information and arguments.[32]

The Framers' vision of deliberative democracy was not populist or necessarily majoritarian. Instead, "procedures and institutions" would be designed to "have the capacity to check or moderate unreflective popular sentiments."[33] Elections would help to ensure that the values of the representatives match the values of "the people." But because of the representatives' greater knowledge and experience, as well as the legislature's well-designed institutional settings and processes, the policies they chose might not be the most popular, at least in real time.

Twenty-first-century American government still reflects the Framers' design for deliberative institutions—we still have a bicameral Congress, a president and executive "departments," and a federal judiciary, all interacting in both actual and metaphorical dialogue. Yet the modern concept of "deliberative democracy" is much broader and less elitist than what the Framers imagined. For contemporary theorists and democratic practitioners, the idea of democratic deliberation now embraces any form of policy-oriented dialogue in which communication among the discussants induces all participants to reflect upon their policy preferences in non-coercive fashion.[34] A government so structured as to empower such dialogue to help shape policy choice is a deliberative democracy. As explained by political scientist John S. Dryzek: "Authentic democracy . . . can . . . be said to exist to the degree that reflective preferences influence collective outcomes."[35]

In Professor Bessette's account of deliberative democracy, Congress, as envisioned by the Framers, was expected to be the most conspicuous site of democratic deliberation in the American system.[36] Other scholars have emphasized courts as deliberative venues, whether focusing on jury deliberations, deliberations between litigants and the court, or deliberations within panels of judges or Justices.[37] More recently, Jerry Mashaw has argued that the executive establishment comprising our vast network of regulatory agencies may qualify as the preeminent site of democratic deliberation, especially as its processes have been structured by requirements for reason-giving imposed on agencies by courts, statutes, or executive orders.[38]

Yet not all democratic deliberation occurs within the halls of government institutions. Communication scholars have identified the larger "public sphere" as the figurative "discursive space in which individuals and groups associate to discuss matters of mutual interest and, where possible, to reach a common judgment about them."[39] Democratic deliberation among the citizenry and within civil society may produce collective action without state intervention, as when neighborhood groups manage common spaces informally. But discussion in the public sphere may also engage the state. This could happen through elections, but it could happen as well through court cases, legislative hearings, administrative proceedings, or through petitions and protests. The greater the possibilities for citizens to affect collective outcomes through authentically inclusive and non-coerced discourse—dialogue that is ongoing and not limited by the election calendar—the stronger will be a nation's claim to deliberative democracy.

This discussion should clarify the inquiry that I have posited as a proper guide in resolving ambiguous separation of powers questions posed by our often Delphic constitutional text: "What reading of the Constitution would most strengthen both the electoral and deliberative democratic sides of America's hybrid democracy?" Such a method holds out the best hope of strengthening the legitimacy of our constitutional system. But how can this work? The answer is to treat questions regarding the powers of the president and the relationship of the president to the other branches of government as questions, in essence, of contemporary institutional design. A constitutional controversy in the face of ambiguity can then be understood as asking which version of institutional design now will best support the pillars of democracy as just outlined. At this moment in history, I would go yet one step further: Democratic constitutionalism should prioritize democracy's deliberative side, at least to the extent of not allowing the tenuous links between elections and policy outcomes to excuse a reduction in deliberative opportunities. Our electoral processes incorporate "distortions of the democratic process long abandoned by most democracies."[40] That reality counsels the value in protecting and expanding the ways in which democracy can be strengthened and legitimated through non-electoral means.

Let me illustrate with three concrete cases, the outcomes of which jive with a democracy-driven approach to constitutional interpretation, even if the Supreme Court did not explain itself in those terms. For example, the Supreme Court in 2014 was called upon for the first time to interpret the scope of the president's so-called recess appointments power.[41] In the ordinary case, the president is required to get the Senate's consent in order to appoint the so-called "principal officers" in any federal agency, such as a cabinet secretary or member of a regulatory commission. Moreover, when Congress creates an "inferior officer"—perhaps an agency's general counsel—it may still require by statute that the Senate's advice and consent be required for that officer, as well. The Constitution, however, provides for the eventuality that the president might want or need to fill an office even when the Senate is not around. Section 2 of Article II provides: "The President shall have power to fill up all vacancies that may happen during the recess of the Senate, by granting commissions which shall expire at the end of their next session."[42]

Beginning with the George W. Bush administration, the Senate began to organize its periods of adjournment so that, at least according to the Senate, these periods of adjournment would not count as being long enough to be the kind of "recess" that would trigger the president's recess appointments power. No matter how long the Senate as a working body might be out of town, it would convene in a so-called "pro forma" session every three days.[43] In such a "pro forma" session, a Senator who lived relatively close by would come into the Senate chamber, gavel the empty room to order, and adjourn roughly a minute later. Because the breaks between these sessions lasted only three days, the three-day intervals, according to the Senate, would be too short to count as recesses during which presidents could make appointments without prior Senate approval.

In 2010 and 2011, President Obama was involved in a dispute with the Republican-led Senate, which refused to confirm any of his regular nominees to the National Labor Relations Board. He decided to appoint three members to the Board during one of the three-day breaks between "pro forma" sessions. When the Board so staffed decided a case against the Noel Canning Company, Noel Canning challenged the Board as having been unconstitutionally appointed.

The case really presented three interpretive issues. First, did a vacancy "happen during the recess of the Senate" even if the office first became vacant while the Senate was meeting, as was the case for the NLRB? In other words, did "happen" mean "first arise," which would not cover the NLRB vacancies, or did it mean "happen to exist," which would? Second, would a period of adjournment *during* a so-called session of the Senate, which typically runs from January to November or December, count as a recess? Or did "recess" refer only to the break *between* sessions of the Senate? Obama made his appointments in the midst of a Senate session, but during a period of adjournment. Finally, was a three-day hiatus between "pro forma" sessions long enough to be a "recess" for Article II purposes? Given the particular facts of the case, President Obama could win only if the clause permitted appointments even to vacancies that occurred prior to the recess, only if a recess could occur during a session of the Senate, and only if a three-day hiatus between pro forma sessions could count as a recess. The Court decided the first two issues for the president, but the last for the Senate. It concluded, based on historical practice, that breaks in Senate proceedings had to last at least ten days to be deemed a recess for purposes of presidential appointments.[44]

The Supreme Court's decision was based on a combination of pragmatism—if a vacant office is disabling to the government, what difference should it make when the office became vacant or why the Senate is unavailable for consultation?—and customary institutional practice. Because of what they took to be Article II's linguistic ambiguity, the five-justice majority thought none of the interpretive issues could be resolved on purely originalist grounds.[45] By way of contrast, the Scalia-authored concurrence would have decided against the president on the basis that, as interpreted by the concurrence, the relevant clause was intended to empower the president only *between* sessions of the Senate and only with regard to vacancies first arising during such recesses.[46] The three-day issue would have been superfluous.

Scalia's argument that the issues before the Court were free from ambiguity was a weak one. The Third Circuit, deciding the same issue in a different case (albeit also on the side of Noel Canning and thus, of the Senate) had thoroughly demonstrated the lack of any definitive original public meaning.[47] But the decision of the Supreme Court majority, which made it harder for a president to evade the Senate's confirmation role, is plainly consistent with the ideal of deliberative democracy. In combining the president's unilateral power of nomination with the Senate's collective entitlement to participate in the appointments process, the Constitution sets up an important opportunity for interbranch dialogue. The confirmation process, which has come to involve not only a Senate vote, but committee hearings, as well, even invites direct public participation in that dialogue. Unfortunately, that "dialogue" can descend into partisan stalemate, which is what threatened to happen to President Obama. But in interpreting the meaning of "recess," if an interpretive thumb is to be placed on the side of dialogue or unilateralism, it is appropriate under democratic principles to prefer dialogue.

Yet Congress will not always prevail in decisions favoring deliberative democracy. An important counterexample is the 1983 case of *Immigration and Naturalization Service v. Chadha*, which held unconstitutional a congressional process called the "legislative veto."[48] The legislative veto is a mechanism by which Congress, without enacting a new statute, can effectively change the scope of authority it had delegated to an executive branch agency through an earlier statute. As discussed in chapter 3, almost everything that federal administrative agencies do in domestic affairs is a consequence of statutes that empower them to implement Congress's goals. If a later Congress is unhappy with how an agency has implemented such statutory power, it can always enact a new statute either to void the agency's specific decision or to redraw the boundaries of the agency's authority more narrowly. A well-known example occurred in 1984 when Congress, having empowered the Department of Transportation in the 1960s to mandate safety devices for automobiles, took away the department's power to require ignition interlocks—devices that would either make noise or prevent a car from starting altogether until all passengers fastened their seat belts.[49] Despite the safety effectiveness of the devices, consumers hated them, and Congress changed the law to narrow its earlier grant of power to the agency.

Enacting statutes, however, is always time-consuming business. Not only must an issue appear compelling enough to command legislative attention, but the two Houses of Congress need to reach an agreement that the president is willing to sign into law. (Reaching the two-thirds vote to overturn a presidential veto is a very heavy political lift.) As a result, Congress, throughout the twentieth century, wrote into a variety of statutes an easier way to override agency action taken pursuant to those statutes. Over two hundred statutes provided that the authorities vested by those statutes in various agencies could be nullified either by a vote of both Houses that did not need the president's signature (a "two-House veto") or even by a nullifying vote in just one House of Congress (a "one-House veto").[50]

Jagdish Chadha's case involved a provision of the Immigration and Nationality Act (INA) that allowed the attorney general to suspend the deportability of an otherwise deportable alien in cases of "extreme hardship," provided that the applicant met certain other requirements, as well. Mr. Chadha, who had overstayed his student visa, applied successfully for that relief. The INA also provided, however, that Congress could overturn an attorney general's grant of hardship relief through a one-House veto. For reasons never officially explained, the House of Representatives, without hearing or debate, voted to nullify the order allowing Mr. Chadha to remain lawfully in the United States.

The Supreme Court held the legislative veto unconstitutional on the ground that Congress was effectively enacting new legislation—a revocation of the attorney general's decision—without passing a new statute, thus violating the requirement that laws be enacted by both Houses of Congress and, absent an override, with the approval of the president. The one-House veto, according to the Court, was an especially offensive violation because it dispensed not only with the president's involvement, but also with the requirement of bicameralism.

For an originalist, however—at least for an originalist focused on constitutional text—the Court's explanation should not really be deemed satisfactory. The Constitution is quite specific about the congressional acts that need to be sent to the president for his approval or veto. Under the so-called Presentment Clauses—referring to the requirement of "presentment" of legislation to the president for approval or veto—the acts covered include "[e]very bill which shall have passed the House of Representatives and the Senate," and "[e]very order, resolution, or vote to which the concurrence of the Senate and House of Representatives may be necessary (except on a question of adjournment)."[51] A one-House veto is not a "bill" and, by definition, it is not a vote requiring the concurrence of both Houses. A one-House veto is thus not covered by the wording of these clauses. Making the matter yet more complicated is the fact that Congress, from the beginning, has adopted any number of so-called "concurrent resolutions"—that is, votes of both Houses that are not sent to the president, most often to communicate legislative sentiment on some subject.[52] Hence, even within their precise terms, these clauses of the Constitution have not been followed without exception.

In dissent, Justice White argued that the legislative veto should be regarded as an appropriate device for keeping major policy-making decisions in the hands of an elected Congress.[53] Because the Court so regularly defers to Congress's determinations that broad policymaking authorities should be delegated to unelected agencies, then, in White's view, it is appropriate also to defer to Congress's decision to subject those authorities to more efficient congressional pushback. For his part, Justice Powell emphasized the unusual—perhaps unique—context in which Congress reserved to itself legislative veto authority regarding the administrative adjudication of an individual's application for a government benefit.[54] The Court, he argued, should deem such interference with administrative adjudication to be a violation of due process. On the other hand, he thought it should hold off on deciding (as the Court shortly would) that legislative vetoes were also unconstitutional with regard to the kind of general policymaking that goes into rulemaking—a decision, for example, to require all car manufacturers to install ignition interlocks.

The majority, however, went in another direction. It inferred that the purpose of the Presentment Clauses was to reach all congressional action "legislative in its character and effect."[55] The Court implicitly defined such initiatives as comprising any action having "the purpose and effect of altering the legal rights, duties and relations of persons . . . all outside the legislative branch."[56] Because the one-House veto would affect the legal relations of the attorney general, other Executive Branch officials, and Chadha, it was "legislative in character and effect," and thus covered implicitly by the Presentment Clauses. The Court thus rebuffed Congress's argument that the legislative veto was merely the exercise of a quasi-administrative judgment that the INA authorized Congress to make. It rejected the view that, because the INA had been enacted by both Houses and with presidential approval, Congress had respected the requirements of legislative process.

Deliberative democracy provides a more direct route to the majority's conclusion. Justice White is plainly correct that the legislative veto enables Congress to exercise oversight more vigorously over unelected administrators and thus respects democracy to that extent. But legislative vetoes are troubling from the standpoint of deliberative democracy in a surprising number of ways. First, the availability to Congress of the legislative veto takes pressure off the legislative branch to reach hard decisions through dialogue prior to the enactment of a statute. When a difficult question arises regarding the terms of a delegation of administrative power, the temptation would always exist for contending parties to compromise around a general grant of power tempered only by the prospect of a legislative veto that could be exercised in the future. Second, a bill containing a legislative veto presents a president with a less clear understanding of what is really being presented for approval or veto. To that extent, interbranch dialogue is also rendered less substantive.

Moreover, administrative decisions subject to legislative veto typically involve prior public dialogue under the management of the executive branch. In a case like Mr. Chadha's, the only such input may have been his own application for relief. But in the usual case—a general regulation adopted through notice-and-comment rulemaking—the agency will have had to spend significant time both soliciting and responding to public input. An agency is not required to respond individually to each comment it receives. But an agency that issues a rule without explicitly noting all significant issues raised by public comment and offering some response to those issues risks being found "arbitrary and capricious" by a reviewing court.[57] Yet the pressure to avoid a legislative veto may greatly reduce an agency's attentiveness to public input. A legislative veto is fatal to an agency regulation in a way that responding lackadaisically to public comments may or may not be.

Also, as Mr. Chadha's case illustrates, the deliberation within Congress over whether to issue a legislative veto may be far less than what would accompany ordinary legislation. There was no hearing or floor debate concerning the merits of the attorney general's decision regarding Mr. Chadha.[58] Without public reasoning, it is hard for anyone to hold the decision maker—in this case, Congress—accountable for its decisions.

Finally, as an important study of legislative vetoes showed, the impact of their inclusion in various statutes was not really because they were ever exercised; they rarely were. Rather, the prospect of a legislative veto would empower legislative staff to telephone agency administrators off-the-record and pressure those administrators to resolve issues according to the policy preferences of whomever the staff represented.[59] Two notable theorists of deliberative democracy, Amy Gutmann and Dennis Thompson, have emphasized in their work how publicity and accountability are key to authentic deliberation.[60] The possibility of legislative veto typically triggered a process of interbranch deliberation that would fail on both counts.

Yet a third case consistent with the needs of deliberative democracy—a decision that serves the deliberative needs of all branches of government—is *United States v. Nixon*, the 1974 Supreme Court decision requiring President Nixon to comply with a special prosecutor's subpoena for the Watergate tapes.[61] *Nixon* was the first Supreme Court decision to acknowledge the existence of a constitutionally protected executive privilege covering presidential communications. Earlier that year, Raoul Berger, a seminal figure in originalist constitutionalism had published a book, *Executive Privilege: A Constitutional Myth*, arguing on historical grounds that no such privilege for presidential confidentiality existed.[62]

Yet the Supreme Court upheld the executive privilege as a matter of general principle because of "the President's need for complete candor and objectivity from advisers."[63] It was feared such candor might be compromised if those advising the president anticipated "public dissemination of their remarks."[64] At the same time, the Court determined that the principle was not absolute: "The generalized assertion of privilege must yield to the demonstrated, specific need for evidence in a pending criminal trial."[65] The Court expressly reserved any question about the circumstances, if any, in which presidents could validly claim executive privilege against Congress.[66] Yet both Congress and Nixon's White House successors have interpreted the *Nixon* decision as stating a general principle of balancing.[67] That is, the president is entitled to the confidentiality of his discussions unless another branch of government has a "demonstrated, specific need" for the information in question in order to carry out its proper constitutional functions. Such a balancing test manages to underscore the importance of full and frank deliberation within the executive branch, while recognizing at the same time that disclosure of the communications at issue may be necessary to enable the courts or Congress to conduct the informed deliberations at the heart of their own respective constitutional functions.

DEMOCRACY THEN AND NOW

The general idea that courts should implement the Constitution with an eye toward perfecting or at least protecting the quality of representative democracy is not new. I have already cited the importance of that idea to the jurisprudence of the Warren Court. Yet as far back as one of the Marshall Court's most enduringly significant decisions—the 1819 case of *McCulloch v. Maryland*—the Court showed sensitivity to issues of representation.[68] *McCulloch* held it unconstitutional for individual states to tax federal entities like the National Bank of the United States. Part of the Court's reasoning was that, although the funds for paying such levies would dip into the pockets of the taxpaying voters of every state, the officials voting to impose the tax would represent only the voters from their own state.[69]

Such legislators would have no accountability for the costs imposed on the citizens of other states. For nearly a century, the Court has implemented the same idea in holding unconstitutional a wide variety of state regulations that affect interstate commerce, the costs of which fall disproportionately on out-of-state (and thus unrepresented) interests.[70]

In a similar vein, a famous 1938 footnote set forth a Supreme Court suggestion that legislation might receive more intense constitutional scrutiny if the challenged statutes were "directed at particular religious, or racial minorities."[71] The legislative process might have gone awry because "prejudice against discrete and insular minorities may be a special condition, which tends seriously to curtail the operation of those political processes ordinarily to be relied upon to protect minorities, and which may call for a correspondingly more searching judicial inquiry."[72] In other words, the unelected judiciary might have a special role in amplifying the voices of those whose political power is muted by the force of racism or other forms of bigotry. In 1980, the late John Hart Ely published *Democracy and Distrust: A Theory of Judicial Review*, which expanded on this idea, arguing that the judiciary should be especially protective of those individual rights that are critical to free and fair elections and should limit constitutional review on behalf of groups whose participation in elections was not limited by law.[73]

Scholars have also pressed the relevance of deliberative democracy to constitutional interpretation. Not long after the 1980 publication of a work by Joseph Bessette I cited earlier, the deliberation theme was picked up by legal scholar Cass Sunstein, whose work in both constitutional and administrative law has emphasized the Framers' hope that "the structure of government [would] lead political actors to pursue a general public good."[74] Courts, Sunstein argued, might opt in that spirit for doctrinal innovations designed "to ensure that what emerges" from the legislative process "is genuinely public rather than a reflection of existing relations of private power."[75] Sunstein cast his ideas as a variation on what he called the "republican" tradition of political thought in the founding era:

> Its animating principle was civic virtue. To the republicans, the prerequisite of sound government was the willingness of citizens to subordinate their private interests to the general good. Politics consisted of self-rule by the people; but it was not a scheme in which people impressed their private preferences on the government. It was instead a system in which the selection of preferences was the object of the governmental process.[76]

An influential article the following year by Harvard professor Frank Michelman termed this variation on early thought "civic republicanism."[77] And in 1992, law professor Mark Seidenfeld built on this line of thought to argue that civic republicanism provides a strong justification for what he variously calls the "bureaucratic" or "administrative" state. That is, well-structured administrative policymaking might best vindicate the belief of the "modern civic republicans" that the Constitution is "an attempt to ensure that government decisions are a product of deliberation that respects and reflects the values of all members of society."[78] A similar argument, recast explicitly in "deliberative democracy" terms and emphasizing the importance of reason giving, has more recently been made by Jerry Mashaw.[79]

Aside from a few scholars focused on administrative policy making, however, modern writers about deliberative democracy have mostly focused their pro-democracy prescriptions on the constitutional dimensions of individual rights, such as equal protection. There has been less writing on the importance of deliberative democracy for reshaping our constitutional understanding of the presidency or, indeed, reshaping our understanding of the basic enterprise of constitutional interpretation. Yet the need at this very moment to "democratize" our reading of the Constitution in general could hardly be greater. Democratic constitutionalism should involve the candid use of democratic values to resolve ambiguities in constitutional construction and should root the application of constitutional principles in an assessment of contemporary democratic needs.

The imperative to focus early twenty-first-century constitutional interpretation on strengthening democracy is as urgent as the late eighteenth- and early nineteenth-century imperative to focus constitutional interpretation on nation building. The Trump administration was both a symptom and an accelerator of democratic decline. Trump was relentless in attacking institutions that are the mainstays of pluralistic dialogue in the United States—the press, the courts, and any part of the civil service not utterly in thrall to his belligerent self-regard.[80] His resistance to Congress's oversight powers was unprecedented in scope. As noted above, the fundamental premise of democratic governance is equal respect for the interests of all citizens. Yet rather than cultivating unity and mutual acceptance, he "pitted us against one another along lines of race, sex, religion, citizenship, education, region, and—every day of his presidency—political party."[81]

But Trump was able to pursue so antidemocratic a course largely because he was plowing ground made fertile by four decades of ideological warfare, party polarization, expanding economic inequality, and the anti-democratic features built into the structure of our electoral politics, such as gerrymandering, the malapportionment of the Senate, and the operation of the electoral college. The weakening of democracy afflicts every level of government. States under the political control of a single party—most often, the Republicans—resolutely try to make it more difficult to vote and often push public policy decisions through a legislature without even a pretense of consideration for competing views. No doubt intensifying the weakening of democracy, local journalism and the accountability local reporters provide have been decimated since the 1990s.[82]

The 1980 election of Ronald Reagan followed and further energized a backlash against the liberalism of the 1960s and 1970s, which had seemed to run out of steam in the face of the 1970s' economic crises.[83] The consequent rise of neoliberalism in public policy led to a steady weakening of the public sector. The successor to Great Society liberalism was an extreme insistence that markets will outperform government and that individuals are entirely responsible for their own life opportunities. Neoliberals sold the idea, as explained by Ganesh Sitaraman, that "instead of governments, corporations, and unions balancing the interests of all stakeholders, the primary regulator of social interests should be the marketplace."[84] The steady defunding of government predictably undermined its competence, which not so coincidentally fed the neoliberal narrative of government-as-problem. The Trump administration's unprecedented nepotism and elevation of loyalty over ability made this trend worse—with deadly consequences in the mismanagement of the coronavirus pandemic.[85]

Neoliberalism undermined the very idea at the heart of Madisonian constitutionalism—the hope that government might be so organized as to champion a public interest above faction. Neoliberalism regards all interests as "special interests." In the eyes of neoliberalism, oil companies seeking protection from competition by sustainable fuels and women campaigning for affordable childcare are engaged in morally and civically equivalent phenomena. Neoliberal economics also ignores the economics of public goods, most especially the importance of non-market-based support for assets like national defense or public health—goods from which individuals can benefit without reducing their availability to others and from which no one can be excluded.[86] Such goods cannot be efficiently priced, which means that private firms cannot maximize profits by investing in their creation. Over-reliance on markets inevitably thus leads to their underproduction. Since

1980, the weakening of the public sector resulting from such underinvestment has been exacerbated as the philosophy of private-sector supremacy has empowered business interests "to strip-mine public assets for the benefit of private interests."[87]

Political polarization has deepened as neoliberalism has intensified economic inequality and as national leaders have played on people's resentments. The George W. Bush administration squandered a moment of intense national unity following September 11 in pursuit of its highly partisan Iraq war policy. Alienation on the right fed by economic and cultural resentment has been matched by alienation on the left fed by the ability of those in power to dodge accountability for their disastrous decision-making, whether it be the invasion of Iraq and the consequent destabilization of the entire Middle East or the subprime mortgage debacle that fueled the economic recession of 2008.

Leadership in a polity so polarized is unlikely to honor the democratic imperative of equal consideration for all. And for the individual citizen, both the formal manipulation of political institutions—by gerrymandering, for example—and the seeming remoteness of the technocratic state may well combine to defeat any feeling of authentic political efficacy. Regarding the current predicament of the administrative state, political economist William Davies has written: "The civil and gentlemanly dimension of expert knowledge never includes everyone as a participant, and can be actively oppressive. . . . Even if people don't feel violently oppressed, they often feel belittled and irrelevant to the style of knowledge being generated by economists, statisticians, and financial reporters."[88] Whether caused by these circumstances or simply coincident with them, research suggests we may be living in a time when "only a small fraction of Americans prioritize democratic principles in their electoral choices when doing so goes against their partisan affiliation or favorite policies."[89] That is, despite their professed devotion to democracy, voters may elevate candidates who suit their political agenda over politicians who take positions supportive of "core democratic principles, including free and fair elections, civil liberties, and checks and balances."[90]

Pro-democracy constitutional interpretation cannot by itself solve all these problems any more than John Marshall's iconic decisions could assure a strong foundation for a fledgling national government. What these challenges demonstrate, however, is the primacy that democracy deserves at this moment among the values competing for constitutional prominence. Indeed, if the resolution of constitutional disputes requires interpreters to identify "the spirit of the Constitution," it is conspicuous not only how deeply the Framers worried about the quality of representative accountability, but also how much of the formal amendment process from 1789 forward has been devoted to perfecting democracy. The First Amendment protects the press, as well as rights of expression and association that are central to democratic governance. The Twelfth Amendment fixed the most immediate problems with the electoral college system. The Civil War Amendments (Thirteenth, Fourteenth, and Fifteenth) ended slavery, guaranteed due process and equal protection, and prohibited voting discrimination based on race. The Seventeenth Amendment established popular election for the Senate. The Nineteenth guaranteed women's suffrage. The Twenty-Second Amendment eliminated any authoritarian threat that might have been posed by future breaches of the presidential two-term limit norm. The Twenty-Third Amendment enfranchised citizens of the District of Columbia in presidential elections. The Twenty-Fourth ended poll taxes in federal elections. The Twenty-Sixth reduced the voting age to eighteen. All in all, eleven of the Constitution's twenty-seven amendments were designed explicitly to strengthen or expand our democratic institutions. The very text of the Constitution has moved steadily in the direction of greater democracy. If good faith constitutional interpretation in the "construction zone" entails recourse to the "spirit of the Constitution," it is hard to gainsay that the quality of democratic governance is at the heart of that spirit.

Prioritizing current democratic need over "original public meaning," when they conflict, is not to say that the past is no source of guidance in responding to contemporary challenges. The problems of twenty-first-century democracy are not wholly unrelated to the dilemmas facing eighteenth-century Americans in the design of republican institutions. Institutional practices that have worked well for decades, if not centuries, should enjoy a presumption of acceptability. How our forebears thought about and reacted to the challenges of sound governance may certainly teach us lessons.

But we must be aware that what we mean by democratic inclusion today is not how democracy was understood in the early Republic. Summing up the work of fellow legal historians Gerald Leonard and Saul Cornell, as well as reflecting her own ongoing research, Mary Sarah Bilder describes the populist ferment of the early nineteenth century as marking "the unsettling transformation of [an] aristocratic-tinged constitutional republic into a partisan white male democracy."[91] As Leonard and Cornell recount, "The ascendancy of democratic ideology and the expansion of political rights among white men in the Jacksonian period rested on an explicitly racist [and we might add sexist] understanding of civic capacity, not on a truly universalist egalitarianism."[92]

Twenty-first-century democratic constitutionalism thus aligns as an abstract matter with the Framers' preoccupation with government by and for "We, the People," but it is not backward looking in its search for legitimacy. It is an attempt to candidly resolve constitutional ambiguity by acknowledging our most pressing contemporary constitutional needs.

The next chapter lays out what I take to be the implications of democratic constitutionalism for those issues concerning the presidency that I highlighted in chapters 2 and 3 regarding control of the bureaucracy. It also explores other separation of powers controversies and investigates both the strengths and limits of the democratic approach. Intriguingly, when pressed for a normative defense of presidentialism that resonates in contemporary needs, presidentialists also stress democracy. Yet the next chapter will also show that the link of presidentialism to democracy is mostly an illusion, as is the claim that presidentialism is simply following a "dead" constitutional text.

PART THREE

Democracy's Chief Executive

SIX

Democracy's Presidency

SHOULD DEMOCRATIC CONSTITUTIONALISM become the lens through which we view the presidency, we would not read Article II as a charter for the "entitled executive" that four decades of aggressive presidentialism have produced. A democratic constitutionalist approach would instead prioritize two key, intertwined values in resolving the construction of ambiguous constitutional text regarding the distribution of government powers. One of those values is the preference for more inclusive democratic deliberation both within and among the branches of government. Ordinarily, the more transparent the deliberation, the better. The second value is the rule of law, which implies preeminent concerns for accountability and reasoned decision-making. Democratic constitutionalism would also be hospitable to respecting long-standing patterns of interbranch interaction in deciding on questions regarding the scope of presidential and congressional power. Accommodations reached by elected representatives of "the people" deserve a presumption of respect. That respect, however, should not always freeze in place patterns of interaction that could be improved through more inclusive deliberation, reasoned decision-making, and accountability. A key constitutional premise—that Congress makes law and the executive branch faithfully implements law—remains as a limit on the interbranch accommodations that are permissible.

In many instances, democratic constitutionalism's answer to questions of Article II interpretation will resemble the answers that other approaches yield. For example, in some respects, democratic constitutionalists would reach the same answers as textualists because the constitutional text is in some key details unambiguous—the length of the president's term, the existence (if not boundaries) of some specific Article II powers, and the age and citizenship requirements to be president, for example. Language would also preclude us from trying out some institutional innovations, such as a separately elected attorney general, which, however desirable, would be irreconcilable with the text.[1]

Some issues would also be resolved just as historically competent original-ists would prefer. That is because some of the problems facing contemporary democracy resonate strongly in the challenges confronting the founding generation, and it is unsurprising that we would meet them similarly. For example, as I discuss further below, both originalism and democratic con-stitutionalism argue for a broad reading of impeachable "high crimes and misdemeanors," not limited by the terms of the federal criminal code. On a number of key questions, however, democratic constitutionalism points readily toward constitutional readings that originalists would likely resist. An example is the permissibility of presidents entering into international agree-ments authorized by majorities of the House and Senate, not two-thirds of the Senate alone.

Following some discussion of our democracy's current institutional needs, this chapter tours the separation-of-powers disputes of recent decades to draw a portrait of a small-d democratic presidency. The picture differs from the one drawn by our post-Reagan aggressive presidentialists. Even where original-ism and democratic constitutionalism point to similar conclusions, the path from democratic constitutionalism to sensible contemporary interpretation is shorter, and its normative underpinnings clearer and more compelling.

THE NEEDS OF DEMOCRACY

Before getting down to cases, it is important to be more concrete about what it means to strengthen democracy. If American democracy were solely a form of electoral democracy, we might be content with Robert Dahl's catalog of six political institutions required by large-scale democracy. These are:

1. Elected officials;
2. Free, fair, and frequent elections;
3. Freedom of expression;

4. Alternative sources of information;

5. Associational autonomy; and

6. Inclusive citizenship.[2]

Dahl's list encompasses the democratically representative decision makers themselves, the processes by which they are chosen, and an array of individual rights that are necessary for "the people" genuinely to control the policy-making agenda and to participate effectively as well-informed voters.

To achieve the yet more complex form of hybrid democracy to which the United States aspires, however, requires two other kinds of institutions, as well. That is because democracy cannot draw sustenance from periodic elections alone. One is the opportunity between elections for genuine policy dialogue both within and outside government. The more deliberation is required within and among the branches of government in order to make policy, the more opportunities will exist for interested citizens to interject their views into those deliberations. In this way, deliberation is advanced both by the constitutional checks and balances design—features such as bicameralism, the veto power, and judicial review—and by the processes Congress has set up for both its internal decision-making (e.g., hearings) and for decision-making by the executive branch (e.g., notice-and-comment rulemaking).

The second indispensable institution is the rule of law itself. Certain procedural and substantive elements will characterize any plausible version of what constitutes "rule of law," even if as a concept it may be highly contested.[3] A rule of law regime must be "regular," in the sense of preventing officials from exercising power at mere whim, and "public," which means that the law must be accessible to those obliged to follow it.[4] In Paul Gowder's thoughtful account, what ties the rule of law to democracy is also a requirement of "generality" in the formulation and execution of law. That is, whether in drafting law or in exercising enforcement discretion, officials "must treat like cases and individuals alike, treating them differently only if there is a relevant distinction between them."[5] In this way, the rule of law helps to fulfill democracy's promises of equal respect for the interests of all.[6]

The legal philosopher Jeremy Waldron has further articulated a version of the rule of law that is especially apt given the realities of public administration. Our constitutional system is one in which both elected officials and the appointees they supervise frequently enjoy significant discretion that is not bound by hard bright-line rules. Such discretion may even be critical in relatively low-visibility bureaucratic settings, which means that officials can often exercise their discretion without any real expectation of sanction for illegality. In such settings

> the Rule of Law consists in issues being settled by ... legal processes, procedures of deliberation and reason-giving that are focused on antecedent legal materials rather than political advantage, and in a form of deference on the part of the contesting parties that is motivated by the stake they have, along with their fellow citizens, in the integrity of the legal and constitutional order.[7]

Under this conception of the rule of law, legal interpretation becomes a form of inter-temporal dialogue, a way of assuring those democratic decisions made by the people's representatives at Time 1 are not ignored when relevant at Time 2. When executive branch lawyers attend to statutes conscientiously, they bring to bear multiple politically accountable voices of earlier times. These earlier lawmakers themselves had to reach consensus in order to create binding rules. Attending thoughtfully at a later moment to their handiwork can thus bring to bear a range of interests and concerns that might not otherwise be vigorously articulated, much less treated as binding, when key decisions are made now. Attending to these voices through professionally recognized forms of interpretation is a critical way in which government officials and their lawyers breathe life into the rule of law.[8] At the same time, such attention can also shed light on those voices that may have been ignored or subordinated in the making of law. Knowledge of such exclusion can come into play in deciding how ambiguities in the law ought today to be interpreted.

The rule of law on which democracy depends is dependent in part on the quality of formal institutions, such as judicial review or resort to the Office of Legal Counsel. But as I wrote in my 2009 book, *Madison's Nightmare*, for such an account of the rule of law to be plausible, "the written documents of law must be buttressed by a set of norms, conventional expectations, and routine behaviors that lead officials to behave as if they are accountable to the public interest and to legitimate sources of legal and political authority."[9] In a checks-and-balances system, democracy-reinforcing norms, cooperative arrangements, and informal coordination activities are as important as formal rules. A persistent question for democratic constitutionalists faced with separation-of-powers questions will thus be, "What are the institutional designs most likely to support both the structured and unstructured institutions of democratic life?"

Presidentialists have responded to this argument by stressing what they believe is the democratic pedigree of their own view of the Constitution. Steven Calabresi, a cofounder of the Federalist Society and arguably the scholar most important to the modern efflorescence of unitary executive theory, stated the key premise of the argument in an article written over twenty-five years ago: "The President is unique in our constitutional system as being the only official who is accountable to a national voting electorate and no one else."[10] From this fact, two related virtues supposedly follow. One is that presidents are uniquely situated to focus their decision-making on the national interest, as opposed to the interests of particular states or even smaller congressional districts. Further, because of this supposed accountability to the national electorate, the president is uniquely positioned to help counter what James Madison called the spirit of "faction." Madison famously wrote: "By a faction, I understand a number of citizens, whether amounting to a majority or a minority of the whole, who are united and actuated by some common impulse of passion, or of interest, adverse to the rights of other citizens, or to the permanent and aggregate interests of the community."[11] The president, purportedly representing the interests of all, is supposedly less likely to be corrupted by faction. As hypothesized by Professor Calabresi, "A foreign or domestic faction (or interest group) will find it far more costly to 'purchase' the President and his national constituency than it would be for such a faction (or interest group) to purchase some much smaller, more regional constituency."[12]

This argument, unfortunately, does not bear out in practice.[13] Presidents, as shown by political scientists, are "like members of Congress in that they too seek 'particularistic' policies favoring one region or constituency at the cost of the whole."[14] In our current moment of political polarization, it is easy to see why. We do not actually have a national election for president, but fifty-one elections in the states and D.C. to choose electors from each jurisdiction. All but two states have winner-take-all systems, and most states are so predictably Republican or Democratic in their leanings that presidential candidates (and presidents) need not concern themselves much with their votes. The focus is instead on "battleground" states, which pose for presidents an ever-present temptation of favoritism in the competition for governmental largesse.

As far as the president's "uniqueness" in having a national perspective "above faction," the presidentialist argument mistakenly compares the position of the president to that of individual representatives or even congressional committees. Legislative decisions must win the favor of a majority, at least, in each House of Congress. Individual members of Congress may well be parochial in their allegiances, but there is no a priori reason why Congress, as a collectivity, is less likely than the president to balance competing concerns in a way that reflects the national interest. What is notable, however, is that even a presidentialist like Calabresi looks to democratic accountability as the modern source of normative legitimacy for his theory of executive power. Democratic constitutionalism responds to a set of values that nearly all positions on the political spectrum purport to embrace.

THE DOMESTIC PRESIDENCY

Our tour of the small-d democratic presidency can begin by reviewing some of the issues that have provoked separation-of-powers controversies concerning the "domestic presidency." On the domestic front, the questions that go most directly to the heart of presidentialism involve the president's supervisory authority over the rest of the executive branch. Is it unconstitutional, as presidentialists insist, for Congress to insulate federal officers from at-will removability by the president? May the president take over and perform personally the statutory duties Congress has assigned to other officers? May the president command how other officers exercise whatever policy discretion is entailed in fulfilling those duties? Presidentialists answer all three questions affirmatively.

Chapter 4 debunked on originalist grounds the presidentialists' supposedly originalist case for their position. Despite the Roberts Court's insistence otherwise, the founding generation would likely not have understood the executive power as guaranteeing the president unlimited removal authority over administrative officials; statutes conditioning removal on something like "inefficiency, neglect, or malfeasance" fully respect the president's duty to take care that the laws be faithfully executed and do not deprive the president of powers that Article II originally enshrined.

But democratic constitutionalism points with yet greater firmness toward this conclusion. That is because an executive branch focused entirely on the policy predilections of a single individual, with officials regarding themselves as extensions of the president's will and not as responsible actors in their own right, is likely to be an executive branch in which policy dialogue is stunted and relatively nontransparent. In the realm of foreign affairs and war powers, where the historical case for presidential command is arguably greatest, episode after episode shows the dangers of too tightly controlled a deliberative environment—from Vietnam,[15] to Iraq,[16] to Libya.[17] The tighter a president's control over subordinates, the less incentive there is for administrators to speak freely and to listen to voices other than those coming out of the White House.[18] A pluralistic environment for executive-branch policy making is more likely to support vigorous, open, and reasoned dialogue between government agencies and the constituencies most directly affected by their work.[19] And the more loci that exist for meaningful policy input, the more opportunities are presented for members of the public to influence policy outputs.

Even when Congress does not protect an officer from at-will removability, there is no reason to interpret Article II as giving the president complete policy command over agencies in which Congress has vested specific statutory duties. The president's influence will inevitably be significant; agencies are headed by political appointees the resident has selected. In cases of genuine impasse with an appointee dischargeable at will, however, it ought to be understood that the president's choices are limited to accepting the officer's preferred course of action or replacing that officer and shouldering whatever political repercussions follow. Even Andrew Jackson thought as much.[20] Conflicts of that magnitude will likely be rare, but themselves can give rise to appropriate dialogue between the political branches, both to investigate the conflict and to review the president's choice of a new nominee.

There is a natural fit between the presidentialists' assertions as to the broad scope of Article II executive power and an equally formalist assertion as to the limited scope of Congress's Article I legislative powers. The latter position typically takes two forms. One, for which Justice Clarence Thomas has become the most prominent judicial advocate, is that the Supreme Court should resurrect what originalists take to be the limited meanings of Article I's categories of legislative authority. The prime target is Congress's power to "regulate Commerce ... among the several states."[21] As interpreted by the Supreme Court, this power over interstate commerce comprises authority to "regulate the use of the channels of interstate commerce . . . , to regulate and protect the instrumentalities of interstate commerce, or persons or things in interstate commerce, even though the threat may come only from intra-state activities," and "to regulate those activities having a substantial relation to interstate commerce, i.e., those activities that substantially affect interstate commerce."[22] This broad construction has been sufficient to uphold federal legislation concerning civil rights, environmental protection, and even a good deal of criminal activity also subject to control by the states. For his part, Justice Thomas would prefer to interpret "regulat[ing] commerce" as confined to legislation regarding "selling, buying, and bartering, as well as transporting for these purposes,"[23] thus abandoning the "substantial relation to interstate commerce test." In his view, a broad construction is belied by the fact that, "despite being well aware that agriculture, manufacturing, and other matters substantially affected commerce, the founding generation did not cede authority over all these activities to Congress."[24] Even the current very conservative Supreme Court majority, however, seems little inclined to go so far.

Where the Court's current composition makes significant movement more plausible, however, is with regard to what administrative lawyers call "the nondelegation doctrine." This is the rule that Congress may not enact statutes delegating to the executive branch so limitless a scope for administrative policy making that Congress has effectively abdicated the legislative power which is constitutionally vested only in the legislative branch. Conversely, as understood by the Court, "a statutory delegation is constitutional as long as Congress 'lay[s] down by legislative act an intelligible principle to which the person or body authorized to [exercise the delegated authority] is directed to conform.'"[25] This test has been interpreted with sufficient laxness that only two statutes have ever been overturned as so lacking in standards as to be unconstitutional; both were voided in 1935.[26] By contrast, the Court has upheld statutes that, for example, allow broadcast licenses to be issued consistent with the "public interest, convenience, or necessity,"[27] or allow the setting of commodity prices that are "fair and equitable."[28] As a consequence, Congress has been able to vest authority in the executive branch to enact a far larger volume of specific rules for the governance of private activity than Congress itself now enacts on an annual basis.[29] It is a fair statement that it is the nondelegation doctrine that has allowed Congress to give shape to the contemporary administrative state.

An early opinion by Justice Gorsuch, however, which Chief Justice Roberts and Justice Thomas both joined, argued that the Court should dramatically tighten up its approach. The anti-delegation justices would allow Congress to confer authority on administrative agencies only to "fill up the details" for policies significantly specified by statute, to engage in the threshold fact-finding that would trigger a statute's operation, or to perform functions that are simply not legislative in character.[30] Depending on how such an approach is implemented, the tighter constraint on delegation could eviscerate much of the regulatory activity in which the federal government has engaged since the 1960s.[31]

Professor Prakash, whose work on originalism I have mentioned earlier, has not explicitly endorsed the Gorsuch view, although he says he "shares [the] misgivings" of "some who doubt the constitutionality of the countless delegations of legislative power that litter the US code."[32] This is not surprising. As an originalist who sees in the 1787 document a formalist division between legislative, executive, and judicial powers, Prakash insists that many of the rules agencies make are "just laws by another name."[33] The "nebulous generalities," he says, that satisfy the Supreme Court's current nondelegation test, "impose no real limits on the delegations to agencies,"[34] with the consequence that Congress is abdicating lawmaking power.

Whether originalism, pursued rigorously, condemns the nondelegation doctrine turns out, however, to be a controversial question. Law professors Julian Davis Mortenson and Nicholas Bagley have argued that, at the founding, "there was no constitutional problem with delegating the authority to make rules so long as Congress did not irrevocably alienate its power to legislate."[35] In their view, the Framers would have had nothing in mind like the nondelegation doctrine in either the conventional form or the version championed by Justice Gorsuch. Challenging them, Professor Ilan Wurman argues that it was the Framers' view that "Congress could not delegate its legislative power to the Executive."[36] He states his conclusion, however, with some caution:

> Although the history is messy, there is significant evidence that the Founding generation adhered to a nondelegation doctrine, and little evidence that clearly supports the proposition that the Founding generation believed that Congress could freely delegate its legislative power.[37]

Wurman's riposte, however, has suffered an implicit and compelling surrebuttal from legal historian Nicholas Parrillo.[38] Parrillo has rediscovered the vast and largely unconstrained rulemaking power that Congress authorized when it enacted the "direct tax" of 1798. As Parrillo explains, the taxing scheme erected by Congress depended on the rulemaking activities of federal administrative boards created in every state to insure that assessors' valuations of real estate would "'appear to be just and equitable'—a phrase undefined in the statute and not a term of art."[39] Not only was rulemaking by the federal boards largely discretionary, hugely impactful, and beyond judicial review, but it was "accepted as constitutional by the Federalist majority and Jeffersonian opposition in 1798 and also by the Jeffersonians when they later took over."[40] Such agreement is powerful evidence either that "the boards' power was consistent with original meaning," or that, over a short period of time, the Constitution's meaning came to be settled in a manner embodied in the practice.[41] As Parrillo observes: "Vesting administrators with discretionary power to make politically-charged rules domestically affecting private rights was not alien to the first generation of lawmakers who put the Constitution into practice."

The debate among these first-rate scholars, although fascinating, helps to illustrate what is bizarre about using originalism as the primary guide to constitutional interpretation. What is at stake is the capacity of our national government in the twenty-first century to address regulatory issues that are critical to public health and social welfare. Regulation is needed to:

- reduce negative spillover costs that parties to market exchanges don't bear fully, such as pollution; ...

- regulate the market to protect consumers and investors—both from corporate predation (collusion, fraud, harm) and from individuals' own myopic behavior (smoking, failing to save, underestimating economic risks);

- provide or require certain insurance protections, notably against the costs of health care and inadequate retirement income; and

- soften the business cycle and reduce the risk of financial crises.[42]

Crippling the regulatory process through too great a constraint on congressional delegation could undermine both American prosperity and our collective capacity to combat such urgent problems as climate change. It seems all but insane to decide that Congress's capacity to create administrative programs depends on whether the balance of "equivocal" and "unequivocal" evidence" regarding eighteenth-century understanding of an eighteenth-century text leans more in one direction or the other, especially if ambiguities in the evidence "preclude any kind of categorical conclusion." In the hands of judges, who are, of course, not trained historians and who possess no special competence at judging historical evidence, it is all too likely that ambiguities in the historical record will simply be resolved in whatever direction is consistent with the judges' personal ideology or philosophical inclinations.[43] The exercise is likely to be shallow, tendentious, and oblivious to what is practically at stake.

Democratic constitutionalism points decisively to the right answer here: within extremely broad limits, it should be up to Congress to decide the scope of authority properly handed to administrative bodies to deal with regulatory issues. As Jerry Mashaw has forcefully contended, the democratic pedigree of the modern federal administrative establishment is at least as strong as that of Congress itself. Agencies, he argues, operate under a system of "'reasoned administration,' [which] may provide the most democratic form of governance available to us in a modern, complex, and deeply compromised political world."[44] Unlike legislators, administrative rule makers must not only engage in a dialogue with the public about the content of rules, but must explain in transparent terms how they have or have not responded to the issues that members of the public have brought to their attention. They must explain themselves with sufficient clarity to persuade the public and often a reviewing court that they understand the goals they are pursuing, that they grasp the state of the world and how it falls short of Congress's goals, that their proposed initiatives conform to the relevant statutory criteria for action, and that their initiatives can reasonably be expected to promote the relevant goals, given the facts as currently known.[45] The combination of accountability to elected policy makers and the demand that administrators exercise power on the basis of knowledge thus respects both the majoritarian and deliberative sides of American democracy."[46] However imperfect the system, it aspires to a form "of administrative governance that is well-informed, highly participatory, complexly interconnected with political and legal monitors, and insulated against (although surely not immune from) the seizure of power for private or partisan advantage."[47]

Professor Prakash's anxiety about this system, however, is not rooted solely in formalist constitutional theory. Although he champions the presidentialist claim of complete bureaucratic control, he sees the source of dangerously burgeoning presidential power not in Article II, but in the breadth of Congress's delegations of administrative authority. Presidents, he points out, not only exploit the "letter" of such broad delegations but go beyond them through methods of statutory interpretation that ignore congressional intent. Presidents are reinforced in this tendency by Congress's typical failure to react critically in response. Later presidents cite apparent acquiescence by the legislative branch in their predecessors' generous statutory interpretations as confirming the accuracy of those interpretations. Prakash argues that attributing to the president comprehensive at-will firing authority and the power to command all subordinates in the exercise of their discretion would make the president a far less powerful figure if Congress simply conferred less discretionary authority on the executive branch.[48]

Professor Prakash's stance is analytically coherent, but unattractive from the standpoint of democracy. After all, the converse of the Prakash position is also coherent, namely, broad delegations of discretionary regulatory power to agencies would portend far less of a risk of authoritarianism if the president were not deemed to have comprehensive firing authority and constitutionally vested power to command how all discretionary decisions are made within the executive branch. The stance I am advocating—allowing Congress broad authority to delegate but giving administrators some degree of independence from direct presidential command—is doubly sound for democracy. By accommodating both the pro-delegation decisions of elected Congresses and the capacity of elected presidents to influence, even if not command, how subordinates make decisions, this understanding of separation-of-powers doctrine gives weight to the force of electoral democracy. In accepting the legitimacy of administrative rulemaking, however, especially as disciplined by requirements of administrative reason giving, my interpretation also aligns regulatory policy making with the aspirations of deliberative democracy. This is not to deny Professor Prakash's observation that any president sitting atop a highly empowered administrative establishment will have the potential to be a strong president, but a strong presidency need not be authoritarian. That is the argument I am making.

Congress's authority to create independent agencies should be understood also to extend to the chartering of independent officers within the executive branch charged with conducting audits and investigations of executive branch performance. Such officers are currently referred to as inspectors general, and Congress categorically permits their removal by the president.[49] Instead of restricting the president's power to removal for good cause, Congress has so far required only that the president communicate to Congress, in writing, the reasons for any such removal at least thirty days before the removal takes effect.[50] Congress imposed this requirement in the apparent hope that demanding a presidential statement of reasons would elicit a sufficiently specific statement to both discipline presidents from springing to dismissals too readily and give Congress, in cases of removal, an adequate basis for oversight. Trump, however, disappointed any such hope. He repeatedly fired inspectors general who had released findings embarrassing to the administration; Trump informed Congress only that he no longer possessed the "fullest confidence" in the IGs thus removed.[51] In the name of faithful execution of the laws—an indispensable element of democratic accountability—Congress should be allowed to go further to protect IGs from arbitrary discharge.[52]

Going beyond civil contexts, it is also especially important to recognize the danger in treating presidents as having comprehensive personal control over the machinery of criminal prosecution. The idea that the Constitution would protect the president's discretion to corruptly obstruct the criminal investigation of his own conduct and that of his family and associates is so obviously repugnant to concern for the rule of law that the centrality of the rule of law to democratic constitutionalism should be enough to settle the point.

Chapter 3 highlighted other issues regarding the domestic presidency worthy of brief review. For example, the Supreme Court's decision in *Lucia v. SEC* threatens to generate a politicization of administrative adjudication by requiring agency heads who are political appointees to involve themselves directly in the selection of administrative law judges (ALJs).[53] Yet Congress structured the ALJ system in the precise hope of depoliticizing administrative adjudication by reducing the appearance of partiality when an agency directly appoints the judges who adjudicate its disputes. Fights on this issue have centered on whether ALJs in various contexts are "officers." The implication is that agency heads authorized by statute to appoint inferior "officers" may not constitutionally subdelegate that authority within their agencies to place it in more independent hands. Democratic constitutionalism suggests precisely the opposite result. In the name of the rule of law, a policy like the SEC's, under which ALJ selection was delegated to a subordinate employee, should be counted as satisfying the Article II appointments requirement so long as the delegation does not appear to be irrevocable and the individuals appointed are engaged entirely in adjudicatory functions.

Chapter 3 also reviewed the use of presidential executive orders to centralize oversight of government regulation in the Office of Management and Budget. The president's constitutional entitlement to seek information from the heads of executive agencies and the obligation to take care that the laws be faithfully executed anticipate some significant role for the president in managing the executive branch. That role, in turn, legitimates require-ments that agencies report to the White House on how their initiatives fare under the administration's favored rubrics for policy analysis, including cost-benefit analysis. Democratic constitutionalism requires, however, that requirements for reporting and analysis not be administered in ways that undermine any agency's legally vested authority. The process should leave unimpaired each agency's capacity to pursue Congress's regulatory aims in a manner that respects both public input and an appropriate role for exper-tise in decision-making. The Reagan, Clinton, and Obama executive orders on federal regulation went as far as is constitutionally permissible in these respects; the Trump order requiring agencies to identify rules for revocation as a condition for issuing new rules and to observe an OMB-imposed ceil-ing for the aggregate annual cost of their regulatory initiatives was uncon-stitutional—and revoked by President Biden on the day he took office.[54] Without statutory authority for OMB that Congress has not yet enacted, a president undermines democratic policy making by requiring agencies to adhere to policy making criteria that are simply not sanctioned by the respective agencies' organic and authorizing statutes.

Among the recent presidential innovations in asserting more aggressive control over the bureaucracy, chapter 3 reviewed the use of presidential sign-ing statements—declarations offered by presidents upon signing statutes into law that also purport to object to the constitutionality of portions of those statutes. Such statements arguably augment the democratic process of interbranch dialogue and permit greater oversight of the executive branch by both Congress and the public.[55] What was objectionable in their use, espe-cially in the George W. Bush and Trump administrations, was the dubious constitutional theories they often proffered.[56] Moreover, the sheer volume of such statements[57] may generate a dangerous organizational psychology among executive branch lawyers to resist every imaginable limitation on presidential prerogative, no matter how inconsequential, and to minimize the core presidential obligation of faithful execution of Congress's legislative directions.[58]

A final set of bureaucratic moves especially worrisome from a democratic constitutionalist standpoint are presidential efforts to avoid the Senate confirmation process. The Senate's success in using so-called "pro forma sessions" to forestall excessive use of the recess appointments power is inadequate to keep a determined president from working around the need for Senate confirmation. Chapter 3 recounted Trump's aggressiveness using "acting administrators" to fill positions that would normally require Senate confirmation for presidential appointees—known to D.C. lawyers as PAS positions. For example, the Defense Department was headed by acting secretaries for over half of 2019.[59] Acting secretaries headed the Department of Homeland Security for over half of Trump's four years in office; there was no confirmed secretary later than April 10, 2019.[60] As also recounted in chapter 3, Trump brought in the politically loyal director of the Office of Management and Budget to serve simultaneously as acting head of the Consumer Finance Protection Bureau.[61] He appointed as acting attorney general a Justice Department lawyer who had held no prior PAS position in the Trump administration at all.[62]

Nonetheless, how Congress should protect the Senate's constitutional authority presents complicated issues. A president's ability to appoint acting administrators is often critical to effective government. As described in a report of the Administrative Conference of the United States, "Vacancies in PAS and other high-level positions may lead to agency inaction, generate confusion among nonpolitical personnel, and lessen public accountability."[63] The problem is chronic at the start of a new administration, when there has presumably been a complete changeover in cabinet positions and many other top agency posts. It is also typical for many PAS officers to leave their positions before the end of a presidential term, which could leave an agency in limbo for months.[64]

To facilitate an appropriate use of acting administrators, Congress enacted the Federal Vacancies Reform Act of 1998.[65] For most agencies, the Vacancies Act "specifies who can serve in an acting capacity, for how long, and in what positions."[66] Congress sometimes provides also in an agency-specific statute the order of succession that should be followed in cases of vacancy. The Justice Department has taken the position that, unless an agency-specific statute explicitly makes its order of succession exclusive, the president has the option of following either the agency-specific statute or the generic Vacancies Act.[67] The terms of the Vacancies Act are generous enough to presidents to permit the unconventional uses of acting administrators that Trump especially seemed to prefer. The Trump administration demonstrated the capacity of norms-challenging presidents to significantly reduce the Senate's advice-and-consent role by exploiting the Act's broad grants of presidential discretion.

One can thus imagine congressional efforts to modify the Federal Vacancies Reform Act to disincentivize presidential efforts to evade the Senate's confirmation authority. One obvious change would be an amendment providing that the Act was not to be used to replace the head of any agency that is explicitly governed by a statute specifying the order of succession for that agency. Another would be to make clear that the Act is not available for choosing acting administrators to replace administrators that the president has fired. A third would clarify that acting appointees chosen for positions ordinarily protected against at-will discharge—recall that Congress allows some agency heads to be discharged only for inefficiency, negligence, malfeasance, or other good cause—enjoy similar protection until either their terms expire or they are replaced by Senate-confirmed appointees. The latter two sorts of limitations might elicit presidentialist objections that such limits would somehow burden constitutionally vested presidential authority to fire administrative officials. From a democratic constitutionalist point of view, however, all would be permissible efforts to reinforce the necessity for interbranch dialogue in the appointment of principal officers in the executive branch.

THE GLOBAL PRESIDENCY

Of course, domestic policy making is hardly the only context in which recent presidents have raised difficult constitutional issues concerning their exercise of power. Presidents since World War II have deployed military force and conducted foreign policy with conspicuous unilateralism. The few constitutional challenges to reach the Supreme Court have produced mixed results, sometimes affirming the role of both Congress and the judiciary in checking and balancing executive initiative,[68] but sometimes reaffirming the breadth of presidential discretion.[69] Especially from the perspective of deliberative democracy, it is remarkable how little genuine policy dialogue outside the executive branch is currently required in establishing the global posture of the United States.

Regarding war powers, it might well be said that presidents have followed a particular variety of living constitutionalism, but not one guided by democratic aims. Scholars often treat the Korean War as the pivotal moment.[70] On his own initiative, President Truman bombed North Korea and deployed two army divisions to help repel an invasion of South Korea by the North. His moves were unproblematic under international law; the young United Nations Security Council had issued a resolution asking member states to assist the South. U.S. participation on the South Korean side was thus consistent with the United Nations Treaty. What Truman lacked was any kind of congressional approval. Claiming he did not need it, he referred to the military conflict as a "police action" and insisted we were not formally at war.[71] The lack of explicit authorization, however, was likely decisive in the Supreme Court's rejection in the famous *Youngstown* case of Truman's attempted takeover of the steel mills to assure a continued flow of materiel to support the Korean war effort.[72]

In the wake of *Youngstown*, presidents since Truman have not tried to engage the United States in land wars on this scale without at least some modicum of congressional approval.[73] But they have evolved a doctrine under which there is virtually no limit on military deployments of lesser scope.

Textually, what is at stake is the allocation of military authorities rooted in Articles I and II of the Constitution. Article II names the president "commander in chief of the Army and Navy of the United States, and of the militia of the several states, when called into the actual service of the United States."[74] Congress, for its part, is empowered by half a dozen Article I clauses explicitly referring to military affairs, specifically the powers:

1. To declare war, grant letters of marque and reprisal, and make rules concerning captures on land and water;

2. To raise and support armies, [provided] no appropriation of money to that use shall be for a longer term than two years;

3. To provide and maintain a navy;

4. To make rules for the government and regulation of the land and naval forces;

5. To provide for calling forth the militia to execute the laws of the union, suppress insurrections and repel invasions; and

6. To provide for organizing, arming, and disciplining, the militia, and for governing such part of them as may be employed in the service of the United States, reserving to the states respectively, the appointment of the officers, and the authority of training the militia according to the discipline prescribed by Congress.[75]

Given what seems on its face to be Congress's far weightier and more extensive military authorities, one might guess that the deployment of military force would always—at least in cases short of invasion—require advance legislative authorization. That is not how matters stand.

In April 2018, the Trump Administration engaged in the bombing of Syria in response to a chemical weapons attack allegedly sponsored by the Syrian government.[76] In a memorandum supporting the legality of the attack, OLC laid out the all-but-limitless authority presidents currently claim under Article II to deploy military force without prior congressional authorization.[77] Unlike its claims in domestic authority, however, the Trump administration's war powers claims were not innovative. The Obama administration's view was nearly identical[78] and itself represented what was essentially the view of the George W. Bush administration before it.[79]

The presidentialist war powers doctrine comes down to this: "The President, as Commander in Chief and Chief Executive, has the constitutional authority to deploy the military to protect American persons and interests without seeking prior authorization from Congress."[80] Such authority exists so long as the military deployment falls short of the kind of "war" that, pursuant to the Declare War Clause, only Congress may sanction. To qualify as a "war" requiring congressional authorization, the military action must amount to "a sustained, full-scale conflict with another Nation."[81] For more "limited hostilities," the "President's authority to direct U.S. military forces arises from Article II of the Constitution, which makes the President the 'Commander in Chief of the Army and Navy of the United States,' and vests in him the Executive Power."[82] This bold claim is supposedly tempered by a recognition that the president may exercise his unilateral power only under certain conditions: first, the president must "reasonably determine that the [planned] action serves important national interests."[83] Second, "the 'anticipated nature, scope and duration' of the conflict" should not suggest that hostilities "might rise to the level of a war under the Constitution."[84]

In broad strokes, this has been the presidentialist position at least as far back as the Nixon administration.[85] Yet it has nothing to do with originalism. The division between military conflicts that are and are not "war" within the meaning of Article I is cut entirely from whole cloth. Moreover, the legal opinions of recent administrations make clear that requiring a president to "reasonably determine that the [planned] action serves important national interests" is effectively no limit at all once a president determines to act. That is because the interests that have been asserted as meeting this standard include supporting the credibility of international alliances and institutions—part of the Obama administration's rationale for joining in the bombing of Libya[86]—and promoting regional stability, an interest emphasized by the Trump administration in justifying the bombing of Syria.[87] Harvard law professor Jack Goldsmith, who headed OLC during part of the George W. Bush administration, observed in 2013 that the "national interest" test "places no limit at all on the president's ability to use significant military force unilaterally."[88]

John Yoo, the Berkeley law professor probably best known for authoring the so-called "Torture Memo" to justify the Bush administration's post-9/11 harsh interrogation techniques,[89] has tried to give the presidentialist position an originalist defense.[90] The argument is all but universally acknowledged, however, to be preposterous.[91] For his part, Alexander Hamilton said of the president's commander-in-chief power:

> It would amount to nothing more than the supreme command and direction of the military and naval forces, as first General and admiral of the Confederacy; while that of the British king extends to the *declaring* of war and to the *raising* and *regulating* of fleets and armies, all which, by the Constitution under consideration, would appertain to the legislature.[92]

Following Trump's bombing of Syria and recognizing the distance presidents have traveled since 1787, Keith Whittington, a leading theorist of constitutional originalism, penned an essay to which he gave the title, "R.I.P. Congressional War Power."[93]

There is something jarring in the ease with which presidentialist lawyers, so aggressive in advancing originalism in defense of unilateral executive theory, have embraced a framework for presidential war powers so thoroughly at odds with the Framers' understanding. It suggests again that it is not so much originalism that drives presidentialism, but rather presidentialism that provides the lens through which original sources are weighed, interpreted, or, as with war powers, ignored. For its part, the Johnson administration, which proffered Congress's Gulf of Tonkin resolution as legislative authority for massive escalation in Vietnam, did offer an explicit "living originalism" view of presidential war powers by deploying the "moderate originalist" technique of elevating the relevant level of generality.[94] In a much-noted white paper, State Department legal advisor Leonard Meeker made a two-step pseudo-originalist Article II argument: Step One was recognizing that the Framers changed the wording of Congress's power regarding war from "make war" to "declare" war. This was to avoid any implication that the president could not act on his own to repel sudden attacks. Step Two was the suggestion that, although the Framers presumably "had in mind attacks upon the United

States," "the world has grown much smaller" since 1787, and "an attack on a country far from our shores can impinge directly on the nation's security."[95] From this observation, Meeker derives the conclusion: "The Constitution leaves to the President the judgment to determine whether the circumstances of a particular armed attack are so urgent and the potential consequences so threatening to the security of the United States that he should act without formally consulting the Congress."[96] In other words, the president gets to say whether a contemporary armed attack abroad is threatening in the same way that an invasion would have been in 1787.

In recent decades, presidents have broadened U.S. doctrine regarding the use of force for "self-defense," which also expands the opportunities for unilateral presidential deployments. Under international law, self-defense is an exception to the ordinary prohibition against the use of force between states. As national security expert Rebecca Ingber has explained, however, U.S. presidents have invoked "self-defense" as a rationale for military force in the face of both actual and supposedly imminent attacks and against both nation-states and non-state actors; "self-defense" has also been invoked when enemies have attacked U.S. armed forces, but not U.S. territory.[97] Such attacks are all but inevitable when the United States, at the invitation of another government—the government of Iraq, for example—offers military support to that government for its own national defense. The Biden administration was barely a month old, when, on February 25, 2021, it conducted what Biden called "a targeted military strike against infrastructure in eastern Syria used by Iran-supported non-state militia groups."[98] As Biden explained in a letter to Congress:

> Those non-state militia groups were involved in recent attacks against United States and Coalition personnel in Iraq, including the February 15, 2021, attack in Erbil, Iraq, which wounded one United States service member, wounded four United States contractors, including one critically, and killed one Filipino contractor. These groups are also engaged in ongoing planning for future such attacks.[99]

It is the Authorization to Use Military Force that Congress enacted in 2002 which is supposed to legalize our military operations on Iraq's behalf in Syria.[100] But the early Biden strike demonstrates how a president can build on seemingly well-delimited authority to deploy armed force across international boundaries by treating even the ordinary use of force against U.S. troops as an attack on the United States itself.[101]

Leonard Meeker's defense of Vietnam escalation gestured toward Framer intent. But what chiefly bolstered his argument, and what undergirds more recent presidents' ambitious claims for unilateral discretion, is an idea that has proved critical to separation of powers law nearly from the beginning—an idea often called "settlement by practice." Settlement by practice is the notion that, when constitutional text is sparse and its import is uncertain, the legal meaning may be settled by the behavior of government over time. For example, although the Constitution does not specify who determines our recognition of foreign governments—that is, whether Congress or the president determines what authority is sovereign over foreign territory—President Washington claimed that power as his own, and Congress has accepted that assertion ever since. A 2015 Supreme Court opinion relies on history as confirming that the president's power to receive ambassadors and public ministers should be understood to include the recognition power, as well.[102]

Settlement by practice provides pretty much the entire basis for the version of presidentialist war powers doctrine that prevails in the executive branch.[103] OLC has repeatedly urged, because Congress has so often acquiesced in presidential deployments of military force without prior authorization, that settlement-by-practice confirms that the president is acting constitutionally when exercising that power.

Arguing from settlement-by-practice raises a host of questions—not least because the pattern of interbranch accommodation thought to settle constitutional meaning is often debatable as to its contours and implications. Yet the idea is an old one and, for the federal courts, inescapable. Though some justices may occasionally appear willing to upset long-established interbranch modes of operation, the prospect is understandably uncomfortable for unelected jurists surveying the handiwork of the elected branches. In his important 1819 opinion upholding Congress's authority to charter a national bank, Chief Justice John Marshall wrote:

> [A] doubtful question, one on which human reason may pause, and the human judgment be suspended, in the decision of which the great principles of liberty are not concerned, but the respective powers of those who are equally the representatives of the people, are to be adjusted; if not put at rest by the practice of the government, ought to receive a considerable impression from that practice.[104]

It is just this mode of argument on which the defenders of presidential war power are dependent.

From a democratic point of view, some version of settlement-by-practice makes sense. The people's chosen officials in the two elected branches may create a stable pattern of repeated action regarding the interplay of legislative and executive power that reflects a suitable accommodation of the Constitution's ambiguous text to the needs of governance. But settlement-by-practice should be respected only as a presumption, not as the final word. Congress, for example, should have room under the Constitution to cut back on a prior pattern of acquiescence in executive power and to begin to insist on a reinvigorated legislative role. It is one thing for courts to treat a pattern of congressional acquiescence as a kind of tacit authorization to the executive branch to act in certain limited circumstances. It would be a far more radical position to argue that the passivity of earlier Congresses has so effectively amended the Constitution as to be beyond Congress's authority to remedy. If one Congress cannot bind a future Congress in the sense of explicitly narrowing the authority of the later legislature to legislate,[105] it is hard to see how earlier Congresses can bar a later Congress from rethinking the wisdom of its tacit acquiescence.

In the waning years of the Vietnam War, Congress enacted the War Powers Resolution over the veto of President Nixon precisely to reclaim legislative authority over the introduction of "United States armed forces into hostilities."[106] Congress took a four-step approach to reform. Step one was enacting a specific, limited understanding of the scope of the president's commander-in-chief power.[107] Step two was requiring that the president, "in every possible instance," consult with Congress before "introducing United States Armed Forces into hostilities or into situations where imminent involvement in hostilities is clearly indicated by the circumstances."[108] Step three was mandating that the president report promptly to Congress on virtually all combat-equipped military deployments, except those involving a formal declaration of war.[109] Step four was requiring that, with certain exceptions, presidents terminate within sixty or, in some cases, ninety days any deployments for which reports had been required, unless Congress subsequently authorized lengthening the president's use of the armed forces.[110]

Nearly forty years later, it is obvious that the WPR has not ended unilateral presidential war making. It certainly has not reshaped the Justice Department's legal theories as to the scope of presidential war power. That does not mean the WPR has been without helpful impacts. Although Republican administrations have periodically reasserted their belief in the unconstitutionality of the WPR, all presidents since 1973 have filed reports consistent with its requirements. The Reagan administration, when it was determined to station Marines in Lebanon for an extended period, negotiated with Congress to obtain a specific statutory sunset of eighteen months, rather than sixty days.[111] With regard to the George H. W. Bush administration operations in Somalia and Clinton administration actions in Bosnia, it likewise seems clear that each of the elected branches used the ambiguity of its own powers—and the ambiguity of the legal status of our military deployments—to help leverage its bargaining position over the course of events.[112] A less vigilant Congress—the Congress of the 1960s, for example—could easily have allowed any of these engagements to become a version of Vietnam. In each case, however, Congress used the WPR and its own claims of authority to force the executive to sharpen its articulation of American objectives, respond to contrary positions regarding the executive branch's foreign policy analyses, and share substantial information with Congress. In every case also, Americans witnessed a better-informed and more substantial intra-governmental debate over military policy than the executive mustered in the Vietnam era. In the cases of Lebanon and Somalia, Congress helped set the stage for a relatively early withdrawal of ground troops. In the case of Bosnia, congressional pressure presumably helped curtail what might have been a temptation to commit United States ground troops even prior to the Dayton accords.[113]

The WPR has nonetheless proved less powerful than it might have because it muddied its message of limitation in two ways. First, Section 2(c) took a seemingly stringent position on presidential authority:

> The constitutional powers of the President as Commander-in-Chief to introduce United States Armed Forces into hostilities, or into situations where imminent involvement in hostilities is clearly indicated by the circumstances, are exercised only pursuant to (1) a declaration of war, (2) specific statutory authorization, or (3) a national emergency created by attack upon the United States, its territories or possessions, or its armed forces.

But Section 8 arguably undercut the force of Section 2 by providing: "Nothing in this joint resolution—(1) is intended to alter the constitutional authority of . . . the President." The latter language left it open to the Justice Department to argue that the WPR did not limit the president's authority to launch short-term unilateral military deployments without meeting the conditions of Section 2. Indeed—and here is the second way the WPR muddied the waters—by mandating a sixty-day sunset for any military operation for which the president is required to submit a report, the WPR seemingly invited the interpretation that military engagements shorter than sixty days were still within the scope of Congress's acquiescence.[114]

Reforms remain possible and within Congress's power to pursue. Even if there were a stronger originalist defense of extensive unilateral presidential war power, democratic constitutionalism would argue strongly for a requirement of congressional authorization for military action. To be sure, such authorization and its antecedent deliberations do not insure wise policy. The invasion of Iraq, fully supported under domestic law by a 2002 congressional authorization to use military force, still stands as perhaps the greatest geopolitical blunder in U.S. history. It not only destabilized the Middle East by creating new openings for radical extremists, but also strengthened Iran by weakening Iraq as a checking-and-balancing regional competitor. Yet the inability of process to guarantee wisdom is not an argument against trying.

Intriguingly, one package that would have represented a significant improvement over the WPR is the "Use of Force Act" proposed in 1995 by then Senator Joseph Biden.[115] Although its terms explicitly accept the position that the Constitution by itself confers some military authority on the president, it would require consultation "before any use of force abroad." It would not only impose the sixty-day limit on unilateral deployments, but would also eliminate funding for any military operation that, except under terms consistent with the Act, exceeded the sixty days. Perhaps most important, it would provide authority for federal courts to declare that the terms of the Act have been violated. Such a framework should be deemed squarely within Congress's constitutional authority "to make rules for the government and regulation of the [armed] forces."

It might be argued that acknowledging such broad power in Congress to regulate the use of the military pays too little attention to Leonard Meeker's mid-60s argument. He was surely correct that threats geographically distant from American shores can now pose threats to the United States that were inconceivable in 1787. The problem is that focusing solely on the capacity of harm from abroad is attending to only one aspect of how life has changed since the Founding. It is also true that a twenty-first-century military misadventure by the United States will have far worse consequences both for us and for other nations than an unjustified armed deployment by the American president in 1787. Given our superpower status—not to mention firepower—the consequences of American action abroad for good or ill necessarily loom larger than at the Founding. Democratic deliberation ought to precede our inevitably consequential military commitments.

In addressing the most glaring example of this point, law professors Bob Bauer, Jack Goldsmith, and Dakota Rudesill[116] have made compelling arguments for a framework statute to govern American use of nuclear weapons. As Rudesill bluntly puts the matter, "Concentration of discretion to use the world's most destructive weapons in one person, the President of the United States" is simply intolerable given the stakes.[117]

Under the reform specifically proposed by Bauer and Goldsmith, Congress would acknowledge presidential power to launch a nuclear strike without more specific legislative authority only in response to an incoming nuclear attack or "in self-defense in extreme circumstances to defend the vital interests of the United States or its allies."[118] Congressional consultation would be required, however, prior to the use of force should the president receive intelligence that its use might be required in the latter circumstance.[119]

Because the argument I am offering puts so strong a thumb on the side of legislative deliberation, it is important to acknowledge that putting theory into practice faces one obvious obstacle: Congress's seeming resistance to making hard deliberative choices. Over two decades have passed since al Qaeda's 9/11 attack on the Twin Towers. Throughout those decades and beyond, presidents engaging foreign terrorists militarily have continued to rely on the authorizations to use military force enacted in the immediate wake of 9/11 or the following year, with regard to Iraq.[120] Repeated calls from both Republicans and Democrats for Congress to update its statutory charter for such action produced nothing but draft proposals.[121] The executive branch has been all too comfortable with the situation. Even as the Obama administration offered its own draft legislation, it seemed to put little energy into getting it passed. Making constitutional checks and balances meaningful if a "checking" branch prefers inaction is a critical problem that I will address at length in chapter 7.

In principle, however, there is a democratic constitutionalist interpretation of war powers that honors both the importance of genuine deliberation before any sustained commitment of the U.S. military to foreign combat and the permissibility for our democratically elected officials to work out an acceptable framework for short-term presidential military deployments. As OLC concedes, the president may commit U.S. armed forces to "sustained, full-scale conflict with another Nation" only with explicit congressional authorization for that operation.[122] With regard to short-term deployments, however, the president should be deemed constitutionally required to obtain prior congressional authorization to the degree—but only to the degree—Congress has demanded. And even when the president has initiated a short-term military deployment on a constitutionally permissible basis, Congress retains the ability to regulate the scope and duration of that deployment should it wish to do so.

A similar set of principles is needed to honor the demands of democratic constitutionalism in foreign affairs more generally. Just as Articles I and II assign military authorities to the elected branches, so, too, are a variety of powers mentioned with specific reference to foreign affairs more generally. In addition to such foreign affairs powers as the Executive Power Vesting Clause may convey, Article II expressly assigns to the president the powers to make treaties, to appoint U.S. ambassadors, and to receive the ambassadors and "other public Ministers" sent to the U.S. by other nations.[123] The first two powers are conditioned, however, on the concurrence of the Senate, whether by two-thirds in the case of treaties or a majority in the case of appointments. As for Congress, in addition to its military powers, which obviously carry foreign policy implications, Article I places in legislative hands the powers to "regulate commerce with foreign nations," "establish a uniform rule of naturalization," and "define and punish piracies and felonies committed on the high seas, and offenses against the law of nations."[124] All of these have obvious implications for foreign policy. And, of course, to the extent the Constitution has vested foreign affairs powers in the president, Congress may make laws "necessary and proper" for carrying those powers into effect.

Again, given the balance of text, one might suspect that it is Congress that has the upper hand in making foreign policy, but, as with war powers, such is not the case. Four factors have coincided to give the president a conspicuous upper hand in the domain of foreign policy. To begin with, institutional features give the president first mover advantage in dealing with other countries. As Hamilton observed in *The Federalist*, the unitary character of the executive means that the president can decide on policy more quickly, communicate that policy more directly, and take advantage of confidential information (in both receiving it and creating it) not readily available to the legislative branch.[125]

Second, Congress has, by statute, delegated enormous decision-making authority to the president in the management of foreign affairs. One especially significant such piece of legislation is the International Economic Emergency Powers Act.[126] Trump invoked the Act when threatening to put tariffs on all Mexican imports in response to what he declared to be an emergency caused by illegal immigration.[127] Other presidents had invoked IEEPA to freeze the assets of foreign governments, such as when in 1979 President Jimmy Carter responded to the Iranian hostage crisis by blocking assets owned by the Iranian government from passing through the U.S. financial system.[128]

Third, the president's position is buttressed by the frequent reluctance of federal courts to second-guess the executive branch on foreign policy matters. In some cases, courts show extraordinary reluctance to second-guess the accuracy or even good faith of executive branch fact-finding.[129] Other cases may be treated as nonjusticiable either because plaintiffs lack standing[130] or because the issue is deemed a political question committed to the elected branches for resolution between them.[131]

Fourth, and quite unfortunately, misleading Supreme Court dicta from a 1930s case, United States v. Curtiss-Wright Export Corp., have undergirded repeated executive branch legal arguments that the Framers intended for the president to have an all-but-illimitable berth for unilateral action in foreign relations.[132] Nonetheless, the scope of the president's foreign affairs powers may seem ripe for reconsideration, especially in light of a 2015 Supreme Court decision that cautioned against overreliance on the Curtiss-Wright dicta. The case of Zivotofsky ex rel. Zivotofsky v. Kerry raised the question whether Congress could legislatively require the executive branch to permit U.S. citizens born in Jerusalem to indicate on their passports that Israel was their nation of birth.[133] Prior to the Trump administration, both Republican and Democratic presidents had instructed the State Department to name only "Jerusalem" and not either "Israel" or "Palestine" as the place of birth in such cases. They did so in order to preserve America's hoped-for role as an honest broker between Israelis and Palestinians in negotiating issues related to sovereignty over Jerusalem. In a 5–4 decision, the majority held that a passport designation that a Jerusalem-born U.S. citizen was born in Israel would implicate the president's exclusive authority over the recognition of other countries, a power implied by the president's authority to receive ambassadors from other nations.[134] Congress, in the Court's view, could not intrude on that power. Nonetheless, the majority pointedly rejected any broader claim of presidential control over foreign policy. Justice Kennedy, speaking for the majority, wrote:

United States v. Curtiss–Wright Export Corp. does not support a broader definition of the Executive's power over foreign relations that would permit the President alone to determine the whole content of the Nation's foreign policy. The Executive is not free from the ordinary controls and checks of Congress merely because foreign affairs are at issue.[135]

Two justices who dissented from the majority's holding in this case nonetheless agreed about the executive branch's habitual over-reading of *Curtiss-Wright*.[136]

The democratic preference for legislative deliberation to precede executive action helps to explain the Supreme Court's decision in a major case rebuffing the George W. Bush administration. *Medellín v. Texas* involved a habeas corpus application by a Texas death row inmate who challenged his conviction on the ground that, as a Mexican national, he had been entitled under the Vienna Convention on Consular Relations to notification, upon his arrest, of his right to inform the Mexican consulate of his detention.[137] With regard to Medellín and fifty other Mexican nationals, the International Court of Justice held that, because the defendants had not been informed of their rights, they were now entitled to a post-conviction review and reconsideration of their respective state-court convictions and sentences in the United States. Texas courts refused, however, to hear Medellín's Vienna Convention claim because Medellín had failed to raise it either at trial or on direct appeal, as Texas procedural law required. Following the judgment of the ICJ, however, President Bush issued a memorandum to the attorney general, stating that "the United States will discharge its international obligations under the decision of the International Court of Justice . . . by having State courts give effect to the decision in accordance with general principles of comity in cases filed by the 51 Mexican nationals addressed in that decision."[138] Medellín then refiled his habeas petition, arguing that Texas was bound to hear his case following the president's memorandum.

In a 6–3 decision, the Supreme Court reversed. Pivotal to the decision was the distinction between what are called "self-executing" and "non-self-executing" treaties. As a nation-state, the United States operates under two systems of law, international and domestic. When we join a treaty, such as the Vienna Convention on Consular Relations, international law binds us to adhere to its provisions; if we do not, injured parties may seek redress through international institutions, such as the International Court of Justice. But those obligations do not always become enforceable automatically as a matter of domestic law; that is, parties injured by U.S. treaty violations are not always entitled immediately to seek relief in U.S. domestic courts. Sometimes a treaty may provide that its obligations become part of domestic law automatically—those treaties are "self-executing." But if a treaty is not self-executing, its terms become enforceable in U.S. courts only if Congress makes those terms binding domestically through statutory law.

The distinction between self-executing and non-self-executing treaties makes a big difference in terms of who participates in domestic lawmaking. If a treaty is self-executing, it becomes domestic law once the president negotiates the treaty, two-thirds of the Senate approves it, and the president affixes his or her signature. In that scenario, however, the House of Representatives plays no role. In the case of a non-self-executing treaty, however, the implementing legislation must go through the ordinary Article I process. That is, both the House and Senate must approve the legislation, and the president must sign it unless it is enacted over a veto. The Article I process relaxes the requirement of Senate concurrence because only a majority is needed for a statute to pass. But the House now gets a voice, which may or may not make it more difficult for a president to follow through on our treaty commitments.

Medellín held that the Vienna Convention was not self-executing. In every case, the Court said, the nature of the treaty is to be divined in the first instance from its text. But the chief justice's opinion for five justices added that, where the impact of a treaty could be to displace state law, self-execution should not be inferred absent a clear statement of intent.[139] This could amount to something of a presumption that treaties should not be deemed part of domestic law until both Houses of Congress participate in making that decision. The Court further held that, without implementing legislation, the president's foreign affairs powers did not give him authority to impose obligations on a state pursuant to a non-self-executing treaty. Were the president able to do so, the president would effectively be making law, not executing it.

From the standpoint of democratic constitutionalism, the majority approach is sensible. Plainly, the two-thirds requirement for Senate treaty approval suffices to ensure intense deliberation between the president and the Senate to secure that approval. Nonetheless, because the House and Senate are structured differently and their members relate differently to their respective constituencies, including the House in major policy decisions likely expands the range of issues under consideration, as well as the opportunities for democratic public input.

This is not to say that there are no institutional costs involved in the preference for two-house deliberation. Empowering presidents to make treaties, but then leaving their implementation to a separate legislative process, may put U.S. credibility at risk when the president negotiates with foreign powers. Other countries' doubts whether the president can ultimately deliver on promises may impede the forming of agreements that would be in the national interest. In Medellín's case specifically, there was a cost to the rule of law when Texas was able to evade a right that should have been observed under the Vienna Convention.

It is even arguable that the needs of democracy cut both ways on this question. Because the president is the one elected official who represents the national polity, it could be said that honoring our commitment to electoral democracy counsels for making it easier, not harder for presidents to translate the results they have negotiated with Senate approval into domestic law. After all, Americans elected the president to do a job. Any hurdles placed in the way of implementing treaties as domestic law tilt the United States in a more isolationist direction vis-à-vis the community of nations and may make it more difficult for the president to engage constructively in at least certain aspects of international diplomacy.

I would still argue, however, that the normative commitments of deliberative democracy should take precedence, especially given the antidemocratic features built into our electoral politics. Hamilton's famous defense for giving the president provisional veto power also provides a strong argument not to exclude the House from debates about incorporating our international obligations into domestic law:

> The oftener [a] measure is brought under examination, the greater the diversity in the situations of those who are to examine it, the less must be the danger of those errors which flow from want of due deliberation, or of those missteps which proceed from the contagion of some common passion or interest. It is far less probable, that culpable views of any kind should infect all the parts of the government at the same moment and in relation to the same object, than that they should by turns govern and mislead every one of them.[140]

As a practical matter, whether or not courts entertain a presumption in favor of non-self-executing treaties may seem to recede in importance because recent presidents have presented so few treaties to the Senate. The number of international agreements that take the form of treaties is vastly outnumbered by so-called executive agreements—that is, agreements that the president negotiates either on his own authority or pursuant to authority that Congress has delegated to the president, but which do not require a Senate supermajority. Agreements that presidents negotiate on their own are necessarily limited to those few specific powers—like the power of recognition—that presidents have been deemed to hold exclusively or in which Congress has acquiesced. Yet more common is the latter group—the so-called congressional-executive agreements. These are agreements that Congress, by statute, first authorizes the president to negotiate. The authorizing statute is likely to provide, as well, that the agreement will enter into force after Congress approves the negotiated text by subsequent legislation. Such agreements are especially common in the field of international trade, which is subject to Congress's explicit power to regulate "Commerce with foreign Nations."

There is a nontrivial originalist argument against congressional-executive agreements. The Constitution's specificity with regard to the making and approval of treaties suggests an early understanding that "only a treaty could pledge the good faith of the United States on matters of major international importance," and "presidents could make treaties only after securing the consent of two thirds of the Senate."[141] Thus while an originalist like John Yoo admits the permissibility of congressional-executive agreements in areas, like foreign trade, over which Congress has "plenary constitutional authority," he disputes their permissibility in areas "over which the President and Congress possess concurrent and potentially conflicting powers," presumably including national security.[142]

For its part, the Justice Department has taken the position that the choice of instrument for international agreement—treaty or congressional-executive agreement—is a matter for the elected branches to work out on their own politically; history "undermines any dogmatic claim" that a particular kind of agreement need take the form of a treaty.[143] Professor Oona Hathaway has gone yet further in her analysis, arguing that congressional-executive agreements are actually superior from a democratic point of view.[144] She makes a series of strong arguments, pointing out first that exclusion of the House from treaty making "was originally justified by a need for secrecy and a desire to have the Senate function as a council of advisors in the treaty-making process."[145] Yet, as Hathaway points out, "these rationales were almost immediately undermined by actual practice."[146] After the Senate delayed giving George Washington advice he requested on a treaty negotiation then in process, he resolved never again to seek advice except in writing and usually upon treaties already reduced to text.[147] "'Advice and consent' had devolved to just 'consent'" by the end of Washington's presidency.[148]

The House inevitably makes the process of international law making more democratic because it is the one House of Congress apportioned by population and is, by virtue of its members' shorter terms, more closely connected to popular sentiment. Hathaway cites Robert Dahl as supporting the view also that, compared with the Senate supermajority requirement, "majority action by both Houses is more 'democratic'—in the sense that majority rule is an essential element of democratic procedure."[149] It is also the case that international law now covers virtually the entire range of topics on which the House would ordinarily have a legislative voice: "Modern international law is about everything from education to tax policy to torture. In this era, the exclusion of the House from participation in international lawmaking is increasingly dissonant."[150]

Finally, although any Senate supermajority requirement may lead to the defeat of treaties that enjoy strong popular support, getting to two-thirds may mean "playing to the polarized extremes of modern American politics."[151] It is obstacle enough that most such agreements, like all other regular legislation, must get by the Senate's three-fifths filibuster rule. That is why Congress, in authorizing congressional-executive agreements, sometimes preempts Senate filibuster practice by creating a "fast-track" process for review of the president's handiwork.[152] Even if a filibuster is possible, however, getting a two-thirds vote of the Senate requires the same level of consensus that the Constitution demands for removing an impeached official from office or sending a constitutional amendment to the states for possible ratification. The rarity of those events is testament to the difficulty of achieving that kind of agreement.

More generally, democratic constitutionalism also supports construing Congress's implied powers to give it extensive regulatory control—should it decide to exercise such control—over the executive branch processes through which decisions about foreign affairs get made. Such controls, as detailed by Professor Rebecca Ingber, may involve numerous questions of institutional design. These details can affect the dynamics of consultation within the executive branch; the prescription of administrative processes, such as certification, before certain decisions can be implemented; and the designation of specific "deciders," in order to ensure that certain kinds of perspective predominate with regard to different kinds of decisions.[153] Such process controls do not ensure wise policy and do not achieve the same level of political accountability as would direct legislation. Yet leaving decision-making authority within the executive branch, while subject to regulated processes may "provide a means of Congressional influence on policy while still benefiting from the executive branch advantages of information, expertise, and dispatch."[154] Contrary to the notion that the president has sole authority in foreign affairs decision-making, a democratic interpretation of the separation of powers strongly supports Congress's entitlement to proceed in this manner.

THE ACCOUNTABLE PRESIDENCY

In the president's conduct of either domestic or global affairs, it is critical that he or she remain accountable to the other branches of government. Madison famously explained how the mutual accountability of the branches was essential to keep each in its constitutional place. The lack of external controls adequate to check the abuse of power could be cured only "by so contriving the interior structure of the government as that its several constituent parts may, by their mutual relations, be the means of keeping each other in their proper places."[155]

For any branch of government to check the actions of another, however, the "checking branch" must have access to information. Congress, of course, offers potentially the strongest balancing force against an overreaching executive. Yet presidents in varying degrees—and with varying degrees of success—have insisted on their right to withhold from Congress at least some of the information that would shed light on executive branch performance.

Many of these claims have at least the virtue of bipartisanship. Since the Reagan administration, presidents of both parties have generally claimed authority to determine that Congress's need for documents or testimony in general may be overcome by the executive's need for confidentiality when Congress has not articulated its need for information in relation to specific proposals for legislation that are under consideration.[156] Presidents of both parties have likewise exercised executive privilege to withhold open law enforcement files from mandatory disclosure.[157] These claims are rooted not only in executive privilege, as it protects presidential communications, but also in the risk of further politicizing executive branch decisions to charge or not charge criminal offenses. Finally, multiple administrations have insisted that the president's immediate White House advisers are absolutely immune from compelled testimony before Congress. The claims of absolute adviser privilege are supposedly rooted in the immunity of the president from compulsory testimony and the presumptively privileged nature of any conversations with the president about which an adviser might be asked.[158] Presidents have even insisted that this immunity extends to former advisers no longer in White House employ.[159]

It is not clear that any of these positions reads the Constitution correctly. Intriguingly, both the old-style originalist Raoul Berger and the "original public meaning" scholar Saikrishna Prakash deny any originalist constitutional basis for executive privilege claims against Congress.[160] The most recent cases to elicit at least a district court order on the merits have not gone well for the executive branch.[161] Yet presidents have been able to persist largely because of the difficulty of getting quick and authoritative resolutions to executive privilege disputes in court. Congress's desire to obtain specific documents and to hear from specific witnesses is typically time-bound, which creates a significant disincentive to undertake lengthy interbranch litigation.

As in other areas of separation of powers controversy, the Trump administration was more assertive than its predecessors in stonewalling Congress. First, contrary to all prior executive branch precedent, the Trump White House insisted it would not turn over any records in connection with the House impeachment inquiry or cooperate in providing witnesses.[162] It asserted the right to determine for itself the legitimacy of the impeachment inquiry and to deny Congress's entitlement to investigate potential corruption in the president's discharge of constitutionally vested discretionary functions.[163] The previously conventional executive branch view, that a congressional impeachment investigation always trumps any privilege claim, goes back as far as the Washington administration.[164]

Second, and arguably of greater significance to run-of-the-mill congressional oversight, the Trump administration asserted a right to make "protective claims" of executive privilege, even as to information that might ultimately not be legally privileged. Since 1982, presidents of both parties have dealt with potential privilege claims against Congress pursuant to a procedure President Reagan outlined in a presidential memorandum.[165] Reagan's memo recognized that, properly speaking, a claim of executive privilege must be lodged by the president. Should an agency or department head determine that compliance with a congressional subpoena would raise a "substantial question of executive privilege," the memo instructs that officer to immediately consult the attorney general (through the Office of Legal Counsel) and to notify White House counsel. If any of these three individuals, following consultation, believes privilege should be claimed, White House counsel would present the matter to the president for resolution. Of course, all this would take time. Thus, the memorandum provided:

> Pending a final Presidential decision on the matter, the Department Head shall request the Congressional body to hold its request for the information in abeyance. The Department Head shall expressly indicate that the purpose of this request is to protect the privilege pending a Presidential decision, and that the request itself does not constitute a claim of privilege.[166]

As depicted in the Reagan memorandum, a congressional committee that received a "protective claim" could expect a definitive resolution "as promptly . . . as possible," accompanied presumably with a legal explanation of the basis for the president's claim.

An early Trump administration "protective claim" came in testimony by Attorney General Jeff Sessions. In June 2017 testimony to the Senate Intelligence Committee, Sessions refused to answer whether Trump had ever expressed frustration to him concerning Sessions's decision to recuse himself from the Justice Department's investigation of the 2016 election campaign. He likewise would not answer whether Trump ever discussed with him the firing of FBI Director James Comey. While emphasizing that Trump had not claimed privilege as to his testimony, Sessions insisted it would be "premature" for him to answer and thus "to deny the president a full and intelligent choice about executive privilege."[167] Unfortunately, there was no apparent follow-up to this colloquy, no deadline set by the committee for the president to claim privilege, and no subsequent demand for answers. Such constitutional choreography put the committee in a triple bind. Its questions went unanswered. It had no formal claim of privilege to litigate. And holding Sessions in contempt would have been pointless, given that the executive branch will not prosecute a case of contempt against a federal official who refuses to testify on grounds of presidential privilege.[168]

By May 2019, the Justice Department had built upon the "protective claim" idea a supposed constitutional corollary: Federal officers subpoenaed for congressional depositions to which they were not allowed to bring agency lawyers could ignore those subpoenas. Because agency counsel would be better able to spot significant potential questions of privilege, "the exclusion of agency counsel impairs the President's ability to exercise his constitutional authority to control privileged information of the Executive Branch." Moreover, based on unitary executive theory, "the exclusion undermines the President's ability to exercise his constitutional authority to supervise the Executive Branch's interactions with Congress."[169]

What one can see in the behavior of the executive branch since Reagan and accelerated in the Trump administration is the development within the executive branch of a complex body of purported legal doctrine regarding the president's entitlement to resist congressional oversight. That doctrine is based on historically dubious premises and shows little to no regard for the respect owed to Congress's constitutionally based oversight role. From the standpoint of democratic constitutionalism, the question is whether Congress must acquiesce in it. Could Congress prescribe by statute the process by which presidents would be bound either to assert or disavow potential claims of privilege? Would it be entitled to prescribe a statutory fast-track litigation process to protect its rights to information? The answer to both questions must be affirmative. Whatever past practice has been, there cannot be a constitutionally based entitlement of the executive branch to unilaterally stonewall congressional investigations without any legal or institutional accountability.

Congressional investigations are a critical source of public information about government operations. To stonewall Congress is also significantly to preempt the public's capacity to monitor the authorities they have put in place. Even our presidentialist Supreme Court majority has observed that, "Without information, Congress would be shooting in the dark, unable to legislate 'wisely or effectively.'"[170] The same Court quoted with approval the characterization of Congress's investigating function by then-professor Woodrow Wilson:

> It is the proper duty of a representative body to look diligently into every affair of government and to talk much about what it sees. It is meant to be the eyes and the voice, and to embody the wisdom and will of its constituents. Unless Congress have and use every means of acquainting itself with the acts and the disposition of the administrative agents of the government, the country must be helpless to learn how it is being served.[171]

In addition to ignoring subpoenas, the Trump administration also resisted explicit requirements, both statutory and constitutional, to report certain kinds of information to Congress. For example, in 2017, Congress enacted a requirement that, within ninety days, the president would have to "submit to the appropriate congressional committees a report on the legal and policy frameworks for the United States' use of military force and related national security operations."[172] This imposed on the Trump administration a legal obligation to provide a report giving Congress the same kind of information that the Obama administration provided on its own initiative in December 2016.[173] In 2019, Congress amended the requirement to make it an annual report, due no later than March 1.[174] The administration did not comply, even though it did reveal that changes had been made to the Obama 2016 policy frameworks.[175]

According to two national security experts who filed suit[176] to compel the release of the required report: "The missing March 1 report would provide an unparalleled amount of information regarding Trump's own views of his authority as president, in a single location and with a level of certainty that is otherwise difficult to achieve."[177] As Congress realized when it enacted the reporting requirement, legislative deliberations about the scope of the president's authority and military engagements are obviously hampered if Congress is denied a comprehensive presentation of the president's interpretation of his or her legal authority and strategic objectives in using military force. There is no persuasive constitutional argument, originalist or otherwise, that presidents may resist providing such information to Congress.

Chapter 1 recounted Trump's refusal, throughout his administration, to provide Congress with information that would enable that body to determine his compliance with the Constitution's Emoluments Clauses. In litigation brought by the District of Columbia and the State of Maryland,[178] which asserted that Trump had violated the rules regarding both domestic[179] and foreign[180] emoluments, legal scholar Seth Barrett Tillman offered an arguably startling interpretation that would have exempted Trump from the foreign emoluments rule altogether. Unlike the ban on domestic emoluments, which applies singly to the president, the constitutional requirement for congressional approval to accept any foreign emolument applies to any "Person holding any Office of Profit or Trust under" the United States. Tillman argued that the Framers would not have understood the president to be an official covered by this phrase.[181] The district court rejected the argument, after examining the relevant constitutional text as a whole, assessing both the original public meaning of the disputed clause and its likely constitutional purpose, and reviewing subsequent practice and precedent in the executive branch regarding the meaning of foreign emoluments.[182] The court persuasively found that Tillman's argument was unconvincing on all these grounds.

But what if there were more to the Tillman argument than the district court granted? The core of Tillman's argument was that "in the Colonial Period the phrase 'Office under the Crown' was a commonly-used drafting convention that referred only to appointed—not elected—positions."[183] Perhaps it is not unimaginable that, with George Washington as everyone's guess as to who would hold the first presidency, the founding generation might have been concerned less for the corruption of their elected officials than those who held power solely by virtue of appointment. But, in modern parlance, it plainly does no violence to the phrase, "Person holding any Office of Profit or Trust," to include the president within its purview. One would be hard pressed to posit any plausible contemporary democratic or rule-of-law purpose that would argue for a presidential exemption. The very possibility that a president's singular focus on the interests of the United States might be compromised by the prospect of enrichment from official foreign benefactors threatens to undermine the president's oath to execute his office "faithfully." In short, even if Tillman were correctly channeling the understanding of George Washington–besotted Framers, twenty-first century Americans would have no sound reason to be bound by so limited a prophylactic against corruption. In sum, regarding both the emoluments question and executive privilege claims against Congress, the pro-deliberation, pro-checks-and-balances presumptions of democratic constitutionalism point decisively toward limits on executive power.

An important accountability issue that helped frame the Mueller investigation into Trump's possible obstruction of justice was whether sitting presidents are subject to criminal indictment. Justice Department regulations[184] required Mueller, as a special counsel, to accept the Justice Department's existing view of the question, which was that incumbent presidents may not be indicted.[185] In the waning months of the Clinton administration, OLC had written an opinion holding that an incumbent president would not be amenable to indictment or trial while in office.[186] In doing so, it reiterated a stance that OLC took during the Nixon administration.[187] Yet Independent Counsel Kenneth Starr, who led the Clinton Whitewater and Monica Lewinsky investigations, had solicited an outside opinion on the indictment question from the late law professor Ronald D. Rotunda, one of the most prominent conservative constitutional scholars of his generation. Professor Rotunda concluded that the indictment of a sitting president would be constitutional, citing a long string of Supreme Court opinions supporting the proposition that "no one is above the law."[188]

In evaluating the OLC position, it is noteworthy that the opinion begins with a concession of constitutional ambiguity. In both 1973 and 2000, OLC rejected the view that the Impeachment Clause was properly read as precluding criminal proceedings against a sitting president.[189] In 1973, however, OLC opined that a temporary presidential immunity was implicit in the separation of powers because an adjudication of the president's criminal culpability—even preliminarily through indictment—would be uniquely destabilizing to an entire branch of government, and the diversion of attention to criminal proceedings would hamstring a president's ability to fulfill his or her constitutional role. Reaching the same bottom-line conclusion, but taking account of twenty-seven years of intervening case law, the 2000 OLC concluded that "the proper doctrinal analysis requires a balancing between the responsibilities of the president as the sole head of the executive branch against the important governmental purposes supporting the indictment and criminal prosecution of a sitting president."[190] In OLC's view, "the proper balance supports recognition of a temporary immunity from such criminal process while the President remains in office."[191] OLC found it impermissible not only to incarcerate a convicted president, but even to compromise the president's "constitutionally contemplated leadership role" by triggering "public stigma and opprobrium" with an indictment, and to hamper the performance of official duties by imposing on a president "the mental and physical burdens of assisting in the preparation of a defense."[192] One conspicuous problem with this balancing analysis, however, is that the mental and physical burdens to which OLC refers, along with the opprobrium of being criminally charged, are very nearly the same as the burdens attending impeachment, a constitutionally sanctioned process. The one potentially distinctive burden would be the threat of incarceration, which could simply be accommodated through a delay in sentencing. That, indeed, was Professor Rotunda's conclusion.

Professor Rotunda's opinion letter looked more deeply into the 1787 constitutional debates and concluded, *contra* OLC, that the omission of any explicit presidential immunity to match that of members of Congress was intentional.[193] His analysis of constitutional structure and relevant legal precedent led him to the same conclusion. It is unmistakable, however, that Professor Rotunda was significantly driven by the rule-of-law premise embedded in democratic constitutionalism, although he did not express himself in those terms. For example, although not relying on the point, he starts his analysis with the observation that "democracies in other countries do not recognize a principle that an individual would be above the law and privileged to engage in criminal activities simply because he or she is the President, Premier, Prime Minister, Chief Executive, or Head of State."[194] He goes on to argue: "If the Constitution prevents the President from being indicted for violations of one or more federal criminal statutes, even if those statutory violations are not impeachable offences, then the Constitution authorizes the President to be above the law."[195]

Mueller's reasoning based on the OLC opinion buttresses the Rotunda fear. Despite a commission entitling him to report on crimes connected with the 2016 campaign, Mueller declined to state a judgment whether Trump committed obstruction of justice. He reasoned that if a sitting president is immune from indictment and prosecution, two unfortunate consequences would follow from a special counsel finding that the president's conduct constituted a federal offense. First, it would create the same kind of burden as an indictment: "'The stigma and opprobrium' could imperil the President's ability to govern."[196] Moreover, unlike the indictment of an ordinary criminal defendant who could clear his name at a trial, "a prosecutor's judgment that crimes were committed, but that no charges will be brought, affords no such adversarial opportunity for public name-clearing before an impartial adjudicator."[197] Given a president's unique access to media and the base of political support he or she enjoys, Mueller's latter point seems a weak makeweight. If the logic of OLC's position demands prosecutorial reticence even to reach a judgment as to criminality, then a sitting president truly is above the law for the duration of his or her term.[198]

THE LIMITS OF DEMOCRATIC CONSTITUTIONALISM AS INTERPRETIVE STRATEGY

The portrait I have painted of the presidency as viewed through the lens of democratic constitutionalism sometimes matches and sometimes diverges from the likeliest interpretations yielded by "originalism done well." Unlike originalism, democratic constitutionalism posits the living as the authorized deciders of constitutional meaning and seeks to meet the most pressing needs of inclusive, deliberative, and responsive contemporary governance. But democratic constitutionalism does not promise, any more than originalism done well, completely determinate ways of resolving matters that the Constitution leaves ambiguous. Democratic constitutionalists may disagree among themselves as to proper constitutional outcomes for at least two reasons.

First, like virtually all actual, real-life, putatively originalist judges, adaptive constitutionalist judges would follow a common law method that looks to multiple sources of interpretive guidance in constructing constitutional meaning. The textual coherence of the Constitution as a whole, historical practice, judicial precedent, the pragmatic implications of the contending positions, and, yes, Framer expectations still play a legitimate role in educating judgment. Democratic constitutionalism does not exclude these aids to interpretation, even as it de-prioritizes "original public meaning." (Remember, originalists resort to these additional tools, as well.) Because different interpreters may weigh the persuasive force of these different aids differently, even those ultimately guided by democratic constitutionalist principles will not all land on the same answer to a difficult question. The presumptions built into democratic constitutionalism may sometimes give way to other legitimating factors.

Second, in a complex democratic system such as ours, the demands of democracy may seem to support alternative "living Constitution" arguments based on different assessments of how democratic principles relate to a particular controversy. One interpretation might seem to strengthen the electoral side of our democratic practice, while another might favor the deliberative side.

The indeterminacy that results from both sources of uncertainty is well illustrated by the question posed by the Trump impeachments of whether "high crimes and misdemeanors" encompass only forms of misconduct that are also criminal offenses under the United States Code. Trump's lawyers, most famously Harvard law professor Alan Dershowitz, tried proffering an originalist argument in favor of so restricting the range of impeachable offenses. Dershowitz appeared to go even further, arguing that misconduct, to be impeachable, must be both a statutory crime and "a violation of trust and injury to society."[199]

The kindest thing to say about the crimes-only argument is that it was made also by Benjamin Curtis, the Supreme Court Justice who acted as counsel to Andrew Johnson during the nation's first presidential impeachment trial.[200] But then, as now, it was an implausible reading of 1787. There is near unanimity among both legal scholars and historians that the phrase "high crimes and misdemeanors" was intended to encompass all offenses that, in the words of the late legal scholar Charles L. Black Jr., "so seriously threaten the order or political society as to make pestilent and dangerous the continuance in power of their perpetrator."[201] Black's statement echoes the formulation of Hamilton in Federalist 65:

> The subjects of [the Senate's] jurisdiction are those offenses which proceed from the misconduct of public men, or, in other words, from the abuse or violation of some public trust. They are of a nature which may with peculiar propriety be denominated POLITICAL, as they relate chiefly to injuries done immediately to the society itself.[202]

Justice Joseph Story, whose *Commentaries on the Constitution* remain the preeminent such volumes from the early Republic, took a similar view.[203] In fact, virtually every leading contemporary legal scholar, bridging a wide political and philosophical spectrum, has concurred.[204] It is a position adopted by the House Judiciary Committee for both the Nixon and Trump impeachments.[205]

At first blush, it might well seem obvious that democratic constitutionalism should lead to the same interpretation. The criminal code cannot encompass all those possible abuses of power or betrayals of the presidential oath so serious as to place our democratic order in jeopardy. The impeachment process galvanizes a moment of national deliberation unparalleled except perhaps at the time of a presidential election. Should a majority of the House of Representatives and two-thirds of the Senate concur that a president has so undermined the integrity of the constitutional system as to warrant removal, the demands of deliberative democracy will have been met. Impeachment for such "high crimes and misdemeanors," even if technically not statutory crimes, remains an invaluable safeguard against corruption and possible despotism. This is an adaptive argument that also ratifies the wisdom of the Framers.

Professor Stephen Griffin, however, has proffered an alternative "living Constitution" argument that supports a different conclusion. His argument is that the advent of political parties and what he calls "the party-political logic" of the Johnson, Nixon, and Trump impeachments replaced the Hamiltonian vision with "a constitutional order in which presidents could be impeached only when the opposing party controlled Congress and then only for committing indictable crimes or, at least, significant violations of law."[206] Griffin does not offer a normative argument that the displacement of the Hamiltonian vision is a good (or bad) thing. Rather, he offers his interpretation of the Impeachment Clause as a historically accurate description of where the Constitution has landed in a world in which "interactions between the president and Congress are 'party-political,' that is, deeply influenced by partisan allegiances and the always-pressing need to advance the interests of one's own party."[207]

The fact that Professor Griffin and I reach different adaptive, "living Constitution" interpretations reflects both sources of indeterminacy I mentioned above. I give greater weight to the persistent historical dominance of the Hamiltonian view than does Griffin; he gives greater weight to the pragmatic implications of party politics. Moreover, although Griffin does not frame his conclusion with a democratic defense, it is easy to see that one is possible. When Hamilton wrote, he represented a generation hostile to political parties. Theirs was a vision of presidents selected essentially on the basis of good character and public achievement. The statement by Chief Justice Roberts in his opinion for the *Seila Law* majority that "the Framers made the President the most democratic and politically accountable official in Government" is entirely anachronistic.[208] Not only was the president *not* to be chosen directly by "the People," the president was not necessarily to be chosen even by intermediary officials—state legislators, for example—who were popularly elected. Instead, state legislators would determine for each state how that state's electors would be chosen. Our still-imperfectly democratic election process did not become institutionally fixed until the Age of Jackson.[209] One could argue that, however imperfect a modern president's democratic mandate, the far-more-democratic character of the office now as compared to 1787 argues for a higher threshold of wrongdoing to support ousting the elected chief executive. Removal of a modern president would undo the previously expressed will of citizen-voters. Furthermore, insofar as impeachment now follows a "party-political logic," it might be urged that respecting the predominance of political parties in shaping contemporary political institutions is a good thing given that parties remain the predominant vehicles for mobilizing political activism among the voting public at large. Seen in this light, a now-limited role for impeachment might be seen as reflecting a much deeper commitment to electoral democracy, as compared to that of the Framers.

The facts that the two arguments just outlined assign different weights to different aids to interpretation and that a democratic defense for each is possible lead me to two concluding points. The first is that I still believe that what I would call the adaptive, living Hamiltonian view is superior. Although each modern president brings to the office more democratic electoral bona fides than our early presidents, the institutions that sit in judgment of the president—the House and Senate—are also democratically chosen. Any impeachment hearings and trial emanating from House and Senate decisions will occasion extensive democratic deliberation both within and beyond Congress. Given the two-term limit imposed by the Twenty-Second Amendment, the discipline imposed on presidents by the desire for reelection disappears after being reelected once, while the oversight of Congress is ever present. Moreover, impeachment can be consequential for our democracy even if the Senate acquits a president. Much will depend on popular reaction. Thus, for example, in initially egging on the Democratic House to impeach him for his importuning of Ukraine, Trump was perhaps thinking that, like Bill Clinton, he would enjoy a positive bump in the polls due to the partisan action against him. That never happened. Despite the Senate's acquittal, the public did not think the House's judgment was unfair or that the offense on which it focused was inconsequential.[210] I am clearly speculating by this point, but I believe it now well established that a president's use of official acts to leverage foreign assistance to his or her reelection campaign is an impeachable offense. In this regard, history may attribute greater significance to the single pro-conviction vote of Utah senator Mitt Romney, himself a former Republican presidential candidate, than to the party-line acquittal votes of his fellow Senate Republicans.

My second point is that interpreters arguing on democratic principle whether the "living Hamiltonian" interpretation or the "living party-political logic" interpretation is superior would at least be arguing about the right thing. Neither seeks to define "high crimes and misdemeanors" by scouring ancient texts in the hope they could make the decision for us. Both arguments—the one I sincerely believe and the one I have been presumptuous enough to craft for Professor Griffin—locate the authority to interpret the Impeachment Clause in the present, not the past. And both arguments strive to align ambiguous constitutional text with an interpretation best meeting the needs of democratic constitutionalism. That is how the separation of powers and Article II specifically should be approached in the twenty-first century.

SEVEN

Breaking the Grip of Presidentialism

THE ANALYSIS SO FAR has pointed to two very different conceptions of our chief executive. The *presidentialist* version treats the chief executive as the singular constitutional vessel for all power vested in the executive branch. Even authority Congress delegates to an agency becomes authority delegated to the president, who may personally command how each officer of the executive branch discharges their discretionary functions—at the threat of at-will discharge. The democratic constitutionalist view of Article II also ascribes to the president important powers under Article II, both explicit and implicit. But all are subject to congressional oversight, and most are subject to legislative control, at least as to process. This view of the presidency multiplies the opportunities for both formal and informal interbranch policy dialogue, as well as opening more options for public input into executive branch decision-making. It recognizes the democratic character of both elected branches of government and prioritizes checks and balances, as well as the rule of law, over executive branch expediency.

The democratic constitutionalist president need not be a weak chief executive. The unique visibility of the office will always give the president an unmatched capacity for political mobilization. Congress may continue to delegate broad authorities to the executive branch; the president, by choosing and supervising agency heads, will have a profound influence over the government's policy direction pursuant to those statutes. The veto power will continue to ensure that the White House has an outsized role in the content of legislation. Yet the chief executive should also be deeply conscious of his or her ultimate dependence on Congress for virtually all of a president's capacity to set the direction of government spending and to alter the public's legal duties and entitlements through regulation and administrative adjudication.

However appealing the latter picture may be, the two conceptions of the presidency are importantly not symmetrical. Legal scholars, judges, and executive branch lawyers—mostly conservative—have sought to legitimate the presidentialist conception of Article II by purveying a set of putatively originalist theories as to the Constitution's guarantees of presidential authority. If they are right, then we are legally required to have a unilateral presidency, unless the Constitution is amended. Presidents may implement their ideas simply by continuing to act unilaterally, which they will all but inevitably have political incentives to do.

On the other hand, the more democratic reading of Article II is chiefly a narrative of the authorities granted to Congress and to the courts to check and balance the president, *should they choose to do so*. Congress could limit the president's authority to remove administrators. Congress could set ground rules for U.S. foreign policy. Congress could limit the president's options for deploying U.S. military force. Congress might demand information from the executive branch more resolutely. Courts could enforce vigorously whatever limitations on presidential unilateralism Congress enacts. But all these moves would require initiative, and institutional incentives for initiative beyond the executive branch may be anemic. Should Congress and the courts forbear in the exercise of their constitutional authority, the presidentialist version of executive power wins by default. Inertia, in other words, favors presidentialism, even if legal history and interpretive soundness do not.[1]

The upshot of this asymmetry is that proper understanding of the Constitution is by itself but a parchment-thin bulwark against the threat of authoritarianism rooted in presidentialism.[2] Congress, the courts, and voters need to embrace the cause of democracy. Change is imperative. Yet at this moment in our history, three critical circumstances impede meaningful change. The first is the existence of a Supreme Court majority still committed to the myth of the unitary presidency.[3] Litigants challenging the executive must argue on these justices' terms to have any hope of prevailing for their clients. Reading recent opinions, lawyers and law students may too readily accept presidentialist narratives as if they treat history accurately, which they do not. Myths recede slowly.

The second is the supine posture of Congress, an institution in which allegiance to party has overcome allegiance to institutional integrity. Those of us who served in the 1970s Justice Department can recall Democratic majorities in Congress no less deferential to a Democratic president than they had been to Republicans, at least in the conduct of oversight. This is no longer the case for either party. A bipartisan duo of political scientists, both preeminent observers of the legislative branch, Thomas Mann and Norm Ornstein, bemoan a Congress gripped by "the permanent campaign, the collapse of the center . . . , the growing ideological polarization of the parties, the transformation of intense partisanship into virtually tribal politics, and [a] decline in accountability."[4]

The third is the public's fickleness when it comes to supporting politicians who are committed to democratic principles and checks and balances. Unfortunately, we tend to be fans of executive restraint and forbearance mostly when we do not share the incumbent president's objectives.[5] If our candidate prevailed in the most recent election—and even more if we believe there exists a crisis to be addressed—presidential assertiveness suddenly looks like a good thing.

For these reasons, breaking the grip of presidentialism requires a two-track agenda. First, there must be a set of institutional reforms within government to counter presidential unilateralism and strengthen executive accountability. The second is a set of broader democratic reforms to create the conditions under which reforms of the first kind have a more realistic chance of adoption.

CHANGING GOVERNMENT FROM WITHIN

A Congressional Agenda

The judiciary can help to recalibrate separation of powers law, but its role is chiefly one of deciding cases that others bring to the courts' attention. Courts are poorly positioned to take the creative lead in re-balancing our constitutional democracy. That role belongs to Congress, which possesses a considerable arsenal of powers for checking the executive.[6] Unfortunately, Congress has weakened itself as a checking institution in a variety of ways.[7] Since the mid-90s, there has been a shift of power and resources away from the committees and toward the leadership of the House and Senate. The drop in rank-and-file staff numbers has correlated with less committee activity, less rigor in routine oversight, and a seeming inability to get even normal business done in a timely fashion.

Congress's ills arguably have less to do with constitutional design than with the political agendas of the particular senators and representatives we elect. For example, it is the members of Congress who have decided to allocate their staff budgets increasingly to their home districts, rather than supporting legislative activity in Washington. Many members try to be in Washington only from Tuesday through Thursday, dramatically reducing the opportunities for interaction. What Mann and Ornstein observed in 2006 about committee deliberation seems to be borne out still: "Committee deliberation on controversial legislation has become increasingly partisan and formalistic, with the serious work being done by the committee chair, party leadership, administration officials, and lobbyists."[8] As two other political scientists wrote in 2018: "By any available measure, the U.S. Congress is not currently functioning at a high level. The number of laws being passed is near an all-time low, while the number of issues that the institution is gridlocked on stands at an all-time high."[9]

One could argue, of course, that a gridlocked Congress may show the success of the legislative branch at mirroring a highly polarized country. But Americans are not polarized on everything. Large majorities support more protective firearms regulation,[10] a path to citizenship for undocumented immigrants who arrived in the U.S. as children,[11] and a higher minimum wage.[12] Americans across all party lines overwhelmingly favor allowing the federal government to negotiate with drug companies on prescription drug prices.[13] For a variety of reasons, some institutional and some cultural, we frequently live, as Dahlia Lithwick has written, under minority rule.[14] Congress often fails to represent significant bipartisan policy consensus among the public as a whole.

A Congress determined to re-democratize the executive branch would focus primarily on five areas: presidential involvement in agency decision-making generally, protecting the rule of law, curbing presidential unilateralism in war making, reforming the president's emergency powers, and increasing presidential accountability.

With regard to the president's relationship involvement in agency administrative processes, Congress should bring that activity within the purview of the Administrative Procedure Act.[15] It should demand a process that reveals the ways, if any, in which the Office of Management and Budget or other White House sub-agencies induced changes in whatever substantive rules are issued by executive branch agencies. The record should be sufficient to enable reviewing courts to determine whether the policies put forward by agencies are consistent with their statutory mandates and not dominated by political considerations unrelated to the rulemaking record.

Regarding agency adjudication, Congress should depoliticize as much as possible the selection procedures for all quasi-judicial agency functionaries. If the formal appointment of administrative judges is to be conducted by politically appointed agency heads, Congress should make that process a technical formality, while leaving actual selection in the hands of career officials. Alternatively, Congress should vest the appointment of adjudicatory officers in the courts of law, removing the process altogether from White House influence.

It is imperative also to repair the Federal Vacancies Reform Act.[16] As argued in chapter 6, Congress should insist that the order of succession in specific agency statutes be followed when Congress has provided such an order. When the president is given alternatives for filling vacancies that would ordinarily require Senate confirmation, it should not be permissible to appoint acting officials who have not been confirmed to any position (at least beyond a new administration's first months), to place functions in the hands of appointees from outside agencies, or to leave those functions indefinitely in the hands of persons to whom powers have been delegated without formally reassigning them.

To protect the rule of law, Congress should reform the current discharge-at-will system for both agency inspectors general and for United States attorneys.[17] Because of their inferior officer status, the cleanest process might be a provision for judicial appointment, perhaps aided by a commission system that would provide the appointing courts with slates of duly vetted, highly qualified candidates, at least for U.S. attorney positions. U.S. attorneys should also serve for terms of years, subject to removal only for good cause.

Congress could also usefully buttress checks and balances in interpreting separation of powers law by creating an office of first-class lawyers to serve the legislative branch in the way the Justice Department's Office of Legal Counsel serves the executive. They would be able to address questions of executive and legislative power with the same degree of skill and sophistication as OLC, but with institutional roots in Congress, not the presidency. Having first-rate competition in the world of legal analysis might prod OLC to be yet more protective of the rigor and integrity of its opinions.

The Trump administration, like others before it, dramatized the importance to the rule of law of reform of the pardon power. At the very least,

Congress should enact its understanding that presidential self-pardon is impermissible. But as Keith Whittington has observed, real reform requires a constitutional amendment.[18] Because of public revulsion against both Trump's politicized use of the pardon power and Bill Clinton's pardons for both his brother and a fugitive financier and longtime supporter, Marc Rich, it might be possible to mobilize a bipartisan supermajority to move such an amendment forward.[19] The amendment should preclude presidential self-pardon and authorize Congress to legislate a quasi-judicial process for entertaining and making recommendations to the president concerning pardon applications. In drafting its proposed amendment, Congress should also consider whether to ban lame-duck pardons after a president has faced his or her last opportunity for reelection.

A Congress intent on restoring itself as a check on executive overreach must attend to the difficult, but urgent question of war powers. Two legislative projects are imperative. One is an updated charter for the use of force in response to international terrorism. Military operations against terrorist groups in the third decade of the century should no longer be based on a 2002 Authorization to Use Military Force in Iraq.[20] Even more problematic has been the reliance of every president since 9/11 on the 2001 AUMF against al Qaeda and its supporters.[21] The Obama administration cited the 2001 AUMF in support of operations not only in Afghanistan, but also in Syria, Somalia, Libya, and Yemen.[22] In some cases, the executive branch has relied on the AUMF as authority to confront groups that were not in existence in 2001, including some that are competitors with, not supporters of al Qaeda. Congress needs to consider against which armed groups the use of force should be authorized, as well as a process for fast-track consideration of future presidential proposals to add other groups to the list. It should do the same with regard to naming the countries in which the use of force will be authorized against new state actors. Congress should require that any force undertaken pursuant to its new resolution comply with the requirements of international law. And most important, the AUMF should have a sunset provision, requiring deliberation over reauthorization on a periodic basis.[23]

The second project is a rewrite of the War Powers Resolution (WPR) as a permanent framework for the use of military force more generally. As noted earlier, one thoughtful draft rewrite of the WPR was a "Use of Force Resolution" introduced by then-Senator Joseph Biden, which would have repealed the War Powers Resolution and substituted for it a far more detailed and potentially restrictive regulation of presidential power.[24] It generally followed the WPR's strategy of requiring reports and consultation to insure presidential accountability, but added a critical element: potential judicial review to enable members of Congress to seek declaratory relief in the face of presidential violations. Subsequent to the introduction of the Biden proposal, however, the Supreme Court has proven reluctant in other contexts to permit individual members of legislative bodies to sue on the basis of those bodies' institutional interests.[25] As a result, what Congress should authorize is a process whereby, via concurrent resolution, the House and Senate may designate the Speaker of the House and the Senate majority leader to bring such a suit on behalf of the legislative branch. The new WPR should put such a resolution on a fast-track process and exempt it from filibusters. Such a process "may increase the likelihood that Congress will succeed in challenging the usurpation of its constitutional role in deciding whether and when to wage war."[26]

Congress should also reexamine the ease with which it has permitted presidents to exercise broad economic powers in the face of putative national emergencies. Under current law, the president's declaration of a national emergency triggers his ability to use a variety of emergency statutes Congress has enacted.[27] The statute to which presidents turn most often is called the International Economic Emergency Powers Act (IEEPA).[28] Both presidents and presidential candidates have used or proposed to use the IEEPA not for short-term exigent measures, but to achieve broad policy goals that ought clearly to involve intense congressional deliberation. Trump, for example, cited the Act as the potential basis for imposing retaliatory tariffs on goods from Mexico and for possibly ordering U.S. companies to leave China. Bernie Sanders once suggested that, if elected president, he would have used executive authority to impose sanctions on companies threatening "national and global [greenhouse gas] emissions reductions goals."[29] As urged by former State Department official Peter Harrell: "Regardless of whether one agrees or disagrees with these policies, they are the type of far-reaching actions that should be subject to strong checks and balances, not executive fiat."[30] Rather than necessarily narrowing the grounds for which emergencies can be declared, Congress should, as Harrell recommends, require much more detailed reporting to Congress concerning the putative benefits to U.S. policy interests from any emergency measures undertaken, as well as an estimate of the costs to U.S. interests resulting from those measures. Congress should also "amend IEEPA to require an affirmative congressional vote to continue IEEPA actions beyond an initial period of time, such as six months or a year, with actions automatically lapsing if Congress fails to act."[31] Congress's authority to act in this area is beyond doubt. Not only is the regulation of commerce with foreign nations explicitly within Congress's enumerated constitutional powers, but Congress has frequently legislated to require specific administrative procedures as prerequisite to executive branch action in pursuing national security.[32]

Finally, although any effort in this regard will be politically fraught, a process must be created to assure some meaningful accountability for executive branch malfeasance, including malfeasance by the president. Even if incumbent presidents could be prosecuted, however, it seems implausible that any such initiative would be undertaken by a Justice Department under the incumbent president's supervision. The president's misconduct would have to be so manifest and so corrupt as to defy political exculpation. Both party and public must have abandoned the president all but entirely.

The prospect of past presidential criminality poses similarly difficult problems. Even if confronted with compelling evidence of a former president's felonies while in office, the political minefield facing a successor administration will be daunting. If the successor president is of the same party, then prosecution risks splintering his or her political base. If the successor president is of a different party, then partisan challenges to the legitimacy of the prosecution may make it extremely difficult to get traction on other pressing public priorities.

A Congress intent on protecting the rule of law should attend to these difficulties. There needs to be as nonpartisan an investigative and prosecutorial process as possible for examining serious allegations of criminality by past presidents. In the wake of independent counsel probes regarding, first, Iran-Contra and then, later, Whitewater and the Lewinsky scandal, both parties were eager to abandon the independent counsel provisions of the 1978 Ethics in Government Act when they lapsed.[33] The independent counsel law remains, however, the best model available for investigating and possibly prosecuting a former president and that president's family and close associates, if implicated in felonies relating to the former president's time in office. An important amendment might be the requirement that the judicial panel appointing an independent counsel must choose a distinguished individual with past prosecutorial experience who belongs to the party of the past president. This might help reduce any public sense that one party is simply trying to weaken the political opposition.

The Supreme Court poses a twin set of obstacles to achieving a presidency less conducive to authoritarianism. One is its current membership. Even if Congress pursued the ambitious agenda I have suggested, the ascension to the Supreme Court of Justice Gorsuch to succeed Justice Scalia, and of Justice Kavanaugh to replace Justice Kennedy, produced the most executive-indulgent Court since World War II—and that was even before the appointment of the avowed originalist, Justice Amy Coney Barrett, to succeed the late Justice Ruth Bader Ginsburg.[34] As repeated cases have shown, Chief Justice Roberts, an alumnus of the Reagan administration, still adheres to the originalist myth of the unitary executive.[35] A current Supreme Court majority thus remains enamored of an exaggerated version of the president's constitutional prerogatives, creating the possibility that the Court would turn back at least some of the most important congressional measures aimed at restoring the rule of law. Absent the current justices' rethinking of their approach to Article II, the cure for this problem must be the appointment of justices more skeptical of unitary executive theory and presidential unilateralism than the current Court.

The second problem is structural. The absence of electoral accountability and the constitutional guarantee of life tenure made the federal judiciary a counter-majoritarian institution from its inception. But counter-majoritarian does not have to mean undemocratic. The framers understood their new governmental design to be revolutionary in its approach to representation, but it was important that the people had a hand, whether direct or indirect, in constituting every branch of government. Moreover, each branch partook of government's fiduciary obligation to pursue the true welfare of all the people.[36] In the words of James Wilson:

> The executive and judicial powers are now drawn from the same source, are now animated by the same principles, and are now directed to the same ends, with the legislative authority: they who execute, and they who administer the laws, are so much the servants, and therefore as much the friends of the people, as those who make [the laws].[37]

Closer to our time, Alexander Bickel famously argued that the federal judiciary was uniquely positioned to uphold long-term values that the Constitution reflected, but which might be unduly subordinated if decision-making were left entirely to elected officials.[38] A Court so positioned might make important contributions to democracy's deliberative character. Along these lines, Robert Post and Reva Siegel have argued that, in articulating constitutional values, courts interact in democracy-enhancing ways with nonjudicial political actors and social movements. The public may adopt, resist, or transform those articulations—reactions that may, in dialectic fashion, shape further rounds of constitutional adjudication. Post and Siegel "use the term 'democratic constitutionalism' to denominate these complex and interdependent relationships between constitutional law and politics."[39]

At a time of hyper-partisanship, however, faith in such a democratic judicial role becomes difficult to sustain. The "sets of beliefs and knowledge" held even by jurists purporting to share the same general values may become so "radically different" from one another that the application of those views to concrete disputes by a Supreme Court majority becomes less and less a credible signal of reliable constitutional understanding.[40] The public begins to perceive different wings of the Court as defined more by party than by jurisprudence. In this way, lifetime tenure for judges—and especially justices—diminishes in its attractiveness as a way of ensuring the robust representation of long-term constitutional values.[41] Lifetime tenure rather maximizes the value of a coveted prize for presidents and senators intent on entrenching the worldview of one political party rather than another.

The temptation of entrenchment was all too obvious in how Senate Republicans responded to the recent Supreme Court vacancies. Their refusal in 2016 to entertain any Obama nomination to succeed Justice Scalia was an unprecedented act of institutional hardball.[42] Obama's nominee, Judge Merrick Garland of the U.S. Court of Appeals for the District of Columbia Circuit, should have cruised to confirmation, but Republicans stonewalled the nomination on the supposed ground that a Supreme Court vacancy arising in the last year of a president's term ought only to be filled after the voters had decided the impending presidential contest. Following Trump's election, the Senate, led by Republican majority leader Mitch McConnell, abolished the sixty-vote requirement to get an up-or-down confirmation vote for Neil Gorsuch.[43] With the backing of fifty-four senators, Gorsuch took the Scalia seat, joining Justice Thomas among the Court's most enthusiastic supporters of broad executive power.[44]

The appointment of Amy Coney Barrett to succeed Ruth Bader Ginsburg betrayed the same yearning for entrenchment. Although Republican justices outnumbered their Democratic colleagues 5–4 in 2020, political conservatives suspected Chief Justice John Roberts of insufficient fealty to the hard-right Trump agenda because of several critical, high-profile decisions for which he had joined the Court's more liberal wing.[45] Ginsburg's passing on September 23, 2020, gave Trump what he regarded as an urgent opportunity to appoint a "safe" sixth justice just in case legal disputes concerning the November 2020 election should elicit Supreme Court involvement.[46] Republicans abandoned their objection to filling Supreme Court vacancies in close proximity to a presidential election. Instead, Trump nominated Barrett on September 26, and on October 26, 2020—just over a month since Ginsburg's death—the Senate confirmed Barrett's appointment on a near-party lines vote. Only Susan Collins, a Maine Republican facing reelection, joined the Democrats in protest against the rushed proceedings. Republican Senators argued that Democrats would do the same if they had an equivalent opportunity. This was equivalent to admitting it would have been irrational for a party intent on clinging to power to have done otherwise.[47]

Although the Democrats retook control of the Senate in 2021, the slimness of their majority foredoomed the most dramatic possible short-term responses. For example, with a 6–3 right-wing majority on the Court, Congress could expand the Court to a bench of thirteen, creating four new seats for a Democratic president to fill, and then trim the Court back to a bench of nine, depending on the order of subsequent retirements. A more long-term approach would be engineering reforms in the Court's dynamics through statutory changes that would limit the number of years a justice would sit on the Supreme Court—serving the remainder of their life tenure on a lower court—and perhaps randomize the panels of justices who would decide individual cases.[48] Such innovations would significantly reduce the prospects for partisan manipulation of Supreme Court outcomes. Lowering the stakes surrounding the appointment of each individual justice would help protect American democracy because "capturing the referees," including court systems, is a building block of authoritarianism.[49]

Internal Executive Branch Reform

Pro-democracy structural changes in either the Supreme Court or the executive branch could be mandated only through legislation (or less likely, constitutional amendment). Presidents, however, could take their own voluntary steps to bolster a rule-of-law culture within the executive branch. The real disadvantage of any such approach is that what one president may erect, another may just as easily disassemble.

Nonetheless, if law is to function yet more effectively as a constraint on executive authority, the relationship of White House lawyers to the Justice Department—specifically, to the Office of Legal Counsel—needs recalibration.[50] Structurally, OLC is inevitably in a precarious position, not unlike that of an "outside" law firm hired by in-house counsel. On one hand, the legal opinions of OLC are of value only to the extent that the office enjoys respect for both its quality of analysis and independence. Yet an office wholly at arm's length from the White House and indifferent to the political consequences of its opinions will be asked less frequently to opine on sensitive issues. Maintaining a judicious balance between "independent" and "supportive" is not easy, and arriving at that balance requires attention to norms that are not entirely susceptible to written specification.

I share a view expressed by other OLC alumni—I served under President Carter and more briefly under President Reagan—that the pendulum has swung too far toward the role of presidential enabler.[51] The office has too often cheapened the currency of its opinions by providing analyses that were notably weak on the law. The most notorious example is widely known as the Torture Memo, which purported to approve the legality of the Bush administration's harsh interrogation techniques in the wake of 9/11.[52] Under Trump, perhaps the most dubious example was an opinion approving a decision by the Treasury Secretary not to provide the president's tax returns to the House Ways and Means Committee, despite what looked like a plain statutory duty to do so.[53] Not only was the reasoning of the latter opinion highly questionable, but it was unclear why OLC would be involved at all in a question relating far more directly to the political fortunes of the incumbent president than to the institution of the presidency. An OLC in this mode looks too much like a mere extension of the White House Counsel's office.

The temptation to keep one's lawyers closer rather than more distant is not limited to presidents of only one party. During my own OLC service in the Carter administration, we generally took the role of "outside counsel" seriously, generally keeping at arm's length. The Obama administration, by way of contrast, "adopted an interagency 'lawyers' group' model for deciding almost all important national security legal questions."[54] As recounted by Professor Jack Goldsmith, a former OLC head himself, the task force model "emphasizes deliberation, equities-consideration, consensus-building, and error avoidance."[55] But, as he acknowledges, "the lawyers' group tends to be White-House-centered, and White House-centered deliberations can (not must) undermine the already fragile independence of legal advice that OLC, operating as a semi-detached entity in the Justice Department, is designed to provide."[56] OLC arguably compromised its independence further under Obama by circulating legal advice in the form of tentative drafts. As Goldsmith observes, this practice "can . . . make legal conclusions an implicit topic of bargaining . . . [and] can diminish OLC's influence overall to the extent it makes OLC in practice one voice among many."[57]

Measuring the merits and demerits of different counseling models is obviously a tricky business, but it must be observed that the Obama-era task force model proved no guarantee of the best lawyering. The White House chose to ignore OLC's view and put forth a notably weak argument for remaining militarily engaged in Libya beyond the sixty-day period allowed under the War Powers Resolution.[58] To its credit, the administration relied on a statutory stretch rather than an assertion of constitutional prerogative.[59] But the entire Libya episode did not end well for U.S. interests. In retrospect, following a more conventional view of the law might have been better, not just as lawyering, but as policy.

The credibility of OLC ultimately depends on the quality of its leadership and the attitudes of the president and attorney general. It is difficult to see how the office can recover and maintain its reputation unless the attorney general insists on, and the president accepts, its distinctiveness. The cost of greater independence may be less intimate involvement with some high-profile issues, but the benefit is likely to be greater impact regarding those matters on which it does opine. Bruce Ackerman some years ago suggested reforming OLC by reconstituting it as a formal executive branch tribunal for addressing separation of powers questions.[60] But so formally independent an entity cannot play a potentially invaluable role of "outside counsel" to the White House that carefully navigates the balance between independence and enablement. A better course is to keep OLC in its current structural position, but under different norms.[61]

A president can also take steps to rebalance the influence of political and career policy makers by rebuilding the civil service. Blake Emerson and Jon D. Michaels have outlined a series of steps President Biden (and his successors) could take to replace overaggressive presidentialism with a more balanced form of "civic governance."[62] One thing presidents can do is take steps toward "depoliticizing the work of government lawyers, scientists, engineers, social workers, and law enforcement officers."[63] In addition, a president can beef up recruitment efforts, using the "bully pulpit" to highlight the important work of career bureaucrats and directing agency heads to engage fully in the policy-making process with the "essential cohort of career, expert policy analysts, scientists, lawyers, and social workers within [each] agency."[64] Although all such reforms are subject to rescission by a later president, they can help restore deliberative norms which, if helpful in producing good policy, may counsel their retention from administration to administration.

REINVIGORATING DEMOCRACY

Our institutions of government, if intent on restoring the Madisonian model of checks and balances, would do well to pursue the agenda I have outlined. Though hardly radical in form, the recommended steps would amount to a significant recalibration of power between the elected branches of the federal government. The problem in hoping for such reforms, however, is simply stated: The individuals currently enjoying significant political power have largely acquired their clout by "playing" the separation-of-powers "game" within existing rules. They have no obvious incentive to change the rules that have already made them powerful. This means that some form of external shock must be administered to induce change. Changes in the political landscape need to produce public clamor for a form of governance more pluralistic than aggressively presidentialist. For that to happen—if we want a government rededicated to democratic norms and accountability to the rule of law—democracy and the rule of law must be experienced as lived realities by more Americans.

I earlier identified as the normative premises of democracy a promise of equal respect for all, as well as inclusive opportunities to experience the exercise of meaningful influence in collective public decision-making. I have discussed how the rule of law, with commitments to transparency, publicity, and official accountability is essential to making civic equality a reality. The fact is, however, that even as America asserts its preeminence on the world stage as a constitutional democracy, these ideals are not satisfied equally well for all groups of Americans. Most obviously, as law professors Kate Andrias and Benjamin I. Sachs have succinctly stated: "At every stage of the electoral and governing process, wealthy Americans dominate."[65] Andrias and Sachs point to extensive political science research confirming what many citizens already suspect: "[F]or Americans below the top of the income distribution, any association between preferences and policy outcomes is likely to reflect the extent to which their preferences coincide with those of the affluent."[66]

Economic inequality worsened in the decades leading up to the Trump administration. According to the Pew Research Center, the top-fifth of U.S. households, in terms of earnings, have steadily brought in a larger share of the country's total income over the last five decades, with middle-class incomes growing at a slower rate than upper-tier incomes. The racial income gap between whites and Blacks has held steady since 1970, while the wealth gap between America's richest and poorer families more than doubled from 1989 to 2016. All in all, these trends have given the United States the highest rate of income inequality among all the G7 nations.[67] To their credit, some individual possessors of great wealth have chosen to devote considerable resources to strengthening democracy, but they are the exception. In general, "the wealthiest people and interest groups use their wealth to reshape laws and regulations in ways that benefit themselves."[68] Dramatic economic inequality erodes the social solidarity on which democracy depends.

What political scientists have identified as the link between economic and political inequality applies also with regard to America's racial hierarchy. Over forty years ago, the late Derrick A. Bell Jr. articulated what he called the "interest-convergence thesis": "The interest of blacks in achieving racial equality will be accommodated only when it converges with the interests of whites."[69] What made *Brown v. Board of Education* possible, he argued, was that, by 1954, "whites in policymaking positions [were] able to see the economic and political advances at home and abroad that would follow abandonment of segregation."[70] School desegregation remedies faltered, however, over the succeeding decades. The interests of Black families in educational equity were seen to conflict with the interests of white families in preserving traditional patterns of local control over schools and in exercising their preference to avoid racially integrated classrooms.[71] The Supreme Court effectively protected the latter interests.[72]

The Supreme Court's race jurisprudence is unfortunately consistent with Bell's diagnosis. Civil rights advocates in the 1960s and early 1970s argued for a "disparate impact" view of the Fourteenth Amendment's Equal Protection Clause. Under a disparate impact approach to equality, a law disproportionately burdening the interests of a racial minority or of one sex would be deemed unconstitutional absent a compelling, racially neutral justification for leaving the law in place. The Burger Court decided, however, that laws disproportionately burdensome to one race[73] or one sex[74] are unconstitutional only if adopted with the intention to inflict that harm. The power of constitutional law to enforce the democratic promise of equal concern diminished as litigation was thus confined to fighting only the most manifest efforts to inflict racial or sexual subordination. The interests of the racial majority could dominate the interests of racial minorities so long as the majority's motivation was not substantially—or provably—one of racial animosity.

The persistence of cross-cutting inequalities, even as various groups intensified their demands for inclusion and social justice, laid the groundwork for polarizing the American electorate. As different groups of non-privileged voters experienced the precariousness of their own influence over government, tensions between them escalated. Racial conflict and economic insecurity paved the way for the ascension of would-be leaders "exciting [people's] jealousies and apprehensions," and eager "to throw affairs into confusion, and bring on civil commotion."[75] Such demagogues inevitably offer their own ascent to power as the cure for the resentments they stoke. Polarization accelerates a vicious cycle potentially fatal to democracy.[76] By undermining social tolerance, bipartisan cooperation, and democratic norms, polarization frustrates each citizen's ability to see his or her welfare linked to the welfare of all fellow citizens, which, in turn, continues to deepen the corrosive impact of polarization on the nation's social and political fabric.

To remedy this situation, the recitation of democracy and rule of law as abstract ideals is not enough to rally people against the dangers of authoritarianism. Nor is it enough for government to direct its reformist intentions entirely toward its own internal machinery. A realistic theory of democratic renewal must encompass "the normative principles that animate democracy and the structure of the political avenues, coalitions, and equilibriums that could sustain the institutional realization of those principles in large-scale, modern societies."[77] Citizens must again be able to experience the achievements of democratic self-government through their own participation. In the words of George Packer: There is no remedy except the exercise of [democratic] muscles that have atrophied."[78]

A government program directed at reenergizing American democracy should pursue at least five goals. First, reduce barriers to democratic participation in existing institutions. Second, shore up those institutions on which citizens rely for relevant and credible information about public affairs. Third, strengthen the capacity of citizens to engage with information. Fourth, generate opportunities and motivation for meaningful public engagement. Fifth, help enable less wealthy and other underrepresented groups to "build organizations capable of countervailing the political power of the wealthy."[79]

In terms of reducing existing barriers, we must reverse the determination of too many state governments to alter election rules in ways that make it difficult to dislodge incumbents. It is not only that gerrymandered election districts pack one party into as few seats as possible, while the party in power maximizes its "safe" seats. Strict ID laws, cutbacks in voting days and locations, and tendentious "purges" of voter rolls have all been deployed to make voting more difficult for underrepresented groups.[80] Congress, however, has explicit constitutional power to "make or alter ... Regulations" regarding "[t]he Times, Places and Manner of holding Elections for Senators and Representatives."[81] Congress should exercise that power to make registration and voting easier and the counting of votes more secure. Such efforts could bolster public confidence that officeholders genuinely represent the choice of voters. Toward this end, states should also adopt election rules that award victories only to majority winners. In many elections, no one candidate will represent the first choice of most voters.[82] To counter polarization, however, office holding should go only to those who, for a majority of voters, represent at least the most acceptable of the widely supported candidates.

Citizens cannot successfully govern themselves if they do not know what is going on in their communities, their states, and the country at large. Yet a collapse in print advertising has resulted in a disastrous reduction in state and local news reporting. Research from the University of North Carolina has shown nearly eighteen hundred local newspapers closed between 2004 and 2018.[83] Consolidation in ownership over many of the remaining papers along with a reduction in investment in newsrooms mean that "many more have lost the ability to comprehensively cover their communities."[84] The loss, to be clear, is in the availability of reporting specifically, not journalism in general. We are flooded with "information," but not with fact-gathering by trained investigators. Given the loss in resources devoted to apprising the public of what their governments are doing, recent decades, as Princeton sociologist Paul Starr has remarked, have proven a good time to be a corrupt local official—many fewer trained eyes are watching.[85]

It is time for America to redress its overreliance on private commercial markets to sustain adequate news reporting. Civic information is a public good—one person's consumption does not reduce its availability to others, and those who fail to pay for it cannot be excluded from the benefits that follow from its circulation. Yet exclusive reliance on private markets for the generation of public goods inevitably results in their underproduction relative to potential social benefit. Policies such as tax-enabled new ownership structures may help some news organizations to survive in the private marketplace. But they are insufficient to generate the support needed for enough professional reporting to undergird successful democratic problem solving. Over the longer run, governments in the United States should move toward the adoption of systems of public subsidies to support news reporting.[86] Although the idea now seems foreign to our traditions of commercially supported and lightly regulated media, government has been involved with the support of American news media ever since the earliest postal subsidies for newspaper delivery.[87] A variety of public funding models are being tried in other Western democracies, and promising moves in the United States have already been seen at the state and local level.[88] Without new nonmarket mechanisms for the support of reporting, Americans will never have the level of trained, professional reporting they need to help ensure government accountability and responsiveness.

Strengthening people's capacity to engage with civic information requires intensifying our support of public education and redoubling support for public libraries. First-rate public education is essential to a healthy democracy. Schooling is the critical institution in helping to prepare young people to become well-informed, critically thinking citizens. But public schools play an additional and invaluable democratic role. They unite all segments of a local community in an ongoing deliberation about what best serves the children of all. There is probably no other public institution that is more successful at drawing into democratic dialogue the fully diverse range of constituencies within a local community. Yet public K–12 education has been under assault for decades, as proponents of "school choice" have worked to steer local funds away from public schools—including those charter schools that are genuinely public—to private and parochial schools, including privately managed charter schools with less public accountability.[89] These movements have drawn on a narrative of public school failure that is largely exaggerated, relying largely on the lower test scores of students in low-income school districts.[90] As with other public sector institutions, the political response to struggling schools has often been to make it yet easier to divert funds away from the already resource-stretched units, which predictably makes it yet harder for them to excel. It is imperative to reverse this trend.

Beyond public schools, the most important "information institution" in any community is likely to be its library. Far from being rendered obsolete through digitization, libraries have taken on even greater importance in guiding citizens through an increasingly complex information ecology. They are typically centers for community meetings and for free public programs, including free after-school enrichment opportunities for children. Libraries are arguably unique in simultaneously celebrating the freedom of the individual to pursue his or her interests in the unconstrained pursuit of knowledge and manifesting the collective power of a democratic community to bond over its common interests.

The vituperation, ridicule, and hate speech so often infecting public dialogue is, indeed, poisonous. The cultural figure perhaps most responsible for yoking right-wing populist anger to the agenda of beltway Republicans was Rush Limbaugh. The elimination in 1987 of the FCC's Fairness Doctrine, which had required licensed broadcasters to provide multiple points of view on significant public issues, paved the way for Limbaugh's combative brand of misogynist, liberal-hating rhetoric on both radio and television.[91] Bill Clinton's election brought Limbaugh as targets not only the president, but also the First Lady and their twelve-year-old daughter, whom Limbaugh called the "White House dog."[92]

Yet the remedy for our democracy's ills is not, as sometimes suggested, "civility," but engagement. The surface orderliness of government policy making in earlier decades was often purchased at the price of exclusion. We cannot expect communities that have experienced injustice, that have endured marginalization and disrespect, and that have suffered from the neglect of those supposedly responsible for protecting their interests to observe a punctilious formality that feels comfortable to those of us already empowered and protected.[93] A willingness to argue and work through disagreement openly is essential in a democratic polity. But the need to deliberate effectively cannot become a bar to the honest expression of feeling, including grievance. The challenge is how to attract deeper and broader democratic engagement.

The executive branch of the federal government most frequently invites engagement through public hearings and the notice-and-comment process that precedes the issuance of many administrative regulations. The opportunity to engage agencies in these ways can become a focus for the work of civil society institutions, such as public interest groups and political organizations, which are able to participate meaningfully in such exercises.[94]

Although these deliberative opportunities are undoubtedly significant, their scale is unlikely to give many individual citizens the experience of having real influence over the content of the policy decisions that touch their lives.

What could be transformative would be a renaissance in opportunities for so-called ordinary citizens to participate in impactful ways in decision-making in local communities. It is at the level of the local community that citizens can most practicably gather and deliberate meaningfully over their common needs, opportunities, and priorities. Thus, while the federal government no doubt has the greatest resources to sponsor such deliberative opportunities, the federal bureaucracy is not optimally situated to create a strong sense of individual involvement.[95] Congress could thus do a great deal of good by setting up a fund for local deliberative democracy, to be administered perhaps by newly created National Institutes for Democracy modeled on the National Institutes for Health. Although the logistics of such exercises may vary by subject matter and location, funding should be available to local projects only if they meet two critical criteria. First, there must be some structural guarantee that the persons deliberating be representative of the citizenry as a whole—the deliberating body must not be skewed to disproportionately represent any one set of interests within the overall community. Second, whatever the decision put up for deliberation, the local governing body should commit beforehand to adopt whatever decisions the deliberating body makes—or to explain in painstaking detail any determination not to do so. For example, if the issue put before the deliberating citizenry is whether to build an additional runway at the local airport, considering both its economic and environmental impacts, there should be a presumption among those in authority that the deliberative outcome will be followed. Such community deliberations could not be expected to replace more than a small fraction of a governing authority's decision-making, but they could occur often enough and with respect to enough significant issues to generate a strong democratic ethos within the community overall.

Finally, Congress should make it easier for noncorporate interests to organize in order to provide "checks and balances" against the political power of the wealthy. Labor unions represent the paradigm example, but Professors Andrias and Sachs have also explained how local tenants' groups and other forms of social organization can help level the playing field for poor and working-class families to exercise significant economic and political power.[96] Framework statutes can make it easier to form such organizations and to formalize their bargaining rights. Government can promote their growth whether through subsidies, favorable tax treatment, leadership training, or the provision of physical and virtual meeting space.[97]

Measures like those I am advocating are directed toward moving the common understanding of the relationship of government-to-citizens from them-versus-us to "those of us who serve the community by working in government" and "those of us who exercise citizenship in other ways." People need to feel that, with their engagement, public problems can be collectively addressed and democratic government can effectively serve. Stephen Coleman, a leading scholar of political communication and democratic theory, has called the reconfiguration of our governing institutions along the lines I am advocating "direct representation."[98] What he means by this is a system that combines the strengths of both direct democracy—"whereby the interests and values of society are collectively, self-consciously and autonomously determined by citizens rather than ordained by elites"—and political representation—"whereby accountable deliberators are elected to work through the complex details of policy-making and legislation."[99] The virtues Coleman attributes to direct democracy can be realized, however, only if citizens participate.

Reform on this scale is not a short-term project that will produce an immediate big "win." Political theorist Danielle Allen, one of the wisest voices writing today about the urgency of democratic renewal, has said the same: "[S]mall increments of change, multiplied by decades, are what put us where we are. They can also pull us out."[100] She emphasizes the critical role of participation in achieving democratic renewal, and she wisely understands citizen engagement as flowing from a sense of identity:

> People are not so much rational actors as purpose-driven ones. Human goals and values cannot always be represented in financial terms. Can you put a price on family? Empowerment? Self-sacrifice? Love? You cannot. As purpose-driven actors, we develop our values and learn to justify them within the context of communities that give our lives meaning and worth. Human moral equality flows from the human need to be the author of one's own life.[101]

A healthy democracy, as I earlier defined it, is legitimate precisely because it responds to the human need for personal and collective authorship of the kind to which Allen refers.

As Coleman and others have pointed out, the institutions of government can so arrange themselves as to empower citizens to be the "confident and efficacious democratic agents"[102] we need ourselves to be. Avenues of participation—especially through deliberation—help people to develop two essential capacities:

> Democratic citizens must be capable of being recognized as someone who counts; to be respected on their own terms, without being classified or categorized by pre-determined labels or stereotypes. In short, the capacity to manage one's own self-presentation—as an individual, but also as a group or area—is a precondition of democratic dignity.
>
> Democratic citizens must be capable of making a difference to the events, structures and outcomes that shape the world around them. They must not only possess a degree of historical agency that transcends the boundaries of passive spectatorship, but be confident in their capacity to exercise such agency in ways that are not ultimately manipulated, ritualistic or easily nullified.[103]

Our government can structure opportunities for political involvement that empower citizens to experience the "democratic dignity" of which Coleman speaks and which are consequential because they lead to actual legislative and administrative outcomes.[104]

Lest it seem that I have wandered far from ruminations about the presidency and about constitutional interpretation to an excessively wide-angle view of our democratic shortcomings, my argument is this: Presidentialist lawyers, judges, and legal scholars have gone far since 1981 in enabling a too-authoritarian chief executive, rhetorically legitimated by a purportedly originalist reading of the Constitution that misreads history and that attributes to the past, not the present, the power to determine our institutional possibilities. These ideas originally flowered less because of their merits than because they proved congenial to the ascendancy of conservative politics in the wake of the more liberal 1960s and 1970s. The situation can be remedied. But those in government with the power to rebalance the allocation of power will act to reform the presidency only if there is external pressure.

Sustained by the political forces that helped to generate his victory in 2020, President Biden expressed his determination, beginning with his inaugural address, to revivify democratic norms and to promote inclusive politics.[105] But as shown by Biden's unilateral revocation of some of his predecessor's most norm-challenging policies, reforms dependent solely on the character of one incumbent president are as easily repealed as created.[106]

To support more enduring reforms that can come only through constitutional or even legislative change, sustained pressure must come from the citizenry. Achieving successful problem solving through mutual democratic engagement is the necessary path by which now-polarized Americans can regain respect for their mutual legitimacy. Only a people united in their experience that democratic governance based on mutual respect and equal concern is as productive for them as an authoritarian alternative will pull together to preserve and strengthen democratic norms. Public policy should be directed at laying the foundation for that success. To put the bottom line most simply: To protect democracy, we need to reconceptualize the president to be the chief executive of a democracy. But without genuine democracy as the real-world context for that reconceptualization, "democracy's chief executive" will remain more a theory than a reality.

ACKNOWLEDGMENTS

Acknowledgments in a project of this kind are inevitably incomplete. There is too much indebtedness to too many friends and colleagues whose insights have enriched my learning over four-plus decades. I would remiss, however, if I failed to thank Maura Roessner, senior editor at the University of California Press, for her initial outreach to me and for the enthusiastic support she has given this project from the start. Likewise, I will be forever indebted to the Ohio State University and its Moritz College of Law for the encouragement, both intellectual and material, that has helped sustain my work for nearly two decades. This includes the work of two excellent students, John Coming and Jacob Farrell, Moritz College of Law Class of 2022, who provided important research assistance.

A few individuals have contributed inordinately to the book you are holding by reading all or part of earlier versions of the manuscript. I am especially grateful in this regard to my fellow members of the Board of Academic Advisers to the American Constitution Society, who graciously read and reacted to my views on constitutional interpretation; to Richard Pildes and another, anonymous reviewer for the University of California Press, for a variety of important and constructive suggestions; and most emphatically to Garrett Epps, whose detailed notes on the manuscript were invaluable—as has been his friendship and mentorship since our days as college journalists.

In addition, two legal scholars with whom I have had the privilege of coediting legal casebooks—Hal Bruff and Jerry Mashaw—have had a career-long impact on my thinking about issues of executive power, as has another valued mentor, Peter Strauss. Two more recent collaborators, Neil J. Kinkopf and Nicholas R. Parrillo, have also left their mark. My effort to concretize an understanding of executive power that is faithful to democracy and the rule of law is, in some ways, an attempt to articulate a constitutional vision embodied for me in the lives and careers of three extraordinary colleagues from the Carter-era Office of Legal Counsel, each of whom passed too soon—Larry Hammond, Tom Sargentich, and Larry Simms. I often feel that what I am trying to do is to capture their idealism in the form of constitutional analysis.

NOTES

PROLOGUE

1. Randy E. Barnett & Evan D. Bernick, *The Letter and the Spirit: A Unified Theory of Originalism*, 107 GEORGETOWN L.J. 1, 3–4 (2018).

2. Peter L. Strauss, *Overseer, or "The Decider"? The President in Administrative Law*, 75 GEO. WASH. L. REV. 696 (2007).

3. Neal K. Katyal, *Internal Separation of Powers: Checking Today's Most Dangerous Branch from Within*, 115 YALE L.J. (2006).

4. PETER M. SHANE, MADISON'S NIGHTMARE: HOW EXECUTIVE POWER THREATENS AMERICAN DEMOCRACY 28-29 (2009).

5. Calvin TerBeek, *"Clocks Must Always Be Turned Back"*: Brown v. Board of Education *and the Racial Origins of Constitutional Originalism*, 115 AM. POL. SCI. REV. 821,822 (2021).

6. *Id.*

7. *Id.*

8. GRAHAM G. DODDS, THE UNITARY PRESIDENCY 12 (2020).

9. Amanda Hollis-Brusky, *Helping Ideas Have Consequences: Political and Intellectual Investment in the Unitary Executive Theory, 1981–2000*, 89 DENV. U. L. REV. 197, 242 (2011).

10. TerBeek, *supra* note 5, at 2.

11. Stephen Skowronek, *The Conservative Insurgency and Presidential Power: A Developmental Perspective on the Unitary Executive*, 122 HARV. L. REV. 2070, 2096–2100 (2009).

12. *Id.* at 2074.

1. Jeremy Diamond, *Trump Focuses on "Perfect" Ukraine Call Despite Allegations of Broader Pressure Campaign*, CNN (Nov. 4, 2019, 5:52 PM), https://www.cnn.com /2019/11/04/politics/donald-trump-ukraine-perfect-call-defense/index.html.

2. PETER M. SHANE, MADISON'S NIGHTMARE: HOW EXECUTIVE POWER THREATENS AMERICAN DEMOCRACY (2009).

3. Elena Kagan, *Presidential Administration*, 114 HARV. L. REV. 2245, 2282 (2001).

4. George W. Bush, Remarks by the President on Stem Cell Research—Crawford, Texas (Aug. 9, 2001), 2001 WL 896981, at *3 ("I have concluded that we should allow federal funds to be used for research on these existing stem cell lines, where the life and death decision has already been made.")

5. John Cassidy, *What the Collapse of the Trump Foundation Tells Us about Donald Trump*, NEW YORKER (Dec. 20, 2018), https://www.newyorker.com/news/our -columnists/what-the-collapse-of-the-trump-foundation-tells-us-about-donald-trump.

6. Jane Chong, *Donald Trump's Strange and Dangerous 'Absolute Rights' Idea*, THE ATLANTIC (Feb. 20, 2020), https://www.theatlantic.com/ideas/archive/2020 /02/president-trump-absolute-rights/607168/.

7. KEVIN P. PHILLIPS, THE EMERGING REPUBLICAN MAJORITY (1969).

8. Andrew J. Wistrich, Jeffrey J. Rachlinski & Chris Guthrie, *Heart versus Head: Do Judges Follow the Law or Follow Their Feelings?*, 93 TEX. L. REV. 855, 869 (2015).

9. JEREMY D. BAILEY, THE IDEA OF PRESIDENTIAL ADMINISTRATION: AN INTELLECTUAL AND POLITICAL HISTORY 175 (2019).

10. Peter M. Shane, *The Originalist Myth of the Unitary Executive*, 19 U. PA. J. CONST. L. 323, 324 (2016).

11. THE SUPREME COURT OF THE UNITED STATES, https://www.supreme court.gov/about/biographies.aspx (last visited May 18, 2020) (providing a biography of Chief Justice Roberts).

12. THE SUPREME COURT OF THE UNITED STATES, https://www .supremecourt.gov/about/biographies.aspx (last visited May 18, 2020) (providing a biography of Justice Alito).

13. Walter E. Dellinger et al., *Principles to Guide the Office of the Legal Counsel* (Dec. 21, 2004), https://scholarship.law.duke.edu/cgi/viewcontent.cgi?article=2927 &context=faculty_scholarship.

14. *Our Background*, THE FEDERALIST SOCIETY, https://fedsoc.org/our -background.

15. Attorney General William Pelham Barr, UNITED STATES DEPARTMENT OF JUSTICE (Apr. 23, 2021), https://www.justice.gov/ag/bio/barr-william-pelham.

16. U.S. DEPARTMENT OF JUSTICE, COMMON LEGISLATIVE ENCROACHMENTS ON EXECUTIVE BRANCH AUTHORITY (1989), https://www.justice.gov /file/24286/download.

17. *Id.* at 248.

18. *Id.* at 250.

19. *Id.* at 256.

20. *Justice News,* THE UNITED STATES DEPARTMENT OF JUSTICE (Nov. 15, 2019), https://www.justice.gov/opa/speech/attorney-general-william-p-barr-delivers-19th-annual-barbara-k-olson-memorial-lecture.

21. THE DECLARATION OF INDEPENDENCE (U.S. 1776).

22. THOMAS PAINE, COMMON SENSE 67 (Moncure Daniel Conway ed., 3rd ed. 2016) (1776).

23. Andy Grewal, *The Separation of Powers Doctrine May Save Trump from Obstruction Charges,* YALE JOURNAL ON REGULATION (Nov. 19, 2017), https://www.yalejreg.com/nc/the-separation-of-powers-doctrine-may-save-trump-from-obstruction-charges/.

24. John C. Yoo, *Rejoinder: Treaty Interpretation and the False Sirens of Delegation,* 90 Cal. L. Rev. 1305, 1321 (2002) ("Article II's granting of the unenumerated federal executive powers to the President, in combination with his enumerated powers as commander in chief, maker of treaties, and receiver and appointer of ambassadors, makes clear that the President is the sole organ of the nation in its foreign affairs."); John C. Yoo, *The Continuation of Politics by Other Means: The Original Understanding of War Powers,* 84 Cal. L. Rev. 167, 174 (1996) ("The Framers established a system which was designed to encourage presidential initiative in war, but which granted Congress an ultimate check on executive actions. Congress could express its opposition to executive war decisions only by exercising its powers over funding and impeachment.")

25. Saikrishna Prakash, *New Light on the Decision of 1789,* 91 CORNELL L. REV. 1021 (2006).

26. Memorandum from William Barr to Rod Rosenstein, Deputy Attorney General, and Steve Engel, Assistant Attorney General (June 8, 2018), https://assets.documentcloud.org/documents/5638848/June-2018-Barr-Memo-to-DOJ-Muellers-Obstruction.pdf.

27. Department of Health and Human Services Appropriations Act, 1988, Pub. L. No. 100-102, 101 Stat. 1329, 1329-265 (1987).

28. U.S. DEPARTMENT OF JUSTICE, STATUTE LIMITING THE PRESIDENT'S AUTHORITY TO SUPERVISE THE DIRECTOR OF THE CENTERS FOR DISEASE CONTROL IN THE DISTRIBUTION OF AN AIDS PAMPHLET 56 (1988), https://www.justice.gov/file/24041/download

29. *Id.* at 57.

30. *In re Aiken Cnty.,* 645 F.3d 428, 441 (D.C. Cir. 2011).

31. Barr, *supra* note 26.

32. Memorandum from the U.S. Department of Justice, Office of the Legal Counsel, to John A. Rizzo, Senior Deputy General Counsel, Central Intelligence Agency (May 30, 2005), https://www.justice.gov/sites/default/files/olc/legacy/2013/10/21/memo-bradbury2005.pdf.

33. *Id.* at 1–2. ("By its terms, Article 16 is limited to conduct within "territory under [United States] jurisdiction." We conclude that territory under United States

Jurisdiction includes, at most, areas over which the United States exercises at least de facto authority as the government. Based on CIA assurances, we understand that the interrogations do not take place in any such areas. We therefore conclude that Article 16 is inapplicable to the CIA's interrogation practices and that those practices thus cannot violate Article 16.")

34. PETER M. SHANE, MADISON'S NIGHTMARE: HOW EXECUTIVE POWER THREATENS AMERICAN DEMOCRACY 89–95 (2009).

35. Interview by David Frost with Richard Nixon, President of the United States (May 1977).

36. Al Gore, Former Vice President, Restoring the Rule of Law (Jan. 16, 2006) (transcript available at https://web.archive.org/web/20061102082525/http://www.draftgore.com/exec_power.htm).

37. Id.

38. Id.

39. Martin S. Flaherty, *The Most Dangerous Branch*, 105 Yale L.J. 1725 (1996).

40. SAIKRISHNA BANGALORE PRAKASH, IMPERIAL FROM THE BEGINNING: THE CONSTITUTION OF THE ORIGINAL EXECUTIVE (2015).

41. Id. at 321.

42. MAX FARRAND, 1 THE RECORDS OF THE FEDERAL CONVENTION OF 1787, at 65 (1911).

43. Id. at 66 (remarks of James Wilson). As recorded in the Farrand compilation of the records of the Constitutional Convention, Wilson said: "We must consider two points of Importance existing in our country—the extent & manners of the United States—the former seems to require the vigour of Monarchy, the manners are agt. a King and are purely republican—Montesquieu is favor of confederated Republicks—I am for such a confedn. if we can take for its basis liberty, and can ensure a vigorous execution of the laws." *Id.* at 71.

44. Barr, *supra* note 26.

45. Id.

46. Brief for Petitioner at 48–49, Trump v. Mazars USA, LLP, 140 S. Ct. 660 (2019).

47. HAROLD H. BRUFF, BAD ADVICE: BUSH'S LAWYERS IN THE WAR ON TERROR 162–163 (2009).

48. Charlie Savage, *Explaining Executive Privilege and Session's Refusal to Answer Questions*, N.Y. TIMES (June 15, 2017), https://www.nytimes.com/2017/06/15/us/politics/executive-privilege-sessions-trump.html.

49. ROBERT S. MUELLER, III, 2 REPORT ON THE INVESTIGATION INTO RUSSIAN INTERFERENCE IN THE 2016 PRESIDENTIAL ELECTION (2019), https://www.justice.gov/storage/report_volume2.pdf.

50. Id. at 157.

51. Id. at 9.

52. Id. at 169.

53. 18 U.S.C. § 1505.

54. Mueller Report, *supra* note 49, at 8.

55. Josh Blackman & Seth Barrett Tillman, *The 'Resistance' vs. George Washington*, WALL STREET JOURNAL (Oct. 15, 2017, 6:13 PM), https://www.wsj.com/articles/the-resistance-vs-george-washington-1508105637.

56. U.S. CONST. art. II, § 1, cl. 7.

57. U.S. CONST. art. I, § 9, cl. 8.

58. Amended Complaint at 82, District of Columbia v. Trump, 344 F. Supp. 3d 828, 835 (D. Md. 2018) (No. 8:17-cv-1596-PJM).

59. Darren Samuelsohn, *State Department, U.S. embassies promoted Trump's Mar-a-Lago*, POLITICO (Apr. 24, 2017, 3:50 PM), https://www.politico.com/story/2017/04/24/state-department-us-embassy-mar-a-lago-237537.

60. Toluse Olorunnipa et al., *Trump has awarded next year's G-7 summit of world leaders to his Miami-area resort, the White House said*, WASH. POST (Oct. 17, 2019, 6:59 PM), https://www.washingtonpost.com/politics/trump-has-awarded-next-years-g-7-summit-of-world-leaders-to-his-miami-area-resort-the-white-house-said/2019/10/17/221b32d6-ef52-11e9-89eb-ec56cd414732_story.html.

61. *Id.*

62. District of Columbia v. Trump, 344 F. Supp. 3d 828, 835 (D. Md. 2018).

63. Blumenthal v. Trump, 373 F. Supp. 3d 191, 194 (D.D.C.), cert. denied, 382 F. Supp. 3d 77 (D.D.C. 2019), vacated, No. CV 17-1154 (EGS), 2019 WL 3948478 (D.D.C. Aug. 21, 2019), and motion to certify appeal granted, No. CV 17-1154 (EGS), 2019 WL 3948478 (D.D.C. Aug. 21, 2019), and vacated as moot, 949 F.3d 14 (D.C. Cir. 2020).

64. Id. at 204.

65. 26 U.S.C. § 6103(f).

66. Letter from Steven T. Mnuchin, Secretary of the Treasury, Dep't of the Treasury, to Richard E. Neal, Chairman on the Committee on Ways and Means, U.S. House of Representatives (May 17, 2019), https://fm.cnbc.com/applications/cnbc.com/resources/editorialfiles/2019/05/17/Secretary-Mnuchin-Letter-to-Chairman-Neal-2019-05-17.pdf.

67. Congressional Committee's Request for the President's Tax Returns Under 26 U.S.C. § 6103(f), 43 Op. Atty. Gen. __ (June 13, 2019).

68. *Id.* at 1.

69. *Id.* at 11.

70. *Id.* at 16. In 2021, the House Ways Committee—now reassembled in a new Congress—re-issued its demand, and OLC repudiated its 2019 advice. OLC's 2021 opinion concludes that, "applying the proper degree of deference due the Committee," the Treasury Secretary is required by statute to comply with the committee's demand. Ways and Means Committee's Request for the Former President's Tax Returns and Related Tax Information Pursuant to 26 U.S.C. § 6103(f)(1), 45 Op. O.L.C. __, at 4 (July 30, 2021).

71. Brief for Petitioner at 20–21, Trump v. Mazars USA, LLP, 140 S. Ct. 660 (2019). In Trump v. Mazars, U.S., LLP, No. 19-715 (U.S. Jul. 9, 2020), Chief Justice

Roberts, writing for a seven-Justice majority, rejected arguments for narrowing the scope of Congress's investigative authority. Although "Congress may not issue a subpoena for the purpose of 'law enforcement,'" *id.* at 17, "Congress's responsibilities extend to 'every affair of government,'" *id.* at 19. Its investigative power "encompasses inquiries into the administration of existing laws, studies of proposed laws, and 'surveys of defects in our social, economic or political system for the purpose of enabling the Congress to remedy them.'" *Id.* at 16.

72. *Id.* at 21, 45–46.

73. *Id.* at 48–49.

74. Peter M. Shane, Madison's Nightmare: How Executive Power Threatens American Democracy 9–10 (2009).

75. *White House Communications with the DOJ and FBI*, Protect Democracy (Mar. 8, 2017), https://protectdemocracy.org/agencycontacts/. For the Biden Administration policy, *see* Memorandum from Dana Remus, Counsel to the President, to All White House Staff re: Prohibited Contacts with Agencies and Departments (July 21, 2021), https://www.whitehouse.gov/wp-content/uploads/2021/07/White-House-Policy-for-Contacts-with-Agencies-and-Departments.pdf.

76. Carrie Johnson & Jessica Taylor, *Trump Fires Acting Attorney General for Refusing to Defend Immigration Order*, NPR (Jan. 30, 2017), https://www.npr.org/2017/01/30/512534805/justice-department-wont-defend-trumps-immigration-order.

77. Andrew Prokop, *Trump Has Now Admitted He Fired Comey Because of the Russia Investigation*, Vox (May 11, 2017, 7:40 PM), https://www.vox.com/2017/5/11/15628276/trump-comey-fired-russia.

78. 28 U.S.C. § 532

79. @realDonaldTrump, Twitter (July 24, 2019, 6:43 AM), https://twitter.com/realdonaldtrump/status/1153994026099630081; @realDonaldTrump, Twitter (Nov. 14, 2019, 11:52 PM), https://twitter.com/realdonaldtrump/status/1195202834645405698; @realDonaldTrump, Twitter (Aug. 14, 2018, 8:15 AM), https://twitter.com/realdonaldtrump/status/1029355952414371841.

80. John Wagner, *Trump Says He Nominated Sessions As Attorney General Even Though He Wasn't 'Equipped' for the Job*, Wash. Post (May 8, 2020, 2:24 PM), https://www.washingtonpost.com/politics/trump-says-he-nominated-sessions-as-attorney-general-even-though-he-wasnt-equipped-for-the-job/2020/05/08/78f369be-912f-11ea-9e23-6914ee410a5f_story.html.

81. Robert S. Mueller, III, Report on the Investigation into Russian Interference in the 2016 Presidential Election (2019), https://www.justice.gov/storage/report_volume2.pdf; Bob Bauer, *What the Mueller Report Reveals about the Presidency*, The Atlantic (Apr. 19, 2019), https://www.theatlantic.com/ideas/archive/2019/04/mueller-report-special-counsel-limits/587488/.

82. Andrew Restuccia, *Trump Issues Pardon for Lewis 'Scooter' Libby*, POLITICO (Apr. 13, 2018, 5:12 PM), https://www.politico.com/story/2018/04/13/trump-pardon-scooter-libby-522055.

83. Kaitlan Collins et al., *Trump Pardons Dinesh D'Souza—and Hints at More Celebrity Pardons*, CNN (May 31, 2018, 1:24 PM), https://www.cnn.com/2018/05/31/politics/trump-dinesh-dsouza-pardon/index.html.

84. *Id.*

85. Michael A. Robinson, *Trump Pardoned a Soldier Convicted of Murder. Is He Hurting Military Effectiveness?*, WASH. POST (May 14, 2019, 7:25 AM), https://www.washingtonpost.com/politics/2019/05/14/trump-pardoned-soldier-convicted-murder-is-he-hurting-military-effectiveness/.

86. *Id.*

87. Julie Hirschfeld Davis & Maggie Haberman, *Trump Pardons Joe Arpaio Who Became Face of Crackdown on Illegal Immigration*, N.Y. TIMES (Aug. 25, 2017), https://www.nytimes.com/2017/08/25/us/politics/joe-arpaio-trump-pardon-sheriff-arizona.html.

88. Brian Tashman, *Arizona Voters Deserve to Know Joe Arpaio's True Record of Brutality and Abuse*, ACLU (June 27, 2018, 11:30 AM), https://www.aclu.org/blog/criminal-law-reform/arizona-voters-deserve-know-joe-arpaios-true-record-brutality-and-abuse.

89. Davis & Haberman, *supra* note 87.

90. *Id.*

91. Darren Samuelsohn & Meridith McGraw, *Possible Pardons Loom for Former Trump Aids*, POLITICO (Dec. 9, 2019, 5:03 AM), https://www.politico.com/news/2019/12/09/possible-pardons-loom-former-trump-aides-078480.

92. Maggie Haberman and Michael S. Schmidt, *Trump Gives Clemency to More Allies, Including Manafort, Stone and Charles Kushner*, N.Y. TIMES (Dec. 20, 2021, updated Jan. 17, 2021), https://www.nytimes.com/2020/12/23/us/politics/trump-pardon-manafort-stone.html.

93. Paul R. Verkuil, *Why Government Professionals Matter*, THE REGULATORY REVIEW (Dec. 4, 2017), https://www.theregreview.org/2017/12/04/verkuil-government-professionals-matter/.

94. Jenna Johnson & Matea Gold, *Trump Calls the Media 'the Enemy of the American People'*, WASH. POST (Feb. 7, 2017, 6:07 PM), https://www.washingtonpost.com/news/post-politics/wp/2017/02/17/trump-calls-the-media-the-enemy-of-the-american-people/.

95. *Donald Trump under fire for mocking disabled reporter*, BBC (Nov. 26, 2015), https://www.bbc.com/news/world-us-canada-34930042.

96. Glen Kessler et al., *President Trump Made 18,000 False or Misleading Claims in 1,170 Days*, WASH. POST (Apr. 14, 2020, 3:00 AM), https://www.washingtonpost.com/politics/2020/04/14/president-trump-made-18000-false-or-misleading-claims-1170-days/.

97. Johnson & Gold, *supra* note 94.

98. Daniel Dale & Tara Subramaniam, *Fact Check: Trump Falsely Denies Saying Two Things He Said Last Week*, CNN (Mar. 30, 2020, 7:58 AM), https://www.cnn.com/2020/03/29/politics/fact-check-coronavirus-briefing/index.html.

99. GEORGE ORWELL, 1984, at 81 (Signet Classic ed. 1961).

100. *Trump's Daily Schedule v Obama and Bush*, BBC (Jan. 9, 2018), https://www.bbc.com/news/world-us-canada-42610275; Kaitlan Collins, *Exclusive: White House Stops Announcing Calls with Foreign Leaders*, CNN (July 25, 2018, 1:06 AM), https://www.cnn.com/2018/07/24/politics/foreign-leaders-call-white-house/index.html.

101. In His Own Words: The President's Attacks on the Courts, BRENNAN CENTER FOR JUSTICE (Feb. 14, 2020), https://www.brennancenter.org/our-work/research-reports/his-own-words-presidents-attacks-courts.

102. Mica Rosenberg & Andrew Chung, *Trump Complicates Travel Ban Case by Grumbling at Justice Department*, REUTERS (June 5, 2017), https://www.reuters.com/article/us-britain-security-usa-trump/trump-complicates-travel-ban-case-by-grumbling-at-justice-department-idUSKBN18W1BR.

103. Cristiano Lima, *White House Slams 'Egregious' Ruling On Sanctuary Cities*, POLITICO (Apr. 26, 2017, 12:24 AM), https://www.politico.com/story/2017/04/26/white-house-slams-egregious-court-ruling-on-sanctuary-cities-237615.

104. *Supra* note 101.

105. Letter from Pat A. Cipollone, Counsel to the President, to Nancy Pelosi, Speaker of the House of Representatives et al. (Oct. 8, 2019), https://games-cdn.washingtonpost.com/notes/prod/default/documents/7cb26618-e770-45ef-9c45-bdd5554ce201/note/9608d380-f0df-4e07-8b08-8f326b723626.pdf#page=1; Matthew Callahan & Reuben Fischer-Baum, *Where the Trump Administration Is Thwarting House Oversight*, WASH. POST (Oct. 11, 2019), https://www.washingtonpost.com/graphics/2019/politics/trump-blocking-congress/.

106. Glenn Thrush & Maggie Haberman, *Bannon Is Given Security Role Usually Held for Generals*, N. Y. TIMES (Jan. 29, 2017), https://www.nytimes.com/2017/01/29/us/stephen-bannon-donald-trump-national-security-council.html.

107. Alex Gangitano, *281 Lobbyists Have Worked in Trump Administration: Report*, THE HILL (Oct. 15, 2019, 1:31 PM), https://thehill.com/business-a-lobbying/465865-281-lobbyists-have-worked-in-trump-administration-report.

108. Tim Marcin, *Donald Trump vs. Rex Tillerson: Their History of Insults, Including the President's Latest 'Dumb as a Rock' Tweet*, NEWSWEEK (Dec. 7, 2018, 5:50 PM), https://www.newsweek.com/donald-trump-vs-rex-tillerson-insults-1250396; Chelsea Cox, *11 Times Trump Has Ripped Jeff Sessions*, CNN (Nov. 8, 2019, 1:28 PM), https://www.cnn.com/2019/11/08/politics/jeff-sessions-donald-trump-insults/index.html.

109. Joel Rose, *How Trump Has Filled High-Level Jobs without Senate Confirmation Votes*, NPR (Mar. 9, 2020, 5:04 AM), https://www.npr.org/2020/03/09/813577462/how-trump-has-filled-high-level-jobs-without-senate-confirmation.

110. Brett Samuels, *Trump Learns to Love Acting Officials*, THE HILL (Apr. 14, 2019, 10:30 AM), https://thehill.com/homenews/administration/438660-trump-learns-to-love-acting-officials.

111. Maggie Haberman et al., *Dan Coats to Step Down as Intelligence Chief; Trump Picks Loyalist for Job*, N.Y. TIMES (July 28, 2019), https://www.nytimes.com/2019/07/28/us/politics/dan-coats-intelligence-chief-out.html.

112. Martin Matishak & Quint Forgey, *John Ratcliffe Won't Be Trump's Next National Intelligence Director*, POLITICO (Aug. 2, 2019, 4:57), https://www.politico.com/story/2019/08/02/trump-rep-ratcliffe-out-of-the-running-to-be-national-intelligence-director-1445150.

113. *Id.*

114. David Priess, *The Potential Trouble with Nominating a DNI from Trump's Central Casting*, LAWFARE (July 30, 2019, 12:09 PM), https://www.lawfareblog.com/potential-trouble-nominating-dni-trumps-central-casting.

115. *Id.*

116. Cory Bennett & Caitlin Oprysko, Trump to Nominate Rep. John Ratcliffe Again as Intel Chief, POLITICO, (Feb. 28, 2020, 7:18 PM), https://www.politico.com/news/2020/02/28/trump-to-nominate-rep-john-ratcliffe-again-as-intel-chief-118239.

117. Chris Riotta, *Jared Kushner 'Granted Top-Level Security Clearance against the Advice of White House Specialists'*, INDEPENDENT (Jan. 25, 15:50), https://www.independent.co.uk/news/world/americas/us-politics/jared-kushner-security-clearance-trump-white-house-job-fbi-a8746341.html.

118. Peter Overby, *Change to President Trump's Trust Lets Him Tap Business Profits*, NPR (Apr. 3, 2017, 8:53 PM), https://www.npr.org/2017/04/03/522511211/change-to-president-trumps-trust-lets-him-tap-business-profits.

119. Curt Devine & Maegan Vazquez, *Trump-Branded Properties Charged Federal Government at Least $1.2 Million, Records Show*, CNN (Mar. 12, 2020, 2:16 PM), https://www.cnn.com/2020/03/12/politics/trump-branded-properties-charge-taxpayers-a-million-invs/index.html.

120. Amir Vera, *President Trump's Tweet on California Wildfires Angers Firefighters, Celebrities*, CNN (Nov. 12, 2018, 3:29 PM), https://www.cnn.com/2018/11/11/politics/california-wildfires-trump-tweets/index.html.

121. Zach Beauchamp, *Trump's Puerto Rico Tweets Are the Purest Expression of His Presidency*, VOX (Sep. 13, 2018, 1:20 PM), https://www.vox.com/2018/9/13/17855268/trump-hurricane-maria-puerto-rico-tweets.

122. Jeremy Diamond, *Trump on Harvey Destruction: 'We Are One American Family'*, CNN (Aug. 28, 2017, 12:30 PM), https://www.cnn.com/2017/08/28/politics/donald-trump-hurricane-harvey-response-texas/index.html.

123. David Jackson, *Trump Defends Response to Charlottesville Violence, Says He Put It 'Perfectly' with 'Both Sides' Remark*, USA TODAY (Apr. 26, 2019, 1:51 PM), https://www.usatoday.com/story/news/politics/2019/04/26/trump-says-both-sides-charlottesville-remark-said-perfectly/3586024002/.

124. *Trump to Congresswomen of Colour: Leave the US*, BBC (July 15, 2019), https://www.bbc.com/news/world-us-canada-48982172.

125. Spencer Kimball, *Trump Calls Baltimore a 'Disgusting, Rat and Rodent Infested Mess' in Attack on Rep. Elijah Cummings*, CNBC (July 27, 2019, 5:08 PM), https://www.cnbc.com/2019/07/27/trump-calls-baltimore-a-disgusting-rat-and-rodent-infested-mess-in-attack-on-rep-elijah-cummings.html.

126. Ben Lefebvre, *Zinke to Leave Interior amid Scandals*, POLITICO (Dec. 15, 2018, 9:24 AM), https://www.politico.com/story/2018/12/15/zinke-interior -secretary-leave-trump-1066653.

127. Glenn Thrush, *Ben Carson's HUD Spends $31,000 on Dining Set for His Office*, N.Y. TIMES (Feb. 27, 2019), https://www.nytimes.com/2018/02/27/us/ben -carson-hud-furniture.html.

128. Gregory Wallace et al., *Wilbur Ross' Financial Disclosure Rejected by Federal Ethics Agency*, CNN (Feb. 19, 2019, 6:28 PM), https://www.cnn.com/2019/02/19 /politics/wilbur-ross-financial-disclosure/index.html.

129. Karen DeYoung, *Inspector General Finds Politically Motivated Harassment at State Department*, WASH. POST (Aug, 15, 2019, 7:33 PM), https://www.washington post.com/national-security/inspector-general-finds-politically-motivated-harassment -at-state-department/2019/08/15/2208a432-bf9f-11e9-9b73-fd3c65ef8f9c_story.html.

130. Tracy Jan, *Trump HUD Appointee's Twitter 'Likes' Violated Federal Law. She Will Not Be Punished*, WASH. POST (Sep. 18, 2019, 4:47 PM), https://www .washingtonpost.com/business/2019/09/18/trump-hud-appointees-twitter-likes -violated-federal-law-she-will-not-be-punished/.

131. Peter Baker, *Trump Is Urged to Fire Kellyanne Conway for Hatch Act Viola- tions*, N.Y. TIMES (June 13, 2019), https://www.nytimes.com/2019/06/13/us/politics /kellyanne-conway-hatch-act.html.

132. Bob Bauer, *Rules and Norms in the Trump Presidency: The Risks and Rewards of 'Playing It Straight' on the Inside*, LAWFARE (Sep. 19, 2019), https://www .lawfareblog.com/rules-and-norms-trump-presidency-risks-and-rewards-playing-it -straight-inside.

133. Bob Bauer, *The President and His Lawyers*, LAWFARE (Mar. 12, 2018), https://www.lawfareblog.com/president-and-his-lawyers.

134. Texas v. United States, 945 F.3d 355 (5th Cir. 2019); *see also* David Gans, *To Save and Not to Destroy: Severability, Judicial Restraint, and the Affordable Care Act*, AMERICAN CONSTITUTION SOCIETY (Dec. 4, 2019), https://www.acslaw .org/issue_brief/briefs-landing/to-save-and-not-to-destroy-severability-judicial -restraint-and-the-affordable-care-act/.

135. Caitlin Dickerson, *Migrant Children Are Entitled to Toothbrushes and Soap, Federal Court Rules*, N. Y. TIMES (Aug. 15, 2019), https://www.nytimes.com/2019 /08/15/us/migrant-children-toothbrushes-court.html.

136. Daniel Marans, *Customs and Boarder Officials Defy Court Order on Lawful Residents*, HUFFPOST (Jan. 29, 2017, 3:17 AM), https://www.huffpost.com/entry /dulles-airport-feds-violated-court-order_n_588d7274e4b08a14f7e67bcf.

137. Caroline Kenny, *Trump: 'I Have the Absolute Right to Pardon Myself'*, CNN (June 4, 2018), https://www.cnn.com/2018/06/04/politics/donald-trump-pardon -tweet/index.html; Greg Sargent, *Trump: I Have the 'Absolute Right' to Declare a National Emergency If Democrats Defy Me*, WASH. POST (Jan. 9, 2019, 4:29 PM), https://www.washingtonpost.com/opinions/2019/01/09/trump-i-have-absolute -right-declare-national-emergency-if-democrats-defy-me/.

138. Jason Lemon, *Trump Insists the Constitution's Article II 'Allows Me to Do Whatever I Want'*, NEWSWEEK (June 16, 2019, 2:58 PM), https://www.newsweek.com/trump-insists-constitution-allows-do-whatever-want-1444235.

139. Rafi Schwartz, *Here's Trump Screaming in Front of a Plane about How He Has Unlimited Power*, SPLINTER NEWS (July 12, 2019, 1:31 PM), https://splinternews.com/heres-trump-screaming-in-front-of-a-plane-about-how-he-1836314919.

140. Interview with Richard Nixon, *supra* note 35.

141. Peter M. Shane, *When Inter-Branch Norms Break Down: Of Arms-for-Hostages, Orderly Shutdowns, Presidential Impeachments, and Judicial Coups*, 12 CORNELL J. L. & PUB. POL'Y 503, 514 (2003).

142. *Id.* at 515.

143. Interview by James S. Young et al. with William P. Barr, Attorney General, U.S. Dep't of Justice (Apr. 5, 2001), https://millercenter.org/the-presidency/presidential-oral-histories/william-p-barr-oral-history-assistant-attorney-general.

144. Neil Devins, *Signing Statements and Divided Governments*, 16 WM & MARY BILL RTS. J. 63 (2007).

145. Neil Kinkopf & Peter M. Shane, Signed Under Protest: A Database of Presidential Signing Statements, 2001–2009 (Version 2.0), (Ohio State Pub. Law Working Paper No. 141), https://papers.ssrn.com/sol3/papers.cfm?abstract_id=1748474.

146. *Alexander Hamilton (1789–1795)*, U.S. DEPARTMENT OF THE TREASURY, https://home.treasury.gov/about/history/prior-secretaries/alexander-hamilton-1789-1795 (last visited May 22, 2020).

147. JACK GOLDSMITH, THE TERROR PRESIDENCY: LAW AND JUDGMENT INSIDE THE BUSH ADMINISTRATION 88–89 (2009).

148. U.S. DEPARTMENT OF JUSTICE, AUTHORIZATION FOR CONTINUING HOSTILITIES IN KOSOVO (2000), https://www.justice.gov/file/19306/download.

149. LOUIS FISHER, PRESIDENT OBAMA: CONSTITUTIONAL ASPIRATIONS AND EXECUTIVE ACTIONS 217 (2018).

150. Nicolas Bagley, *Legal Limits and the Implementation of the Affordable Care Act*, 164 U. PENN. L. REV. 1715 (2016).

151. Spencer Mestel, *How Bad Ballot Design Can Sway the Results of an Election*, THE GUARDIAN (Nov. 19, 2019, 2:00 PM), https://www.theguardian.com/us-news/2019/nov/19/bad-ballot-design-2020-democracy-america.

152. Edward B. Foley, *The Electoral College and Majority Rule: Restoring the Jeffersonian Vision for Presidential Elections* (Ohio State Pub. Law Working Paper No. 429), https://papers.ssrn.com/sol3/papers.cfm?abstract_id=3067992.

CHAPTER 2. THE "CHIEF PROSECUTOR" MYTH

1. Memorandum from William Barr to Rod Rosenstein, Deputy Attorney General, and Steve Engel, Assistant Attorney General (June 8, 2018), https://assets

.documentcloud.org/documents/5638848/June-2018-Barr-Memo-to-DOJ-Muellers
-Obstruction.pdf.

2. *Id.* at 1.

3. *Id.* at 11.

4. *Id.*

5. *Id.* at 13.

6. *Id.* at 14.

7. Carpenter v. United States, 138 S. Ct. 2206, 2209 (2018).

8. In re Aiken Cnty., 396 U.S. App. D.C. 107, 645 F.3d 428 (2011).

9. Memorandum from William Barr to Rod Rosenstein, *supra* note 1, at 11.

10. Lawrence B. Solum, *Communicative Content and Legal Content*, 89 NOTRE DAME L. REV. 479, 498 (2013); for a helpful review of ambiguities as to the meaning of "original public meaning," see Richard H. Fallon Jr, *The Meaning of Legal "Meaning" and Its Implications for Theories of Legal Interpretation*, 82 U. CHI. L. REV. 1235 (2015).

11. See, e.g., ANTONIN SCALIA, A MATTER OF INTERPRETATION: FEDERAL COURTS AND THE LAW (1998).

12. Saikrishna Prakash, *The Essential Meaning of Executive Power*, 2003 U. ILL. L. REV. 701, 716 (2003) (quoting Samuel Johnson's dictionary of 1773).

13. Peter M. Shane, *Prosecutors at the Periphery*, 94 CHI.-KENT L. REV. 241, 241–242 (2019).

14. Peter M. Shane, *The Originalist Myth of the Unitary Executive*, 19 U. PA. J. CONST. L. 323 (2016) (hereafter, "Originalist Myth").

15. GA. CONST. of 1789, Art. III, § 5 ("The judges of the superior court and attorney general shall have a competent salary established by law, which shall not be increased nor diminished during their continuance in office, and shall hold their commission during the term of three years."); MD. CONST. of 1776, Arts. XL ("That the Chancellor, all Judges, the Attorney-General, Clerks of the General Court, the Clerks of the County Courts, the Registers of the Land Office, and the Registers of Wills, shall hold their commissions during good behaviour, removable only for misbehaviour, on conviction in a Court of law."), XLVIII, LII, and LIII; MASS. CONST. of 1780, pt. 2, ch. II, § 1, art. IX ("All judicial officers, the attorney-general, the solicitor-general, all sheriffs, coroners, and registers of probate, shall be nominated and appointed by the governor. . . ."); N.J. CONST. of 1776, para. XII. ("That the Judges of the Supreme Court shall continue in office for seven years: the Judges of the Inferior Court of Common Pleas in the several counties, Justices of the Peace, Clerks of the Supreme Court, Clerks of the Inferior Court of Common Pleas and Quarter Sessions, the Attorney-General, and Provincial Secretary, shall continue in office for five years. . . ."); N.C. CONST. of 1776, Arts. XIII ("That the General Assembly shall, by joint ballot of both houses, appoint Judges of the Supreme Courts of Law and Equity, Judges of Admiralty, and Attorney-General, who shall be commissioned by the Governor, and hold their offices during good behavior."), XXI, and XXX; VA. CONST. of 1776, pars. 35 ("The two Houses of Assembly shall, by joint ballot, appoint Judges of the Supreme Court of Appeals, and General Court,

Judges in Chancery, Judges of Admiralty, Secretary, and the Attorney-General, to be commissioned by the Governor, and continue in office during good behaviour.") and 37. The statement in Joan Jacoby's seminal work on the history of private prosecution that only five of the first thirteen Constitutions mentioned the Attorney General explicitly erroneously omits North Carolina. JOAN E. JACOBY, THE AMERICAN PROSECUTOR: A SEARCH FOR IDENTITY 22 (1980).

16. Shane, *supra* note 14, at 338–339.

17. *Id.* at 340.

18. Ilan Wurman has criticized this argument in part on the ground that the early attorneys general were not prosecutors; their removal from complete gubernatorial control is thus supposedly not probative of the constitutional character of the prosecutorial function. Ilan Wurman, *In Search of Prerogative*, 70 DUKE L.J. 93, 151 n. 251 (2020). Wurman's point, however, is not persuasive. Attorneys general were obviously government lawyers, both counseling other government actors and representing their respective states in court. They were thus involved directly in the faithful execution of law, whether or not they appeared personally in court as criminal prosecutors. States conceptualizing their attorneys general as judicial officers thus implicitly endorsed the idea that an official—presumably including a prosecutor—could be outside complete gubernatorial control and yet involved in the execution of law. (Professor Wurman's argument also fails to address states such as Connecticut, Vermont, and, in short order, Tennessee, in which judicial appointments of state's attorneys occurred at the county level. Whatever the functions of these states' attorneys general, the county-level state's attorneys were presumably doing the same job as federal district attorneys.) Professor Wurman is correct that the district attorneys were administratively linked to the Department of State, but it is not clear that the relationship was supervisory, as opposed to one of administrative convenience. It could be a revealing historical project to see if any of the early district attorneys thought they had any actual accountability, other than financial, to the Department of State. There is no mention of the district attorneys in early legislation regarding the Department of State, and it is interesting, in this connection, that both the U.S. attorney general and the district attorneys are chartered in the *Judiciary* Act of 1789 (emphasis added).

19. Shane, *supra* note 14, at 367.

20. *Id.* at 350–351.

21. *Id.* at 348.

22. *Id.*

23. Prakash, *supra* note 12, at 760.

24. Shane, *Originalist Myth, supra* note 14, at 337–338.

25. 554 U.S. 570, 600–01 (2008).

26. "Our interpretation is confirmed by analogous arms-bearing rights in state constitutions that preceded and immediately followed adoption of the Second Amendment. Four States adopted analogues to the Federal Second Amendment in the period between independence and the ratification of the Bill of Rights. Two of them—Pennsylvania and Vermont—clearly adopted individual rights unconnected

to militia service. Pennsylvania's Declaration of Rights of 1776 said: "That the people have a right to bear arms for the defence of themselves and the state." § XIII, in 5 Thorpe 3082, 3083 (emphasis added). In 1777, Vermont adopted the identical provision, except for inconsequential differences in punctuation and capitalization. See VT. CONST., ch. 1, § XV, in 6 id., at 3741." *Id.* at 600–601.

27. See, e.g., JERRY L. MASHAW, CREATING THE AMERICAN CONSTITUTION: THE LOST ONE HUNDRED YEARS OF ADMINISTRATIVE LAW 40–44 (2012).

28. *Id.* at 40.

29. *Id.* at 41–42.

30. Judiciary Act of 1789, §35, 1 Stat. 73, 92–93 (codified as amended at 28 U.S.C. §1257).

31. HOMER CUMMINGS AND CARL MCFARLAND, FEDERAL JUSTICE: CHAPTERS IN THE HISTORY OF JUSTICE AND THE FEDERAL EXECUTIVE 16 (1937).

32. John G. Heinberg, *Centralization in Federal Prosecutions*, 15 MO. L. REV. 244, 246 (1950).

33. Jacoby, *supra* note 15, at 7–8.

34. *See generally* Allen Steinberg, *From Private Prosecution to Plea Bargaining: Criminal Prosecution, the District Attorney, and American Legal History*, 30 CRIME & DELINQUENCY 568 (1984). Indeed, vestiges remained as late as the 1950s because a majority of states still permitted private prosecution for misdemeanors. Id. at 586. On the post-Constitution vestiges of private participation in federal criminal prosecution, see Harold J. Krent, *Executive Control over Criminal Law Enforcement: Some Lessons from History*, 38 AM. U. L. REV. 275, 293–296 (1989).

35. Jacoby, *supra* note 15, at 23.

36. *Id.* at 20–21.

37. The decentralization of federal prosecution is yet further illustrated by the role early Congresses sanctioned for state officials in the enforcement of federal law. Krent, *supra* note 34, at 303–309.

38. In his thoughtful defense of the president as "Chief Prosecutor," Professor Saikrishna Prakash makes much of the fact that "in England, the king was regarded as the constitutional prosecutor of all offenses." He writes further: "Following the Lockean tradition, William Blackstone claimed that, in the state of nature, everyone enjoyed the executive power to punish those who transgressed the laws of nature." Saikrishna Prakash, *The Chief Prosecutor*, 73 GEO. WASH. L. REV. 521, 547 (2005). The problem with this argument is precisely an equation of "executive power" in the Lockean sense with executive power as understood in 1789. Locke famously considered that the executive power embraced not only what Americans came to understand as executive power, but also judicial power, given that both entailed the application of general rules to specific cases or individuals. When Americans embraced Montesquieu's separation of legislative, executive, and judicial powers, they were necessarily dividing a host of Crown powers between the executive and the judiciary. The fact that prosecution was constitutionally lodged with the Crown did not take it outside the realm of judicial power in the American sense. Suri Ratnapla,

John Locke's Doctrine of the Separation of Powers: A Re-Evaluation, 38 AM. J. JURIS. 189, 189 (1993) ("Locke often treated judicial power as part of the executive power and his threefold separation of legislative, executive, and federative powers does not correspond to the constitutional model which was eulogized by Montesquieu and adopted in modern constitutions to greater or lesser extents.").

39. Susan Low Bloch, *The Early Role of the Attorney General in Our Constitutional Scheme: In the Beginning There Was Pragmatism*, 1989 DUKE L.J. 561 (1989).

40. Their entitlement to engage in private practice continued until 1953. EXECUTIVE OFFICE FOR UNITED STATES ATTORNEYS, BICENTENNIAL CELEBRATION OF THE UNITED STATES ATTORNEYS 1789–1989, at 3 (1989) (unpaginated document). Until 1896, the district attorneys were paid entirely by fees, rather than salary. ALBERT LANGELUTTIG, THE DEPARTMENT OF JUSTICE OF THE UNITED STATES 68 (1927).

41. Bloch, *supra* note 39, at 586.

42. *Id.*

43. *Id.*

44. *Id.* at 587–588.

45. Cummings and McFarland, *supra* note 31, at 147–153.

46. Jed Handelsman Shugerman, *The Creation of the Department of Justice: Professionalization without Civil Rights or Civil Service*, 66 STAN. L. REV. 121, 131–32 (2014).

47. Cummings and McFarland, *supra* note 31, at 143–144.

48. *Id.* at 144.

49. *Id.*

50. Saikrishna Prakash, *The Chief Prosecutor*, 73 GEO. WASH. L. REV. 521 (2005).

51. U.S. CONST., art. III.

52. Plaut v. Spendthrift Farm, Inc., 514 U.S. 211 (1995).

53. U.S. CONST., art. II, §§ 2–3.

54. According to a House of Representatives count, presidents, as of August, 2017, had exercised "regular" vetoes a total of 1,508 times and "pocket" vetoes another 1,066 times. There have been 111 overrides, amounting to just over 4 percent of the total. Presidential Vetoes, https://history.house.gov/Institution/Presidential-Vetoes/Presidential-Vetoes/.

55. The Jewels of the Princess of Orange, 2 Opin. A.G. 482 (1831).

56. An Act concerning the Attorney-General and the Attorneys and Marshals of the several Districts, 37th Cong., 1st Sess., Chap. 37, § 1, 12 Stat. 285 (1861).

57. 27th Cong., 3d Sess., Chap. 93, § 2, 12 Stat. 768 (Mar. 3, 1863).

58. 28 U.S.C. § 546(d).

59. Second Enforcement Act, ch. 99, § 2, 16 Stat. 433 (1871) (codified as amended at 2 U.S.C. § 9 (2000), 28 U.S.C. §§ 1357, 1442, 1446–1447, 1449–1450 (2000)).

60. *Ex parte Siebold*, 100 U.S. 371, 373 (1879).

61. *Id.* at 397 (emphasis added).

62. Yaselli v. Goff, 12 F.2d 396, 404 (2d Cir. 1926), *aff'd*, 275 U.S. 503 (1927). See also Gregoire v. Biddle, 177 F.2d 579, 580 (2d Cir. 1949).

63. Imbler v. Pachtman, 424 U.S. 409 (1976).

64. Fed. R. Crim. Proc., Rule 42 (a)(2).

65. United States v. Arpaio, 906 F.3d 800, 803 (9th Cir. 2018).

66. "Prosecution of individuals who disregard court orders (except orders necessary to protect the courts' ability to function) is not an exercise of '[t]he judicial power of the United States,'" U.S. Const., Art. III, §§ 1, 2." Young v. U.S. ex rel. Vuitton et Fils S.A., 481 U.S. 787, 815 (1987) (Scalia, J., concurring in the judgment).

67. U.S. CONST. art. II, § 3.

68. Andrew Kent, Ethan J. Leib & Jed Handelsman Shugerman, *Faithful Execution and Article II*, 132 HARV. L. REV. 2111 (2019).

69. U.S. CONST. art. VI, cl. 3.

70. U.S. CONST. art. II, § 1, cl. 8.

71. THE FEDERALIST NO. 44 (James Madison).

72. 18 U.S.C. § 1503(a).

73. U.S. CONST. art. I, § 8, cl. 18.

74. Morrison v. Olson, 487 U.S. 654 (1988).

75. *Id.* at 696.

76. JERRY L. MASHAW, RICHARD A. MERRILL, AND PETER M. SHANE, ADMINISTRATIVE LAW: THE AMERICAN PUBLIC LAW SYSTEM 245–246 (6th ed. 2009), citing PETER M. SHANE & HAROLD H. BRUFF, THE LAW OF PRESIDENTIAL POWER 455–456 (1988).

77. Ethics in Government Act of 1978, Pub. L. No. 95-521, 92 Stat. 1824 (codified as amended in 28 U.S.C. §591(a)).

78. 28 U.S.C. § 592(a).

79. 28 U.S.C. § 592(a).

80. 28 U.S.C. §592(c)(1).

81. 28 U.S.C. § 594(a).

82. 28 U.S.C. § 596(a)(1).

83. Morrison v. Olson, 487 U.S. at 690.

84. Memorandum from William Barr to Rod Rosenstein, *supra* note 1, at 11.

85. U.S. CONST. art. II, § 2, cl. 1.

CHAPTER 3. POLITICIZING THE "DEEP STATE"

1. *Eisenhower Executive Office Building*, WHITEHOUSE.GOV, https://www.whitehouse.gov/about-the-white-house/eisenhower-executive-office-building/ (last visited October 25, 2021).

2. Exec. Order No. 12,291, 3 C.F.R. 127 (1981), *reprinted as amended in* 5 U.S.C. § 601 (1988).

3. Exec. Order No. 11,030, 27 Fed. Reg. 5847 (June 21, 1962) (to be codified at 1 C.F.R. § 19.2).

4. JERRY L. MASHAW, RICHARD A. MERRILL, PETER M. SHANE, ELIZABETH MAGILL, MARIANO-FIORENTINO CUÉLLAR, AND NICHOLAS PARRILLO,

Administrative Law: The American Public Law System 271–272 (West Group, 8th ed. 2019).

5. *Americans' Civics Knowledge Increases during a Stress-Filled Year*, Annenberg Public Policy Center (Sept. 14, 2021), https://www.annenbergpublic policycenter.org/2021-annenberg-constitution-day-civics-survey/

6. U.S. Const. art. I, § 8; *id.* amend. XIV, § 5.

7. U.S. Const. art. I, § 8, cl. 18.

8. *City of Arlington v. FCC*, 569 U.S. 290, 315 (2013) (Roberts, J., dissenting).

9. Michael Asimow, Sourcebook on Federal Administrative Adjudication Outside the Administrative Procedure Act 1–4 (2019), available at https://www.acus.gov/sites/default/files/documents/Federal %20Administrative%20Adj%20Outside%20the%20APA%20-%20Final.pdf.

10. Maeve P. Carey & Daniel T. Shedd, Cong. Research Serv., 7-5700, Federal Regulations and the Rulemaking Process (2014).

11. Maeve P. Carey, Cong. Research Serv., R40356, Counting Regulations: An Overview of Rulemaking, Types of Federal Regulations, and Pages in the Federal Register 6–7 (2014).

12. Yakus v. United States, 321 U.S. 414, 425–427 (1944); Whitman v. Am. Trucking Ass'ns, 531 U.S. 457, 472–473 (2001).

13. 5 U.S.C. § 706.

14. Food, Drug and Cosmetic Act of 1938, 21 U.S.C.A. §§ 348 (food additives), 360b (new animal drugs), and 379e (color additives).

15. Federal Trade Commission Act of 1914, 15 U.S.C. §§ 41–58.

16. Dale Pollak, *The Federal Trade Commission's Deception Enforcement Policy*, 35 DePaul L. Rev. 125 (1985).

17. National Traffic and Motor Vehicle Safety Act, Pub. L. 89-563, § 103(a), 80 Stat. 718, 719 (1966).

18. National Traffic and Motor Vehicle Safety Act, § 102(1).

19. Federal Motor Vehicle Safety Standards, 49 C.F.R. §§ 571.101–571.110.

20. Jennifer L. Selin and David E. Lewis, Sourcebook of United States Executive Agencies (2d ed. 2018).

21. U.S. Const. art. II, § 2, cl. 2.

22. 5 U.S.C. § 553.

23. 5 U.S.C. § 554, 556–557.

24. Motor Vehicle Mfrs. Ass'n of U.S., Inc. v. State Farm Mut. Auto. Ins. Co., 463 U.S. 29 (1983).

25. See, e.g., Federal Trade Commission Act of 1914, 15 U.S.C. § 41.

26. Jane Manners and Lev Menand, *The Three Permissions: Presidential Removal and the Statutory Limits of Agency Independence*, 121 Colum. L. Rev. 1, 4, 6 (2021).

27. Federal Trade Commission Act of 1914, 15 U.S.C. § 41.

28. National Labor Relations Act of 1935, 29 U.S.C. § 153(a).

29. 15 U.S.C. § 2053(a).

30. Some agency heads are understood to enjoy tenure protection although the statute authorizing their agency is silent on the question. The Securities and

Exchange Commission is a prominent example. Free Enter. Fund v. Pub. Co. Accounting Oversight Bd., 561 U.S. 477 (2010).

31. In re Aiken Cty., 645 F.3d 428, 438 (D.C. Cir. 2011) (Kavanaugh, J., concurring).

32. SAIKRISHNA BANGALORE PRAKASH, IMPERIAL FROM THE BEGINNING: THE CONSTITUTION OF THE ORIGINAL EXECUTIVE 195–202 (2015).

33. *Id.* at 95.

34. It is not for nothing that the leading exceptional case, Humphrey's Ex'r v. United States, 295 U.S. 602 (1935), was not brought by the late dismissed officer, but by his estate for back pay. In February 2021, Roger Severino, head of the Department of Education's Office of Civil Rights under the Trump Administration, sued President Biden after Biden fired him from the Council of the Administrative Conference of the United States (ACUS). The Council is largely an advisory group overseeing what is itself mostly an advisory organization. Because its members have no statutory tenure protection, the suit appears all but frivolous. It thus seems a reasonable speculation that Severino brought the suit hoping to entice the judiciary to generate yet further opinions supportive of unitary executive theory. Mark Joseph Stern, *Biden's Justice Department Is Walking into a Trap Set by Trump Appointees*, SLATE (May 28, 2021), https://slate.com/news-and-politics/2021/05/biden-trump -severino-trap.html. His spouse, Carrie Severino, runs the Judicial Crisis Network, a non-profit organization advocating conservative judicial appointments.

35. Peter M. Shane, *The Originalist Myth of the Unitary Executive*, 19 U. PA. J. CONST. L. 323, 338 (2016).

36. U.S. CONST., art. II, § 2, cl. 2.

37. The Constitution now explicitly uses the phrase "principal officers" in connection with the decision-making body entitled to determine that the president is "unable to discharge the powers and duties of his office." U.S. CONST. amend. XXV, § 4.

38. See, e.g., United States v. Germaine, 99 U.S. 508 (1878).

39. Ethics in Government Act of 1978, Pub. L. No. 95-521, 92 Stat. 1824.

40. Morrison v. Olson, 487 U.S. 654 (1988).

41. *Id.* at 672.

42. *Id.*

43. *Id.* at 716 (Scalia, J., dissenting).

44. 28 U.S.C.A. § 599 (originally enacted as Ethics in Government Act of 1978, Pub. L. No. 95-521, 92 Stat. 1824).

45. Peter M. Shane, *Presidents, Pardons, and Prosecutors: Legal Accountability and the Separation of Powers*, 11 YALE LAW & POL. REV. 361, 401 (1993).

46. S. REP. NO. 104-280 (1996).

47. Edmond v. United States, 520 U.S. 651 (1997).

48. Asimow, *supra* note 9, at 1.

49. Kent Barnett, *Against Administrative Judges*, 49 U.C.D. L. Rev. 1643, 1652 (2016).

50. *Id.*

51. Asimow, *supra* note 9.

52. 5 C.F.R. § 930.206(a)–(b).

53. Attorney General Manual on the Administrative Procedure Act, 5–6 (1947) https://www.regulationwriters.com/downloads/AttorneyGeneralsManual.pdf.

54. 5 U.S.C. § 556.

55. Barnett, *supra* note 49, at 1652.

56. *Id.* at 1709–1718.

57. *Id.* at 1654.

58. Lucia v. SEC, 138 S. Ct. 2044 (2018).

59. Exec. Order No. 13,843, 83 Fed. Reg. 32,755 (July 10, 2018) (to be codified at 5 C.F.R. 6.2).

60. Memorandum from The Solicitor General, U.S. Dep't of Justice, to the Agency General Counsels 9 (on file with Reuters), https://static.reuters.com /resources/media/editorial/20180723/ALJ--SGMEMO.pdf.

61. Brief for Respondent Supporting Petitioners at 39, Lucia v. SEC, 138 S. Ct. 2044 (2018) (No. 17-130).

62 Exec. Order No. 13,892, 55 Fed. Reg. 55,239 (Oct. 9, 2019) (to be codified at 5 U.S.C. § 551).

63. PHH Corp. v. Consumer Fin. Prot. Bureau, 881 F.3d 75 (D.C. Cir. 2018).

64. *Supra* note 62.

65. Asimow, *supra* note 9, at 21.

66. Lydia Zepeda, *The Costs of U.S. Immigration Policies*, 56 CAL. W. L. REV. 203 (2019).

67. Benslimane v. Gonzales, 430 F.3d 828 (7th Cir. 2005).

68. *Id.* at 829.

69. *Id.*

70. *Id.* at 830.

71. *Attorney General Alberto R. Gonzales Outlines Reforms for Immigration Courts and Board of Immigration Appeals*, U.S. DEP'T OF JUSTICE (Aug. 9, 2006), https://www.justice.gov/archive/opa/pr/2006/August/06_ag_520.html.

72. *An Investigation of Allegations of Politicized Hiring by Monica Goodling and Other Staff in the Office of the Attorney General* 137, U.S. DEP'T OF JUSTICE (July 28, 2008), https://oig.justice.gov/sites/default/files/legacy/special/s0807/final.pdf.

73. Charlie Savage, *Vetted Judges More Likely to Reject Asylum Bids*, N.Y. TIMES (Aug. 23, 2008), https://www.nytimes.com/2008/08/24/washington/24judges .html.

74. U.S. CONST. art. II, § 2, cl. 3.

75. Act of February 13, 1795, ch. 21, 1 Stat. 415.

76. Federal Vacancies Reform Act of 1998, 5 U.S.C. 3345–3349d.

77. Emily Stewart & Jen Kirby, *Judge Rules Mick Mulvaney Is in Charge of CFPB, for now*, VOX (Nov. 28, 2017), https://www.vox.com/policy-and-politics /2017/11/27/16704796/cfpb-english-mulvaney-trump-cordray.

78. Mike Scarella, *How Paul Clement Is Defending Obama's Consumer Protection Bureau*, LAW.COM (Jan. 15, 2020), https://www.law.com/nationallawjournal/2020/01/15/how-paul-clement-is-defending-obamas-consumer-protection-bureau/.

79. Mark Joseph Stern, *Matthew Whitaker's Appointment as Acting Attorney General Is Illegal*, SLATE (Nov. 8, 2018), https://slate.com/news-and-politics/2018/11/matthew-whitaker-jeff-sessions-replacement-illegal.html.

80. *Id.*

81. Alan Gomez, *Who is Kevin McAleenan, Trump's Acting Homeland Security Chief after Kristjen Nielsen Leaves?*, USA TODAY (Apr. 8, 2019), https://www.usatoday.com/story/news/politics/2019/04/08/kevin-mcaleenan-trump-border-chief-dhs-secretary-kirstjen-nielsen/3397977002/.

82. Priscilla Alvarez et al., *TSA Administrator Expected to Temporarily Fill No. 2 Role at Homeland Security*, CNN (Apr. 10, 2019), https://www.cnn.com/2019/04/09/politics/acting-deputy-secretary-dhs-resignation/index.html.

83. Under the DHS Orders of Succession and Delegations of Authority for Named Positions, as amended on April 10, 2019, the top eleven individuals in the order of succession were:

1. Deputy Secretary
2. Undersecretary for Management
3. Commissioner of U.S. Customs and Border Protection
4. Administrator of the Federal Emergency Management
5. Director of the Cybersecurity and Infrastructure Security Agency
6. Under Secretary for Science and Technology
7. Under Secretary for Intelligence and Analysis
8. Administrator of the Transportation Security Agency
9. Director of U.S. Immigration and Customs Enforcement
10. Director of U.S. Citizenship and Immigration Services
11. Under Secretary for Strategy, Policy, and Plans

On June 1, 2020, the DHS.gov site indicated that the secretary was an acting official. In addition, positions 1, 2, 3, 6, 7, 9, and 10 were filled by acting administrators or a "senior official performing the duties of the office. https://web.archive.org/web/20200531203501/https://www.dhs.gov/leadership

84. Brett Samuels, *Trump Learns to Love Acting Officials*, THE HILL (Apr. 14, 2019), https://thehill.com/homenews/administration/438660-trump-learns-to-love-acting-officials.

85. Myers v. United States, 272 U.S. 52 (1926).

86. THE FEDERALIST No. 77 (Alexander Hamilton).

87. Myers v. United States, 272 U.S. at 111–114.

88. Jed Handelsman Shugerman, The Decisions of 1789 Were Anti-Unitary: An Originalism Cautionary Tale (May 8, 2020), available at https://ssrn.com/abstract=3596566; see also Saikrishna Prakash, *The Essential Meaning of Executive Power*, 2003 U. Ill. L. Rev. 701, 794–796 (2003).

89. Myers v. United States, 272 U.S. at 178 (McReynolds, J., dissenting).

90. Humphrey's Ex'r v. United States, 295 U.S. 602, 623 (1935).

91. *Id.* at 618–619.

92. *Id.* at 626.

93. *Id.* at 632.

94. *Id.* at 628.

95. Morrison v. Olson, 487 U.S. 654, 691 (1988).

96. *Id.* at 696.

97. *Id.* at 691.

98. Free Enter. Fund v. Pub. Co. Accounting Oversight Bd., 561 U.S. 477 (2010).

99. *Id.* at 498.

100. Brian P. Smentkowski & Aaron M. Houck, *Brett Kavanaugh*, ENCYCLO-PAEDIA BRITANNICA (last visited June 19, 2020), https://www.britannica.com/biography/Brett-Kavanaugh.

101. *In re Aiken Cnty.*, 645 F.3d 428 (D.C. Cir. 2011).

102. *Id.* at 441, 446 (Kavanaugh, J., concurring).

103. In re Aiken Cnty., 725 F.3d 255, 262–266 (D.C. Cir. 2013).

104. PHH Corp. v. Consumer Fin. Prot. Bureau, 839 F.3d 1 (D.C. Cir. 2016), *on reh'g en banc,* 881 F.3d 75 (D.C. Cir. 2018).

105. 839 F.3d at 8.

106. 881 F.3d at 84–91.

107. Seila Law LLC v. Consumer Fin. Protection Bureau,140 S. Ct. 2183 (2020). In a 6–3 opinion, the Court subsequently adhered to and arguably broadened the reach of *Seila Law* when it invalidated the statutory limitation on the President's power to remove the director of the Federal Housing Finance Agency, another single-headed agency. Collins v. Yellen, 141 S. Ct. 1761 (2021). Unlike *Seila Law*, which arguably implied that single-headed independent agencies might be permissible if they did not wield significant executive authority, the *Collins* Court held that "the nature and breadth of an agency's authority is not dispositive in determining whether Congress may limit the President's power to remove its head." *Id.* at 1784. Based on *Seila Law* and *Collins*, the Justice Department advised President Biden that he could ignore the statutory provision protecting the tenure of the commissioner of the Social Security Administration and fire that official at will. Constitutionality of the Commissioner of Social Security's Tenure Protection, 45 Op. OLC __ (July 8, 2021).

108. Jim Tozzi, *OIRA's Formative Years: The Historical Record of Centralized Review Preceding OIRA's Founding,* 63 ADMIN. L. REV. 37 (2011).

109. Executive Order No. 11,821, 3 C.F.R. 926 (revoked 1977).

110. A study by the American Bar Association echoed this position. ABA COMMISSION ON LAW AND THE ECONOMY, FEDERAL REGULATION: ROADS TO REFORM (1979).

111. Murray Weidenbaum, *Regulatory Process Reform from Ford to Clinton,* REGULATION, at 20, (Winter 1997). Available at https://www.heartland.org/_template-assets/documents/publications/5376.pdf.

112. Executive Order No. 12,044, 43 Fed. Reg. 12,661, *revoked* by Executive Order No. 12291, 46 Fed. Reg. 13,193.

113. *Id.* at § 3 (b)(1).

114. Weidenbaum, *supra* note 111, at 21.

115. *Id.* at 22.

116. Youngstown Sheet & Tube Co. v. Sawyer, 343 U.S. 579 (1952).

117. *Id.* at 635–639 (Jackson, J., concurring).

118. Paperwork Reduction Act of 1980, 44 U.S.C. § 3504(a).

119. Exec. Order No. 12,291, 3 C.F.R. 127 (1981), § 1(a)(1), *reprinted as amended in* 5 U.S.C. § 601 (1988).

120. *Id.,* § 3(a).

121. *Id.,* § 1(d).

122. *Id.,* § 3(f)(1).

123. *Id.,* § 3(f)(2).

124. *Id.,* § 3(f)(3).

125. Peter M. Shane, *Presidential Regulatory Oversight and the Separation of Powers: The Constitutionality of Executive Order No. 12,291*, 23 ARIZ. L. REV. 1235 (1981). Mine was not a unanimous scholarly verdict. Morton Rosenberg, *Beyond the Limits of Executive Power: Presidential Control of Agency Rulemaking Under E.O. 12,291*, 80 MICH. L. REV. 193 (1981).

126. Gillian B. Metzger, *The Constitutional Duty to Supervise*, 124 YALE L. J. 1836 (2015).

127. *Proposed Executive Order Entitled "Federal Regulation"*, U.S. DEP'T OF JUSTICE (Feb. 13, 1981), https://www.justice.gov/file/22586/download.

128. *Attorney General: William French Smith*, U.S. DEP'T OF JUSTICE (updated June 26, 2017), https://www.justice.gov/ag/bio/smith-william-french.

129. *Statute Limiting the President's Authority to Supervise the Director of the Centers for Disease Control in the Distribution of an AIDS Pamphlet*, U.S. DEP'T OF JUSTICE 48 (Mar. 11, 1988), https://www.justice.gov/file/24041/download.

130. *Id.* at 49.

131. *Original Meaning Jurisprudence: A Sourcebook*, U.S. DEP'T OF JUSTICE (Mar. 12, 1987), https://www.ncjrs.gov/pdffiles1/Digitization/115083NCJRS.pdf.

132. Guidelines on Constitutional Litigation, U.S. DEP'T OF JUSTICE (Feb. 19, 1988) https://babel.hathitrust.org/cgi/pt?id=pur1.32754077977712&view=1up&seq=9.

133. The Constitution in the Year 2000: Choices Ahead in Constitutional Interpretation, U.S. DEP'T OF JUSTICE (Oct. 11, 1988), https://babel.hathitrust.org/cgi/pt?id=mdp.39015014943511&view=1up&seq=2.

134. *Supra* note 132, at 10.

135. Marine Mammal Protection Act, 16 U.S.C. ch. 31, § 1413.

136. Peter M. Shane, *Political Accountability in a System of Checks and Balances: The Case of Presidential Review of Rulemaking*, 48 ARK. L. REV. 161, 165–172 (1995).

137. *Id.* at 166.

138. Memorandum for Heads of Executive Departments and Agencies from the Vice President re: Regulatory Review Process, at 1 (Mar. 22, 1991) (on file with author).

139. Paperwork Reduction Act, Pub. L. No. 96-511, 94 stat. 2812 (1980) (codified as amended at 44 U.S.C. §§ 3501–3521.

140. Kitty Dumas, *White House Pulls the Rug Out on Regulatory Review Deal*, 48 CONG. Q. WKLY. REP. 1475 (1990).

141. Caroline DeWitt, Comment, *The President's Council on Competitiveness: Undermining the Administrative Procedure Act with Regulatory Review*, 6 ADMIN. L.J. 759, 762–63 (1993).

142. New York v. Reilly, 969 F.2d 1147, 1149 (D.C. Cir. 1992).

143. *Id.* at 1151.

144. *Id.*

145. *Id.* at 1152 n.9.

146. *Id.* at 1153.

147. Claudia O'Brien, *White House Review of Regulations under the Clean Air Act Amendments of 1990*, 8 J. ENVTL. L. & LITIG. 51, 92–93 (1993).

148. *Id.*

149. DeWitt, *supra* note 141, at 762–63 n.11.

150. Bob Woodward & David S. Broder, *Quayle's Quest: Curb Rules, Leave "No Fingerprints,"* WASH. POST (Jan. 9, 1992) at A1, A17 (describing the council's role in a dispute with EPA over the regulatory definition of protected "wetlands").

151. Michael Kranish, *The Remaking of Dan Quayle*, BOSTON GLOBE (Nov. 13, 1991), at 16, 17.

152. Exec. Order No. 12,866, 51,735 (1993), *reprinted as amended in* 5 U.S.C. § 601 (Supp. 1993).

153. *Id.* at 51,735–51,736.

154. *Id.* at 51,735.

155. Exec. Order No. 12,291, 46 Fed. Reg. 13,193 (1981), *reprinted as amended in* 5 U.S.C. § 601 (1988).

156. Exec. Order No. 12,866, 58 Fed. Reg. at 51,736.

157. *Id.*

158. *Id.* at 51,735, 51,742.

159. *Id.*

160. *Id.*

161. *Id.* at 51,742–51,743

162. OLC, Memorandum for Hon. David Stockman, Director, Office of Management and Budget re: Proposed Executive Order Entitled "Federal Regulation" (Feb. 13, 1981), *excerpted at* PETER M. SHANE, HAROLD H. BRUFF, AND NEIL J. KINKOPF, SEPARATION OF POWERS LAW: CASES AND MATERIALS 592–594 (4th ed., 2018). Intriguingly, although the advice regarding independent agencies appeared in the original OLC memorandum approving Exec. Order 12,291, it was edited out of the version made public on the Justice Department website, https://www.justice.gov/file/22586/download.

163. Exec. Order No. 12,866, 58 Fed. Reg. at 13,193.

164. Exec. Order No. 12,291, 46 Fed. Reg. at 13,194–13,195.

165. Exec. Order No. 12,866, 58 Fed. Reg. at 51,743.

166. *Id.* at 51,744.

167. *Id.*

168. Exec. Order No. 13,422, 72 Fed. Reg. 2,763 (Jan. 18, 2007), *revoked by* Exec. Order No. 13,497.

169. *Id.* at 2,764–2,765.

170. Presidential Memorandum Regarding Regulatory Review, 2009 DAILY COMP. PRES. DOC. (Apr. 23, 2009).

171. Lawrence Lessig & Cass R. Sunstein, *The President and the Administration*, 94 COLUM. L. REV. 1, 93–94 (1994).

172. Exec. Order No. 13,563, 76 Fed. Reg. 3,821 (Jan. 18, 2011),

173. Exec. Order No. 13,579, 76 Fed. Reg. 70,913 (July 11, 2011).

174. Letter from Cass R. Sunstein, Director, Office of Information and Regulatory Affairs, to Lisa Jackson, Administrator, Environmental Protection Agency 1 (Sep. 2, 2011), https://obamawhitehouse.archives.gov/sites/default/files/ozone _national_ambient_air_quality_standards_letter.pdf.

175. Elena Kagan, *Presidential Administration*, 114 Harv. L. Rev. 2245, 2249 (2001).

176. Cheney v. United States Dist. Court, 542 U.S. 367, 373 (2004).

177. U.S. GOV'T ACCOUNTABILITY OFFICE, GAO-03-894, PROCESS USED TO DEVELOP THE NATIONAL ENERGY POLICY 2 (2003).

178. Ass'n of Am. Physicians & Surgeons v. Clinton, 302 U.S. App. D.C. 208 (1993).

179. Neil J. Kinkopf and Peter M. Shane, *Signed under Protest: A Database of Presidential Signing Statements, 2001–2009* (2009), http://papers.ssrn.com/sol3 /papers.cfm?abstract_id=1485715.

180. Parnia Zahedi, From Czars to Commissars: Centralizing Policymaking Power in the White House (Unpublished paper 2019), available at https://www .acslaw.org/wp-content/uploads/2019/06/Parnia_Zahedi_Cudahy_Submission .pdf; see also Barbara L. Schwemle, Todd Garvey, Vivian S. Chu, and Henry B. Hogue, The Debate over Selected Presidential Assistants and Advisors: Appointment, Accountability, and Congressional Oversight (Cong. Res. Service Mar. 31, 2014), available at https://fas.org/sgp/crs/misc/R40856.pdf.

181. Zahedi, *supra* note 180 (manuscript at 6).

182. Joyce A. Green, *Presidential Signing Statements*, COHERENT BABBLE (last visited June 22, 2020), https://coherentbabble.com/listBHOall.htm.

183. David G. Savage, *Supreme Court Rules for "Dreamers," Rejects Trump's Repeal of Immigration Program*, L.A. TIMES (June 18, 2020), https://www.latimes .com/nation/la-na-court-obama-immigration-20160418-story.html

184. Exec. Order No. 13,771, 82 Fed. Reg. 9,339 (Jan. 30, 2017).

185. *Id.* at 9,339–9,340.

186. Memorandum from Paul Ray, Acting Administrator, Office of Information and Regulatory affairs, to Regulatory Policy Officers at Executive Departments and Agencies and Managing and Executive Directors of Commissions and Boards 5 (June 26, 2019), https://www.whitehouse.gov/wp-content/uploads/2019/06/2019 -Fall-Agenda.pdf.

187. Exec. Order No. 13,771, 82 Fed. Reg. at 9,339.

188. REINS Act, H.R. 26, 115th Cong. (as passed by House, Jan. 5, 2017); Regulatory Accountability Act, H.R. 115th Cong. (as passed by House, Jan. 11, 2017).

189. Exec. Order No. 13,771, 82 Fed. Reg. at 9,340.

190. Administrative Procedure Act, 5 U.S.C. §706(2)(a).

191. Citizens to Pres. Overton Park, Inc. v. Volpe, 401 U.S. 402, 416 (1971).

192. Richard J. Pierce Jr., *Is a Ceiling on Regulatory Costs Reasonable?*, THE REGULATORY REVIEW (Sep. 30, 2019), https://www.theregreview.org/2019/09/30 /pierce-ceiling-regulatory-costs/.

193. Zahedi, *supra* note 180 (manuscript at 7, 8).

194. *Id.* at 15; see also Dan Diamond, *Drug Pricing Takes Center Stage on the Hill*, POLITICO (Jan. 29, 2019, 10:00 AM), https://www.politico.com /newsletters/politico-pulse/2019/01/29/drug-pricing-takes-center-stage-on-the -hill-493120.

195. Brianna Ehley and Sarah Karlin-Smith, *Kellyanne Conway's "Opioid Cabinet" Sidelines Drug Czar's Experts,* POLITICO (Feb. 6, 2018, 5:18 AM), https:// www.politico.com/story/2018/02/06/kellyanne-conway-opioid-drug-czar-325457.

196. Jerry L. Mashaw & David Berke, *Presidential Administration in A Regime of Separated Powers: An Analysis of Recent American Experience*, 35 YALE J. ON REG. 549, 604 (2018).

197. Exec. Order No. 13,767, 82 Fed. Reg. 8,797 (Jan. 25, 2017); Proclamation No. 9,645, 82 Fed. Reg. 45,161 (Sep. 24, 2017).

198. Exec. Order No. 13,813, 82 Fed. Reg. 48,385 (Oct. 12, 2017).

199. Exec. Order No. 13,792, 82 Fed. Reg. 20,429 (Apr. 26, 2017).

200. Exec. Order No. 13,927, 82 Fed Reg. 35,165 (June 4, 2020).

201. Exec. Order No. 13,813, 82 Fed. Reg. at 48,386.

202. OLC, Memorandum Opinion for the Secretary of the Interior re: Consultation with the Council of Economic Advisers on the Surface Mining Control and Reclamation Act, 3 Op. O.L.C. 21 (1979), available at https://www.justice.gov/file /21831/download.

203. *Id.* at 21.

204. *Id.* at 22.

205. *Id.*

206. Steve Benen, *Trump: Constitution Gives Me 'The Right to Do Whatever I Want'*, MSNBC (July 24, 2019), http://www.msnbc.com/rachel-maddow-show /trump-constitution-gives-me-the-right-do-whatever-i-want.

207. HAROLD H. BRUFF, UNTRODDEN GROUND: HOW PRESIDENTS INTERPRET THE CONSTITUTION 2–4 (2015).

1. ERIC J. SEGALL, ORIGINALISM AS FAITH 62–64 (2018).

2. JOHN YOO, THE POWERS OF WAR AND PEACE: THE CONSTITUTION AND
FOREIGN AFFAIRS AFTER 9/11 (2008).

3. Memorandum from William Barr to Rod Rosenstein, Deputy Attorney
General, and Steve Engel, Assistant Attorney General (June 8, 2018), https://assets
.documentcloud.org/documents/5638848/June-2018-Barr-Memo-to-DOJ-Muellers
-Obstruction.pdf.

4. About ED, U.S. DEP'T OF EDUCATION, https://www2.ed.gov/about/landing
.jhtml (last visited June 26, 2020); Peter Kastor, *The Early Federal Workforce*, BROOK-
INGS 2 https://www.brookings.edu/wp-content/uploads/2018/05/the-early-federal
-workforce-by-p-kastor.pdf?utm_campaign=Brookings%20Executive%20Education
&utm_source=hs_email&utm_medium=email (last visited June 26, 2020).

5. JACK BALKIN, LIVING ORIGINALISM (2011); Thomas B. Colby and Peter J.
Smith, *Living Originalism*, 59 DUKE L.J. 239 (2009).

6. ANTONIN SCALIA, A MATTER OF INTERPRETATION: FEDERAL COURTS
AND THE LAW 47 (1997). To be "constrained" in constitutional interpretation,
however, is not necessarily the same thing as being "restrained" in the exercise of
judicial power to overcome the judgments of elected officials. Keith E. Whittington,
The New Originalism, 2 GEO. J.L. & PUB. POL'Y 599, 609 (2004) (explaining that
defenders of the "new originalism," discussed below, take constitutional fidelity, not
judicial restraint, to be the normative value underpinning their methodology). For
an intellectual history of modern-day originalist theory, together with a supremely
helpful analysis of disagreements within the "family" of originalist approaches, see
Lawrence B. Solum, *Originalism and Constitutional Construction*, 82 FORDHAM L.
REV. 453, 456 (2013).

7. Richard S. Kay, *Originalist Values and Constitutional Interpretation*, 19
HARV. J. L.& PUB. POL'Y 335, 336–337 (1996).

8. "The judicial power of the United States shall not be construed to extend to
any suit in law or equity, commenced or prosecuted against one of the United States
by citizens of another state, or by citizens or subjects of any foreign state." U.S.
CONST., AMEND. XI.

9. Hans v. Louisiana, 134 U.S. 1, 15–16 (1890) ("[T]he cognizance of suits and
actions unknown to the law . . . was not contemplated by the Constitution when
establishing the judicial power of the United States. . . . The suability of a State
without its consent was a thing unknown to the law."); Alden v. Maine, 527 U.S.
706, 722 (1999) ("The text and history of the Eleventh Amendment . . . suggest that
Congress acted not to change but to restore the original constitutional design.").

10. Fitzpatrick v. Bitzer, 427 US 445 (1976).

11. Alden v. Maine, 527 U.S. 706 (1999) (no unconsented federal suits against a
state in state court brought by that state's own citizens); *Hans v. Louisiana* (1890)

(no unconsented federal suits against a state in federal court brought by that state's own citizens).

12. Paul Brest, *The Misconceived Quest for the Original Understanding*, 60 B.U. L. REV. 204 (1980).

13. H. Jefferson Powell, *The Original Understanding of Original Intent*, 98 HARV. L. REV. 885 (1984).

14. "The new originalism is focused less on the concrete intentions of individual drafters of constitutional text than on the public meaning of the text that was adopted." Whittington, *supra* note 6, at 609. Prominent judicial examples of what purports to be the method at work include District of Columbia v. Heller, 554 U.S. 570, 128 S. Ct. 2783 (2008) and NLRB v. Noel Canning, Co., 573 U.S. 513, 134 S.Ct. 2550, 2578 (2014) (Scalia, J., concurring in the judgment).

15. A fascinating complication has been introduced into the scholarly debate over new originalism by evidence that substantial numbers of voters in New York and Pennsylvania were informed largely by versions of the Constitution that appeared in Dutch and German translations, respectively. This introduces the prospect that, in important ways, English-speaking and non-English-speaking voters during the ratification period may well have understood the Constitution differently. Christina Mulligan, Michael Douma, Hans Lind, and Brian Patrick Quinn, *Founding-Era Translations of the Constitution*, 30 CONST. COMMENTARY 2 (2016), available at http://ssrn.com/abstract=2486301 or http://dx.doi.org/10.2139/ssrn.2486301.

16. Saikrishna Prakash, *The Essential Meaning of Executive Power*, 2003 U. ILL. L. REV. 701, 716 (2003) (quoting Samuel Johnson's dictionary of 1773).

17. Victoria Nourse, *Reclaiming the Constitutional Text from Originalism: The Case of Executive Power*, 106 CAL. L. REV. 1 (2018).

18. *Id.* at 12.

19. *Id.*

20. *Id.* at 12–13.

21. *Id.* at 17.

22. "Article II, § 1, cl. 1, of the Constitution provides: 'The executive Power shall be vested in a President of the United States.' . . . [T]his does not mean *some of* the executive power, but *all of* the executive power." 487 U.S. at 705 (Scalia, J., dissenting) (emphasis in the original).

23. The article "the" before "executive power" does not require comprehensiveness, given that we often use "the" to refer also to things that are divisible. "The dessert was my favorite part of the meal," means exactly the same as, "Dessert was my favorite part of the meal," and neither formulation implies that I am the only diner at any meal who got dessert. Likewise, "The dog is a human's faithful companion," means exactly the same as, "Dogs are a human's faithful companion."

24. U.S. CONST. art. II, § 2.

25. U.S. CONST. art. I, § 8 (emphasis added).

26. William Maclay, one of Pennsylvania's first two Senators, made this suggestion, which the Senate rejected. E. Garrett West, *Congressional Power over Office*

Creation, 128 YALE L. J. 166, 188 (2018), citing THE DIARY OF WILLIAM MACLAY, reprinted in 9 DOCUMENTARY HISTORY OF THE FIRST FEDERAL CONGRESS OF THE UNITED STATES OF AMERICA 1789–1791, at 1, 83 (Charlene Bangs Bickford et al., eds. 1988).

27. U.S. CONST. art. II, § 2.

28. *In re Hennen*, 38 U.S. 230, 254 (1839).

29. THE FEDERALIST, No. 77 (Alexander Hamilton).

30. JOSEPH STORY, COMMENTARIES ON THE CONSTITUTION OF THE UNITED STATES 272–273 (R. D. Rotunda and J. E. Nowak, eds. 1987).

31. U.S. CONST. art. II, § 2.

32. Akhil Reed Amar, *Constitutional Redundancies and Clarifying Clauses*, 33 VAL. U. L. REV. 1, 13 (1998).

33. It is hard to explain how all the power to implement law is the president's when Congress explicitly vests authority in other officials to administer the laws. Professor Prakash implicitly offers a way around this conundrum in arguing that the president is constitutionally entitled to execute the statutes of the United States personally, should he choose to do so. That suggestion implicitly reconceptualizes Congress's charges to specific agencies as, effectively, delegations to the president with an expression of congressional preference as to the president's sub-delegate. But it is doubtful that Congress has ever viewed its administrative statutes in this manner. When Congress wants the president to shoulder personal responsibility for the exercise of administrative authority, it vests such authority in the president explicitly. It likewise authorizes by statute the presidential sub-delegation of such duties to Senate-confirmed officials of his choice, provided that no such sub-delegation "relieve[s] the president of his responsibility in office for the acts of any such head or other official designated by him to perform such function." 3 U.S.C. § 301.

34. Cf., Peter L. Strauss, *Overseer, or "The Decider"? The President in Administrative Law*, 75 GEO. WASH. L. REV. 696, 728–730 (2007).

35. John S. Ehrett, *Against Corpus Linguistics*, 108 GEO. L.J. ONLINE 50, 51 (2019).

36. Morrison v Olson, 487 U.S. 654, 703 (1988) (Scalia, J., dissenting).

37. Peter M. Shane, *The Originalist Myth of the Unitary Executive*, 19 U. PA. J. CONST. L. 323, 338–339 (2016).

38. SAIKRISHNA PRAKASH, IMPERIAL FROM THE BEGINNING: THE CONSTITUTION OF THE ORIGINAL EXECUTIVE 95 (2015).

39. Shane, *supra* note 37, at 357.

40. Myers v. United States, 272 U.S. 52, 118 (1926).

41. Prakash, *supra* note 16, at 794–795.

42. WILLIAM BLACKSTONE, COMMENTARIES ON THE LAWS OF ENGLAND (1765–1770).

43. *Myers v. United States*, 272 U.S. at 118.

44. Daniel D. Birk, *Interrogating the Historical Basis for a Unitary Executive*, 73 STAN. L. REV. 175 (2021).

45. *Id.* at 205, 220-221.

46. *Id.* at 226.

47. *Id.* at 229.

48. Jed Handelsman Shugerman, *The Decisions of 1789 Were Non-Unitary: The First Congress, Removal by Judiciary, and the Imaginary Unitary Executive (Part II)* 2–3 (Fordham Law Legal Studies Research, Working Paper No. 359,7496), https:// papers.ssrn.com/sol3/papers.cfm?abstract_id=3597496. For its participants, the debate over the status of public administrators in the new government was also a debate over whether public administrators had their own constitutional status or were solely to be viewed as instruments of the President. Those advocating the former position "forced the first Congress to address a constitutional dilemma commonly associated with the rise of the modern administrative state: how much responsibility to require of administration and how much autonomy to allow it?" Brian J. Cook, *Subordination or Independence for Administrators? The Decision of 1789 Reexamined*, 52 PUB. ADMIN. REV. 497, 501 (1992).

49. An Act for Establishing an Executive Department, to be Denominated the Department of Foreign Affairs, ch. 4, § 2, 1 Stat. 28, 29 (1789).

50. John F. Manning, *The Means of Constitutional Power*, 128 HARV. L. REV. 1, 46 n. 271 (2014).

51. *Id.* at 46.

52. Saikrishna Prakash, *New Light on the Decision of 1789*, 91 CORN. L. REV. 1021, 1032 (2006); Jed Handelsman Shugerman, *The Indecisions of 1789: Strategic Ambiguity and the Imaginary Unitary Executive (Part I)*, at 23 (May 8, 2020), https://ssrn.com/abstract=3596566.

53. Shugerman, *supra* note 52, at 37.

54. Christine Kexel Chabot, *Is the Federal Reserve Constitutional? An Originalist Argument for Independent Agencies* NOTRE DAME L. REV. (forthcoming) (manuscript at 3), https://papers.ssrn.com/sol3/papers.cfm?abstract_id=3458182.

55. Sinking Fund Act of Aug. 12, 1790, ch. 47, 1 Stat. 186.

56. Chabot, *supra* note 54 (manuscript at 3).

57. JERRY L. MASHAW, CREATING THE AMERICAN CONSTITUTION: THE LOST ONE HUNDRED YEARS OF AMERICAN ADMINISTRATIVE LAW (2012).

58. *Id.* at 40.

59. 1 ANNALS OF CONG. 635, 637 (1789) (Joseph Gales & William W. Seaton eds., 1834–56).

60. Prakash, *supra* note 52, at 1071.

61. Act of Mar. 3, 1797, ch. 20, § 1, 1 Stat. 512, 512.

62. Act of Mar. 3, 1817, ch. 45, § 10, 3 Stat 366, 367.

63. Walter Dellinger and H. Jefferson Powell, *The Constitutionality of the Bank Bill: The Attorney General's First Constitutional Law Opinions*, 44 DUKE L.J. 110, 131 (1994).

64. Alexander Hamilton, *Report on a National Bank* (Dec. 13, 1790), in 1 REPORTS OF THE SECRETARY OF THE TREASURY OF THE UNITED STATES,

PREPARED IN OBEDIENCE TO THE ACT OF THE 10TH MAY, 1800, at 54; *see also*
JOHN THOM HOLDSWORTH AND DAVIS R. DEWEY, THE FIRST AND SECOND
BANKS, OF THE UNITED STATES, S.Doc. 571, 61st Cong., 2d Sess. 19–22 (1910)
(republished in 2012).

65. Mashaw, *supra* note 57, at 47.

66. Act of Feb. 25, 1791, Ch. 10, § 7, par. V, 1st Cong., 3d Sess., 1 Stat. 191, 193
(establishing a quorum of seven).

67. Mashaw, *supra* note 57, at 47.

68. James Madison, *Speech in Congress Opposing the National Bank* (Feb. 2,
1791), in JAMES MADISON: WRITINGS: WRITINGS 1772–1836, at 480, 482 (1999).

69. PAUL BREST, SANFORD LEVINSON, ET AL., PROCESSES OF CONSTITU-
TIONAL DECISIONMAKING: CASES AND MATERIALS 30 (6th ed. 2015).

70. Alexander Hamilton, *Opinion on the Constitutionality of an Act to Establish
a Bank*, 8 PAPERS OF ALEXANDER HAMILTON 97 (1965), available at http://avalon
.law.yale.edu/18th_century/bank-ah.asp; Thomas Jefferson, *Opinion on the Constitutionality of the Bill for Establishing a National Bank*, 19 PAPERS OF THOMAS
JEFFERSON 275 (1974), available at http://avalon.law.yale.edu/18th_century/bank
-tj.asp; Edmund Randolph, *The Constitutionality of the Bank Bill* (Feb. 12, 1791), in
H. JEFFERSON POWELL, THE CONSTITUTION AND THE ATTORNEYS GENERAL
3 (1999);

71. Shane, *supra* note 37, at 338.

72. MICHAEL W. MCCONNELL, THE PRESIDENT WHO WOULD NOT BE
KING: EXECUTIVE POWER UNDER THE CONSTITUTION 256, 258–262 (2020).

73. *Id.* at 167.

74. Andrew Kent, Ethan J. Leib & Jed Handelsman Shugerman, *Faithful Execution and Article II*, 132 Harv. L. Rev. 2111, 2118 (2019).

75. Charles Tiefer, *The Constitutionality of Independent Officers as Checks on
Abuses of Executive Power*, 63 B.U. L. Rev. 59, 90 (1983).

76. Peter M. Shane, *The Originalist Myth of the Unitary Executive*, 19 U. PA. J.
CONST. L.

323, 341 (2016).

77. *Id.* at 342.

78. THE FEDERALIST NO. 39 (James Madison).

79. Segall, *supra* note 1, at 192.

80. *Id.* at 15–35.

81. David A. Strauss, *Common Law, Common Ground, and Jefferson's Principle*,
112 YALE L.J. 1717, 1721–1722 (2003).

82. 15 THE PAPERS OF THOMAS JEFFERSON 23, 26, 27 (Princeton University
Press ed., 1958).

83. SEAN WILENTZ, THE RISE OF AMERICAN DEMOCRACY: JEFFERSON TO
LINCOLN 122 (2005)

84. ALEXANDER KEYSSAR, THE RIGHT TO VOTE: THE CONTESTED HIS-
TORY OF DEMOCRACY IN THE UNITED STATES 5 (2009).

85. U.S. CONST. art. V.

86. Congress chooses whether state ratification may be accomplished by the state legislatures or whether state conventions must be called for that purpose. Congress, however, has invoked the latter process only once, with regard to the Twenty-First Amendment, which repealed Prohibition.

87. U.S. CONST. art. 1, § 8, cl. 1.

88. VANESSA K. BURROWS, CONG. RESEARCH SERV., RL34607, ADMINISTRATIVE LAW JUDGES: AN OVERVIEW 2 (2010); Kastor, *supra* note 4, at 2.

89. Derick Moore, *Fun Facts: From Counties Named Liberty to $368.6M Worth of Fireworks Sold*, U.S. Census Bureau (July 2, 2019), https://www.census.gov /library/stories/2019/07/july-fourth-celebrating-243-years-of-independence.html ("The U.S. population was 2.5 million in 1776. It is more than 130 times larger today at 330 million"); *Strengthening the Federal Workforce*, WHITEHOUSE.GOV 65, https://www.govinfo.gov/content/pkg/BUDGET-2019-PER/pdf/BUDGET -2019-PER-4-3.pdf ("About 1.7 million of the approximately 2.1 million direct Federal employees live outside of the Washington, D.C., metro area") (last visited June 28, 2020).

90. Eric J. Segall, *The Constitution Means What the Supreme Court Says It Means*, 129 HARV. L. REV. F. 176, 184–185 (2015–2016).

91. *Id.* at 184–185; Strauss, *supra* note 81, at 1742–1743.

92. William N. Eskridge Jr. & Philip P. Frickey, *Statutory Interpretation as Practical Reasoning*, 42 STAN. L. REV. 321, 332–333, 340–341 (1990).

93. Manning, *supra* note 50, at 17; ANTONIN SCALIA & BRYAN A. GARNER, READING LAW: THE INTERPRETATION OF LEGAL TEXTS (2012).

94. Quoted in Patricia M. Wald, *Some Observations on the Use of Legislative History in the 1981 Supreme Court Term*, 68 IOWA L. REV. 195, 214 (1983).

95. District of Columbia v. Heller, 554 U.S. 570 (2008).

96. U.S. CONST. Amend. II.

97. Saul Cornell, *Heller, New Originalism, and Law Office History: Meet the New Boss, Same as the Old Boss*, 56 UCLA L. REV. 1095 (2009); Enrique Schaerer, *What the Heller: An Originalist Critique of Justice Scalia's Second Amendment Jurisprudence*, 82 U. CIN. L. REV. 795 (2014).

98. District of Columbia v. Heller, 554 U.S. at 577.

99. *Id.* at 577-78.

100. *Id.* at 720–721, 586–587.

101. CORPUS OF FOUNDING ERA AMERICAN ENGLISH (COFEA), https://lcl .byu.edu/projects/cofea/ (last visited June 29, 2020).

102. Josh Blackman & James C. Phillips, *Corpus Linguistics and the Second Amendment*, HARV. L. REV. BLOG (Aug. 7, 2018), https://blog.harvardlawreview .org/corpus-linguistics-and-the-second-amendment/.

103. *Id.*

104. Christopher J. Peters, *Originalism, Stare Decisis, and Constitutional Authority* (2013), http://scholarworks.law.ubalt.edu/all_fac/879 ("I doubt many

originalists would be comfortable with an Equal Protection Clause that did not protect gender equality, for example, or with a Free Speech Clause that did not protect commercial speech, or with an Establishment Clause that forbade only official state churches supported with tax dollars; yet even the most creative originalists would be hard-pressed to anchor these interpretations in the original understandings"); 44 Liquormart, Inc. v. Rhode Island, 517 U.S. 484, 517 (1996) (Scalia, J., concurring) (stating that the first amendment's preservation of free speech is "indeterminable." In such cases, he will take guidance as to what the constitution forbids "from the long accepted practices of the American people").

105. DAVID A. STRAUSS, THE LIVING CONSTITUTION 25–29 (2010).

106. Michael W. McConnell, *The Fourteenth Amendment: A Second American Revolution or the Logical Culmination of the Tradition*, 25 LOY. L. A. L. REV. 1159, 1162 (1992).

107. *Obergefell v. Hodges*, 135 S. Ct. 2584 (2015).

108. Brief for Petitioner, Obergefell v. Hodges, 135 S. Ct. 2584 (2015) (No. 14-556).

109. Keith E. Whittington, *Constructing a New American Constitution*, 27 CONST. COMMENT. 119 (2010).

110. *Id.* at 130–131.

111. Randy E. Barnett & Evan D. Bernick, *The Letter and the Spirit: A Unified Theory of Originalism*, 107 GEO. L.J. 1, 1 (2018); Steven J. Burton, *More on Good Faith Performance of a Contract: A Reply to Professor Summers*, 69 IOWA L. REV. 497, 504–505 (1984); Steven J. Burton, *Breach of Contract and the Common Law Duty to Perform in Good Faith*, 94 HARV. L. REV. 369, 369 (1980).

112. Barnett & Bernick, *supra* note 111, at 36.

113. *Id.* at 28, 36.

114. *Id.* at 37.

115. *Id.* at 46.

116. *Id.* at 15, 38.

117. Wickard v. Filburn, 317 U.S. 111 (1942).

118. Gibbons v. Ogden, 22 U.S. (9 Wheat.) 1, 195 (1824).

119. Bolling v. Sharpe, 347 U.S. 497 (1954); Harper v. Va. State Bd. of Elections, 383 U.S. 663 (1966).

120. Bolling v. Sharpe, 347 U.S. at 498.

121. Harper v. Va. State Bd. of Elections, 383 U.S. at 666.

122. Strauss, *supra* note 81, at 1750.

123. Breedlove v. Suttles, 302 U.S. 277 (1937).

124. Strauss, *supra* note 81, at 1724.

125. Carrington v. Rash, 380 U.S. 89 (1965).

126. Reynolds v. Sims, 377 U.S. 533 (1964).

127. Harper v. Va. State Bd. of Elections, 383 U.S. at 668.

128. BENJAMIN N. CARDOZO, THE NATURE OF THE JUDICIAL PROCESS 66 (1921).

CHAPTER 5. INTERPRETING DEMOCRACY'S CONSTITUTION

1. Jonathan Easley, *Scalia: Constitution Is 'Dead Dead Dead,'* THE HILL (Jan. 29, 2013, 2:11 PM), https://thehill.com/blogs/blog-briefing-room/news/279789-scalia -constitution-is-dead-dead-dead.

2. Aaron Blake, *Neil Gorsuch, Antonin Scalia and Originalism, Explained,* WASH. POST (Feb. 1, 2017), https://www.washingtonpost.com/news/the-fix/wp /2017/02/01/neil-gorsuch-antonin-scalia-and-originalism-explained/.

3. Eric J. Segall, *The Constitutional Means What the Supreme Court Says It Means,* 129 Harv. L. Rev. F. 176, 181–82 (2015–2016); David A. Strauss, *Common Law, Common Ground, and Jefferson's Principle,* 112 Yale L.J. 1717, 1718 (2003).

4. McCulloch v. Maryland, 17 U.S. (4 Wheat.) 316, 415 (1819).

5. *Id.* at 407.

6. District of Columbia v. Heller, 554 U.S. 570, 627 (2008).

7. *Id.* at 627.

8. *Id.* at 627–628.

9. Section 1 of the proposed amendment reads, "Section 1: Equality of rights under the law shall not be denied or abridged by the United States or by any state on account of sex."

10. Compare Bostock v. Clayton County, Georgia, 590 U.S. __, 140 S. Ct. 1731 (2020).

11. Lawrence B. Solum, *Originalism and Constitutional Construction,* 82 FORD-HAM L. REV. 453, 453 (2013).

12. DAVID A. STRAUSS, THE LIVING CONSTITUTION 25–29 (2010).

13. On the centrality of making such judgments to common law reasoning, see STEVEN J. BURTON, AN INTRODUCTION TO LAW & LEGAL REASONING (2007).

14. McCulloch v. Maryland, 17 U.S. (4 Wheat.) at 407.

15. JERRY L, MASHAW, REASONED ADMINISTRATION AND DEMOCRATIC LEGITIMACY: HOW ADMINISTRATIVE LAW SUPPORTS DEMOCRATIC GOVERNMENT 158 (2018).

16. *See generally* Max Lerner, *John Marshall and the Campaign of History,* 39 COLUM. L. REV. 396 (1939).

17. David E. Bernstein, *Lochner Era Revisionism, Revised: Lochner and the Origins of Fundamental Rights Constitutionalism,* 92 GEO. L.J. 1, 3 (2003).

18. Raoul Berger, *The Activist Legacy of the New Deal Court,* 59 WASH. L. REV. 751,752 (1984).

19. GEOFFREY R. STONE & DAVID A. STRAUSS, DEMOCRACY AND EQUAL-ITY: THE ENDURING CONSTITUTIONAL VISION OF THE WARREN COURT (2020); VINCENT BLASI, BURGER COURT: THE COUNTER-REVOLUTION THAT WASN'T (1983).

20. MARK V. TUSHNET, A COURT DIVIDED: THE REHNQUIST COURT AND THE FUTURE OF CONSTITUTIONAL LAW (2005).

21. Marcia Coyle, The Roberts Court: The Struggle for the Constitution (2020).

22. Emily Bazelon, *How Will Trump's Supreme Court Remake America?*, N.Y. Times (Feb. 28, 2020), https://www.nytimes.com/2020/02/27/magazine/how-will-trumps-supreme-court-remake-america.html.

23. David E. Pozen, *Constitutional Bad Faith*, 129 Harv. L. Rev. 885, 896–897 (2016).

24. Seila Law v. CFPB, 591 U.S. ___, 140 S. Ct. 2183, 2224 (2020) (Kagan, J., dissenting).

25. Segall, *supra* note 3, at 181–182.

26. Richard H. Fallon Jr., *Legitimacy and the Constitution*, 118 Harv. L. Rev. 1787, 1795–1801 (2005).

27. *Id.* at 1797; Allen Buchanan, *Political Legitimacy and Democracy*, 112 Ethics 689, 702 (2002).

28. Robert C. Post, Constitutional Domains 7 (1995).

29. Robert A. Dahl, *What Political Institutions Does Large-Scale Democracy Require?*, 120 Poli. Sci. Q. 187, 188 (2005).

30. Rucho v. Common Cause, 139 S. Ct. 2484, 2509 (2019) (Kagan, J., dissenting).

31. Joseph M. Bessette, The Mild Voice of Reason: Deliberative Democracy and American National Government 1 (1994).

32. A great deal of scholarly work has since been done to refine the idea of deliberative democracy. Some legal scholars have urged the pursuit of a kindred ideal they call "civic republicanism," which, like "deliberative democracy," aims to arrive at the public good not just through elections, but by engaging the citizenry in an ongoing and inclusive dialogue. As explained by Mark Seidenfeld, "the demand for deliberative government means that before the government acts, it must engage in public discourse about whether the action will further the common good." Mark Seidenfeld, *A Civic Republican Justification for the Bureaucratic State*, 105 Harv. L. Rev. 1511, 1529 (1992). I will use the "deliberative democracy," rather than the "civic republican" frame for my analysis because the tie to republican thought—and the controversies over whether civil republicanism is really republicanism at all—are beside the point for my purposes.

33. Bessette, *supra* note 31, at 1.

34. John S. Dryzek, Deliberative Democracy and Beyond 2 (2002).

35. *Id.*

36. Bessette, *supra* note 31, at 1–2.

37. John Rawls, Political Liberalism 231 (1993).

38. Jerry L. Mashaw, *Prodelegation: Why Administrators Should Make Political Decisions*, 1 J. L. Econ. & Org. 81, 95 (1985).

39. Gerard A. Hauser, Vernacular Voices: The Rhetoric of Publics and Public Spheres 61 (1999).

40. Matthew Graham and Milan Svolik, *Democracy in America? Partisanship, Polarization, and the Robustness of Support for Democracy in the United States*, 114 Am. Poli. Sci. Rev. 392, 406 (2020).

41. NLRB v. Canning, 573 U.S. 513 (2014).

42. U.S. Const., Art. II, § 2, cl. 3.

43. Jordain Carney, *Senate Schedules More Pro Forma Sessions after Trump Demands Adjournment*, The Hill (Apr. 16, 2020), https://thehill.com/homenews/senate/493201-senate-schedules-more-pro-forma-sessions-after-trump-demands-adjournment.

44. NLRB v. Canning, 573 U.S. at 515.

45. *Id*. at 533–534.

46. *Id*. at 575 (Scalia, J., concurring in the judgment).

47. NLRB v. New Vista Nursing & Rehab., 870 F.3d 113 (3d Cir. 2017).

48. INS v. Chadha, 462 U.S. 919 (1983).

49. Jerry L. Mashaw & David L. Harfst, The Struggle for Auto Safety (1990).

50. Ins v. Chadha, 462 U.S. at 1003–1013 (White, J., dissenting).

51. U.S. Const. art I, §7, cl 2–3.

52. *Concurrent Resolution*, United States Senate, https://www.senate.gov/legislative/common/briefing/leg_laws_acts.htm.

53. Ins v. Chadha, 462 U.S. at 967–968 (White, J., dissenting).

54. *Id*. at 959–960 (Powell, J., concurring).

55. *Id*. at 952.

56. *Id*.

57. United States v. Nova Scotia Food Prods. Corp., 568 F.2d 240, 249 (2d Cir. 1977).

58. I.N.S. v. Chadha, 462 U.S. at 927–928; Barbara Hinkson Craig, Chadha: The Story of an Epic Constitutional Struggle (1988).

59. *See generally* Harold H. Bruff & Ernest Gellhorn, *Congressional Control of Administrative Regulation: A Study of Legislative Vetoes*, 90 Harv. L. Rev. 1369 (1977).

60. Amy Gutmann & Dennis Thompson, Democracy and Disagreement (1998).

61. United States v. Nixon, 418 U.S. 683 (1974).

62. Raoul Berger, Executive Privilege: A Constitutional Myth (1974).

63. United States v. Nixon, 418 U.S. at 706.

64. *Id*. at 705.

65. *Id*. at 713.

66. *Id*. at 712, n. 19.

67. Letter from Fred F. Fielding, Counsel to the President, to Patrick Leahy, U.S. Senate et al. (Mar. 20, 2007) (on file with author), https://legacy.npr.org/documents/2007/mar/doj_senate/fielding_letter032007.pdf; Assertion of Executive Privilege with Respect to Clemency Decision, 23 Op. Att'y Gen. 4,6 (1999), https://presnellonprivileges.com/wp-content/uploads/2020/03/OLC-Opinion-September-16-1999-Clinton.pdf.

68. McCulloch v. Maryland, 17 U.S. (4 Wheat.) 316 (1819).

69. *Id.* at 435–436.

70. Pike v. Bruce Church, 397 U.S. 137 (1970).

71. United States v. Carolene Prod. Co., 304 U.S. 144, 153 n. 4 (1938).

72. *Id.*

73. JOHN HART ELY, DEMOCRACY AND DISTRUST: A THEORY OF JUDICIAL REVIEW (1980).

74. Cass R. Sunstein, *Interest Groups in American Public Law*, 38 STAN. L. REV. 29, 85 (1985).

75. *Id.* at 86.

76. *Id.* at 31.

77. Frank I. Michelman, *Traces of Self-Government*, 100 HARV. L. REV. 4, 74 (1986).

78. Seidenfeld, *supra* note 32, at 1514.

79. Jerry L. Mashaw, *Reasoned Administration: The European Union, the United States, and the Project of Democratic Governance*, 76 GEO. WASH. L. REV. 99, 101–102 (2007).

80. SUSAN HENNESSEY & BENJAMIN WITTES, UNMAKING THE PRESIDENCY, DONALD TRUMP'S WAR ON THE WORLD'S MOST POWERFUL OFFICE (2020).

81. George Packer, *We Are Living in a Failed State*, THE ATLANTIC (June 2020), https://www.theatlantic.com/magazine/archive/2020/06/underlying-conditions /610261/.

82. Steven Waldman & Charles Sennott, *The Crisis in Local Journalism Has Become a Crisis of Democracy*, WASH. POST (Apr. 11, 2018), https://www .washingtonpost.com/opinions/the-crisis-in-journalism-has-become-a-crisis-of -democracy/2018/04/11/a908d5fc-2d64-11e8-8688-e053ba58f1e4_story.html.

83. GANESH SITARAMAN, THE GREAT DEMOCRACY: HOW TO FIX OUR POLITICS, UNRIG THE ECONOMY AND UNITE AMERICA 9 (2019).

84. *Id.* at 5.

85. Packer, *supra* note 81.

86. SITARAMAN, *supra* note 83, at 27–28.

87. Packer, *supra* note 81.

88. WILLIAM DAVIES, NERVOUS STATES: DEMOCRACY AND THE DECLINE OF REASON 59-60 (2018).

89. Graham and Svolik, note 40, at 406.

90. *Id.* at 392.

91. GERALD LEONARD & SAUL CORNELL, THE PARTISAN REPUBLIC: DEMOCRACY, EXCLUSION, AND THE FALL OF THE FOUNDERS' CONSTITUTION, 1780–1830S (2019); Mary Sarah Bilder, *White Male Aristocracy*, BALKANIZATION (Apr. 30, 2020). https://balkin.blogspot.com/2020/04/white-male-aristocracy.html

92. GERALD LEONARD AND SAUL CORNELL, THE PARTISAN REPUBLIC: DEMOCRACY, EXCLUSION, AND THE FALL OF THE FOUNDERS' CONSTITUTION, 1780S–1830S, at 167 (2019).

1. On the case for its desirability, see Garrett Epps, The Ill-Made Prince: A Modest Proposal for a New Article II 43 (Aug. 8, 2009) (unpublished manuscript) *available at* https://papers.ssrn.com/sol3/papers.cfm?abstract_id=1445643.

2. Robert Dahl, *What Political Institutions Does Large-Scale Democracy Require?* 120 POL. SCI. Q. 187, 188–189 (2005).

3. Jeremy Waldron, *Is the Rule of Law an Essentially Contested Concept (in Florida)?*, 21 LAW & PHIL. 137, 140–144 (2002).

4. PAUL GOWDER, THE RULE OF LAW IN THE REAL WORLD 12–18 (2016).

5. *Id.* at 28.

6. *Id.* at 40–41.

7. *Id.* at 147.

8. PETER M. SHANE, MADISON'S NIGHTMARE: HOW EXECUTIVE POWER THREATENS AMERICAN DEMOCRACY 11–12, 83 (2009).

9. *Id.* at 116.

10. Steven G. Calabresi, *Some Normative Arguments for the Unitary Executive,* 48 ARK. L. REV. 23, 59 (1995).

11. THE FEDERALIST, No. 10, at 46 (Clinton Rossiter, ed. 1961) (James Madison).

12. Calabresi, *supra* note 10, at 38.

13. William P. Marshall, *Why the Assertion of a "Nationalist" Presidency Does Not Support Claims for Expansive Presidential Power*, 12 J. CONST. L. 549 (2010).

14. JEREMY D. BAILEY, THE IDEA OF PRESIDENTIAL REPRESENTATION: AN INTELLECTUAL AND POLITICAL HISTORY 6 (2019).

15. ROBERT S. MCNAMARA, IN RETROSPECT: THE TRAGEDY AND LESSONS OF VIETNAM (1995).

16. THOMAS E. RICKS, FIASCO: THE AMERICAN MILITARY ADVENTURE IN IRAQ (2006); JACK GOLDSMITH, THE TERROR PRESIDENCY: LAW AND JUDGMENT INSIDE THE BUSH ADMINISTRATION (2007).

17. SAMANTHA POWER, THE EDUCATION OF AN IDEALIST: A MEMOIR (2019).

18. William V. Luneberg, *Civic Republicanism, the First Amendment, and Executive Branch Policymaking*, 43 ADMIN. L. REV. 367, 403–404 (1991).

19. My argument thus rests primarily on the deliberative side of democratic theory. If, however, one views the matter through an electoral lens, Matthew Stephenson showed over a decade ago that "a moderate degree of bureaucratic insulation from political control alleviates rather than exacerbates the countermajoritarian problems inherent in bureaucratic policymaking." Stephenson shows, that is, that some bureaucratic insulation from political control for individual agencies makes it more, not less likely that agency outcomes will track the preferences of the "median voter." Matthew C. Stephenson, *Optimal Political Control of the Bureaucracy*, 107 MICH. L. REV. 53 (2008).

20. HAROLD H. BRUFF, UNTRODDEN GROUND: HOW PRESIDENTS INTERPRET THE CONSTITUTION 99–100 (2015).

21. U.S. Const. art. I, § 8.

22. United States v. Lopez, 514 U.S. 549, 558–59 (1995).

23. *Id.* at 585 (Thomas, J., concurring).

24. *Id.* at 591 (Thomas, J., concurring).

25. Gundy v. United States, 139 S. Ct. 2116, 2123 (2019).

26. Panama Ref. Co. v. Ryan, 293 U.S. 388 (1935); A. L. A. Schechter Poultry Corp. v. United States, 295 U.S. 495 (1935).

27. Nat'l Broad. Co. v. United States, 319 U.S. 190, 227 (1943).

28. Yakus v. United States, 321 U.S. 414, 427 (1944).

29. Maeve P. Carey, Cong. Research Serv., R43056, Counting Regulations: An Overview of Rulemaking, Types of Federal Regulations, and Pages in the Federal Register 6–7 (2019).

30. Gundy v. United States, 139 S. Ct., at 2136 (Gorsuch, J., dissenting).

31. Gillian E. Metzger, *1930's Redux: The Administrative State Under Siege*, 131 Harv. L. Rev. 1 (2017).

32. Saikrishna Bangalore Prakash, The Living Presidency: An Originalist Argument Against Its Ever-Expanding Powers 257 (2020).

33. *Id.* at 224.

34. *Id.*

35. Julian Davis Mortenson & Nicholas Bagley, *Delegation at the Founding*, 121 Colum. L. Rev. 277 (2021).

36. Ilan Wurman, *Nondelegation at the Founding*, 130 Yale L. J. 1490, 1497 (2021).

37. *Id.* at 1494.

38. Nicholas R. Parrillo, *A Critical Assessment of the Originalist Case against Administrative Regulatory Power: New Evidence from the Federal Tax on Private Real Estate in the 1790s*, 130 Yale L. J. 1288 (2021).

39. *Id.*

40. *Id.*

41. *Id.*

42. Jacob S. Hacker & Paul Pierson, American Amnesia: How the War on Government Led Us to Forget What Made America Prosper 4–5 (2016).

43. Eric J. Segall, *The Constitution According to Justices Scalia and Thomas: Alive and Kickin'*, 91 Wash. U. L. Rev. 1663 (2014); J. Harvie III Wilkinson, *The Role of Reason in the Rule of Law*, 56 U. Chi. L. Rev. 779, 800–801 (1989).

44. Jerry L. Mashaw, Reasoned Administration and Democratic Legitimacy: How Administrative Law Supports Democratic Government 11 (2018).

45. *Id.* at 60–61.

46. *Id.* at 157.

47. *Id.* at 164.

48. Saikrishna Prakash, *The Essential Meaning of Executive Power*, 2003 U. Ill. L. Rev. 701, 708–709 (2003).

49. Inspector General Act of 1978, 5 U.S.C. § 3 (a)–(b).

50. 5 U.S.C. § 3 (b).

51. Jen Kirby, *Trump's Purge of Inspectors General, Explained*, VOX (May 28, 2020), https://www.vox.com/2020/5/28/21265799/inspectors-general-trump-linick-atkinson.

52. Although the *Seila Law* decision reflected the skepticism of presidentialist justices toward administrative independence, it may be a hopeful sign—at least as far as inspectors general are concerned—that the majority seemed open to the possibility that greater independence might be tolerated if the focus of an official's actions were on the executive branch itself, rather than on the general public. As the majority noted, the power of independent counsel upheld in *Morrison v. Olson*, "while significant, was trained inward to high-ranking Governmental actors identified by others, and was confined to a specified matter in which the Department of Justice had a potential conflict of interest." Seila Law LLC v. Consumer Fin. Prot. Bureau, 140 S. Ct. 2183, 2200 (2020).

53. Lucia v. SEC, 138 S. Ct. 736 (2018).

54. Exec. Order No. 13,992, 86 Fed. Reg. 7049 (Jan. 20, 2021).

55. Nelson Lund, *In Defense of Presidential Signing Statements* 1 (George Mason Legal Studies Research Paper No. LS 16-05, 2016), https://papers.ssrn.com/sol3/papers.cfm?abstract_id=2730815.

56. Peter M. Shane, *Presidential Signing Statements and the Rule of Law as an "Unstructured Institution,"* 16 WM. & MARY BILL RTS. J. 231, 232 (2007).

57. Neil J. Kinkopf & Peter M. Shane, *Signed Under Protest: A Database of Presidential Signing Statements, 2001–2009* (Ohio State Pub. L. Working Paper No. 141, 2011), http://papers.ssrn.com/sol3/papers.cfm?abstract_id=1485715.

58. SHANE, *supra* note 8, at 141–142.

59. *United States Secretary of Defense*, WIKIPEDIA, https://en.wikipedia.org/wiki/United_States_Secretary_of_Defense (last visited July 21, 2020).

60. *United States Secretary of Homeland Security*, WIKIPEDIA, https://en.wikipedia.org/wiki/United_States_Secretary_of_Homeland_Security (last visited May 26, 2021).

61. Emily Stewart & Jen Kirby, *Judge Rules Mick Mulvaney Is in Charge of CFPB, For Now*, VOX (Nov. 28, 2017), https://www.vox.com/policy-and-politics/2017/11/27/16704796/cfpb-english-mulvaney-trump-cordray.

62. Caitlin Oprysko, *Whitaker to Stay at Justice Department Following Stint as Acting AG*, POLITICO (Feb. 15, 2019), https://www.politico.com/story/2019/02/15/whitaker-justice-department-attorney-general-counselor-1172109.

63. *Administrative Conference Recommendation 2019–7*, ADMINISTRATIVE CONFERENCE OF THE U.S. (Dec. 12, 2019), https://www.acus.gov/sites/default/files/documents/12122019-adopted-recommendation-post-plenary-actings-dec272019_0.pdf.

64. Anne Joseph O'Connell, *Acting Agency Officials and Delegations of Authority* 1 (Dec. 1, 2019) (report to the Admin. Conf. of the U.S.), https://www.acus.gov/report/final-report-acting-agency-officials.

65. Federal Vacancies Reform Act of 1998, 5 U.S.C. §3345.

66. O'Connell, *supra* note 64, at 1.

67. Designating an Acting Director of the Bureau of Consumer Financial Protection, 41 Op. O.L.C. 5-6 (2017). Congress tried in the FVRA to prevent abuse of the "acting administrator" designation by imposing time limits on any such individual's service. Those limits, however, can be avoided to the extent a vacant position has functions that are deemed to have been delegable to other officers within a department. As OLC interprets the FVRA, "Most, and in many cases all, the responsibilities performed by a PAS officer will not be exclusive, and the Act permits non-exclusive responsibilities to be delegated to other appropriate officers and employees in the agency." Guidance on Application of Federal Vacancies Reform Act of 1998, 23 Op. O.L.C. 60, 72 (1999).

68. See, e.g., Hamdan v. Rumsfeld, 548 U.S. 557 (2006).

69. See, e.g., Zivotofsky v. Kerry, 576 U.S. 1 (2015).

70. STEPHEN M. GRIFFIN, LONG WARS AND THE CONSTITUTION 52 (2013). Presidential historian Michael Beschloss treats Korea as significant, but also as a precedent that built on the acts of earlier war presidents. He argues that "the notion of presidential war took hold step by step." MICHAEL BESCHLOSS, PRESIDENTS OF WAR 585 (2018).

71. Leon Edel, *Truman's 'Police Action'*, N.Y. TIMES (June 10, 1990), https://www.nytimes.com/1990/06/10/books/l-truman-s-police-action-841390.html#:~:text=Truman%20"initially%20mislabeled%20the%20fighting,it%20"a%20police%20action.&text=He%20needed%20the%20U.N.%20to,had%20crossed%20into%20South%20Korea.

72. Youngstown Sheet & Tube Co. v. Sawyer, 343 U.S. 579 (1952).

73. The most protracted post-Korea U.S. war against the government of another nation was the Vietnam War. The major escalation of U.S. involvement in 1965 was supposedly authorized by the Gulf of Tonkin resolution. Gulf of Tonkin Resolution, H.R.J. Res. 1145, 88th Cong. (1964). A Senate Committee study later asserted that the Johnson administration had assured Senators supporting it that the resolution would not be used to legitimate a major land war. National Commitments, S. Rep. No. 129 (Comm. on Foreign Relations), 91st Cong., 1st Sess. (1969). It also appears that the U.S. instigated the incident that led to enactment of the resolution. (History.com Editors, *Gulf of Tonkin Resolution*, HISTORY (Jun. 7, 2019) https://www.history.com/topics/vietnam-war/gulf-of-tonkin-resolution-1).

74. U.S. CONST. art II, § 2, cl. 1.

75. U.S. CONST. art. 1, § 8.

76. Helene Cooper et al., *U.S., Britain and France Strike Syria over Suspected Chemical Weapons Attack*, N.Y. TIMES (Apr. 13, 2018), https://www.nytimes.com/2018/04/13/world/middleeast/trump-strikes-syria-attack.html.

77. Office of Legal Counsel, Memorandum Opinion for the Counsel to the President re: April 2018 Airstrikes Against Syrian Chemical-Weapons Facilities, 42 O.L.C. ___ (May 31, 2018) ["OLC Syria Opinion"], https://www.justice.gov/olc/opinion/file/1067551/download.

78. Authority to Use Military Force in Libya, 35 Op. O.L.C. (Apr. 1, 2011), https://fas.org/irp/agency/doj/olc/libya.pdf.

79. Authority of the President under Domestic and International Law to Use Military Force against Iraq, 26 Op. O.L.C. (Oct. 23, 2002), https://fas.org/irp/agency/doj/olc/force.pdf.

80. OLC Syria Opinion, *supra* note 77, at 3.

81. *Id.* at 4.

82. *Id.*

83. *Id.* at 9.

84. *Id.* at 10.

85. Office of Legal Counsel, Memorandum Opinion for the Special Counsel to the President re: The President and the War Power: South Vietnam and the Cambodian Sanctuaries, 1 Op. O.L.C. 321 (1970), https://www.justice.gov/file/20826/download.

86. Authority to Use Military Force in Libya, 35 Op. O.L.C. (Apr. 1, 2011), at 6, https://fas.org/irp/agency/doj/olc/libya.pdf.

87. OLC Syria Opinion, *supra* note 77, at 11.

88. Jack L. Goldsmith, *What Happened to the Rule of Law?* N.Y. TIMES (Aug. 31, 2013), available at https://www.nytimes.com/2013/08/31/opinion/what-happened-to-the-rule-of-law.html?smid=tw-share.

89. Memorandum from Jay S. Bybee, Assistant Attorney General, to Alberto R. Gonzales, Counsel to the President, re: Standards of Conduct for Interrogation under 18 U.S.C. §§ 2340–2340A, at 1, 34–35 (Aug. 1, 2002), https://www.justice.gov/olc/file/886061/download.

90. JOHN YOO, THE POWERS OF WAR AND PEACE: THE CONSTITUTION AND FOREIGN AFFAIRS AFTER 9/11 (2005), critiqued in Peter M. Shane, *Powers of the Crown*, 68 REV. OF POLITICS 702 (2006).

91. JOHN HART ELY, WAR AND RESPONSIBILITY: CONSTITUTIONAL LESSONS OF VIETNAM AND ITS AFTERMATH (1993). Professor Prakash, whose originalist defenses of unitary executive theory I have earlier critiqued, also dissents on originalist grounds from Yoo's position. PRAKASH, *supra* note 32, at 150–51.

92. THE FEDERALIST, NO. 69, at 386 (Alexander Hamilton) (Clinton Rossiter, ed., 1961, 1999 reprint).

93. Keith Whittington, *R.I.P. Congressional War Power*, LAWFARE (Apr. 20, 2018), https://www.lawfareblog.com/rip-congressional-war-power.

94. Gulf of Tonkin Resolution, H.R.J. Res. 1145, 88th Cong. (1964).

95. Leonard Meeker, *The Legality of United States Participation in the Defense of Viet-Nam*, 54 DEPT. STATE BULL. 474, 484 (1966).

96. *Id.* at 485.

97. Rebecca Ingber, *Legally Sliding into War*, JUST SECURITY (Mar. 15, 2001), https://www.justsecurity.org/75306/legally-sliding-into-war/.

98. A Letter from President Joseph R. Biden Jr. to the Speaker of the House and President pro tempore of the Senate Consistent with the War Powers Resolution

(Feb. 27, 2021), https://www.whitehouse.gov/briefing-room/statements-releases
/2021/02/27/a-letter-to-the-speaker-of-the-house-and-president-pro-tempore-of-the
-senate-consistent-with-the-war-powers-resolution/.

99. *Id.*

100. Authorization for Use of Military Force against Iraq Resolution of 2002,
Pub. L. 107–243, 116 Stat. 1498 (2002).

101. Ryan Goodman, *Legal Questions (and Some Answers) Concerning the U.S.
Military Strike in Syria*, JUST SECURITY (Mar. 1, 2021), https://www.justsecurity
.org/75056/legal-questions-and-some-answers-concerning-the-u-s-military-strike
-in-syria/.

102. Zivotofsky v. Kerry, 576 U.S. at 11–12.

103. Although he did not believe President Truman's handling of the steel
mills met this test, Justice Felix Frankfurter used his opinion in *Youngstown* to
articulate an especially stringent version of settlement-by-practice as applied to
Article II. Youngstown Sheet & Tube Co. v. Sawyer, 343 U.S. 579, 610–11 (1952)
(Frankfurter, J., concurring).

104. McCulloch v. Maryland, 17 U.S. 316, 401 (1819).

105. Fletcher v. Peck, 10 U.S. (6 Cranch) 87, 135 (1810).

106. Veto of War Powers Resolution, 9 WEEKLY COMP. PRES. DOC. 1285–87
(Oct. 24, 1973).

107. War Powers Resolution, Pub. L. No. 93-148, 87 Stat. 555 (1973) (codified as
amended at 50 U.S.C. §§ 1541–1548 (2012 & Supp. 2015)).

108. *Id.* §1542.

109. *Id.* §1543.

110. *Id.* §1544.

111. Those negotiations produced the enactment of the Multinational Force
in Lebanon Resolution (MFLR), Pub. L. 98-119, 97 Stat. 805 (1983). The MFLR
"determined" that the War Powers Resolution had been triggered on August 29,
1983, but expressly authorized the continued presence of U.S. forces in Lebanon for
eighteen months, unless extended, following the date of the MFLR's enactment.
The MFLR also stated the general terms of the Marines' authorized mission, and
provided that authority for their continued presence would expire in less than
eighteen months if any of several specified conditions occurred that would obviate
their deployment.

112. Peter M. Shane, *Learning McNamara's Lessons: How the War Powers Resolution Advances the Rule of Law,* 47 CASE W. RES. L. REV. 1281, 1300–1303 (1997).

113. *Id.*; See also Christopher A. Ford, *War Powers as We Live Them:
Congressional-Executive Bargaining under the Shadow of the War Powers Resolution,* 11 J.L. & POL. 609, 613–620 (1995).

114. Authority to Use Military Force in Libya, 35 Op. O.L.C. 8 (2011), https://
www.justice.gov/file/18376/download.

115. S. 564, 104th Cong., 1st Sess. (1995), https://www.congress.gov/104/bills
/s564/BILLS-104s564is.pdf.

116. Bob Bauer & Jack Goldsmith, After Trump: Reconstructing the Presidency 287–298, 307–314, 376–377 (2020); Dakota S. Rudesill, *Nuclear Command and Statutory Control*, 11 J. Nat. Sec. L. & Pol'y, No. 2, 365 (2021), https://jnslp.com/2021/03/12/nuclear-command-and-statutory-control/.

117. *Id.* at 367.

118. Bauer & Goldsmith, *supra* note 117, at 313.

119. *Id.* at 377.

120. Authorization for Use of Military Force, Pub. L. No. 107-40, 115 Stat. 224 (2001) (codified at 50 U.S.C. § 1541–1548 (2012)); Authorization for Use of Military Force Against Iraq Resolution of 2002, Pub. L. No. 107-243, 116 Stat. 1498.

121. H.R. 5415, 113th Cong. (2014); H.J. Res. 123, 113th Cong. (2014); S.J. Res. 42, 113th Cong. (2014); Message to the Congress on Submitting Proposed Legislation to Authorize the Use of Military Force against the Islamic State of Iraq and the Levant (ISIL) Terrorist Organization 2009, DCPD No. 201500093 (Feb. 11, 2015).

122. OLC Syria Opinion, *supra* note 77, at 4.

123. U.S. Const., Art. II, §§ 2, 3.

124. *Id.*, Art I, § 8, cl. 3.

125. The Federalist No. 70, at 392 (Clinton Rossiter, ed. 1961) (Alexander Hamilton).

126. International Economic Emergency Powers Act, Pub. L. No. 95-223, tit. 11, 91 Stat. 1625 (codified at 50 U.S.C. §§ 1701–1706 (Supp. IV 1980)).

127. Joanna Tan, *Trump Says US Will Impose 5% Tariff on All Mexican Imports from June 10*, CNBC (May 31 2019), https://www.cnbc.com/2019/05/31/trump-says-us-will-impose-5percent-tariff-on-all-mexican-imports-from-june-10.html.

128. Vesting of Iranian Assets, Op. O.L.C. 202 (1980), https://www.justice.gov/sites/default/files/olc/opinions/1980/03/31/op-olc-v004a-p0202_0.pdf.

129. Trump v. Hawaii, 138 S. Ct. 2392 (2018).

130. Al-Aulaqi v. Obama, 727 F. Supp. 2d 1 (D.D.C. 2010).

131. Goldwater v. Carter, 444 U.S. 996 (1979) (plurality opinion).

132. United States v. Curtiss-Wright Export Corp., 299 U.S. 304 (1936).

133. Zivotofsky ex rel. Zivotofsky v. Kerry, 576 U.S. 1 (2015).

134. *Id.* at 32.

135. *Id.* at 3.

136. *Id.* at 66. In a separate dissent, Justice Scalia, writing for himself, Chief Justice Roberts, and Justice Alito, made a strong argument that the inference of presidential power to recognize other nations from Article II and from history does not necessarily support the exclusivity of that power.

137. Medellín v. Texas, 552 U.S. 491 (2008).

138. *Id.* at 503.

139. *Id.* at 517.

140. The Federalist No. 73, at 411 (Alexander Hamilton) (Clinton Rossiter, ed., 1961, 1999 reprint).

141. Prakash, *supra* note 32, at 194–195.

142. John C. Yoo, *Laws as Treaties: The Constitutionality of Congressional-Executive Agreements*, 99 MICH. L. REV. 757, 821 (2001).

143. Memorandum Opinion for the United States Trade Representative re: Whether Uruguay Round Agreements Required Ratification as a Treaty, 18 Op. O.L.C. 232, 240 (1994), https://www.justice.gov/file/20276/download.

144. Oona A. Hathaway, *Treaties' End: The Past, Present, and Future of International Lawmaking in the United States*, 117 YALE L.J. 1236, 1308–12 (2008).

145. *Id.* at 1308.

146. Id. See also *Treaties: A Historical Overview*, U.S. SENATE, https://www.senate.gov/artandhistory/history/common/briefing/Treaties.htm (last visited Oct. 25, 2021).

147. BRUFF, *supra* note 20, at 35–36.

148. Hathaway, *supra* note 144, at 1308.

149. *Id.*

150. *Id.* at 1309.

151. *Id.* at 1310.

152. Agreement between the United States, the United Mexican States, and Canada, Nov. 30, 2018, available at https://ustr.gov/trade-agreements/free-trade-agreements/united-states-mexico-canada-agreement/agreement-between.

153. Rebecca Ingber, *Congressional Administration of Foreign Affairs*, 106 VA. L. REV. 395, 412–437 (2021).

154. *Id.* at 465.

155. THE FEDERALIST No. 51, at 288 (James Madison) (Clinton Rossiter, ed. 1961).

156. Assertion of Executive Privilege in Response to a Congressional Subpoena, 5 Op. O.L.C. 27, 30 (1981) ("It is important to stress that congressional oversight of Executive Branch actions is justifiable only as a means of facilitating the legislative task of enacting, amending, or repealing laws"); Assertion of Exec. Privilege for Memorandum to the President Concerning Efforts to Combat Drug Trafficking, 20 Op. O.L.C. 8, 9 (1996).

157. Response to Congressional Requests for Information Regarding Decisions Made Under the Independent Counsel Act ("Independent Counsel Act"), 10 Op. O.L.C. 68, 75–78 (1986) (explaining the Executive Branch's authority to withhold open and closed law enforcement files from Congress); Prosecution for Contempt of Congress of an Executive Branch Official Who Has Asserted a Claim of Executive Privilege, 8 Op. O.L.C. 101, 117 (1984); Assertion of Executive Privilege in Response to Congressional Demands for Law Enforcement Files, 6 Op. O.L.C. 31, 32–33 (1982). Cf., Assertion of Exec. Privilege Concerning the Special Counsel's Interviews of the Vice President & Senior White House Staff, 2008 WL 5458939, at *3 (O.L.C. July 15, 2008).

158. Memorandum from William H. Rehnquist, Assistant Attorney General, Office of Legal Counsel, re: Power of Congressional Committee to Compel Appearance or Testimony of "White House Staff" (Feb. 5, 1971); Office of Legal Counsel, Memorandum Opinion for the Counsel to the President re: Immunity of

the Assistant to the President and Director of the Office of Political Strategy and Outreach from Congressional Subpoena, (July 15, 2014), https://www.justice.gov /file/30896/download.

159. *Id.* at 1.

160. RAOUL BERGER, EXECUTIVE PRIVILEGE: A CONSTITUTIONAL MYTH (1974); Prakash, *supra* note 32, at 66, 261–264.

161. Comm. on the Judiciary of the United States H.R. v. Miers, 558 F. Supp. 2d 53 (D.D.C. 2008); Comm. on Oversight & Gov't Reform v. Lynch, 156 F. Supp. 3d 101 (D.D.C. 2016); Comm. on the Judiciary v. McGahn, 415 F. Supp. 3d 148 (D.D.C. 2019), *vacated and remanded sub nom.* Comm. on Judiciary v. McGahn, 951 F.3d 510 (D.C. Cir. 2020), *reh'g en banc granted, opinion vacated sub nom.* United States House of Representatives v. Mnuchin, 379 F. Supp. 3d 8 (D.D.C. 2019), *hearing en banc ordered sub nom.* U.S. H.R. v. Mnuchin, 19-5176, 2020 WL 1228477 (D.C. Cir. Mar. 13, 2020).

162. Letter from Pat A. Cipollone, Counsel to the President, to Nancy Pelosi, Speaker of the House of Representatives et al. 2, (Oct. 8, 2019), https://www.nytimes .com/interactive/2019/10/08/us/politics/white-house-letter-impeachment.html#.

163. *Id.* at 5.

164. Jonathan Shaub, *Obstruction of Congress, Impeachment and Constitutional Conflict*, LAWFARE (Jan. 10, 2020), https://www.lawfareblog.com/obstruction -congress-impeachment-and-constitutional-conflict.

165. Ronald Reagan, Memorandum for the Heads of Executive Departments and Agencies (Nov. 4, 1982), reprinted in PETER M. SHANE, HAROLD H. BRUFF, & NEIL J. KINKOPF, SEPARATION OF POWERS LAW: CASES AND MATERIALS 357 (4th ed. 2018).

166. *Id.* at 358.

167. Politico Staff, *Transcript: Jeff Sessions' Testimony on Trump and Russia*, POLITICO (June 13, 2017), https://www.politico.com/story/2017/06/13/full-text-jeff -session-trump-russia-testimony-239503.

168. Prosecution for Contempt of Congress of an Executive Branch Official Who Has Asserted a Claim of Executive Privilege, 17 Op. O.L.C. 101, 101 (1984).

169. Memorandum from Stephen A. Engel, Assistant Attorney General, Office of Legal Counsel, for the Attorney General and the Counsel to the President re: Attempted Exclusion of Agency Counsel from Congressional Depositions of Agency Employees 8 (May 23, 2019), https://assets.documentcloud.org/documents /6150688/2019-05-23-Agency-Counsel.pdf.

170. Trump v. Mazars USA, LLP, 140 S. Ct. 2019, 2031 (2020).

171. *Id.* at 2033, quoting (without attribution) WOODROW WILSON, CONGRESSIONAL GOVERNMENT 303 (1885). The *Mazars* Court omitted the following from its excerpted quote: "and unless Congress both scrutinize these things and sift them by every form of discussion, the country must remain in embarrassing, crippling ignorance of the very affairs which it is most important that it should understand and direct. The informing function of Congress should be preferred even to its legislative function."

172. National Defense Authorization Act for Fiscal Year 2018, Pub. L. 115-91, div. A, title XII, § 1264, 131 Stat. 1283,1689, codified at 50 U.S.C. § 1549.

173. White House Report on the Legal and Policy Frameworks Guiding the United States' Use of Military Force and Related National Security Operations (Dec. 2016), https://www.justsecurity.org/wp-content/uploads/2016/12/framework .Report_Final.pdf.

174. Pub. L. 116-92, § 1261(3).

175. Scott R. Anderson & Benjamin Wittes, *We Filed Suit over Trump's Missing War Powers Report*, LAWFARE (June 9, 2020), https://www.lawfareblog.com/we -filed-suit-over-trumps-missing-war-powers-report.

176. Complaint for Declaratory Relief and Petition for Writ of Mandamus, Wittes v. Trump, 2020 WL 3076568 (D.D.C. June 9, 2020).

177. Anderson & Wittes, *supra* note 175.

178. D.C. v. Trump, 315 F. Supp. 3d 875 (D. Md. 2018), *rev'd on other grounds and remanded sub nom.* In re Trump, 928 F.3d 360 (4th Cir. 2019), *reh'g en banc granted*, 780 F. App'x 36 (4th Cir. 2019), *and on reh'g en banc*, 958 F.3d 274 (4th Cir. 2020), *cert. granted, judgment vacated, and remanded with instruction to dismiss as moot*, 141 S. Ct. 1262 (2021).

179. U.S. CONST. art. II, § 1.

180. U.S. CONST. art. I, § 9.

181. D.C. v. Trump, 315 F. Supp. 3d at 880.

182. D.C. v. Trump, 315 F. Supp. 3d at 882-886.

183. D.C. v. Trump, 315 F. Supp. 3d at 883.

184. 28 C.F.R. § 600.7(a).

185. ROBERT S. MUELLER, III, 2 REPORT ON THE INVESTIGATION INTO RUSSIAN INTERFERENCE IN THE 2016 PRESIDENTIAL ELECTION 1 (2019).

186. *A Sitting President's Amenability to Indictment and Criminal Prosecution*, 24 Op. O.L.C. 222 (2000) (OLC Op.), https://www.justice.gov/sites/default/files /olc/opinions/2000/10/31/op-olc-v024-p0222_0.pdf.

187. Memorandum from Robert G. Dixon Jr., Assistant Attorney General, Office of Legal Counsel, Re: Amenability of the President, Vice President and other Civil Officers to Federal Criminal Prosecution While in Office (Sept. 24, 1973), https://fas.org/irp/agency/doj/olc/092473.pdf.

188. Letter from Ronald D. Rotunda to Kenneth W. Starr re: Indictability of the President (May 13,1998), at 3 and n. 6, https://turtletalk.files.wordpress.com/2018/12 /1998-starr-rotunda-memo-re-indictment-of-sitting-president.pdf.

189. Conversely, OLC also rejected the idea that, because members of Congress have an explicit immunity from criminal investigation via the Speech and Debate Clause, U.S. CONST. art. I, § 6, Article II's comparative silence regarding presidential immunity conclusively demonstrates that presidents have none. 24 Op. O.L.C. at 222.

190. *Id.* at 238.

191. *Id.*

192. *Id.* at 246.

193. Rotunda, *supra* note 188, at 6–7.

194. *Id.* at 12.

195. *Id.* at 5.

196. Mueller, *supra* note 185, at 2.

197. *Id.*

198. Trump also claimed he could relieve himself of criminal liability through self-pardon, a power he said he "absolutely" has. Yet the notion of self-pardon is plainly at odds with a president's obligation to take care that the laws be faithfully executed and the principle of due process that no one should be judge in his own cause. Even though the only explicit constitutional exclusion from the president's pardon power is impeachment, it is implausible under a democratic constitution that sitting presidents could exempt themselves from criminal sanction. Philip Ewing & Scott Neuman, *Trump: I Have 'Absolute' Power to Pardon Myself, But Have Done Nothing Wrong*, NPR (June 4, 2018), https://www.npr.org/sections/thetwo-way /2018/06/04/616724965/giuliani-president-trump-has-constitutional-authority-to -pardon-himself.

199. Quoted in Bob Bauer, *The Trump Impeachment and the Question of Precedent, Part II: The Trouble With Alan Dershowitz's 'Constitutional Argument,'* LAWFARE (Jan. 20, 2020), https://www.lawfareblog.com/trump-impeachment-and -question-precedent-part-ii-trouble-alan-dershowitzs-constitutional-argument.

200. Nikolas Bowie, *High Crimes without Law*, 132 HARV. L. REV. FORUM 59, 60–61 (2018).

201. CHARLES L. BLACK JR., IMPEACHMENT: A HANDBOOK 39–40 (1974).

202. THE FEDERALIST NO. 65, at 364 (Alexander Hamilton) (Clinton Rossiter, ed., 1961, 1999 reprint).

203. JOSEPH STORY, 2 COMMENTARIES ON THE CONSTITUTION § 762 (1833).

204. Patrick McDonnell et al., *What Do Scholars Say about the Impeachment Power?*, LAWFARE (Oct. 29, 2019), https://www.lawfareblog.com/what-do-scholars -say-about-impeachment-power.

205. H.R. REP. No. 1305-93 (1974); H.R. REP. No. 116-346, pt. 2, at 3 (2019).

206. Stephen M. Griffin, *Presidential Impeachment in Tribal Times: The Historic Logic of Informal Constitutional Change*, 51 CONN. L. REV. 413, 419 (2019).

207. *Id.* at 425.

208. Seila Law LLC v. Consumer Fin. Prot. Bureau, 140 S.Ct. 2183, 2203 (2020).

209. BAILEY, *supra* note 14, at 194–195.

210. Giovanni Russonello, *With Impeachment Inquiry in Full Swing, Public Opinion Remains Split*, N.Y. TIMES (Nov. 30, 2019), https://www.nytimes.com/2019 /11/29/us/politics/impeachment-trump-polls.html.

CHAPTER 7. BREAKING THE GRIP OF PRESIDENTIALISM

1. PETER M. SHANE, MADISON'S NIGHTMARE: HOW EXECUTIVE POWER THREATENS AMERICAN DEMOCRACY 27–29 (2009).

2. For comparative evidence showing how "head-of-state control over the executive branch of government provides a pathway to autocracy," see David M. Driesen, *The Unitary Executive Theory in Comparative Context*, 72 HASTINGS L.J. 1, 2 (2020).

3. Seila Law LLC v. Consumer Fin. Prot. Bureau, 140 S. Ct. 2183 (2020).

4. THOMAS E. MANN & NORMAN J. ORNSTEIN, THE BROKEN BRANCH x (2006).

5. Matthew H. Graham & Milan W. Svolik, *Democracy in America? Partisanship, Polarization, and the Robustness of Support for Democracy in the United States*, 114 AM. POL. SCI. REV. 392, 392 (2020).

6. JOSH CHAFETZ, CONGRESS'S CONSTITUTION: LEGISLATIVE AUTHORITY AND THE SEPARATION OF POWERS (2017).

7. Anthony Chergosky & Jason M. Roberts, *The De-Institutionalization of Congress*, 133 POLI. SCI. Q. 475 (2018).

8. MANN & ORNSTEIN, *supra* note 4, at 172.

9. Chergosky & Roberts, *supra* note 7, at 494.

10. Domenico Montanaro, *Americans Largely Support Gun Restrictions to "Do Something" about Gun Violence*, NPR (Aug. 10, 2019), https://www.npr.org/2019/08/10/749792493/americans-largely-support-gun-restrictions-to-do-something-about-gun-violence.

11. Jens Manuel Krogstad, *Americans Broadly Support Legal Status for Immigrants Brought to the U.S. Illegally as Children*, PEW RESEARCH CENTER (June 17, 2020), https://www.pewresearch.org/fact-tank/2020/06/17/americans-broadly-support-legal-status-for-immigrants-brought-to-the-u-s-illegally-as-children/.

12. Leslie Davis & Hannah Hartig, *Two-Thirds of Americans Favor Raising Federal Minimum Wage to $15 an Hour*, PEW RESEARCH CENTER (July 30, 2019), https://www.pewresearch.org/fact-tank/2019/07/30/two-thirds-of-americans-favor-raising-federal-minimum-wage-to-15-an-hour/.

13. Ashley Kirzinger, Audrey Kearney, Mellisha Stokes, Liz Hamel, & Mollyann Brodie, *The Public Weighs in on Medicare Drug Negotiations*, KAISER FAMILY FOUNDATION (Oct 12, 2021), https://www.kff.org/health-costs/poll-finding/public-weighs-in-on-medicare-drug-negotiations/.

14. Dahlia Lithwick, *From Richmond to the Senate Chambers, Minority Rule Rules*, SLATE (Jan. 21, 2020), https://slate.com/news-and-politics/2020/01/richmond-to-impeachment-senate-minority-rule-rules.html.

15. Kathryn E. Kovacs, *Constraining the Statutory President*, 98 WASH. U.L. REV. 63 (2020).

16. 5 U.S.C. § 3345.

17. PAUL C. LIGHT, MONITORING GOVERNMENT: INSPECTORS GENERAL AND THE SEARCH FOR ACCOUNTABILITY (1993); Anne Joseph O'Connell, *Watchdogs at Large*, BROOKINGS (Aug. 6, 2020), https://www.brookings.edu/research/watchdogs-at-large/.

18. Keith Whittington, *Time to Amend the Presidential Pardon Power*, LAWFARE (July 14, 2020), https://www.lawfareblog.com/time-amend-presidential-pardon-power.

19. Josh Gerstein, *Clinton Pardon Records Offer Fuel for Hillary's Foes*, POLITICO (Jan. 28, 2016), https://www.politico.com/story/2016/01/hillary-clinton-pardon-record-218331.

20. Authorization for Use of Military Force Against Iraq Resolution of 2002, Pub. L. No. 107-243, 116 Stat. 1498.

21. Authorization for Use of Military Force, Pub. L. No. 107-40, 115 Stat. 224 (2001) (codified at 50 U.S.C. § 1541–1548 (2012)).

22. White House Report on the Legal and Policy Frameworks Guiding the United States' Use of Military Force and Related National Security Questions (Dec. 2016)

23. Tess Bridgeman, *How to Ensure New Congressional War Authorization Is Not a Blank Check*, JUST SECURITY (Apr. 20, 2018), https://www.justsecurity.org/55147/stop-congressional-war-authorization-blank-check/.

24. S. 564, 104th Cong., 1st Sess. (1995), https://www.congress.gov/104/bills/s564/BILLS-104s564is.pdf.

25. Raines v. Byrd, 521 U.S. 811 (1997); Va. House of Delegates v. Bethune-Hill, 139 S. Ct. 1945 (2019).

26. Oona Hathaway & Geoffrey Block, *How to Recover a Role for Congress and the Courts in Decisions to Wage War*, JUST SECURITY (Jan. 10, 2020), https://www.justsecurity.org/68001/how-to-recover-a-role-for-congress-and-the-courts-in-decisions-to-wage-war/.

27. National Emergencies Act, 50 U.S.C. §§ 1601–1651.

28. International Economic Emergency Powers Act, Pub. L. No. 95-223, tit. 11, 91 Stat. 1625 (codified at 50 U.S.C. §§ 1701–1706 (Supp. IV 1980)).

29. Peter Harrell, *The Right Way to Reform the U.S. President's International Emergency Powers*, JUST SECURITY (Mar. 26, 2020), https://www.justsecurity.org/69388/the-right-way-to-reform-the-u-s-presidents-international-emergency-powers/.

30. *Id.*

31. *Id.*

32. Rebecca Ingber, *Congressional Administration of Foreign Affairs*, 106 VA. L. REV. 395 (2020).

33. 28 U.S.C. § 591–599.

34. Peter M. Shane, *Brett Kavanaugh and the Executive-Indulgent Court*, 44 ADMIN. & REG. L. NEWS 5 (2018).

35. Free Enter. Fund v. Pub. Co. Accounting Oversight Bd., 561 U.S. 477 (2010); Seila Law LLC v. Consumer Fin. Prot. Bureau, 140 S. Ct. 2183 (2020).

36. Peter M. Shane, *Reflections in Three Mirrors: Complexities of Representation in a Constitutional Democracy*, 60 OHIO ST. L.J. 693, 705 (1999).

37. GORDON S. WOOD, THE CREATION OF THE AMERICAN REPUBLIC 1776–1787, at 598 (1969) (quoting James Wilson).

38. ALEXANDER M. BICKEL, THE LEAST DANGEROUS BRANCH: THE SUPREME COURT AT THE BAR OF POLITICS (2d ed. 1986).

39. Robert Post, *Theorizing Disagreement: Reconceiving the Relationship between Law and Politics*, 98 CAL. L. REV. 1319, 1344–1345 (2010). In Siegel's words: "Social

movements change the ways Americans understand the Constitution. Social movement conflict, enabled and constrained by constitutional culture, can create new forms of constitutional understanding—a dynamic that guides officials interpreting the open-textured language of the Constitution's rights guarantees." Reva B. Siegel, *Constitutional Culture, Social Movement Conflict and Constitutional Change: The Case of the De Facto ERA*, 94 CALIF. L. REV. 1323, 1323 (2006). See also Robert Post & Reva Siegel, *Democratic Constitutionalism*, in JACK M. BALKIN & REVA B. SIEGEL, EDS., THE CONSTITUTION IN 2020, at 25 (2009). In my own invocation of "democratic constitutionalism" to refer to a particular approach to adaptive constitutional interpretation, I am using the phrase compatibly but somewhat differently from its important theoretical use by Post and Siegel.

40. I am here drawing on the analysis of polarization by Paul Gowder. Paul Gowder, *The Dangers to the American Rule of Law Will Outlast the Next Election*, CARDOZO L. REV. DE NOVO 126,149 (2020), http://cardozolawreview.com/the-dangers-to-the-american-rule-of-law-will-outlast-the-next-election/.

41. *Id.* at 162.

42. Nina Totenberg, *170-Plus Days and Counting, GOP Unlikely to End Supreme Court Blockade Soon*, NPR (Sep. 6, 2016), https://www.npr.org/2016/09/06/492857860/173-days-and-counting-gop-unlikely-to-end-blockade-on-garland-nomination-soon.

43. Leigh Ann Caldwell, *Republicans Use "Nuclear Option" to Clear the Way for Gorsuch Confirmation*, NBC NEWS (Apr. 6, 2017), https://www.nbcnews.com/politics/congress/senate-democrats-block-neil-gorsuch-s-supreme-court-nomination-n743326.

44. Trump v. Vance, 140 S. Ct. 2412 (2020); Trump v. Mazars USA, LLP, 140 S. Ct. 2019 (2020).

45. National Federation of Independent Business v. Sebelius, 567 U.S. 519 (2012) (upholding the Affordable Care Act); Department of Commerce v. New York, 139 S. Ct. 2551 (2019) (blocking the addition of a citizenship question on the 2020 census as "arbitrary and capricious" under the Administrative Procedure Act); Department of Homeland Security v. Regents of the University of California, 140 S. Ct. 1891 (2020) (blocking the repeal of the Deferred Action for Childhood Arrivals program as "arbitrary and capricious" under the Administrative Procedure Act).

46. David Jackson & Joey Garrison, *Trump Says He Wants to Fill Supreme Court Seat Quickly in Case Justices Need to Settle Election Dispute*, USA TODAY (Sept. 24, 2020), https://www.usatoday.com/story/news/politics/elections/2020/09/23/trump-need-fill-supreme-court-seat-quickly-because-election/3501368001/.

47. Gowder, *supra* note 40, at 162.

48. For a survey of proposals intended to boost the Court's legitimacy, but which are not targeted specifically at redressing the Scalia succession, see Daniel Epps & Ganesh Sitaraman, *How to Save the Supreme Court*, 129 YALE L.J. 148 (2019).

49. Steven Levitsky & Daniel Zablatt, How Democracies Die 78–81 (2018).

50. Bob Bauer & Jack Goldsmith, After Trump: Reconstructing the Presidency 253–277 (2020).

51. On the evolution of OLC in recent decades, see Daphna Renan, *The Law Presidents Make*, 103 Va. L. Rev. 805 (2017).

52. Memorandum for William J. Haynes II, General Counsel of the Department of Defense Re: Military Interrogation of Alien Unlawful Combatants Held Outside the United States, Op. O.L.C. 1 (Mar. 14, 2003), https://www.aclu.org/sites/default/files/pdfs/safefree/yoo_army_torture_memo.pdf.

53. Congressional Committee's Request for the President's Tax Returns Under 26 U.S.C. § 6103(f), 43 Op. O.L.C. 1, 9 (2019). OLC in the early months of the Biden administration withdrew the 2019 opinion. It said the earlier opinion erred "in suggesting that the Executive Branch should closely scrutinize the Committee's stated justifications for its requests in a manner that failed to accord the respect and deference due a coordinate branch of government." Ways and Means Committee's Request for the Former President's Tax Returns and Related Tax Information Pursuant to 26 U.S.C. § 6103(f)(1), 45 Op. O.L.C. __ (July 30, 2021), slip op. at 3.

54. Jack Goldsmith, *More on the Decline of OLC*, Lawfare (Nov 3, 2015, 7:58 AM), https://www.lawfareblog.com/more-decline-olc.

55. *Id.*

56. *Id.*

57. *Id.*

58. Charlie Savage, Power Wars: Inside Obama's Post-9/11 Presidency (2015).

59. *Presidential Powers-Hostilities and War Powers: Hearing on Libya and War Powers Before the Sen. Foreign Relations Comm.*, 112th Cong. 8–9 (2011) (statement of Harold Hongju Koh, Legal Advisor, Department of State), *reprinted* in 1 Pub. L. Misc. 292 (2011),http://journaloflaw.us/1%20Pub.%20L.%20Misc./1-2/JoL1-2,%20PLM1-2,%20Koh-Senate%20committee%202011.pdf; Peter M. Shane, *The Presidential Statutory Stretch and the Rule of Law*, 87 U. Colo. L. Rev. 1231, 1247 (2016).

60. Bruce Ackerman, The Decline and Fall of the American Republic 143 (2013). For a somewhat sympathetic, but largely critical review of Ackerman's argument, see Trevor W. Morrison, *Constitutional Alarmism*, 124 Harv. L. Rev. 1688 (2011). Dean Morrison had previously served both in OLC and in the office of the White House counsel.

61. Walter E. Dellinger et al., *Principles to Guide the Office of the Legal Counsel* (Dec. 21, 2004), https://scholarship.law.duke.edu/cgi/viewcontent.cgi?article=2927&context=faculty_scholarship.

62. Blake Emerson & Jon D. Michaels, *Abandoning Presidential Administration: A Civic Governance Agenda to Promote Democratic Equality and Guard against Creeping Authoritarianism*, 68 UCLA L. Rev. Disc. 418 (2021).

63. *Id.* at 434.

64. *Id.* at 435.

65. Kate Andrias & Benjamin I. Sachs, *Constructing Countervailing Power: Law and Organizing in an Era of Political Inequality*, 130 YALE L.J. 546, 562 (2021).

66. *Id.* at 570.

67. Katherine Schaeffer, *6 Facts about Economic Inequality in the US*, PEW RESEARCH CENTER (Feb. 7, 2020) https://web.archive.org/web/20200401051202 /https://www.pewresearch.org/fact-tank/2020/02/07/6-facts-about-economic -inequality-in-the-u-s/.

68. GANESH SITARAMAN, THE GREAT DEMOCRACY: HOW TO FIX OUR POLITICS, UNRIG THE ECONOMY, & UNITE AMERICA 91 (2019).

69. Derrick A. Bell, Jr., Brown v. Board of Education *and the Interest-Convergence Dilemma*, 93 HARV. L. REV. 518, 523 (1980).

70. *Id.* at 524.

71. *Id.* at 526.

72. See, e.g., Milliken v. Bradley, 418 U.S. 717 (1974). Even worse, the Court has rebuffed voluntary efforts by some white-majority school boards to preserve desegregation through racially conscious remedies. Parents Involved in Community Schools v. Seattle School District No. 1, 551 U.S. 701 (2007).

73. Washington v. Davis, 426 U.S. 229 (1976).

74. Personnel Administrator of Massachusetts v. Feeney, 442 U.S. 256 (1979).

75. Alexander Hamilton, Objections and Answers Respecting the Administration, at Objection XIV (Aug. 18, 1792), https://founders.archives.gov/documents /Hamilton/01-12-02-0184-0002#ARHN-01-12-02-0184-0002-fn-0044-ptr.

76. Pippa Norris, *Voters against Democracy: The Roots of Autocratic Resurgence*, FOREIGN AFFAIRS (May/June 2021), at 174, 178.

77. Steven Klein, *Democracy Requires Organized Collective Power*, J. POLITICAL PHIL., at 4 (May 4, 2021), https://doi.org/10.1111/jopp.12249.

78. George Packer, *Make America Again*, THE ATLANTIC (Oct. 2020), at 48, 57, https://www.theatlantic.com/magazine/archive/2020/10/make-america-again /615478/ (under the headline "America's Plastic Hour Is Upon Us").

79. Andrias & Sachs, *supra* note 65, at 546.

80. FAIR ELECTIONS DURING A CRISIS, AD HOC COMMITTEE FOR 2020 ELECTION FAIRNESS AND DEMOCRACY 1–2 (2020).

81. U.S. CONST., Art. I, § 4.

82. On the potential impact of such reforms on presidential elections, see EDWARD B. FOLEY, PRESIDENTIAL ELECTIONS AND MAJORITY RULE: THE RISE, DEMISE, AND POTENTIAL RESTORATION OF THE JEFFERSONIAN ELECTORAL COLLEGE (2020).

83. PENELOPE MUSE ABERNATHY, THE EXPANDING NEWS DESERT (2018), https://www.usnewsdeserts.com/reports/expanding-news-desert/.

84. Erin Keane, *The U.S. Newspaper Crisis Is Growing: More Than 1 In 5 Local Papers Have Closed since 2004*, SALON (Oct.16, 2018), https://www.salon.com/2018

/10/16/the-u-s-newspaper-crisis-is-growing-more-than-1-in-5-local-papers-have
-closed-since-2004/.

85. Paul Starr, *Goodbye to the Age of Newspapers (Hello to a New Era of Corruption)*, THE NEW REPUBLIC, Mar. 4, 2009, at 28, https://newrepublic.com/article
/64252/goodbye-the-age-newspapers-hello-new-era-corruption.

86. VICTOR PICKARD, DEMOCRACY WITHOUT JOURNALISM? CONFRONTING THE MISINFORMATION SOCIETY 136–163 (2019).

87. Victor Pickard, *Can Government Support the Press? Historicizing and Internationalizing a Policy Approach to the Journalism Crisis*, 14 COMMUNICATION REV. 73, 79 (2011).

88. PICKARD, *supra* note 86, at 151–157.

89. DIANE RAVITCH, SLAYING GOLIATH: THE PASSIONATE RESISTANCE TO PRIVATIZATION AND THE FIGHT TO SAVE AMERICA'S PUBLIC SCHOOLS (2020).

90. DIANE RAVITCH, REIGN OF ERROR: THE HOAX OF THE PRIVATIZATION MOVEMENT AND THE DANGER TO AMERICA'S PUBLIC SCHOOLS (2014).

91. IAN REIFOWITZ, THE TRIBALIZATION OF POLITICS: HOW RUSH LIMBAUGH'S RACE-BAITING RHETORIC ON THE OBAMA PRESIDENCY PAVED THE WAY FOR TRUMP (2019).

92. Amy Bingham, *Chelsea Clinton, Sandra Fluke Unite over Rush Limbaugh Attacks*, ABC NEWS (Apr. 2, 2012), https://abcnews.go.com/blogs/politics/2012/04
/chelsea-clinton-sandra-fluke-unite-over-rush-limbaugh-attacks.

93. *See* JOHN DRYZEK, DELIBERATIVE DEMOCRACY AND BEYOND 57–80 (2000) (discussing and responding to the work of Lynn M. Sanders and Iris Young).

94. Scott R. Furlong & Cornelius M. Kerwin, *Interest Group Participation in Rule Making: A Decade of Change*, 15 J. PUB. ADMIN. RESEARCH AND THEORY 353 (2005); Andrias & Sachs, *supra* note 65, at 579.

95. THEDA SKOCPOL, DIMINISHED DEMOCRACY: FROM MEMBERSHIP TO MANAGEMENT IN AMERICAN CIVIL LIFE (2003); Theda Skocpol & Caroline Tervo, *Resistance Disconnect*, THE AMERICAN PROSPECT (Feb. 4, 2021), https://prospect.org/politics/resistance-disconnect-indivisible-national-local-activists/.

96. Andrias & Sachs, *supra* note 65, at 577–586.

97. *Id.* at 595–631.

98. Stephen Coleman, *Dysfunctional Democracy vs. Direct Representation*, 9 J. APPLIED JOURNALISM & MEDIA STUD. 215 (2020).

99. *Id.* at 215.

100. Danielle Allen, *The Road from Serfdom*, THE ATLANTIC (Dec. 2019), at 94, 101.

101. *Id.* at 99.

102. Coleman, *supra* note 98, at 219.

103. *Id.*

104. On some of the institutional possibilities, see the essay on "Suggested Further Reading," which concludes this volume.

105. Inaugural Address by President Joseph R. Biden Jr., WHITEHOUSE.GOV (Jan. 20, 2021), https://www.whitehouse.gov/briefing-room/speeches-remarks/2021/01/20/inaugural-address-by-president-joseph-r-biden-jr/.

106. Peter M. Shane, *Lessons in Presidential Authority*, REGULATORY REV. (Mar. 29, 2021), https://www.theregreview.org/2021/03/29/shane-lessons-presidential-authority/.

SUGGESTED FURTHER READING

This book traverses five huge areas of study: constitutional history, the history of the presidency, public administration, approaches to constitutional interpretation, and democratic theory. Although the endnotes to each chapter point to my sources for specific propositions, readers may appreciate a more user-friendly guide to some of the most helpful work on these subjects. For better or worse, however, the sheer volume of important books and articles in each area is mountainous, and the mountains are likely to grow between my writing of this book and your reading of it. The guide is, therefore, quite partial and personal. Aside from my own work and some major books and articles that have specifically informed my argument, I have included books and articles that have influenced my thinking more generally, as well as what I consider to be some of the best-written work antagonistic to my views.

PROLOGUE

In addition to foreshadowing the main arguments in this volume, the prologue claims that two ideas I am arguing against—originalism and unitary executive theory—owe their contemporary prominence in part to their attractiveness to political movements that invested institutionally, as well as intellectually, in their development. The political origins of contemporary originalism are explored in Calvin TerBeek, *"Clocks Must Always Be Turned Back"*: Brown v. Board of Education *and the Racial Origins of Constitutional Originalism*, 115 AM. POL. SCI. REV. 1 (2021). On the politics behind unitary executive theory, two helpful studies are Amanda Hollis-Brusky, *Helping Ideas Have Consequences: Political and Intellectual Investment in the Unitary Executive Theory, 1981–2000*, 89 DENV. U. L. REV. 197 (2011), and Stephen Skowronek, *The Conservative Insurgency and Presidential Power: A Developmental Perspective on the Unitary Executive*, 122 HARV. L. REV. 2070, 2096–2100 (2009). Two excellent volumes that address both the history of contemporary unitary executive theory and its many doctrinal manifestations are JEFFREY CROUCH, MARK J. ROZELL & MITCHELL SOLLENBERGER, THE UNITARY EXECUTIVE THEORY: A DANGER TO CONSTITUTIONAL GOVERNMENT (2020), and GRAHAM G. DODDS, THE UNITARY PRESIDENCY (2020).

CHAPTER 1. FROM THE "UNITARY" TO THE "ENTITLED" EXECUTIVE

Chapter 1 draws a line between the set of ideas I am calling "aggressive presidentialism" and the antidemocratic norm-breaking behavior of the Trump administration. But it also describes why his was hardly the first administration to evoke anxieties about excessive presidential unilateralism and why Trump's defeat in 2020 did not end the risk of presidential attacks on democratic norms.

On the centrality of norms to understanding the operation of the presidency, Professor Daphna Renan has written an exceptional analysis, which also helpfully theorizes the institutional forces that undergird (or undermine) norms. *Presidential Norms and Article II*, 131 HARV. L. REV. 2187 (2018). One way of conceptualizing the danger of aggressive presidentialism is that unilateralism exaggerates the personal nature of the presidency at the risk of subverting the institutional. As it happens, Professor Renan has also published an insightful exploration of the inescapable tension in constitutional law between understanding "the president" as an institutional office versus as an individual incumbent. Daphna Renan, *The President's Two Bodies*, 120 COLUM. L. REV. 1119 (2020).

My thinking about our twenty-first-century presidencies has been strongly influenced by a number of excellent books about the Bush, Obama, and Trump administrations. An outstanding insider account of the Bush administration that is simultaneously sympathetic, but critical is JACK GOLDSMITH, THE TERROR PRESIDENCY: LAW AND JUDGMENT INSIDE THE BUSH ADMINISTRATION (2007). A yet more critical academic analysis of presidential lawyering under Bush is HAROLD H. BRUFF, BAD ADVICE: BUSH'S LAWYERS IN THE WAR ON TERROR (2009). Two books by the Pulitzer Prize-winning reporter Charlie Savage provide enlightening accounts of legal struggles within the Bush and Obama administrations, respectively: TAKEOVER: THE RETURN OF THE IMPERIAL PRESIDENCY AND THE SUBVERSION OF AMERICAN DEMOCRACY (2007) and POWER WARS: THE RELENTLESS RISE OF PRESIDENTIAL AUTHORITY AND SECRECY (2017). Another helpful, but more academic assessment of the Obama administration is LOUIS FISHER, PRESIDENT OBAMA: CONSTITUTIONAL ASPIRATIONS AND EXECUTIVE ACTION (2018). The developments under the Trump administration that most shaped my reactions are well covered in SUSAN HENNESSEY &

BENJAMIN WITTES, UNMAKING THE PRESIDENCY: DONALD TRUMP'S WAR ON THE WORLD'S MOST POWERFUL OFFICE (2020).

I have been alarmed about presidentialist assaults on democratic norms since the Reagan and George H. W. Bush administrations. I sought to lay out the problem in *When Interbranch Norms Break Down: Of Arms-for-Hostages, "Orderly Shutowns," Presidential Impeachments, and Judicial Coups*, 12 CORNELL J. L. & PUB. POL. 503 (2003). The post-9/11 norm-breaching by the George W. Bush administration gave me occasion to synthesize my opposition to aggressive presidentialism in MADISON'S NIGHTMARE: HOW EXECUTIVE POWER THREATENS AMERICAN DEMOCRACY (2009). I emphasized then, as I do now, however, that the antidemocratic risks posed by the theory and practice of the unilateral presidency are not limited to any one administration.

CHAPTER 2. THE "CHIEF PROSECUTOR" MYTH

This chapter, discussing the debate over presidential control of criminal prosecution, argues two points: (1) originalism, practiced well, supports the permissibility of legal checks on presidential supervision of criminal prosecution, and (2) a modern, adaptive interpretation of the Constitution produces the same bottom line in even more linear fashion. I have laid out these positions in yet greater detail in two articles: Peter M. Shane, *Prosecutors at the Periphery*, 94 CHI.-KENT L. REV. 241 (2019), and Peter M. Shane, *The Originalist Myth of the Unitary Executive*, 19 U. PA. J. CONST. L. 323 (2016). In some respects, both build upon a yet earlier analysis, Peter M. Shane, *Independent Policymaking and Presidential Power: A Constitutional Analysis*, 57 GEO. WASH. L. REV. 596 (1989). The orientation toward separation of powers law in these and other works has long been influenced also by the scholarship of political scientist William B. Gwyn, including WILLIAM B. GWYN, THE MEANING OF THE SEPARATION OF POWERS (1965); William B. Gwyn, *The Indeterminacy of the Separation of Powers and the Federal Courts*, 57 GEO. WASH. L. REV. 474 (1989); and William B. Gwyn, *The Indeterminacy of the Separation of Powers in the Age of the Framers*, 30 WM. & MARY L. REV. 263 (1989)

The most important arguments on behalf of the presidentialist position I oppose appear in the work of Professor Sai Prakash. SAIKRISHNA BANGALORE PRAKASH, IMPERIAL FROM THE BEGINNING: THE CONSTITUTION OF THE ORIGINAL EXECUTIVE 33 (2015), and Saikrishna Prakash, *The Chief Prosecutor*, 73 GEO. WASH. L. REV. 521 (2005).

On the history of criminal prosecution in the United States, the most complete volume is still JOAN E. JACOBY, THE AMERICAN PROSECUTOR: A SEARCH FOR IDENTITY (1980). An important study that emphasizes the persistence of decentralized power in the evolution of federal prosecution is Leslie B. Arffa, *Separation of Prosecutors*, 128 YALE L.J. 1078 (2019). Two important articles on the early history of the attorney general's office and of federal criminal prosecution are Harold J. Krent, *Executive Control over Criminal Law Enforcement: Some Lessons from History*, 38 AM. U. L. REV. 275 (1989); and Susan Low Bloch, *The Early Role of the Attorney General in Our Constitutional Scheme: In the Beginning There Was Pragmatism*, 1989 DUKE L.J. 561 (1989).

CHAPTER 3. POLITICIZING THE "DEEP STATE": PRESIDENTS AND THE BUREAUCRACY

Chapter 3 broadens the focus on post-Reagan presidentialism from its impact on criminal prosecution to its broader impact on all personnel and policy making in the executive branch. Trump's authoritarian leanings were enabled in part by pro-executive Supreme Court opinions, but also by broadly worded authorities that Congress conferred on presidents by statute—authorities that proved easy to exploit by a president hostile to norms of self-restraint. An excellent analysis revealing the breadth of substantive powers delegated to the resident by statute, as well as by the Constitution is Shalev Roisman, *Presidential Law*, 105 MINN. L. REV. 1269 (2021).

To appreciate the real-world stakes in the debate over presidential administration requires some understanding of both the organization and policy making processes of the federal executive branch. A superb survey of the organizations and personnel systems that constitute the executive establishment is JENNIFER L. SELIN & DAVID E. LEWIS, ADMINISTRATIVE CONFERENCE OF THE UNITED STATES SOURCEBOOK OF UNITED STATES EXECUTIVE AGENCIES (2d ed. 2018). Three important sources for understanding the world of administrative adjudication and the need for reform are MICHAEL ASIMOW, SOURCEBOOK ON FEDERAL ADMINISTRATIVE ADJUDICATION OUTSIDE THE ADMINISTRATIVE PROCEDURE ACT (2019), Kent Barnett, *Against Administrative Judges*, 49 U.C.D. L. REV. 1643 (2016); and Emily S. Bremer, *Reckoning with Adjudication's Exceptionalism Norm*, 69 DUKE L.J. 1749 (2020). With regard to federal administrative rulemaking, the best introduction for non-lawyers (which has plenty of value for lawyers and legal scholars, as well) is CORNELIUS MARTIN KERWIN & SCOTT R. FURLONG, RULEMAKING: HOW GOVERNMENT AGENCIES WRITE LAW AND MAKE POLICY (5th ed. 2018). A favorite resource for lawyers is JEFFREY S LUBBERS, A GUIDE TO FEDERAL AGENCY RULEMAKING (6th ed. 2019).

Appreciating what is at stake in the unitary executive debate also requires awareness of how much policy making discretion the executive branch possesses when implementing its statutory responsibilities. For anyone following the headlines, it may seem puzzling that some of the conservative voices arguing most strenuously for a vigorous conception of Article II power—Justice Neil Gorsuch is a good example—are also advocates for sharper legal constraints on the authority of Congress to give the executive branch a great deal of policy making discretion in the first place. The appearance of paradox disappears, however, if one posits that, in the hands of contemporary conservative constitutionalists, the instrumental aim of both arguments is to shrink the federal administrative enterprise. A unitary right-wing president, like Trump, with largely unchecked authority to curb federal regulatory activity, can be a powerful instrument for undermining the administrative state. So, too, can be a judiciary intent on impeding Congress's enactment of broad regulatory statutes. For an important scholarly assessment of the anti-administrative impulse on the contemporary American right, see Gillian E. Metzger, *Foreword: 1930s Redux: The Administrative State under Siege*, 131 HARV. L. REV. 1 (2017). The importance of the "deep state" to good governance and how presidentialism has threatened to undermine a healthy relationship between politics and administration are topics well explored in STEPHEN SKOWRONEK, JOHN A. DEARBORN, & DESMOND KING, PHANTOMS OF A BELEAGUERED REPUBLIC: THE DEEP STATE AND THE UNITARY EXECUTIVE (2021).

CHAPTER 4: THE ORIGINALIST MIRAGE OF PRESIDENTIAL POWER AND

CHAPTER 5: INTERPRETING DEMOCRACY'S CONSTITUTION

Chapter 4 explains why I think originalism done well does not support the case for presidential unilateralism that undergirds the campaign detailed in chapter 3 for one-person control of the executive branch. It also explains why I do not believe "originalism done well" is an adequate methodological substitute for "originalism done badly" in terms of interpretive method. Chapter 5 lays out the democracy-centered adaptive approach to constitutional interpretation I believe to be better suited to the contemporary United States.

On Founding period history, the strongest originalist arguments for presidentialism are presented in the Prakash volume discussed earlier in connection with chapter 2, and MICHAEL W. MCCONNELL, THE PRESIDENT WHO WOULD NOT BE KING: EXECUTIVE POWER UNDER THE CONSTITUTION 165 (2020). As impressive as these volumes are, however, I find more persuasive the counterarguments of a group of legal historians who, in my judgment, have severely undermined the originalist case for presidentialism and separation of powers formalism more generally. Key articles include:

- Daniel D. Birk, *Interrogating the Historical Basis for a Unitary Executive*, 73 STAN. L. REV. 175 (2021).
- Christine Kexel Chabot, *Is the Federal Reserve Constitutional? An Originalist Argument for Independent Agencies*, 96 NOTRE DAME L. REV. 1 (2020).
- Andrew Kent, Ethan J. Leib, & Jed Handelsman Shugerman, *Faithful Execution and Article II*, 132 HARV. L. REV. 2111 (2019).
- Julian Davis Mortenson, *Article II Vests the Executive Power, Not the Royal Prerogative*, 119 COLUM. L. REV. 1169 (2019).
- Julian Davis Mortenson, *The Executive Power Clause*, 168 U. PENN. L. REV. 1269 (2020).
- Jed Handelsman Shugerman, *The First Congress Rejected Unitary Presidentialism: An Originalist Cautionary Tale*, Fordham Law Legal Studies Research, Working Paper No. 3597496 (2021), https://papers.ssrn.com/sol3 /papers.cfm?abstract_id=3597496, and Fordham Law Legal Studies Research, Working Paper No. 3596566 (2021), https://papers.ssrn.com/sol3/papers.cfm ?abstract_id=3596566
- Jed Handelsman Shugerman, Vesting, 74 STAN. L. REV. __ (2022) (forthcoming), https://papers.ssrn.com/sol3/papers.cfm?abstract_id=3793213.
- Matt Steilen, *How to Think Constitutionally about Prerogative: A Study of Early American Usage*, 66 BUFF. L. REV. 557 (2018).

For general histories of the Founding period, works I have found invaluable are:

- JONATHAN GIENAPP, THE SECOND CREATION: FIXING THE AMERICAN CONSTITUTION IN THE FOUNDING ERA (2018).
- MICHAEL J. KLARMAN, THE FRAMERS' COUP: THE MAKING OF THE UNITED STATES CONSTITUTION (2016).
- JACK N. RAKOVE, ORIGINAL MEANINGS: POLITICS AND IDEAS IN THE MAKING OF THE CONSTITUTION (1996).
- GORDON S. WOOD, THE CREATION OF THE AMERICAN REPUBLIC 1776–1787 (1969).

On the early Congresses' penchant for pragmatism over formalism in institutional design, an outstanding analysis is JERRY L. MASHAW, CREATING THE AMERICAN CONSTITUTION: THE LOST ONE HUNDRED YEARS OF ADMINISTRATIVE LAW (2012).

As for interpretive theory, I find the most thoughtful defense of originalism—even if I remain unpersuaded—to be KEITH E. WHITTINGTON, CONSTITUTIONAL

INTERPRETATION: TEXTUAL MEANING, ORIGINAL INTENT, AND JUDICIAL REVIEW (1999). Professor Whittington also shares online the reading list for his graduate seminar in "Constitutional Originalism." His bibliography provides a very deep dive into the literature of the field, as well as citations to some of the classic works critical of originalism. https://scholar.princeton.edu/sites/default/files/kewhitt/files/constitutional_originalism_syllabus.pdf.

My preferred adaptive approach to interpretation no doubt reflects the influence of the following works:

- Paul Brest, *The Misconceived Quest for the Original Understanding*, 60 B.U. L. REV. 204 (1980).
- RONALD DWORKIN, A MATTER OF PRINCIPLE (1985).
- RICHARD H. FALLON JR., LAW AND LEGITIMACY IN THE SUPREME COURT (2018).
- Victoria Nourse, *Reclaiming the Constitutional Text from Originalism: The Case of Executive Power*, 106 CAL. L. REV. 1 (2018).
- H. Jefferson Powell, *The Original Understanding of Original Intent*, 98 HARV. L. REV. 885 (1984).
- ERIC J. SEGALL, ORIGINALISM AS FAITH (2018).
- DAVID A. STRAUSS, THE LIVING CONSTITUTION (2010).

A number of scholars have sought to bridge the gap between originalist and adaptive approaches. Important works in this vein include JACK BALKIN, LIVING ORIGINALISM (2011) and LAWRENCE LESSIG, FIDELITY & CONSTRAINT: HOW THE SUPREME COURT HAS READ THE AMERICAN CONSTITUTION (2019).

In laying out a version of democratic constitutionalism as interpretive theory, the work on deliberative democracy on which I have drawn most extensively is JOHN DRYZEK, DELIBERATIVE DEMOCRACY AND BEYOND (2000). I have also found invaluable Robert Dahl's synthesis of his approach to democratic theory in ROBERT A. DAHL, ON DEMOCRACY (1998).

Locating democracy at the heart of the "spirit of the Constitution" does greater justice than text-based originalism to just how profoundly certain amendments—most notably, the Fourteenth—changed not only the words of the Constitution, but also the document's underlying normativity. The events surrounding the drafting and adoption of that Amendment are captured in a superb narrative, the title of which captures this idea, GARRETT EPPS, DEMOCRACY REBORN: THE FOURTEENTH AMENDMENT AND THE FIGHT FOR EQUAL RIGHTS IN POST–CIVIL WAR AMERICA (2007). Professor Epps has also authored a deep reading of the constitutional text that, in many respects, reveals just how rich, open-textured, and often puzzling a document it is. GARRETT EPPS, AMERICAN EPIC: READING THE U.S. CONSTITUTION (2013).

CHAPTER 6. DEMOCRACY'S PRESIDENCY

Chapter 6 illustrates how a democratic constitutionalist reading of Article II would resolve a variety of issues raised by the Constitution's elliptical text. Before doing so, I offer a yet more specific account of what I take to be the important institutions to be protected through such an adaptive reading, including the rule of law itself. In elaborating on my own understanding of the rule of law, I have found PAUL GOWDER, THE RULE OF LAW IN THE REAL WORLD (2016), and the writings of Jeremy Waldron to be especially useful, e.g., JEREMY WALDRON, POLITICAL THEORY: ESSAYS ON INSTITUTIONS (2016).

I also thought it important to anticipate and refute two seemingly antiauthoritarian ideas offered by presidentialists. One is the argument offered early by Steven Calabresi that presidentialism is pro-democracy because the president is uniquely representative of the national electorate as a whole. Steven G. Calabresi, *Some Normative Arguments for the Unitary Executive*, 48 ARK. L. REV. 23 (1994). My immediate response to Professor Calabresi appeared as Peter M. Shane, *Political Accountability in a System of Checks and Balances: The Case of Presidential Review of Rulemaking*, 48 ARK. L. REV. 161, 197–202 (1994). Important and more recent work addressing this issue includes B. DAN WOOD, THE MYTH OF PRESIDENTIAL REPRESENTATION (2009). The history of the debate about the representative nature of the presidency is well told in JEREMY D. BAILEY, THE IDEA OF PRESIDENTIAL REPRESENTATION: AN INTELLECTUAL AND POLITICAL HISTORY (2019).

The second argument, offered by Professor Prakash, is that the risks of presidential authoritarianism could be checked if only Congress would delegate less discretionary authority to the executive branch to make policy. SAIKRISHNA BANGALORE PRAKASH, THE LIVING PRESIDENCY: AN ORIGINALIST ARGUMENT AGAINST ITS EVER-EXPANDING POWERS (2020). I contend that his argument is incomplete, but I dissent also from any implication that originalism could provide federal courts a well-founded basis for limiting Congress's authority to delegate broadly. Two important papers influencing my argument are Julian Davis Mortenson & Nicholas Bagley, *Delegation at the Founding*, 121 COLUM. L. REV. 277 (2021), and Nicholas R. Parrillo, *A Critical Assessment of the Originalist Case against Administrative Regulatory Power: New Evidence from the Federal Tax on Private Real Estate in the 1790s*, 130 YALE L. J. 1288 (2021). The affirmative case for the democratic nature of the administrative state is made powerfully in JERRY L. MASHAW, REASONED ADMINISTRATION AND DEMOCRATIC LEGITIMACY: HOW ADMINISTRATIVE LAW SUPPORTS DEMOCRATIC GOVERNMENT (2018). Professor Jon Michaels has gone so far as to argue that something like the current regulatory state ought to be viewed as constitutionally required. JON D. MICHAELS, CONSTITUTIONAL COUP: PRIVATIZATION'S THREAT TO THE AMERICAN REPUBLIC (2017).

My discussion then turns to constitutional ambiguities concerning the president's powers of appointment and removal, bureaucratic supervision, war making, and international diplomacy. The chapter also addresses executive privilege claims against Congress, the susceptibility of presidents to criminal indictment, and the range of "high crimes and misdemeanors" that qualify as constitutional grounds for impeachment. Democratic constitutionalism, I argue, is superior to originalism in interpreting the Constitution with respect to all these questions. The chapter endnotes point to important writing on each subject.

CHAPTER 7. BREAKING THE GRIP OF PRESIDENTIALISM

The concluding chapter argues that the path away from presidentialism will require serious internal government reforms but also the revitalization of American democracy and citizen engagement more generally. On the former subject, two fertile sources of proposals for post-Trump government reform are BOB BAUER & JACK GOLDSMITH, AFTER TRUMP: RECONSTRUCTING THE PRESIDENCY 253–277 (2020), and the twenty-three concise "Good Governance Papers" posted on the *Just Security* blog. Emily Berman, Tess Bridgeman, Ryan Goodman & Dakota S. Rudesill, *The Good Governance Papers: An Introduction*, JUST SECURITY (Oct. 14, 2020), https://www.justsecurity.org/72844/the-good-governance-papers-an-introduction/. For a systematic overview of the powers Congress could employ to check the executive more effectively, JOSH CHAFETZ, CONGRESS'S CONSTITUTION: LEGISLATIVE AUTHORITY AND THE SEPARATION OF POWERS (2017) is excellent.

The literature on democracy is so voluminous that my few recommendations barely qualify as "skimming the surface." Enormous debates attend the definition of democracy, the conditions under which democracy thrives or wanes, the history of democratic practice, the relationship of democracy to constitutional design, the relationship of democracy to human welfare, and much more.

My thinking about the risks of authoritarianism in the contemporary United States has been significantly educated by STEVEN LEVITSKY & DANIEL ZABLATT, HOW DEMOCRACIES DIE (2018). For ideas about U.S. democratic revitalization in the current moment, a good starting point for reading about the struggle for electoral fairness is STACEY ABRAMS, OUR TIME IS NOW: POWER, PURPOSE, AND THE FIGHT FOR A FAIR AMERICA (2020). Two other volumes rich in insight and suggestions are GANESH SITARAMAN, THE GREAT DEMOCRACY: HOW TO FIX OUR POLITICS, UNRIG THE ECONOMY, & UNITE AMERICA (2019), and VICTOR PICKARD, DEMOCRACY WITHOUT JOURNALISM? CONFRONTING THE

MISINFORMATION SOCIETY (2020). An enlightening series of essays on the state of—and necessity for—citizen activism is THEDA SKOCPOL & CAROLINE TERVO, EDS., UPENDING AMERICAN POLITICS: POLARIZING PARTIES, IDEOLOGICAL ELITES, AND CITIZEN ACTIVISTS FROM THE TEA PARTY TO THE ANTI-TRUMP RESISTANCE (2020).

Excellent discussions of concrete possibilities for institutionalizing democratic deliberation more robustly include JAMES S. FISHKIN, DEMOCRACY WHEN THE PEOPLE ARE THINKING: REVITALIZING OUR POLITICS THROUGH PUBLIC DELIBERATION (2018); MICHAEL A. NEBLO, KEVIN M. ESTERLING, & DAVID M. J. LAZER, POLITICS WITH THE PEOPLE: BUILDING A DIRECTLY REPRESEN-TATIVE DEMOCRACY (2018); CAROLYN J. LUKENSMEYER, BRINGING CITIZEN VOICES TO THE TABLE: A GUIDE FOR PUBLIC MANAGERS (2012); JOHN GASTIL & PETER LEVINE, EDS., THE DELIBERATIVE DEMOCRACY HANDBOOK: STRAT-EGIES FOR EFFECTIVE CIVIC ENGAGEMENT IN THE 21ST CENTURY (2005), and STEPHEN COLEMAN & PETER M. SHANE, CONNECTING DEMOCRACY: ONLINE CONSULTATION AND THE FLOW OF POLITICAL COMMUNICATION (2012). The last of these concludes with a brief essay by my coeditor, Stephen Coleman, entitled, "Making the E-Citizen: A Sociotechnical Approach to Democracy," which is a bril-liant synthesis of the ways in which digital information technologies might—or might not—advance robust conceptions of democratic citizenship.

INDEX

Bush, George W., 4, 95, 103, 232n4;
attempts to reset the organizational
psychology of the executive branch,
98–99; enthusiasm for using signing
statements to assert the unconstitutionality of provisions of statutes he was
signing into law, 99–100
Bush, George W., administration of, 9, 10,
71, 146, 156, 174, 178; embrace of aggressive presidentialism by, 27

Calabresi, Steven, 165
Cardozo, Benjamin, 136
Carrington v. Rash, 136
Carson, Ben, 24
Carter, Jimmy, 5, 18, 83, 85, 187; creation of
Regulatory Council, 82; Executive
Order No. 12,044 of, 82
Carter administration, 53
Centers for Disease Control (CDC),
8–9, 87
Chabot, Christine Kexel, 259n54
Chadha, Jagdish, 148–51
checks-and-balances system, 164–65
Cheney, Dick, 19, 27, 98
citizens: democratic citizens, 226; oppor-
tunities for, 224
citizenship, 12, 154, 162, 163, 208, 225,
280n45
Clarridge, Duane, 65
Clean Air Act Amendments (1990), 90, 91
Clinton, Bill, 4, 65, 103, 174, 204, 223;
impeachment of, 65; use of the pardon
power by, 210
Clinton, Hillary Rodham, 19, 98
Clinton administration, 28–29, 92–95, 198
Coats, Dan, 22
Cohen, Michael, 25
Coleman, Stephen, 225–26
Collins, Susan, 215
Collins v. Yellen, 251n107
Comey, James, 19; firing of by Trump,
33–34, 195
Commentaries on the Laws of England
(Blackstone), 118
"Common Legislative Encroachments on
Executive Branch Authority" (Barr), 7
"Common Sense" (Paine), 8

Constitutional Convention (1787), 11, 169
constitutional construction, 132
constitutional interpretation, 145–46;
"common law" conception of constitutional interpretation, 139–40; and
originalism, 170; pro-democracy interpretation of, 156–57; Supreme Court
cases concerning, 146–52; and values,
140–42. *See also* democratic
constitutionalism
"constitutional pluralists, 10–11
Consumer Finance Protection Bureau
(CFPB), 72, 79–80, 175
Consumer Products Safety Commission, 80
Continental Army, 129
Conway, Kellyanne, 24, 102
Conyers, John, 89
Cooper, Charles J., 6, 9, 87
Cornell, Saul, 157–58
Corpus of Founding Era American English
(COFEA), 130–31
Council on Competitiveness, 88, 90; and
the pattern of anti-environmental
interventions, 91–92
Council of Economic Advisors, 82, 103
Council on Wage-Price Stability, 82
criminal prosecution, 40–41, 45, 46, 110,
123, 173, 244n34; decentralized prosecu-
tion, 41; limitation of presidential
influence over, 48
criminal sanction, 47
Curiel, Gonzalo O., 21
Curtis, Benjamin, 201

Dahl, Robert, 162–63, 192
Daniels, Mitch, 92
Darman, Richard, 89
Darman-Conyers pact, 89
Davies, William, 156
Delaney Clauses, 56, 57
Dellinger, Walter, 121–22
democracies, 199–200
democracy, 29, 172; deliberative democracy,
144–45, 147–48, 151, 176, 264n32,
267n19; democratic inclusion, 157;
democratic renewal, 220; democracy
then and now, 152–58; distortions of the
democratic process, 145–46; five goals of

reenergizing American democracy, 220–21; hybrid democracy, 163; needs of, 162–66; normative premises of, 218; reinvigorating democracy, 218–27; and respect for the rule of law, 18; six political institutions required by large-scale democracy, 162–63. *See also* separation of powers, viewed through the lens of democracy

Democracy and Distrust: A Theory of Judicial Review (Ely), 153

democratic constitutionalism, 154, 161–62, 167, 171, 173, 174–75, 192–93; limits of as interpretive strategy, 200–204

Democrats/Democratic Party, 28, 65, 88, 165; Democratic presidents, 104–5

Dershowitz, Alan, 201

district attorneys, 39, 243n18

District of Columbia v. Heller, 38, 130, 133–34, 136, 138

Domestic Policy Council (under Reagan), 7

Dryzek, John S., 144

D'Souza, Dinesh, 19

Eisenhower Executive Office Building, 52

elections, 144

Ely, John Hart, 153

Emerging Republican Majority, The (Phillips), 5–6

Emerson, Blake, 217

Engel, Steven, 32

entitlement, psychology of, 3

Environmental Protection Agency (EPA), 60, 67, 80, 81, 90–91

Equal Employment Opportunity Commission, 67, 80

Ethics in Government Act (1978), 49, 64, 65, 212

Executive Office of Immigration Review (EOIR), 67, 69

executive branch, engagement of through public hearings and the notice-and-comment process, 223–24

executive power, 50, 113, 128–29, 141, 257n23; ambiguities of, 117–25; meaning of in the eighteenth century, 35; unitary character of, 186; vesting of in the president, 45

executive privilege, 12, 151–52, 193–95, 198, 292

Executive Privilege: A Constitutional Myth (Berger), 152

executive theory, unitary, 8–10, 110; renaissance of, 5–8; state of the post-Reagan unitary executive, 102–6

Federal Communications Commission (FCC), 9, 58; Fairness Doctrine of, 223

federal courts, reluctance of to second-guess the executive branch, 187

Federal Drug Administration (FDA), 4

Federal Food, Drug, and Cosmetic Act, 56

Federal Communications Commission (FCC), 58

Federal Reserve System, 9

Federal Trade Commission (FTC), 56–57, 69, 75–76

Federal Vacancies Reform Act (1998 [FVRA]), 72, 175–76, 209, 270n67

Federalist, The, 40, 74, 114–15, 125, 186, 202

Federalist Society for Law and Public Policy Studies ("FedSoc"), 7

Fiers, Alan, 65

First Bank of the United States, 121

Food and Drug Administration (FDA), 56

Ford, Gerald, 5, 83; Executive Order No. 11,821 of, 82

Ford administration, 53

Foreign Emoluments Clause, 15

Formalists, 112

Framers, of the US Constitution, 10, 33, 35, 37, 62–63, 112, 118, 121, 125, 127, 133, 137, 158, 169, 187, 197, 198, 203; on attacks against the United States, 179–80; creation of an "elective monarch" by 11; creation of a navy by, 128; on presidential initiative in war, 233n24; on representative accountability, 157; on the structure of government, 153; view of Congress, 169, 179; vision of, 96, 109, 144; wisdom of, 202

Frankfurter, Felix, 272n103

free Blacks, 127

Freedom of Information Act (FOIA), 92

Free Enterprise Fund, 78, 105

Frost, David, 10, 26

Office of Management and Budget (OMB)
(*continued*)
management responsibility in, 84–85;
"Quality of Life Review" process
in, 81
Office of National Drug Control Policy,
101–2
Office of Personnel Management (OPM),
66, 67, 73
Office of Surface Mining Reclamation and
Enforcement, 103
Olson, Theodore B., 86
originalism, 141, 169, 179, 261–62n104;
bizarreness of using originalism as the
primary guide to constitutional interpretation, 170; and the complexity of
communication, 111–17; constitutional
originalism, 111–12; and judicial creativity, 129–30; "moderate originalism,"
131, 132; new originalism, 112–13, 256n6,
257nn14–15; normative defense of, 129;
old originalism, 112; unbearable light-
ness of, 125–36
Ornstein, Norm, 207, 208
Orwell, George, 21

Packer, George, 220
Paine, Thomas, 8
Palestinians, 187
Parrillo, Nicholas, 169–70
PAS positions, 175, 270n67
Patton, Lynne, 24
*PHH Corp. v. Consumer Finance Protection
Bureau*, 79, 80
Phillips, James C., 130–31
Phillips, Kevin, 5–6
Pierce, Richard J., 101
Plame, Valerie, 19
"plenary constitutional authority," 191
"plenary discretion principle," 8, 13, 110
Poindexter, John, 26
political mobilization, 205
Posner, Richard, 69–70
Post, Robert, 214
Powell, H. Jefferson, 121
Powell, Lewis F., 150
Prakash, Saikrishna, 11, 117–18, 169, 171–72,
194, 244–45n38

presidency: the accountable presidency,
193–200; domestic, 166–76; global,
176–93 *passim*
presidentialism, 3, 4, 5, 109, 166, 179, 205–7;
"originalist" arguments for, 5, 50–51;
and the threat of authoritarianism
rooted in, 206. *See also* presidentialism,
aggressive
presidentialism, aggressive, 25, 27, 104, 217;
defense of, 29–30
presidentialists, 53, 67, 111, 158; and the logic
of presidential resistance to Congress
(doctrinal steps of), 11–12; modern-day,
11, 77, 119
presidential norms, vulnerability of attack
on, 17–25
presidential pardons, 209–10
presidential rhetoric, 105
presidents, 171–72, 187, 215–16, 217–18;
ability to appoint acting administrators,
175; constitutional entitlement to seek
information from heads of executive
agencies, 173–74; control over bureaucracy, 174; and the power of to implement law, 258n33; as politically
motivated in ways similar to members
of Congress, 165–66
Principals Committee of the National
Security Council, 21
prosecutors, limiting of presidential control
over, 49–50
public administrators, debates concerning,
259n48
Public Company Accounting Oversight
Board (PCAOB), 77, 78
public education, 222–23
"public sphere," the, 145

Quayle, Dan, 88

racial conflict, 220
Randolph, Edmond, 41
Ratcliffe, John, 22
Reagan, Ronald, 5, 6, 26, 85, 103, 155, 174,
194–95; Executive Order No. 12,291 of,
53, 83, 88, 89, 253n162
Reagan administration, 3, 5, 7, 26, 53, 83, 86,
93, 95–96, 104, 109, 141, 213; lawyering

Founded in 1893,
UNIVERSITY OF CALIFORNIA PRESS
publishes bold, progressive books and journals
on topics in the arts, humanities, social sciences,
and natural sciences—with a focus on social
justice issues—that inspire thought and action
among readers worldwide.

The UC PRESS FOUNDATION
raises funds to uphold the press's vital role
as an independent, nonprofit publisher, and
receives philanthropic support from a wide
range of individuals and institutions—and from
committed readers like you. To learn more, visit
ucpress.edu/supportus.